Word 2007
All-in-One Desk Reference
For Dummies®

Cheat Sheet

Formatting Commands

Command	Keys
Bold	Ctrl+B
Italic	Ctrl+I
Underline	Ctrl+U
Center	Ctrl+E
Left Align	Ctrl+L
Right Align	Ctrl+R
Justify	Ctrl+J
Normal	Ctrl+spacebar

Editing Commands

Command	Keys
Undo	Ctrl+Z
Cut	Ctrl+X
Copy	Ctrl+C
Paste	Ctrl+V
Select All	Ctrl+A
Find	Ctrl+F
Replace	Ctrl+H
Duplicate	Ctrl+D

Commonly Used Commands

Command	Keys
New	Ctrl+N
Open	Ctrl+O
Save	Ctrl+S
Print	Ctrl+P
Help	F1
New Page	Shift+Enter

Where to Find Familiar Features

Word 2003 Command	Equivalent Word 2007 Command
File➪New	Office➪New
File➪Save	Office➪Save
File➪Page Setup	Page Layout tab, Page Setup group
Edit➪Undo	Quick Access toolbar, Undo
Edit➪Find	Home tab, Editing group, Find
Edit➪Replace	Home tab, Editing group, Replace
View➪Master➪Slide Master	View tab, Presentation Views group, Slide Master
Insert➪Slide	Home tab, Slides group, Add Slide
Insert➪Picture➪Clip Art	Insert tab, Illustrations group, Clip Art
Insert➪Picture➪From File	Insert tab, Illustrations group, Picture
Insert➪Diagram	Insert tab, Illustrations group, SmartArt
Format➪Font	Home tab, Font group, dialog box launcher
Format➪Paragraph	Home tab, Paragraph group, di
Format➪Styles and Formatting	Home tab, Styles group, dialog
Tools➪Spelling and Grammar	Review tab, Proofing group, Sp
Tools➪Letters and Mailings	Mailings tab
Tools➪Templates and Add-Ins	Office➪Word Options, Add-Ins drop-down list and click Go
Tools➪Options	Office➪Word Options
Table➪Draw Table	Inset tab, Tables group, Table

D1441781

For Dummies: Bestselling Book Series for Beginners

Word 2007
All-in-One Desk Reference
For Dummies®

Cheat Sheet

The Word Window

Ribbon

Office Button   Quick Access Toolbar

Help Button

New document   View buttons   Zoom Control

For Dummies: Bestselling Book Series for Beginners

6-16-40

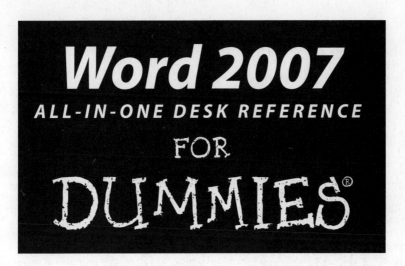

Word 2007
ALL-IN-ONE DESK REFERENCE
FOR
DUMMIES®

by Doug Lowe

BICENTENNIAL
1807
WILEY
2007
BICENTENNIAL

Wiley Publishing, Inc.

Word 2007 All-in-One Desk Reference For Dummies®

Published by
Wiley Publishing, Inc.
111 River Street
Hoboken, NJ 07030-5774
www.wiley.com

Copyright © 2007 by Wiley Publishing, Inc., Indianapolis, Indiana

Published by Wiley Publishing, Inc., Indianapolis, Indiana

Published simultaneously in Canada

For general information on our other products and services, please contact our Customer Care Department within the U.S. at 800-762-2974, outside the U.S. at 317-572-3993, or fax 317-572-4002.

For technical support, please visit www.wiley.com/techsupport.

Wiley also publishes its books in a variety of electronic formats. Some content that appears in print may not be available in electronic books.

Library of Congress Control Number: 2006939587

ISBN: 978-0-470-04058-4

Manufactured in the United States of America

10 9 8 7 6 5 4 3 2 1

1B/RY/QR/QX/IN

WILEY

About the Author

Doug Lowe has written enough computer books to line all the birdcages in California. His other books include *PowerPoint 2007 For Dummies*, *Java All-in-One Desk Reference For Dummies*, and *Networking For Dummies*, Sixth Edition.

Although Doug has yet to win a Pulitzer Prize, he remains cautiously optimistic. He is hopeful that George Lucas will pick up the film rights to this book and suggests *PowerPoint Episode 2,007: The Phantom Presentation* as a working title.

Doug lives in sunny Fresno, California, where the motto is either "We Love Arnold!" or "We Hate Arnold!" (we can't decide which) with his wife, Debbie, and a couple of crazy dogs.

Dedication

To Debbie, Rebecca, Sarah, and Bethany.

Author's Acknowledgments

I'd like to thank the whole crew at Wiley who helped with this edition. Melody Layne got the project rolling and nudged it along when it needed nudging. Project editor Mark Enochs did a great job keeping everything afloat and was very patient as deadlines came and chapters didn't. Copy editor Virginia Sanders did a fantastic job with all the details, including dotting all the t's and crossing all the i's, or something like that. Stuart Stuple gave the entire manuscript a thorough technical review and made many excellent suggestions. And, of course, many other people pitched in.

Publisher's Acknowledgments

We're proud of this book; please send us your comments through our online registration form located at www.dummies.com/register/.

Some of the people who helped bring this book to market include the following:

Acquisitions, Editorial, and Media Development

Project Editor: Mark Enochs

Acquisitions Editor: Melody Layne

Copy Editor: Virginia Sanders

Technical Editor: Stuart Stuple

Editorial Manager: Leah Cameron

Media Development Manager: Laura VanWinkle

Editorial Assistant: Amanda Foxworth

Sr. Editorial Assistant: Cherie Case

Cartoons: Rich Tennant (www.the5thwave.com)

Composition Services

Project Coordinator: Adrienne Martinez

Layout and Graphics: Claudia Bell, Carl Byers, Stephanie D. Jumper, Barbara Moore, Rashell Smith, Erin Zeltner

Proofreaders: John Greenough, Jessica Kramer, Techbooks

Indexer: Techbooks

Anniversary Logo Design: Richard Pacifico

Publishing and Editorial for Technology Dummies

   Richard Swadley, Vice President and Executive Group Publisher

   Andy Cummings, Vice President and Publisher

   Mary Bednarek, Executive Acquisitions Director

   Mary C. Corder, Editorial Director

Publishing for Consumer Dummies

   Diane Graves Steele, Vice President and Publisher

   Joyce Pepple, Acquisitions Director

Composition Services

   Gerry Fahey, Vice President of Production Services

   Debbie Stailey, Director of Composition Services

Contents at a Glance

Table of Contents

Introduction

Welcome to *Word 2007 All-in-One Desk Reference For Dummies,* the book written especially for those of you who use Word on a daily basis and need a handy reference to all the various and sundry things this mighty program can do. This book contains all the basic and not-so-basic information you need to know to get the most out of Word, whether you use it to compose simple letters or write 200-page government grants.

About This Book

Word 2007 All-in-One Desk Reference For Dummies is a big book that's actually made up of nine smaller books, each of which covers a specific aspect of using Word. You find minibooks on such topics as editing your documents, formatting pages, mailings, and customizing Word to make it work the way you want it to.

Word 2007 All-in-One Desk Reference For Dummies doesn't pretend to be a comprehensive reference for every detail of these topics. Instead, this book shows you how to get up and running fast so that you have more time to do the things you really want to do. Designed using the easy-to-follow *For Dummies* format, this book helps you get the information you need without laboring to find it.

Whenever one big thing is made up of several smaller things, confusion is always a possibility. That's why *Word 2007 All-in-One Desk Reference For Dummies* is designed to have multiple access points (I hear an acronym coming on — MAP!) to help you find what you want. At the beginning of the book is a detailed Table of Contents that covers the entire book. Also, each minibook begins with a mini Table of Contents that shows you at a glance which chapters are included in that minibook. Useful running heads appear at the top of each page to point out the topic discussed on that page. And handy thumb tabs run down the sides of the pages to help you quickly find each minibook. Finally, a comprehensive index lets you find information anywhere in the entire book.

This book isn't the kind you pick up and read from start to finish, as though it were a cheap novel. If I ever see you reading it at the beach, I'll kick sand in your face. This book is more of a reference, the kind of book you can pick up, turn to just about any page, and start reading. You don't have to memorize anything in this book. It's a need-to-know book: You pick it up when you need to know something. Need to know how to do a mail merge? Pick up the book. Need to know how to crop an image? Pick up the book. After you find what you need, put the book down and get on with your life.

How to Use This Book

After you find your topic in the Table of Contents or the index, turn to the area of interest and read as much as you need or want. Then close the book and get on with it.

Of course, the book is loaded with information, so if you want to take a brief excursion into your topic, you're more than welcome. If you want to know everything about customizing Word, read the whole minibook on customization. But if you just want to find out how to create a simple keyboard shortcut to apply a style that you use 200 times a day, just read the section on keyboard shortcuts. You get the idea.

If you need to type something, you see the text you need to type like this: **Type this stuff**. In this example, you type **Type this stuff** at the keyboard. An explanation usually follows, just in case you're scratching your head and grunting, "Huh?"

Whenever I describe a message or information that you see on-screen, I present it as follows:

```
A message from your friendly word processor
```

Note: The names of dialog boxes, menu commands, and options are spelled with the first letter of each main word capitalized, even though these letters might not be capitalized on-screen. This format makes sentences filled with long option names easier for you to read. (Haven't we thought of everything?)

How This Book Is Organized

Each of the nine minibooks contained in *Word 2007 All-in-One Desk Reference For Dummies* stands alone. The first minibook covers the basics of using Word. The remaining minibooks cover a variety of Word topics. Even those minibooks that cover familiar ground are packed with techniques and commands you might not know about. You can find something useful in every chapter. Here's a brief description of what you find in each minibook.

Book I: The Brave New Word

This minibook covers the basics you need to get going with Word. Even if you've been using Word for years, you need to read these chapters. Word 2007 introduces an entirely new user interface in which the familiar menus and toolbars are replaced by a gadget called *the Ribbon.* So be sure to familiarize yourself with this new user interface. And you should also take a close look at the chapter on templates. Many Word users don't realize the power of the lowly template.

Book II: Editing and Text Formatting

Here I discuss the ins and outs of editing and formatting your text. You discover basic formatting techniques such as bold and italics as well as a variety of useful editing techniques. The more you use Word, the more it pays to know all the tips and shortcuts that I present in this minibook.

Book III: Formatting Pages

In this minibook, I give you the lowdown on formatting pages. I cover the basics of working with pages and sections, using themes to create great looking pages, and creating advanced features such as columns and lists.

Book IV: Inserting Bits and Pieces

The Ribbon has an entire tab devoted to things you can insert into your document, and this minibook covers the most useful of these bits and pieces. You find out about inserting graphics such as pictures and clip art; using drawing objects such as rectangles and text boxes; formatting visual aids such as charts and diagrams, tables; and so on.

Book V: Publish or Perish

The chapters in this minibook are devoted to various ways you can use Word to share your work with others. First, you'll learn how to use Word's new blogging feature, which lets you use Word as the word processor for your blog site. You'll also learn how to use Word's collaboration and reviewing features, and how to use Word with SharePoint, a server-based collaboration program that integrates with Word.

Book VI: Using Reference Features

This minibook covers all of the features found on the References tab on the Ribbon, including Tables of Contents, footnotes, indexes, and so on.

Book VII: Mailings

In these chapters, I tell you all about creating letters, envelopes, and labels in Word, from single letters to mass mailings using the mail merge feature. You even see how to use Word to send faxes. If you use Word to mail letters to your customers, friends, or relatives, you want to focus especially on Chapters 3 and 4.

Book VIII: Customizing Word

The chapters in this minibook show you how to customize Word so it works the way you want it to. You discover how to customize the user interface, set options, insert fields, and create custom forms.

Book IX: Features for Developers

The last minibook is devoted to readers who want to dig deep into the depths of Word by writing macros using Word's powerful programming language, Visual Basic for Applications (VBA). The chapters in this minibook are not for the faint of heart, but if you're willing to take the plunge, you can make Word do things you never thought possible.

Icons Used in This Book

Like any *For Dummies* book, this book is chock-full of helpful icons that draw your attention to items of particular importance. You find the following icons throughout this book:

Did I tell you about the memory course I took?

Hold it — technical stuff is just around the corner. Read on only if you have your pocket protector.

Pay special attention to this icon; it lets you know that some particularly useful tidbit is at hand — perhaps a shortcut or a little-used command that pays off big.

Danger Will Robinson! This icon highlights information that may help you avert disaster.

Where to Go from Here

Yes, you can get there from here. With this book in hand, you're ready to plow right through the rugged networking terrain. Browse through the Table of Contents and decide where you want to start. Be bold! Be courageous! Be adventurous! And above all, have fun!

Book I

The Brave New Word

"I wrote my entire cookbook in Word. The other programs I saw just didn't look fresh."

Contents at a Glance

Chapter 1: Getting to Know Word 2007

In This Chapter

✔ **Getting Word started**

✔ **Making sense of all the stuff on-screen**

✔ **Dealing with the Ribbon**

✔ **Entering and editing text**

✔ **Printing your document**

✔ **Saving your work**

✔ **Closing a document and quitting Word**

*T*his chapter is an introduction to the very basics of using Word: starting the program; working with the user interface; typing and editing text; printing and saving a document; and perhaps most important of all, quitting Word when you're done. Have fun!

Starting Word

You can start Word in so many different ways that you can probably use a different technique every day for a fortnight. Rather than bore you with the details of every possible way to start Word, I show you the most common way first. Then I show you a couple of shortcuts that are useful if you use Word a lot.

Turn on your computer and then follow these steps to start Word:

1. Get ready.

Light some votives. Take two Tylenol. Put on a pot of coffee. If you're allergic to banana slugs, take an allergy pill. Sit in the lotus position facing Redmond, Washington, and recite the Windows creed three times:

Bill Gates is my friend. Resistance is futile. No beer and no TV make Homer something something . . .

2. Click the Start button.

Find the Start button in the lower-left corner of the Windows display. In Windows XP, it's a round-cornered box with the word *Start* in it. In Windows Vista, it's a round button with a four-colored flag. Either way, clicking the Start button summons the Start menu.

You can quickly summon the Start menu by pressing Ctrl+Esc.

3. Point to All Programs on the Start menu.

Move the cursor up to the word *Programs* and hold it there a moment. Yet another menu appears, revealing a bevy of commands.

In older versions of Windows (prior to Windows XP), All Programs is called simply Programs.

4. Click Microsoft Office on the Start menu and then click Microsoft Office Word 2007.

Your computer whirs and clicks and possibly makes other unmentionable noises while Word comes to life.

The following paragraphs describe some quick ways to start Word. Look into these methods if you use Word frequently and you grow weary of trudging through the depths of the Start menu:

✦ If you use Word frequently, it might appear in an area of the Start menu called the *Frequently Used Program List.* If so, you can start Word by clicking it directly from the Start menu.

If you want Word to always appear at the top of the Start menu, choose Start⇨All Programs⇨Microsoft Office. Then, right-click Microsoft Office Word 2007 and choose the Pin to Start Menu command. This command pins Word to the Start menu, above the Frequently Used Program List.

✦ You can create an icon for Word on your desktop. Then you can start Word by double-clicking its desktop icon. To create a desktop icon for Word, open the Start menu, navigate through All Programs and Microsoft Office, and then right-click Microsoft Office Word 2007 and choose Send To⇨Desktop.

✦ My personal favorite way to start Word is to create an icon for it on the Quick Launch toolbar on the taskbar, right next to the Start button. To create a Quick Launch icon for Word, first create a desktop shortcut as described in the preceding paragraph. Then drag the desktop icon to the Quick Launch toolbar and release the mouse button. To start Word from the Quick Launch toolbar, just click the Word icon once (no need to double-click in the Quick Launch toolbar).

✦ Yet another way to start Word is by using Windows Explorer to browse
to a folder that contains a document you want to edit. Then, double-click
the icon for the document. Windows responds by starting Word and
opening the document you chose.

✦ One more trick before moving on. If you use Word every day, you can set
it to start automatically every time you start your computer. To do that,
navigate your way through the Start menu to the Microsoft Office Word
2007 command. Then drag it into the Startup group under Start⇨All
Programs.

What Is All This Stuff?

When you start Word, it greets you with a screen that's so cluttered with
stuff that you're soon ready to dig out your grandfather's manual typewriter.
The center of the screen is mercifully blank and vaguely resembles a piece of
typing paper, but all around the edges and tucked into every corner are little
icons and buttons, rulers and menus, and whatnot. Figure 1-1 shows the
basic Word screen in all its cluttered glory. The following list points out the
more important parts of the Word screen:

✦ **Title bar:** At the very top of the Word screen is the *title bar,* which displays the name of the document you're working on. The title bar also
includes the standard Minimize, Restore, and Close buttons present in
every window as well as the Quick Access toolbar (described later in
this list).

✦ **The Ribbon:** Across the top of the screen, just below the title bar, is
Word's main user-interface gadget, called the *Ribbon.* If you've worked
with previous versions of Word, you were probably expecting to see a
menu bar followed by one or more toolbars in this general vicinity. After
meticulous research, Microsoft gurus decided that menus and toolbars
are hard to use. So they replaced the menus and toolbars with the Ribbon,
which combines the functions of both. The Ribbon takes some getting
used to, but after you figure it out, it actually does become easier to use
than the old menus and toolbars. The deepest and darkest secrets of
Word are hidden on the Ribbon. Wear a helmet when exploring it.

Note that the exact appearance of the Ribbon varies a bit depending on
the size of your monitor. On smaller monitors, Word might compress the
Ribbon a bit by using smaller buttons and arranging them differently (for
example, stacking them on top of one another instead of placing them
side by side).

For more information about working with the Ribbon, see the section "Unraveling the Ribbon," later in this chapter.

Although Word 2007 has done away with the menus, the keyboard short-cuts (technically called *accelerators*) that were associated with the Word 2003 menu commands still work. For example, to call up the Open dialog box, press Alt, F, and O (for the old File⇨Open command). And to insert clip art, press Alt, I, P, and C (for the old Insert⇨Picture⇨Clip Art command). To keep things simple, this book doesn't specifically mention these accelerators. However, if you remember them from your Word 2003 days, you can continue to use them.

✦ **The Office button (also known as the File menu):** The big colorful logo in the top-left corner of the Word window is called the Office button. You can click it to reveal the program's one and only traditional menu. This is the place to come when you need to open or save files, create new presentations, print a document, and do other file-related chores. It's roughly equivalent to the File menu in previous versions of Word.

✦ **Quick Access toolbar:** Just to the right of the Office button is the *Quick Access toolbar,* also called the *QAT* for short. Its sole purpose in life is to provide a convenient resting place for the Word commands you use the most often.

Initially, this toolbar contains just four buttons: Save, Undo, Redo, and Print. However, you can add additional buttons if you want. To add any button to the QAT, right-click the button and choose Add to Quick Access toolbar. You can also find a pull-down menu at the end of the QAT that lists several frequently used commands. You can use this menu to add these common commands to the QAT.

✦ **Ruler:** Word actually has two rulers: a horizontal ruler and a vertical ruler. The horizontal ruler appears just beneath the Ribbon and is used to set margins and tab stops. The vertical ruler appears on the left edge of the Word window and is used to gauge the vertical position of ele-ments on the page. (If the ruler doesn't appear, you can summon it by clicking the View tab on the Ribbon, then selecting the Ruler check box in the Show/Hide group.)

✦ **Task pane:** The right side of the Word screen is home to the *task pane,* which helps you complete common tasks quickly. When you first start Word, the task pane is hidden. Thus, it doesn't appear in Figure 1-1. Don't worry, the task pane will appear on its own whenever you need it.

✦ **Status bar:** At the very bottom of the screen is the *status bar,* which tells you the page that is currently displayed (for example, Page 5 of 11).

You can configure the status bar by right-clicking anywhere on it. This reveals a list of options that you can select or deselect to determine which elements appear on the status bar.

Figure 1-1:
Word's
cluttered
screen.

✦ **View buttons:** The group of five buttons located to the left of the horizontal scroll bar near the bottom of the screen lets you switch among Word's various document views. You can find out more about these views in the section "The View from Here Is Great."

✦ **Zoom control:** At the bottom-right corner of the screen is a Zoom control, which lets you zoom in for a closer look at your text. The Zoom control consists of a slider that you can slide left or right to zoom in or out, – and + buttons you can click to increase or decrease the zoom factor, and a number that indicates the current zoom percentage. Note that this number is actually a button; if you click it, Word displays a dialog box with additional zoom options.

You'll never get anything done if you feel that you have to understand every pixel of the Word screen before you can do anything. Don't worry about the stuff that you don't understand; just concentrate on what you need to know to get the job done and worry about the bells and whistles later.

Lots of stuff is crammed onto the Word screen — enough stuff that the program works best if you let it run in *maximized* mode. If Word doesn't take over your entire screen, find the boxy-looking Maximize button on the right side of the title bar. (It's the middle of the three buttons.) Click it to maximize the Word screen. Click it again to restore Word to its smaller size.

Unraveling the Ribbon

The Ribbon is Microsoft's new user-interface gadget for not just Word 2007, but also Excel 2007, PowerPoint 2007, and Access 2007. The Ribbon replaces the menus and toolbars found in earlier versions of these programs.

Across the top of the Ribbon is a series of tabs. You can click one of these tabs to reveal a set of controls specific to that tab. For example, the Ribbon in Figure 1-1 (earlier in the chapter) shows the Home tab. Initially, the Ribbon displays the following seven tabs:

✦ **Home:** Basic commands for creating and formatting documents. Here you can find controls for working with the Clipboard, setting the font, formatting paragraphs, applying styles, and using Find and Replace.

✦ **Insert:** Commands for inserting various things into your document, including new pages, tables, pictures, shapes, and other types of illustrations, headers and footers, specially formatted text, and much more! Most of these features are covered in Book IV.

✦ **Page Layout:** Commands that let you tweak the layout of your document's pages. You can apply a theme to your document to set the overall look of the document, or you can control details such as the page margins, background colors, and so on. You find out about these features in Book III.

✦ **References:** Commands that let you create Tables of Contents, footnotes, bibliographies, indexes, and so on. You discover how to use these features in Book VI.

✦ **Mailings:** Commands for creating mail merges. I show you how to use this tab in Book VII.

✦ **Review:** Commands for proofing and adding comments to your documents and tracking changes. For more information, see Chapter 3 of Book V.

✦ **View:** Commands that let you change the view. You can use this tab to switch to different document views, to show or hide certain types of information (such as paragraph marks), and to zoom in for a closer look at your document.

Besides these basic tabs, additional tabs appear from time to time. For example, if you select a picture, a Picture Tools contextual tab appears with commands that let you manipulate the picture. These contextual tabs display in a different color to make them easy to spot. Also, sometimes two or more contextual tabs appear at the same time. For example, if you select a picture within a table, two contextual tabs appear: one for the table, the other for the picture.

The commands on a tab are organized into groups. Within each group, most of the commands are simple buttons that are similar to toolbar buttons in previous versions of Word.

One of the most important differences between the new user interface and the interface from previous versions of Word is that you can't easily customize the Word 2007 user interface. In previous versions, you could easily drag toolbars around to different locations on-screen, add or remove buttons from toolbars, and even create your own toolbars. Microsoft discovered that very few people customized the user interface on purpose, but many people did it by accident . . . and then couldn't figure out how to get things back to normal. As a result, they removed most of the customization features. The only aspect of the user interface you can easily customize is the Quick Access toolbar. For more information, see Chapter 1 of Book VIII.

The View from Here Is Great

On the bottom-right edge of the Word screen (just to the left of the Zoom control) is a series of five View buttons that let you switch among various document views. The following paragraphs describe these five views:

✦ **Print Layout view**, which displays pages exactly as they will appear when printed, complete with columns, headers, footers, and all other formatting details. This is the view you'll work in most.

✦ **Full Screen Reading Layout view**, designed for easy on-screen reading.

✦ **Web Layout view**, which shows how a document appears when viewed by a Web browser, such as Internet Explorer. Web Layout view is the mode you normally work in when you use Word to create HTML documents.

✦ **Outline view**, which lets you work with outlines established via Word's standard heading styles. For more information about using outlines, consult Book II, Chapter 7.

✦ **Draft view**, which formats text as it appears on the printed page with a few exceptions. For example, headers and footers aren't shown. Most people prefer this mode.

Typing and Editing Text

I devote all of Book II to the many and sundry techniques for editing your documents. In the following paragraphs, I just highlight some very basic editing techniques to get you started.

✦ Any text you type is inserted into the document at the location of the *insertion point*. You can move the insertion point around the screen by using the movement keys (the four keys with arrows pointing up, down, left, and right) or by simply clicking at the location you want to move the insertion point to.

✦ In previous versions of Word, you could switch to *Overtype mode* by pressing the Insert key. Then any text you typed replaced the text already on the page. Few people switched to Overtype mode on purpose, and it was all too easy to switch to it by accident. As a result, Microsoft wisely disabled the Insert key for his purpose. (You can reactivate this feature from the Word Options dialog box if you want, but I don't recommend it.)

✦ If you make a mistake (never!), press Backspace to back up, erasing text as you go. For more efficient ways to correct mistakes, refer to Book II.

✦ Press Enter at the end of each paragraph to begin a new paragraph.

Don't press Enter at the end of every line. Word automatically wraps your text to the next line when it reaches the margin.

✦ Press Tab to indent text. Don't press the spacebar repeatedly to indent text; that's a rookie mistake.

Printing Your Masterpiece

After you finish your masterpiece, you might want to print it. I have a lot more to say about printing in Chapter 4 of this minibook. But for now, here's the quick procedure for printing a document:

1. **Make sure that your printer is turned on and ready to print.**

   Check the paper supply while you're at it.

2. **Choose Office⇨Print.**

   This action summons the Print dialog box, as shown in Figure 1-2. The Print dialog box has a myriad of options you can fiddle with to print just parts of your document or to print more than one copy. But to print a single copy of the entire document, you can leave these settings alone.

3. Click OK or press Enter.

Make sure that you say "Print" in a knowing manner, pointing at your printer as you do so. The secret is to fool your printer into thinking you know what you're doing.

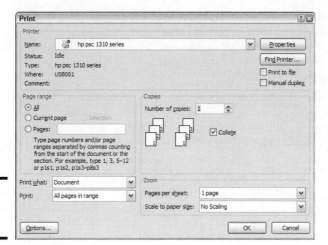

Figure 1-2:
The Print
dialog box.

Saving Your Work

Now that you've spent hours creating your document, you have to save your work to a file. If you make the rookie mistake of turning off your computer before you save your presentation, *poof!* Your work vanishes as if David Copperfield is in town.

Like everything else in Word, you have at least four ways to save a document:

✦ Click the Save button on the Quick Access toolbar.

✦ Choose Office➪Save.

✦ Press Ctrl+S.

✦ Press Shift+F12.

If you haven't yet saved the file to your hard drive, the magical Save As dialog box appears, as shown in Figure 1-3. Type the name that you want to use for the file in the File Name text box and click the OK button to save the file. After you save the file once, subsequent saves update the hard drive file with any changes that you made to the document since the last time you saved it.

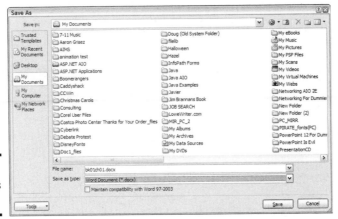

Figure 1-3:
The Save As
dialog box.

Some notes to keep in mind when saving files:

✦ Put on your Thinking Cap when assigning a name to a new file. The file-name is how you can recognize the file later on, so pick a meaningful name that suggests the file's contents.

✦ After you save a file for the first time, the name in Word's title bar changes from *Document1* to the name of your file. This name is simply proof that you saved the file.

✦ Don't work on your file for hours at a time without saving it. I learned the hard way to save my work every few minutes. After all, I live in California, so I never know when a rolling blackout will hit my neighborhood. Get into the habit of saving every few minutes, especially after making a significant change to a document. In fact, I usually save after completing every paragraph. It's also a good idea to save every time you print.

Opening a Document

After you save your document to your hard drive, you can retrieve it later when you want to make additional changes or to print it. As you might guess, Word gives you about 2,037 ways to accomplish the retrieval. Here are the most common:

✦ Choose Office➪Open.

✦ Press Ctrl+O.

✦ Press Ctrl+F12.

Each of these methods pops up the Open dialog box, which gives you a list of files to choose from, as shown in Figure 1-4. Click the file you want, and then click the Open button or press Enter.

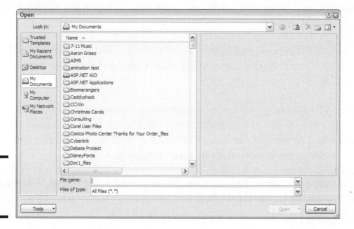

Figure 1-4:
The Open
dialog box.

The Open dialog box has controls that enable you to rummage through the various folders on your hard drive in search of your files. If you know how to open a file in any Windows application, you know how to do it in Word; the Open dialog box is pretty much the same in any Windows program.

The fastest way to open a file from the Open dialog box is to double-click the file that you want to open. This action spares you from having to click the file once and then clicking Open. Double-clicking also exercises the fast-twitch muscles in your index finger.

Word keeps track of files that you've recently opened and displays them on the right side of the Office button menu. To open a file you've recently opened, click the Office button and inspect the list of files that appear on the menu. If the file you want is in the list, click it to open it. (Note that in previous versions, Word displayed only the four most recent documents you've edited. Word 2007 displays 17 recent documents by default, and you can use the Office⇨Word Options command to change the number of recent documents displayed.)

Closing a Document

Having finished your document and printed it just right, you have come to the time to close it. Closing a document is kind of like gathering up your papers, putting them neatly in a file folder, and returning the folder to its proper file drawer. The document disappears from your computer screen. Don't worry: It's tucked safely away on your hard drive where you can get to it later if you need to.

To close a file, choose Office⇨Close. You also can use the keyboard shortcut Ctrl+W, but you need a mind like a steel trap to remember that Ctrl+W stands for Close.

You don't have to close a file before exiting Word. If you exit Word without closing a file, Word graciously closes the file for you. The only reason you might want to close a file is that you want to work on a different file and you don't want to keep both files open at the same time.

If you made changes since the last time you saved the file, Word offers to save the changes for you. Click Yes to save the file before closing or click No to abandon any changes you've made to the file.

If you close all the open Word documents, you might discover that most of Word's commands are rendered useless. (They're grayed out on the menu.) Fear not. Open a document, or create a new one, and the commands return to life.

Exiting Word

Had enough excitement for one day? Use any of these techniques to shut down Word:

✦ Choose Office⇨Exit Word.

✦ Click the X box at the top-right corner of the Word window.

✦ Press Alt+F4.

Bam! Word is history.

You should know a few things about exiting Word (or any application):

✦ Word doesn't let you abandon ship without first considering whether you want to save your work. If you made changes to any documents and haven't saved them, Word offers to save the documents for you. Lean over and plant a fat kiss right in the middle of your monitor — Word just saved you your job.

✦ Never, never, never, ever, never turn off your computer while Word or any other program is running. It's a very bad idea! You'll lose whatever work you've done since the last time you saved, and you run the risk of losing your document altogether and perhaps even corrupting other documents. Always properly exit Word and all other programs that are running before you turn off your computer.

Chapter 2: Managing Your Documents

In This Chapter

✔ **Creating new documents**

✔ **Opening existing documents**

✔ **Finding files gone astray**

✔ **Retrieving files from the Internet**

✔ **Saving your documents and setting Word's file-saving options**

You can't get very far in Word without knowing how to save and retrieve documents on your hard drive, home network, or server. So, this chapter dives head first into the world of Word document management.

Creating a New Document

The easiest way to create a new document in Word is to simply start Word from the Start menu. Then Word creates a blank document named Document1, as shown in Figure 2-1.

When you create a new document this way, the document is based on a template called `Normal.dotm`. A *template* is simply a model document from which new documents are created. New documents based on the `Normal.dotm` template have the following characteristics:

✦ The margins are set at 1 inch from the top and bottom and 1 inch from the left and right. If you want to change these margin settings, turn to Book III, Chapter 1.

✦ The text is formatted using 11-point Calibri. To change the text format, check out Book II, Chapter 2.

✦ The document includes a few (and by "a few" I mean over 100) built-in styles you can use to format headings (you can find 16 as quick styles). To discover how to work with these styles or to create your own styles, see Book II, Chapter 3.

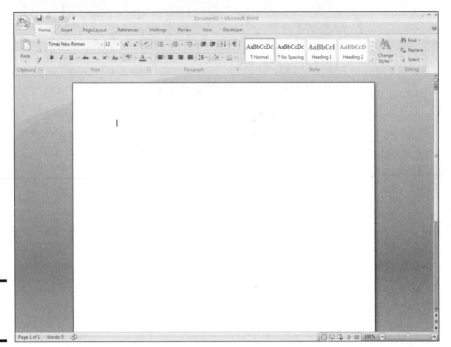

Figure 2-1:
A blank
document.

The `Normal.dotm` template is adequate for generic types of documents, such as book reports and letters to your mom. For more specialized types of documents, you can use other templates that come with Word. Or, you can create your own templates. For more information about working with templates, see Chapter 3 of this minibook.

You can create as many new documents as your heart desires without having to worry about closing any of your other open documents. If you've already started Word, you can create a second (or third, or fourth) new document in one of the following ways:

✦ Choose Office⇨New. This summons the New Document dialog box, shown in Figure 2-2. Next, click the Blank Document icon and then click the Create button to create a new blank document.

✦ Press Ctrl+N. This is the keyboard shortcut for creating a new blank document.

✦ Click the New button on the Quick Access toolbar. The New button doesn't initially appear in the Quick Access toolbar, but you can easily place it there by clicking the Customize Quick Access Toolbar button at the bottom right of the Quick Access toolbar. Then click New from the list of buttons that appears.

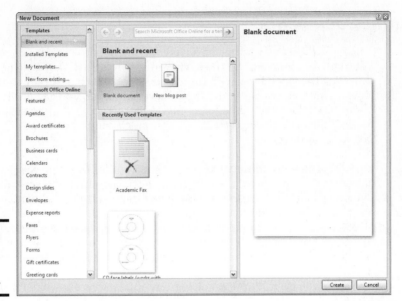

Figure 2-2:
The New
Document
dialog box.

After you create a new document, you can add text and other content, and edit the document however you want. Then, you can save the document to disk as described later in this chapter.

The New Document dialog box provides several alternatives to creating simple blank documents. Another way to create a new document is to choose Office⇨New. When you do, the New Document dialog box appears. It provides several links you can click to create various types of documents:

✦ **Blank Document:** Click this icon to create a blank document, the same as if you click the New Blank Document button.

✦ **New Blog Post:** Click this icon to create a new post at a blogging Web site. For more information, refer to Chapter 1 of Book V.

✦ **Installed Templates:** Click this option (in the left column) to display a list of templates that are available on your computer. For more information about templates, see Chapter 3 of this minibook.

✦ **My Templates:** Click this option to display a list of templates that you have downloaded from Microsoft's Web site and customized for your own use. For more information, see Chapter 3 of this minibook.

✦ **New From Existing:** Click this option to create a new document based on a copy of an existing document.

✦ **Microsoft Office Online:** This section of the New Document dialog box lets you access templates from Microsoft's Web site.

Opening Documents

The most direct way to open a saved document is to choose Office➪Open. Alternatively, you can use the keyboard shortcut Ctrl+O or Ctrl+F12. Or, you can click the Open button on the Quick Access toolbar. Although this button doesn't initially appear in the Quick Access toolbar, you can easily place it there by clicking the Customize Quick Access Toolbar button at the bottom right of the Quick Access toolbar and then clicking Open from the list of buttons that appears.

Ctrl+O is the more intuitive keyboard shortcut for the Office➪Open command ("O" is for "Open"), but Ctrl+F12 is left over from the early days of Windows, before Microsoft programmers decided that keyboard shortcuts make more sense. Rather than drop an antiquated and senseless keyboard shortcut in favor of one that makes sense and is consistent across all Windows applications (or at least is supposed to be), the Word developers at Microsoft decided to leave *both* keyboard shortcuts in place.

However you do it, the Open dialog box appears, as shown in Figure 2-3.

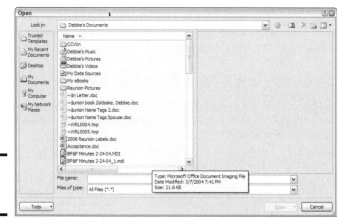

Figure 2-3:
The Open
dialog box.

The most important control in the Open dialog box is the Look In drop-down list. It lists every location where documents might be hiding: all your hard drives, your desktop (you can store documents on the desktop by dragging them there from an Explorer window), your My Documents folder, and a few other locations, such as network drives.

Although the Look In drop-down list is the primary method of navigating through your drives and folders, you can still work your way down through the folder hierarchy by double-clicking folder icons. You can move back up the folder hierarchy by clicking the Up One Level button, which appears next to the Look In field. You can also move up one level in the hierarchy by pressing Backspace.

You can open more than one document at once by selecting several files and clicking the Open button. Use one of the following techniques to select several files:

✦ Hold down the Ctrl key while clicking the files you want to select.

✦ To select a range of files, click the first file in the range, hold down the Shift key, and click the last file in the range.

Changing views

The Open dialog box lets you switch among seven different views of your documents. The Views button at the top of the Open dialog box displays a menu that lets you choose your view:

✦ **Thumbnails:** Displays a large icon that represents the contents of each file. For image files, the thumbnail displays a small view of the image contained in the file. For Windows XP, Word documents don't display useful thumbnails by default, but in Windows Vista they do.

✦ **Tiles:** Displays each document using large icons, with descriptive information listed to the right of each icon.

✦ **Icons:** Displays each document with a medium-sized icon and descriptive information listed below each icon.

✦ **List:** Displays a list of folders and documents with small icons.

✦ **Details:** Displays a list of folders and documents with details, including the filename, type, size, and creation date. *Note:* The headers at the top of the columns are actually buttons; you can sort the list on any of the columns simply by clicking the column's button.

✦ **Properties:** Displays a panel showing various properties for the selected file, including the title, author, template, word count, and other useful information.

✦ **Preview:** Displays a preview of the selected file in a separate pane.

Deleting and renaming documents and folders

You can delete and rename files and folders from the Open dialog box. Here's how:

✦ **To delete a file or folder,** select the file or folder and press Delete.

✦ **To rename a file or folder,** select it by clicking it once and then click the filename again. A text-editing box appears around the file or folder name, allowing you to edit the name. (Don't click it too quickly, or Word thinks you double-clicked and the file or folder opens.)

Setting the default document location

When you call up the Open dialog box, Word initially displays the contents of the folder indicated by the default Document File Location option setting. When you install Word, this option is initially set to the My Documents folder on your computer's local hard drive. However, you can change that location if you want. For example, you might want to set up Word so that the default document location is on a network drive. To do so, follow these steps:

1. **Choose Office⇨Word Options.**

   The Word Options dialog box appears.

2. **Click the Advanced tab on the left side of the Word Options dialog box.**

3. **Use the scroll bar to scroll all the way to the bottom of the Advanced tab.**

4. **Click the File Locations button.**

   The File Locations dialog box appears, as shown in Figure 2-4.

5. **Click Documents and then click the Modify button.**

   This brings up the Modify Location dialog box.

6. **Use the Modify Location dialog box to select the new location for your documents.**

   You can either type the complete path (drive letter and folder) for the location where you want to store documents, or you can use the controls in the Modify Location dialog box to navigate to the folder.

7. **Click OK to return to the File Locations dialog box.**

8. **Click OK again to return to the Word Options dialog box.**

9. **Click OK one more time to dismiss the Word Options dialog box.**

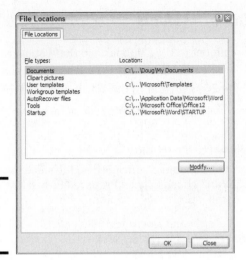

Figure 2-4:
The File
Locations
dialog box.

Using the shortcut menu

You can right-click a folder or document in the Open dialog box to call up a shortcut menu that contains the following commands:

+ **Select:** Selects the document. This option is the same as clicking the document with the left mouse button.

+ **Open:** Opens the document. This option is the same as double-clicking the document or selecting the document and clicking the Open button.

+ **Edit:** The same as Open. (This item doesn't appear in the shortcut menu if the document has been saved as read-only.

+ **New:** Creates a new Word document.

+ **Print:** Prints the document without actually opening it.

+ **Open With:** Lets you open a document using another program besides Word. I don't know why you'd want to do that, but it's good to know you can.

+ **Send To:** This option is one of the most useful commands to appear on the shortcut menu. It allows you to send the selected document to any of several destinations, such as an e-mail recipient, a floppy disk, or a recordable CD-RW drive.

✦ **Cut:** Deletes the document and places it on the Clipboard. Cutting a document allows you to paste it into another folder.

✦ **Copy:** Copies the document to the Clipboard so that you can paste it into another folder.

✦ **Create Shortcut:** Creates a shortcut to the selected document.

✦ **Delete:** Deletes the document or folder. You can achieve the same result by pressing Delete.

✦ **Rename:** Lets you change the document's name.

✦ **Properties:** Displays the document's properties, the same as if you opened the document and chose Office➪Prepare➪Properties. I cover file properties in more detail later in this chapter.

Using the Organize menu in Vista (or the Tools menu in XP)

The Open dialog box displays commands that manipulate the selected document or that sets options that govern how the Open dialog box works. In Vista, the tools discussed here are in the Organize menu (in the upper-right corner of the Open dialog box).

If you're using Windows XP, the Tools menu is located in the top-right corner of the Open dialog box. The commands on the Organize menu and the Tools menu include the following:

✦ **Delete:** Deletes the document or folder. You can achieve the same result by pressing Delete.

✦ **Rename:** Lets you change the document's name.

✦ **Print:** Prints the document without actually opening it.

✦ **Map Network Drive:** Lets you associate a drive letter with a network folder. Don't mess with this command unless you know something about networks.

✦ **Properties:** Displays the document's properties, the same as if you opened the document and chose Office➪Prepare➪Properties. I cover file properties in more detail later in this chapter.

The Tools menu has changed from the XP days. In Vista, the Tools menu is in the lower-middle side on the right in the Open dialog box and contains only the Map Network Drive option. The tools discussed in this section are in the Organize menu in Vista (in the upper-right corner of the Open dialog box).

Using My Places

My Places refers to the band of icons that runs down the left side of the Open dialog box. The following list is similar for Windows Vista. For Windows XP, Word provides the following icons in My Places:

+ **My Recent Documents:** A list of recently used documents.

+ **Desktop:** Your computer's desktop. (I don't recommend storing documents on the desktop. Unlike my real desktop, I like to keep my computer desktop uncluttered.)

+ **My Documents:** Your My Documents folder, which is the normal location for storing documents.

+ **My Computer:** The My Computer folder gives you access to all the hard drives on your computer.

+ **My Network Places:** Lets you access locations available via your network.

You can quickly access any of these document locations by clicking the icon in the My Places bar.

You can add your own locations to the My Places bar. To do so, summon the Open dialog box and navigate to the folder you want to add to My Places. Then right-click anywhere in the My Places bar. The shortcut menu that appears includes a command that lets you add the selected folder to the My Places bar.

In Windows XP, the shortcut menu lets you further customize the My Places bar by moving icons up or down, deleting icons, or switching from large to small icons. (Windows Vista doesn't give you this option, however.)

Opening Recently Used Documents

The right side of the Office menu is dominated by a list of documents you've recently used. You can quickly reopen one of these documents by choosing it from the menu.

Using the Save As Command

The Save As command saves a new file or an existing file under a different name. You can summon this command in two ways:

+ Choose Office⇨Save As.

+ Press F12.

You can also invoke the Save As command by using the Save command for any document that is not yet saved to your hard drive.

Figure 2-5 shows the Save As dialog box, displayed when you invoke the Save As command. As you can see, this dialog box shares many features and controls with the Open dialog box.

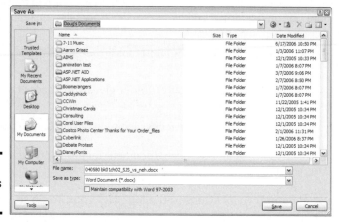

Figure 2-5:
The Save As dialog box.

In the Save As dialog box, navigate to the folder where you want to save the document, type a new name for the document, and click the Save button.

If you want to replace an existing document with the current document, double-click the document you want replaced. Word displays a dialog box asking whether you really want to replace the document. If you click Yes, the existing document is overwritten by the document you're editing.

When you first call up the Save As dialog box, Word takes a wild guess that you want the text in the first paragraph of the document to be the filename. This guess makes sense if the first paragraph is the title of the document, but in most cases, you want to type a more sensible document name.

Like the File Open dialog box, the Save As dialog box contains several buttons. The following list describes the function of each of these buttons:

✦ **Back:** Returns to the previous folder.

✦ **Up One Level:** Moves up the folder hierarchy one level, to the current folder's parent folder.

✦ **Delete:** Deletes the selected file or folder.

✦ **Create New Folder:** Creates a new folder as a subfolder of the current folder. You are prompted to type a name for the new folder.

✦ **Views:** Lets you switch views. For more information, see the section "Changing views," earlier in this chapter.

✦ **Tools:** Brings up the ever-handy Tools menu. For more information, see the section "Using the Organize menu in Vista (or the Tools menu in XP)," earlier in this chapter.

Notice that the Save As dialog box also includes a Save As Type drop-down list. Normally, this field is set to Word Document (*.docx) so that documents are stored in Word format. You can change this setting to save a document in another format.

Not all file types support all of Word's formatting features. Any special formatting not supported by the file type is lost when you save the file. So if you're going to save your masterpiece in one of these formats, you might want to keep a version in Word format, too.

The Office⇨Save As command is interesting in that if you click it square in the middle, it summons the Save As dialog box. However, if you click the arrow at the right side of the Save As command, a menu appears that lets you select the format you want to use for the file. For example, you can choose Office⇨Save As⇨Word 97-2003 Format to save a document in the old format used by Word 97 through 2003. Choosing this command still brings up the Save As dialog box, but with the Save As Type drop-down list set to the file type you selected.

Save Options

You can set several options that affect how files are saved by choosing Office⇨Word Options and then clicking the Save tab on the left, as shown in Figure 2-6.

The following paragraphs describe the effect each of these options has:

✦ **Save Files in This Format:** This option lets you specify the default format for saving files.

✦ **Save AutoRecover Info Every *n* Minutes:** This option automatically saves recovery information at regular intervals. The default setting is to save the recovery information every 10 minutes, but you can change the time interval if you want.

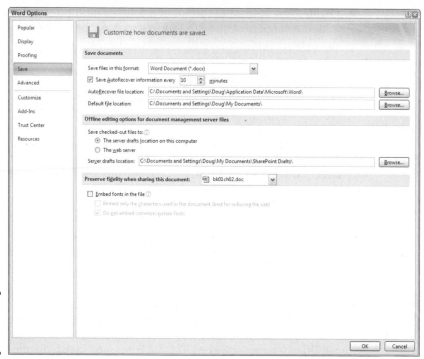

Figure 2-6:
Setting save
options.

✦ **AutoRecover File Location:** With this option, you can set the location where you want the AutoRecover files saved.

✦ **Default File Location:** This option lets you set the default location for Word documents.

✦ **Save Checked-Out Files To:** If you're working with a document-management system such as SharePoint, this option lets you specify where files should be saved when you check them out.

✦ **Embed Fonts in the File:** When you use this option, Word saves TrueType fonts in the document file. This option increases the size of the document file but enables you to copy the file to another system without worrying about whether the other system has the fonts used in the document.

Amazingly, even though Microsoft created a separate tab for Save options, it didn't put all of the Save options on the Save tab. If you switch over to the Advanced tab and scroll down a bit, you can find a Save section that includes more save options:

+ **Prompt Before Saving Normal Template:** This option forces Word to ask for your permission before saving changes to the `Normal.dotm` template. If you're concerned about proliferating changes to this template, enable this option.

+ **Always Create Backup Copy:** If you select this option, Word always saves the previous version of the document as a backup copy each time it saves the document. The backup copy uses the extension BAK.

   Don't rely on the Always Create Backup Copy option as your only backup of important documents. The backup copy created by this option resides on the same drive and in the same folder as the document itself. As a result, if a hard drive failure or other problem renders the drive or folder inaccessible, the backup copy is inaccessible as well. Always back up important documents to a separate hard drive or, better yet, to tape.

+ **Copy Remotely Stored Files onto Your Computer, and Update the Remote File When Saving:** Creates a local copy of documents stored on network or removable drives so that they can be recovered in case you lose access to the network or removable drive.

+ **Allow Background Saves:** Saves documents while allowing you to continue working. This option is activated by default. Don't change it. Just know that it's there and go about your business.

Password Protecting Your Files

Word allows you to protect your sensitive files from snooping eyes by using passwords. You can apply two types of passwords to your documents:

+ A **Password to Open** password prevents users who don't know the password from opening the file. Use this password for files you don't want unauthorized users to examine.

+ A **Password to Modify** password prevents users who don't know the password from saving the file. Use this password for files you don't want unauthorized users to modify.

To password protect a document, follow these steps:

1. **Open the document.**

2. **Choose Office⇨Save As.**

   This brings up the Save As dialog box.

3. Click the Tools button and then click General Options from the drop-down menu that appears.

The dialog box shown in Figure 2-7 appears.

Figure 2-7:
Setting a
password.

4. Type a password in the Password to Open field or the Password to Modify field (or both, if you want to provide a different password for each type of access).

Word displays asterisks as you type the password, which prevents Looky Lous from seeing your password as you type it.

5. Click OK.

6. When Word prompts you to re-enter the password, type it again, exactly as you did the first time.

7. Click OK.

8. Save the file.

After the file is password protected, Word prompts you (or anyone else) to enter the password with the dialog box shown in Figure 2-8. No password, no document.

Figure 2-8:
Entering a
password.

Here are some cautionary tips for working with passwords:

✦ Don't forget your password! If you forget, you can't access your document.

✦ Don't use different passwords for every document. You'll never remember them all. Instead, use the same password for all your documents.

✦ Don't write your password down on a sticky note and stick it on your computer monitor.

✦ Don't use obvious passwords, such as your kids' names, your spouse's name, your dog's name, or the name of your boat.

To remove password protection from a file, open the file (you have to supply the password to do it), choose Office➪Save As, click Tools, click General Options, and then highlight and delete the password. Click OK and save the file.

Chapter 3: Working with Templates

In This Chapter

✔ **Discovering templates**

✔ **Enabling default settings for Word documents**

✔ **Creating documents based on a template**

✔ **Building your own templates**

✔ **Using global templates properly**

✔ **Working with the Organizer**

An entire chapter on templates this early in the book might seem premature, but I want to impress upon you right from the start that understanding templates is one of the keys to using Word as efficiently as possible. You can use Word for years without even knowing what a template is, but either your documents all look the same or you spend way too much time fiddling with the same formatting options over and over again. Besides, the proper use of templates comes up again and again throughout this book, so I might as well get the subject of templates out in the open.

Note that the new themes feature has made it easier to change the appearance of documents without changing templates. For more information about working with themes, turn to Chapter 2 of Book II. However, templates still play a crucial role in the efficient use of Word because they store much more than just formatting information. And, somewhat in contrast to themes, one of the main strengths of templates is that they make it easy to create multiple documents that have a similar, if not identical, appearance.

Understanding How Templates Work

A *template* is a special type of document file used as the basis for formatting your documents. Whenever you create a new document, a template file is the starting point for the new document. The following items are copied from a template into the new document:

✦ **Styles:** Use them to apply paragraph and character formatting quickly. For more information about working with styles, see Book II, Chapter 3.

✦ **Default theme:** The theme used for the document is copied from the template. For more information, see Book III, Chapter 2.

✦ **Margins and other page layout information:** You can use settings such as the paper size, orientation, headers, footers, and so on.

✦ **Text and graphics:** Often referred to as *boilerplate* text, this is the text and graphics that don't change much.

✦ **Building Block entries:** These are sections of text that you can quickly insert into your documents simply by typing a few keystrokes.

✦ **Macros:** Use these miniprograms to automate routine chores. For more information, see Book IX.

Each document has one and only one template attached to it. If you don't specify a template to attach to a new document, Word attaches the generic `Normal.dotm` template, which contains the standard styles such as Normal, Heading 1, Heading 2, and Heading 3, plus default margins, keyboard shortcuts, and so on. You can attach a different template to a document later, and you can copy the styles from the new template into the existing document, if you want. Then you have access to the styles from the new template as well as the existing document.

A template is basically the same thing as a normal document, except that it is given the extension DOTX or DOTM rather than DOCX, as normal documents are. The difference between DOTX and DOTM templates is that DOTM templates allow macros, whereas DOTX templates don't.

Word permits you to open and edit templates as if they're documents, and you can easily convert a document to a template by saving it as a template rather than as a document. The real difference between documents and templates lies in how you use them.

The Normal.dotm Template

When you create a new blank document, Word attaches the `Normal.dotm` template to it. Word obtains the default document format, margins, page orientation, and the standard styles such as Normal, Heading 1, Heading 2, and Heading 3 from the `Normal.dotm` template. In other words, `Normal.dotm` is where Word stores its default settings for any feature controlled by templates.

Computer nerds call `Normal.dotm` a *global template,* which means it is always available in Word, whether or not the document you're working with is attached to it. (We computer nerds love to use the term *global* because we dream of dominating the world someday.) Even if you attach a different template to a document, the settings in `Normal.dotm` are still available because `Normal.dotm` is a global template.

Any changes you make to `Normal.dotm` effectively change Word's default behavior. For example, if you don't like Word's default style for Heading 1 paragraphs, you can change the Heading 1 style in `Normal.dotm`. Or, you can add keyboard shortcuts to `Normal.dotm`. By making careful changes to `Normal.dotm`, you can change Word's behavior to suit your own working style. In effect, you can create your own individualized version of Word.

You can restore your `Normal.dotm` template to its pristine condition by quitting Word and deleting the `Normal.dotm` template. Then, when you restart Word, Word regenerates a standard `Normal.dotm` template. You can find the template in the `C:\Documents and Settings\`*user name*`\ Application Data\Microsoft\Templates` folder. If Word discovers that the `Normal.dotm` template is missing, it reverts to its original default settings and creates a new `Normal.dotm` template. Be aware that when you do delete the template, you lose everything you added to your `Normal.dotm` template.

Creating a New Document Based on a Template

To create a document based on a template other than `Normal.dotm`, you simply select the template you want to use from the New Document dialog box that appears when you choose the Office⇨New command. Click the Installed Templates option on the left to display a list of the templates that are installed with Office 2007, as shown in Figure 3-1. Then select the template you want to use and click Create.

When you create a new document, any text and graphics contained in the template automatically copy into the new document. People often use templates for this purpose to supply text or graphics that always appear in certain types of documents. For example, a Memo Letter template would contain your letterhead. If you attach a template to an existing document, the text and graphics contained in the template don't copy into the document.

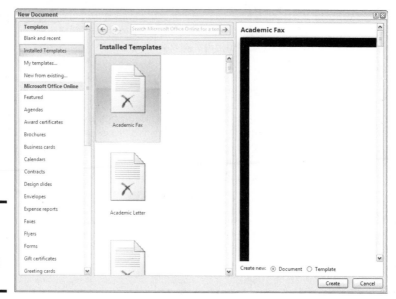

Figure 3-1:
Creating a
document
based on a
template.

Creating a Document from an Online Template

Microsoft maintains an Office Web site that has additional templates you can use for your documents. To create a document by using one of these online templates, make sure you have an active Internet connection and follow these steps:

1. Call up the New Document dialog box.

Choose Office⇨New.

2. Select one of the categories listed under Office Online.

The New Document dialog box displays the templates that are available for the category you selected, as shown in Figure 3-2.

3. Find a template you want to use and then click the Download button.

The template downloads to your computer and automatically creates a new document based on it.

The dialog box shown in Figure 3-3 appears when you attempt to download a template. This dialog box informs you that Microsoft is going to validate your copy of Office before it allows you to download a template from its Web site. Don't worry; Microsoft doesn't snoop around for credit card information or other private information. It just checks a code that indicates whether you obtained your copy of Office legally. Click Continue to proceed.

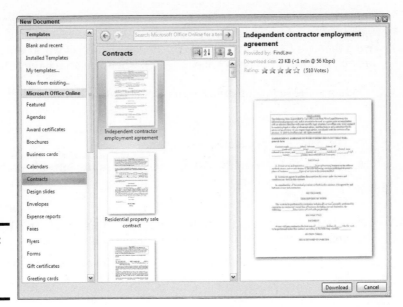

Figure 3-2:
Using an
online
template.

If you don't want to see this dialog box every time you download a template, select the Do Not Show This Message Again check box.

4. **You're done.**

A new document is created from the template you selected.

Figure 3-3:
Microsoft
validates
your copy of
Office
before it lets
you
download
templates.

Changing the Template Attached to a Document

You can change the template attached to a document at any time. When you do, all the macros, keyboard shortcuts, as well as Building Block entries from the new template, automatically copy into the document. Any boiler-plate text or graphics in the template don't copy into the document. Styles from the template are copied into the document only if you select the Auto-matically Update Document Styles option when you attach the template.

To change the template attached to a document, follow these steps:

1. **Choose Office⇨Word Options.**

   The Word Options dialog box appears.

2. **Select Add-Ins from the list of categories on the left side of the Word Options dialog box.**

   The Add-Ins options screen appears.

3. **Select Templates in the Manage drop-down list and then click the Go button (found near the lower-left corner of the dialog box).**

   This brings up the Templates and Add-Ins dialog box, shown in Figure 3-4.

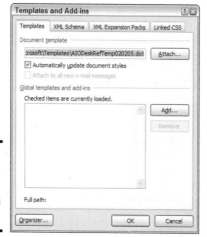

Figure 3-4:
The
Templates
and Add-Ins
dialog box.

If the Developer tab on the Ribbon is visible, you can skip Steps 1 through 3. Instead, just click the Document Template button on the Developer tab to display the Templates and Add-Ins dialog box. For more information, see the next section, "Activating the Developer Tab on the Ribbon."

4. **Click the Attach button.**

   This brings up the dialog box shown in Figure 3-5.

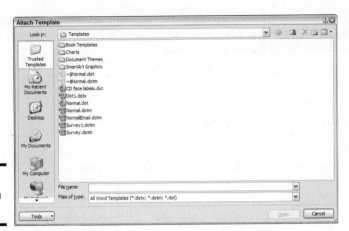

Figure 3-5:
Attaching a
template.

5. **Select the template you want to attach to the document and then click Open.**

   You might have to look in various folders to find the template you want to attach. When you click Open, you're returned to the Templates and Add-Ins dialog box.

You can't go back

Changing the template attached to a document is one of the few Word actions that you cannot undo with the Undo command. As a result, if you inadvertently attach the wrong template to a document, correcting your error can be difficult. That's because when you attach a new template, Word copies elements from the new template into the document but doesn't remove elements from the document derived from the previous template.

To illustrate the type of problem this situation can cause, suppose that you're working on a document that has a handful of custom styles and you mistakenly attach a template that has 50 custom styles. Because you used the Automatically Update Document Styles option,

those 50 styles are copied into your document. The problem arises: How can you get rid of them? You can use the Templates and Add-Ins dialog box to attach the correct template, but the 50 styles copied in from the incorrect template remain in your document! And you can't remove them easily.

To avoid this type of problem, save your document immediately before changing templates. Then, if you're not satisfied with the results after attaching the new template, you can revert to the previously saved version of the document if necessary by closing the document without saving changes and reopening the previously saved copy of the document.

6. **If you want the styles from the template you're attaching to replace the styles in your document, make sure that the Automatically Update Document Styles check box is selected.**

   You'll usually want to select this check box because the most common reason to change templates is to switch to the styles offered by the other template.

7. **Click OK to attach the template.**

If you update styles and your document uses styles to control its formatting, the effects of the new template are immediately visible.

Activating the Developer Tab on the Ribbon

If you plan on working much with templates, you can simplify your life by revealing the Developer tab on the Ribbon. This tab includes a Document Template button, which provides direct access to the Templates and Add-Ins dialog box, eliminating the need to wade through the Word Options dialog box as described in the preceding section. To activate the Developer tab, choose Office⇨Word Options, click the Popular tab, and select the Show Developer Tab In the Ribbon option. Figure 3-6 shows Word with the Developer tab open.

Creating Your Own Templates

Word comes with a collection of templates that let you create a wide variety of document types, but sooner or later you'll almost certainly want to create your own templates. The sections that follow explain everything you need to know about creating and using your own templates.

Converting a document to a template

Suppose that you've been working on a document for hours, toiling with its formats until they're just the way you want them, and you realize that you might want to create other documents with the same formats. Creating a template from this document is a simple matter.

Open the document you want to use to create the template and choose Office⇨Save As to bring up the Save As dialog box. Down at the bottom of the Save As dialog box is a Save As Type drop-down list. The default setting is Word Document. Change this field to Word Template or Word Macro-Enabled Template, depending on whether you want to include macros in the template. Type a name for your template, navigate over to the folder where you want to save the template, and click OK to save the document as a template.

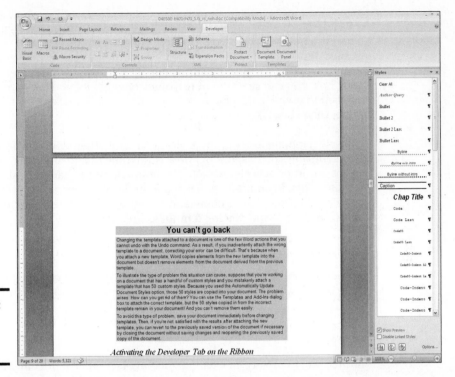

Figure 3-6:
The
Developer
tab.

Before you save your document as a template, take a few moments to improve the template's usefulness. Follow this checklist:

✦ **Remove unnecessary text.** Any text you leave in the template appears in any new documents you create with the template.

✦ **Perfect boilerplate text.** Leave only true boilerplate text that you want to appear in every document based on the template, and make sure that this boilerplate text is exactly as you want it.

To delete all the text from the document, press Ctrl+A to select the entire document and then press Delete.

✦ **Remove any unnecessary styles, macros, and so on that aren't template-worthy.** Leave only those elements you want to be included in documents created from your template.

You might be tempted to open the document, delete text and other unnecessary elements, and then save the document. I caution you against this, though, because deleting an entire document's worth of text and accidentally using Save rather than Save As are easy! To avoid this disaster, save the document as a template before you begin deleting massive amounts of text.

Creating a new template from scratch

To create a new template from scratch, choose Office➪New and select either Installed Templates or My Templates. Select the template you want use as the starting point for your new template. In the lower-right corner of the dialog box, you can see a set of radio buttons that let you indicate whether you want to create a new document or a new template. Select the Template option, then click OK.

Your new template inherits the styles, text, and other elements contained in the template you based it on. Now is the time to add any more styles, macros, or other new elements to the template or to change existing template elements. In addition, you can add boilerplate text and graphics. When you're ready, use the Save command to save the template, assigning it an appropriate name and placing it in the correct folder.

Modifying an existing template

To modify an existing template, choose Office➪Open to call up the Open dialog box. Change the Files of Type list box from Word Documents to Document Templates, and locate and select the template you want to modify. Click Open to open the template, make any changes you want to make, and choose Office➪Save to save the changes. That's all there is to it.

Another way to modify an existing template is to open a document based on the template and change those elements of the document stored in the template rather than in the document. This method is a bit confusing, however: Some elements of a document are stored only in the template, whereas other elements are copied from the template at the time the template is attached and subsequently stored in the document.

The following list indicates how changes to various elements of a document affect the template attached to the document:

✦ **Text:** Any text you add to the document doesn't affect the template. The only way to change boilerplate text in a template is to edit the template directly.

✦ **Direct formatting:** Any direct formatting you apply to the document affects the document only and is not copied back to the template.

✦ **Styles:** When you modify a style, you have the option of applying the change to styles in the current document or to styles in the template. If you apply the change only to the document, the change doesn't affect other documents created from the template.

Boring details about where to store templates

By default, Word stores its templates in the C:\ Documents and Settings*user name*\ Microsoft Office\Templates folder. But you can change the location where templates are stored by choosing Office➪Word Options, clicking the Advanced tab, and then clicking the File Locations button. Then double-click the User Templates option.

You can also specify a location for Workgroup Templates, which are templates you access via a network. Workgroup Templates come in handy if you and other network users need to share a set of common templates. In that case, place the common templates on a network file server and then use the Workgroup Templates option under the File Locations tab to indicate the location of the shared templates.

When you create your own templates, you usually store them in the User Templates folder.

However, if you create a new folder within the User Templates folder, the new folder appears as a separate tab in the dialog box that appears when you click My Templates in the New Document dialog box. You can use this little trick to organize your templates if you create a lot of them.

Word 2007 includes a new Trusted Locations feature that lets you designate certain folders as trusted, which means that documents and templates opened from those locations can be safely opened. You may want to designate your user template folder as a trusted location. To do so, choose Office➪Word Options, click the Trust Center tab, and click the Trust Center Settings button. This brings up a dialog box that lets you designate a folder as a trusted location.

✦ **Macros:** Macros are always stored in a template, so any macros you create or modify are stored in the template, not in the document itself. When you create a macro, you must indicate whether you want the macro stored in Normal.dotm, the attached template, or another global template.

✦ **Customizations:** Changes to custom keyboard shortcuts are stored in the template. You must specify whether you want the change stored in Normal.dotm, the attached template, or a global template.

✦ **Building Blocks:** Changes to Building Blocks are also stored in the template, either Normal.dotm, the attached template, or a global template.

Using Global Templates

A *global template* is a template with macros, Building Blocks, and customized keyboard shortcuts elements available to all open documents regardless of which template is attached to the document. `Normal.dotm` is a global template, which means that its elements are available even in documents attached to some other template. You can add your own templates to the list of global templates if you want, so that their elements also are available globally.

Note that only the macros, Building Blocks, and customization settings in a global template are available to other documents. Styles and boilerplate text contained in global templates aren't available (unless the document happens to be attached to the template).

A global template is a great way to create a library of customized macros. You could place all your macros in the `Normal.dotm` template, but placing them in a separate template for global macros gives you some added flexibility. For example, you can exchange your global macro template with other users without worrying about overwriting their `Normal.dotm` templates. And you can quickly remove all your custom macros by removing the global macro template without losing other custom items in your `Normal.dotm`.

Follow these steps to activate a global template:

1. **Choose Office⇨Word Options.**

   The Word Options dialog box appears.

2. **Select Add-Ins from the list of categories on the left side of the Word Options dialog box.**

   The Add-Ins options screen appears.

3. **Select Templates from the Manage drop-down list and then click the Go button.**

   This brings up the Templates and Add-Ins dialog box, shown back in Figure 3-4.

   If the Developer tab is open, you can skip Steps 1 through 3 and just click the Document Template button on the Developer tab.

4. **Locate the Global Templates and Add-Ins list box.**

   It contains a list of all the currently available global templates, along with buttons to add or remove global templates.

5. **Click the Add button.**

   An Add Templates dialog box appears.

6. **Select the template that you want to make global and then click OK.**

   When you return to the Templates and Add-Ins dialog box, the template you chose appears in the Global Templates and Add-Ins list box.

7. **Click OK.**

   You're done.

TECHNICAL STUFF

Stop me before I tell you about the startup directory

When you add a template to the Global Templates and Add-Ins list, the template remains in the list each time you start Word. However, you must use the Templates and Add-Ins dialog box and select the check box next to the template in the list to make the template global. If you don't want to do that each time you start Word, follow these steps:

1. **Quit Word.**

2. **Double-click the My Computer icon on your desktop. Navigate to the folder that contains the template you want to make global.**

3. **Double-click My Computer again to open a second My Computer window. Double-click the C drive and then navigate to the `C:\Program Files\Microsoft Office\Office\Startup` folder.**

4. **Drag any templates you want to be global ones from the template folder to the Startup folder. Use the right mouse button to drag the template.**

   When you release the right mouse button, a pop-up menu appears.

5. **Choose the Create Shortcut Here command.**

6. **Close both My Computer windows and then start Word.**

Any template files in the `C:\Program Files\Microsoft Office\Office\Winword\Startup` folder automatically load and are made global. If you previously added the template to the Global Templates and Add-Ins list, remove it before following the preceding procedure.

TIP

Check out these tidbits about global templates:

✦ To disable a global template temporarily, open the Templates and Add-Ins dialog box and deselect the template's check box in the Global Templates and Add-Ins list box. To remove the template from the list, select it and click the Remove button.

✦ After you make a template global, it remains global until you quit Word. The next time you start Word, the template is included in the Global Templates and Add-Ins list box, but its check box is deselected so that it isn't active. To activate the template to make it global, open the Templates and Add-Ins dialog box and select the template's check box. See the sidebar, "Stop me before I tell you about the startup directory," to find out how to set up a global template that's active each time you start Word.

How Word Resolves Duplicate Template Elements

When you use global templates, the possibility of duplicate template elements is very real. For example, what happens if a global template has a macro named CopyStyle and the template attached to the document also has a macro named CopyStyle? Which one takes precedence?

The following order of precedence determines which template elements to use when name conflicts occur:

1. The document itself always has first priority. Any element defined directly in the document supersedes any like-named elements in any templates.

2. The template attached to the document is next. Any element defined in the attached template supersedes any like-named elements in Normal.dotm or a global template.

3. The Normal.dotm template is next. Any element that exists in Normal.dotm takes precedence over a like-named element in another global template.

4. Global templates are last. Elements from global templates are used only if the attached template and Normal.dotm don't have a like-named element.

5. If two or more global templates have identically named elements, Word uses the one that comes first in alphabetical order. For example, if Global Template and My Global Macros are both loaded as global templates and both contain a macro named CopyStyle, Word uses the one from Global Template.

Using the Organizer

If you want to move styles *en masse* from one document or template to another, the easiest way is to use the Organizer — Word's tenacious tool for taming templates. The Organizer is especially useful when you create several new styles in a document and you want to copy those files to the document's template.

To copy styles from your document to a template, follow these steps:

1. Open the Templates and Add-Ins dialog box.

You can do that by choosing Office⇨Word Options, clicking the Add-Ins tab, choosing Templates in the Manage drop-down list, and clicking Go.

Or, if the Developer tab is visible on the Ribbon, click the Developer tab and then click the Document Template button in the Templates group. The Templates and Add-Ins dialog box appears. Refer to Figure 3-5.

2. **Click the Organizer button.**

   The Organizer dialog box, shown in Figure 3-7, appears.

Figure 3-7:
The
Organizer
dialog box.

3. **(Optional) If you want to copy styles to a template other than `Normal.dotm`, click the right Close File button, click the Open File button, select the template file, and click Open.**

4. **Choose the styles you want to copy in the left style list (the In list box).**

   To choose several styles, hold down the Ctrl key while clicking style names. To choose a block of styles, click the first style in the block and then hold down the Shift key and click the last style.

5. **Click the Copy button.**

   The styles copy from the document to the template.

6. **Click the Close button.**

The Organizer dialog box is a helpful beast:

✦ You can copy styles from either list in the Organizer dialog box. If you select styles in the right box, the In and To designations switch, and the arrows on the Copy button change to indicate that styles copy from the right list to the left list.

✦ To move styles from the current document to `Normal.dotm`, skip Step 3 in the preceding steps.

✦ Click the down arrow next to the Styles Available In list box on the left side of the Organizer dialog box to reveal a list of style sources that

includes the current document, the currently attached style, and
`Normal.dotm`. To move styles from the attached template to
`Normal.dotm`, select the template from the Styles Available In list.

✦ You can also use the Organizer to delete or rename styles. To delete
styles, select them in either the left or right list; then click the Delete
button. If you've been good, Word asks for confirmation before it deletes
the styles. To rename a style, select it and click the Rename button.
When Word asks for a new name, start typing. (Notice that you can
rename only one style at a time.)

Chapter 4: Printing Your Documents

*T*he Print command. The Printmeister. Big document comin' up. Printin' some pages. The Printorama. The Mentor of de Printor. Captain Toner of the Good Ship Laseroo.

Don't worry — when you print a Word document, no one's waiting to ambush you with annoying one-liners like that guy who used to be on *Saturday Night Live.* Just a handful of boring dialog boxes with boring check boxes. Point-point, click-click, print-print.

Note that many of the printing features described in this chapter — such as collating or scaling — duplicate features that are provided directly by some printers. If your printer has a feature that duplicates a feature provided by Word, it is almost always better to use your printer's feature rather than Word's feature. That's because your printer can provide these features more efficiently than Word can. To find out what features are provided by your printer, click the Properties button when the Print dialog box appears.

Printing the Quick Way

Back in the good old days, before Word 2007, there was a handy Print button right on the Standard toolbar. It was the quickest way to print a single copy of your document on your favorite printer.

Now that the menus and toolbars of old have been supplanted with the Ribbon, you can't find a handy Print button sitting in plain view. But wait!

There is a Print button laying in wait on the Customize menu of the Quick Access toolbar, waiting for you to bring it to the top. I suggest you do so immediately, by following these steps:

1. **Click the Customize Quick Access Toolbar button, located at the far right of the QAT.**

   This reveals a menu of commonly used commands.

 2. **Click the Quick Print button (shown in the margin).**

   This adds the Quick Print button to your Quick Access toolbar.

Now the Quick Access toolbar contains the Quick Print button, which prints your document using the current settings for the Print dialog box, which I explain in the remaining sections of this chapter. Usually, this action results in printing a single copy of all the pages in your document. But if you alter the Print dialog box settings, clicking the Quick Print button uses the altered settings automatically.

Using the Print Dialog Box

For precise control over how you want your document to print, you must conjure up the Print dialog box shown in Figure 4-1. To summon this dialog box, choose Office⇨Print or press Ctrl+P.

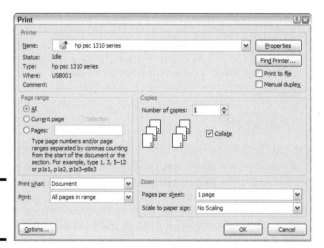

Figure 4-1:
The Print
dialog box.

After you call up the Print dialog box, click OK or press Enter to print a single copy of your entire document. Fiddle around with the settings to print just certain pages, to print more than one copy, or to change other aspects of how your document prints. This section shows you the treasures that lie hidden in this dialog box.

Printing can be es-el-oh-double-ewe, so don't panic if your document doesn't start printing right away. Word printouts tend to demand a great deal from the printer, so sometimes the printer has to work for a while before it can produce a finished page. Be patient. The Print dialog box has every intention of granting your request.

Changing printers

If you're lucky enough to have two or more printers at your disposal, you can use the Name field to pick which printer you want to use. You must first successfully install each printer in Windows — a topic beyond the reach of this humble book but that you find plenty of information about in the appropriate version of Andy Rathbone's *Windows For Dummies* (published by Wiley).

Printing part of a document

When you first use the Print command, the All option is selected so that your entire document prints. The other options in the Print Range portion of the Print dialog box enable you to tell Word to print distinct portions of your document:

✦ **Current Page:** Prints just the current page. Before you invoke the Print command, move to the page you want to print. Then select this option in the Print dialog box and click OK. This option is handy when you make a change to one page and don't want to reprint the entire document.

✦ **Selection:** Prints just the portion of the document you selected before invoking the Print command. First, select the pages you want to print. Then call up the Print command, select the Selection radio button, and click OK. (This option is grayed out in Figure 4-1 because I didn't make a selection before opening the dialog box.)

✦ **Pages:** Lets you select specific pages for printing. You can print a range of pages by typing the beginning and ending page numbers, separated by a hyphen, as in *5-8* to print pages 5, 6, 7, and 8. Or you can list individual pages, separated by commas, as in *4,8,11* to print pages 4, 8, and 11. And you can combine ranges and individual pages, as in *4,9-11,13* to print pages 4, 9, 10, 11, and 13.

Printing more than one copy

The Number of Copies field in the Print dialog box lets you print more than one copy of your document. You can click one of the arrows next to this field to increase or decrease the number of copies, or you can type directly in the field to set the number of copies.

Below the Number of Copies field is a Collate check box. If this box is selected, Word prints each copy of your document one at a time. In other words, if your document consists of ten pages and you select three copies and select the Collate check box, Word first prints all ten pages of the first copy of the document, then all ten pages of the second copy, and then all ten pages of the third copy. If you don't select the Collate check box, Word prints three copies of the first page, followed by three copies of the second page, followed by three copies of the third page, and so on.

The Collate option saves you from the chore of manually sorting your copies. If your document takes forever to print because it's loaded down with heavy-duty graphics, however, you can probably save time in the long run by deselecting the Collate check box. Why? Because many printers are fast when printing a second or third copy of a page. The printer may spend ten minutes figuring out how to print a particularly complicated page, but after it figures it out, the printer can print additional copies in ten seconds each. If you print collated copies, the printer must labor over each page separately for each copy of the document that it prints.

Choosing what to print

The Print What field in the Print dialog box enables you to select which type of output that you want to print. The following choices are available:

+ **Document:** Prints your document. (Duh.)

+ **Document Properties:** Prints information about your document.

+ **Document Showing Markup:** If you enable the Track Changes feature, this option prints your document along with any revision marks.

+ **List of Markup:** Prints a list of revisions made to the document.

+ **Styles:** Prints the styles in the document.

+ **Building Block entries:** Formerly called AutoText entries, this choice prints any AutoText entries in the document.

+ **Key Assignments:** Prints any shortcut keys that are assigned.

Select the type of output you want to print and then click OK or press Enter. Off you go!

Zooming

The Print command has two Zoom options that let you print the text smaller or larger than actual size:

✦ **Pages per Sheet:** This option lets you print more than one page on each sheet of paper. This option is especially useful for creating quick proof pages to make sure your document is laid out properly. It's also useful if your document consists mostly of large text that is still readable when reduced 50 percent or more.

✦ **Scale to Fit Paper:** Adjusts the size of the printed output to fit the paper in the printer. You should usually leave this option deselected.

Playing with print options

If you click the Options button at the bottom left of the Print dialog box, the Word Options dialog box appears, as shown in Figure 4-2. As you can see in this figure, the Display tab is selected so that you can set the basic printing options. (You can also reach this dialog box by clicking the Options button on the Ribbon in Print Preview.)

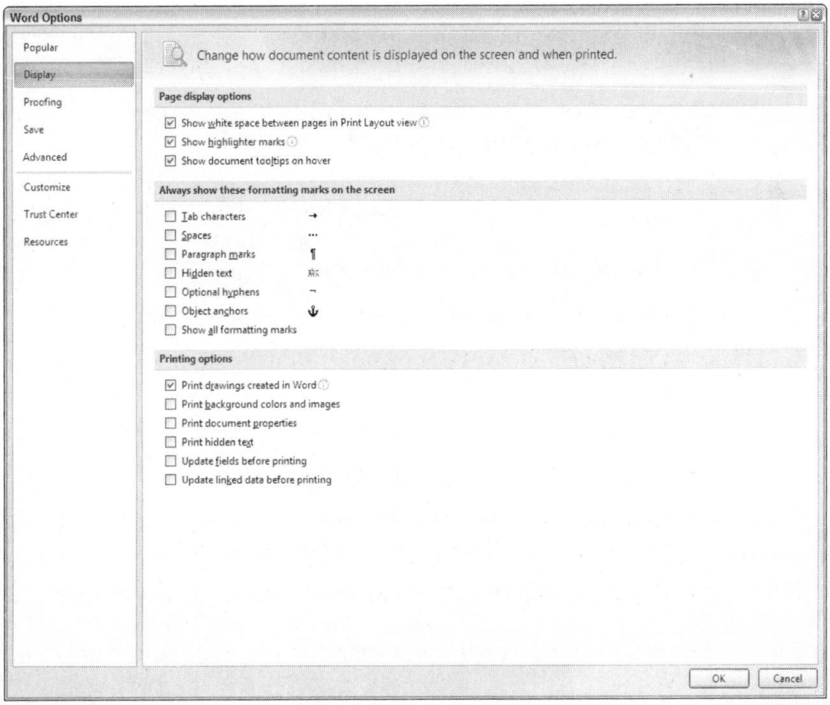

Figure 4-2: The basic print options.

The following options are listed in the Printing Options section of the Display tab:

✦ **Print Drawings Created in Word:** Prints drawing objects.

✦ **Print Background Colors and Images:** Prints background colors and images. These options are disabled by default, as it is easier and cheaper to use colored paper rather than printing color backgrounds.

✦ **Print Document Properties:** Prints document properties on a separate page following the document.

✦ **Print Hidden Text:** Prints any hidden text.

✦ **Update Fields Before Printing:** Updates all of the document's fields before printing the document. You usually leave this option selected.

✦ **Update Linked Data Before Printing:** Updates any linked information in the document before printing it. You usually leave this option selected.

You can find additional printing options in the Print and When Printing This Document sections of the Advanced tab in the Word Options dialog box, as shown in Figure 4-3.

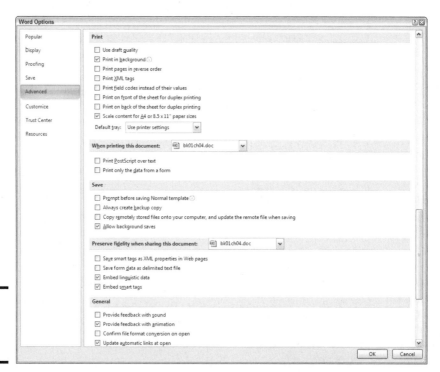

Figure 4-3:
Advanced
printing
options.

The following paragraphs describe the options you can find in the Print section of the Advanced tab:

✦ **Use Draft Quality:** Prints the document in draft format with very little formatting. This option might result in slightly faster printing. But if you're concerned with print speed, I recommend you use your printer's built-in draft mode instead. Most ink-jet printers have a draft-mode feature that prints dramatically faster than normal mode. You can find this option by clicking the Properties button from the Print dialog box.

✦ **Print in Background:** Prints documents in the background, so you can continue working while the document prints. This option is activated by default, so you don't need to worry about it. If you turn this option off, Word refuses to do anything else while it's printing.

✦ **Print in Reverse Order:** Prints the document backwards, starting with the last page in your document. This is useful for printers that stack pages backwards in the output tray. By printing the document backwards, the pages stack in the correct order.

✦ **Print XML Tags:** Prints any XML tags in the document.

✦ **Print Field Codes Instead of Their Values:** Prints field codes rather than field results. Use this option only if your document is filled with fields and you're trying to figure out why they aren't working right.

✦ **Scale Content for A4 or 8.5 x 11" Paper Size:** Automatically adjusts your document to fit the paper size.

✦ **Print on Front of the Sheet for Duplex Printing:** Sets the order of pages on the front of each sheet. Normally, the odd-numbered pages are printed in order on the top of each page. Select this option to reverse the print order of the odd-numbered pages.

✦ **Print on Back of the Sheet for Duplex Printing:** Normally, even-numbered pages are printed in order on the back of each page. Select this option to reverse the print order of the even-numbered pages.

✦ **Default Tray:** Tells the printer to use its default tray.

You can also find two options listed in the When Printing This Document section:

✦ **Print PostScript Over Text:** This option is important only if you're converting documents from Macintosh Word format.

✦ **Print Only the Data From a Form:** Prints the data entered into a form but doesn't print the form itself.

Using the Print Preview Command

The Print Preview feature lets you see how your pages will appear before committing them to paper. To use the Print Preview feature, choose Office➪ Print➪Print Preview. A preview of the printed page appears, as shown in Figure 4-4.

In Print Preview mode, the Ribbon takes on a new form, offering the following controls:

✦ **Print:** Calls up the Print dialog box to print the document.

✦ **Options:** Lets you set the print options. (See the section "Playing with print options" earlier in this chapter.)

✦ **Margins:** Lets you change the page margins.

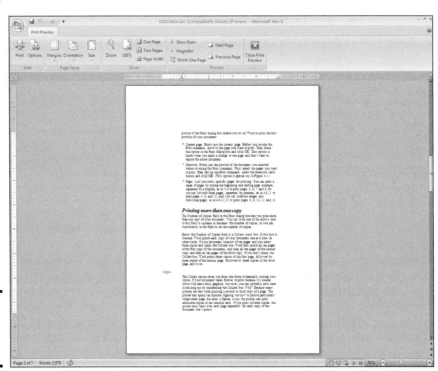

Figure 4-4:
Previewing your printouts.

✦ **Orientation:** Lets you change the page orientation from portrait to landscape (or vice versa).

 ✦ **Size:** Lets you change the paper size.

 ✦ **Zoom:** Lets you zoom in for a closer look.

 ✦ **100%:** Returns the zoom factor to 100 percent.

 ✦ **One Page:** Displays a full page.

 ✦ **Two pages:** Displays two pages side-by-side.

 ✦ **Page Width:** Adjusts the zoom factor to match the page width. You still have to scroll up and down to see the entire page, but not left and right.

 ✦ **Show Ruler:** Shows (or hides) the ruler.

 ✦ **Magnifier:** Activates the Magnifier tool, which lets you zoom in with a single click. This option is activated by default. Deactivating it enables editing of shared files.

 ✦ **Shrink One Page:** Automatically attempts to reduce the length of your document by one page. The reduction is accomplished by subtle means, such as reducing the point size used for your text, rather than by more drastic means such as cutting text.

✦ **Next Page:** Scrolls to the next page.

✦ **Previous Page:** Scrolls to the previous page.

✦ **Close Print Preview:** Closes Print Preview mode so that you can continue editing your document.

Chapter 5: Help!

The ideal way to use Word would be to have an expert sitting patiently at your side, answering your every question with a straightforward answer, gently correcting you when you make silly mistakes, and otherwise minding his or her own business. All you'd have to do is occasionally toss the expert a Twinkie and let him or her outside once a day.

Short of that, the next best thing is to find out how to coax Word itself into giving you the answers you need. Fortunately, Word includes a nice built-in help feature that can provide the answers you're looking for. No matter how deeply you're lost in the Word jungle, help is never more than a few clicks or keystrokes away.

Several Ways to Get Help

As with everything else in Office, more than one method is available for calling up help when you need it. The easiest thing to do would be to yell, "Skipper!!!" in your best Gilligan voice. Otherwise, you have the following options:

✦ **Press F1 at any time.** If you press F1 when you're in the midst of doing something, odds are good that Word offers suggestions for help with just the task you're trying to accomplish. This slick little bit of wizardry is called *context-sensitive help*.

✦ **Click the Help button located just above the right edge of the Ribbon.** This action activates Word's main Help system, shown in Figure 5-1.

✦ **Click the question mark button in the top-right corner of any dialog box.** You receive help that's specific to the dialog box.

✦ **Hover the cursor over an item on the Ribbon.** A ScreenTip bubble appears explaining what the item does. Many of these ScreenTips include the phrase "Press F1 for more help." In that case, you can press F1 to get help specifically about that item.

Figure 5-1:
Help!

Finding Your Way Around the Help System

The Word Help window, shown earlier in Figure 5-1, offers several ways to access the help you need. The following paragraphs describe the various ways you can work your way through Word's Help feature:

✦ **Word Help window links:** You can click any of the links that appear in the Word Help window to display help on a particular topic. For example, if you click the What's New link, you find a page of useful information about the new features of Word 2007.

✦ **Show Table of Contents button:** You can click the Show Table of Contents button (shown in the margin) to display the Table of Contents, which gives you an organized overview of the various help topics. See Figure 5-2. You can then use the Table of Contents to access specific topic pages.

✦ **Search feature:** If you can't find what you're looking for, try entering a word or phrase in the Search text box and clicking the Search button. A list of topics pertaining to the word or phrase you entered appears. For example, Figure 5-3 shows the results of a search for the phrase "mail merge."

What happened to Clippy?

Alexander Graham Bell had Thomas Watson, Batman had Robin, and Dr. Frankenstein had Igor. Everybody needs an assistant, and Office users are no exception. That's why Microsoft decided to bless previous versions of Office with Clippy, a helpful little fellow who offered assistance as you work with Office programs.

Clippy was an animated paperclip that sometimes suddenly morphed onto your desktop with sage advice and suggestions, and even a little idea light that gave you additional Word clues. You could also ask Clippy questions when you weren't sure what to do.

Unfortunately, Clippy wasn't always as helpful as he could have been. In fact, more often than not, he was just annoying. Whenever you typed the word *Dear* in the vicinity of anything that looked like it might be an address, Clippy would pop up and ask whether you were trying to type a letter. And if you asked him a question, many times his answers didn't seem remotely related to the question you were asking.

The developers at Microsoft tried to improve on Clippy with each successive version of Office, but with Office 2007, they finally threw in the towel. Clippy has gone to the great paperclip pile in the sky.

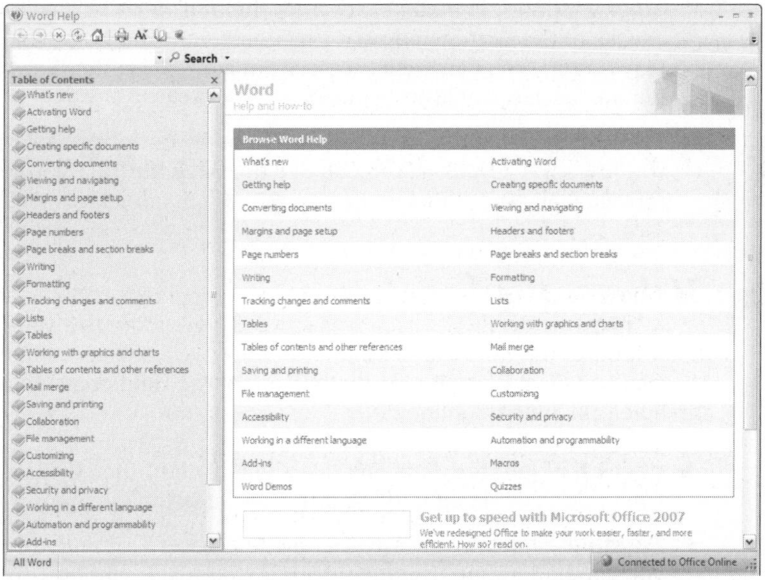

Figure 5-2:
Displaying
the Table of
Contents.

Figure 5-3:
Search
results.

✦ **Pushpin icon:** By default, the Help window always displays on top of other windows. In many cases, this "helpful" feature obscures your access to the Word window. If you don't want the Help window to always stay on top, you can click the pushpin icon. Then the Word Help window minimizes like any other window.

✦ **Back button:** You can retrace your steps by clicking the Word Help window's Back button. You can use the Back button over and over again, retracing all your steps if necessary.

Getting Help on the Internet

In addition to the help that's built in to Word, you can get help from Microsoft's Office Web site. At the bottom of the Help page, you can find three helpful links to online help:

✦ **Check for Updates:** This link takes you to the Office Update home page, where you can download the latest updates to Office programs.

✦ **Training:** This link takes you to the Microsoft Training home page. Here you can find online training tutorials that teach you how to use specific aspects of Word or other Office programs.

✦ **Templates:** This link takes you to a page from which you can download helpful templates.

Book II

Editing and Text Formatting

The 5th Wave   By Rich Tennant

"Having achieved market dominance in the workstation cursor market, we're excited to introduce our line of home cursors called, MyCursor, available in these exciting colors."

Contents at a Glance

Chapter 1: Getting Around Your Documents

In This Chapter

✔ Moving the insertion point

✔ Navigating a document

✔ Returning to your last edit

✔ Browsing with the Document Map

Maybe you remember that Beach Boys tune, "I Get Around." If you do, it's probably stuck in your head now that I've mentioned it, so you can sing it to yourself as you read this chapter and find out the many, many ways you can zip from one part of your document to another.

The Most Basic Way to Move Around a Document

The most basic way to move around a document is to use the arrow keys to move the insertion point one character at a time. The four arrow keys move the insertion point as follows:

Key	Where It Goes
←	Back one character
→	Forward one character
↑	Up one line
↓	Down one line

Admittedly, one character at a time can be a tedious mode of transportation when dealing with a content-heavy document. To speed things up, hold down the Ctrl key while pressing an arrow key, which will move the insertion point as follows:

Key	Where It Goes
Ctrl+←	To the previous word
Ctrl+→	To the next word
Ctrl+↑	To the start of the previous paragraph
Ctrl+↓	To the start of the next paragraph

To take even bigger leaps over the useful information you have entered in your document, use the additional navigation keys generally found above the arrow keys on your keyboard.

Key	Where It Goes
PageUp	To the previous screen
PageDown	To the next screen
Home	To the beginning of the current line
End	To the end of the current line
Ctrl+PageUp	To the previous browse object
Ctrl+PageDown	To the next browse object
Ctrl+Home	To the beginning of the document
Ctrl+End	To the end of the document

Are you confused by the Ctrl+PageUp and Ctrl+PageDown shortcuts? Join the club. These keys work differently depending on the browse object you've selected for use with Word's Go To feature. For more information, see the section "Just Browsing" later in this chapter, where I help you a bit more with that one.

Using the Scroll Bar

If you've ever used a Windows program, you're certainly acquainted with the scroll bar. The scroll bar in Word is the same all over again. Here are a few things you can do with the scroll bar:

✦ Click the arrow buttons at the top or bottom of the scroll bar to scroll the document up or down. The document continues scrolling as long as you hold down the button.

✦ Drag the scroll box (which is sometimes called the *thumb*) to scroll the document up or down. As you drag the scroll box, a balloon appears, indicating the current page number as well as textual information.

✦ Click the scroll bar above or below the scroll box to scroll up or down one screen at a time. Pressing PageUp or PageDown does the same thing.

✦ Just below the scroll bar is a set of three buttons called the *browse control,* which consists of a double-arrow pointing up, a button that looks like a marble, and a double-arrow pointed down. The browse control isn't a part of the scroll bar, but you can use it for navigation. For more information, see the section "Just Browsing," later in this chapter.

✦ The horizontal scroll bar appears toward the bottom of the screen when, for whatever reason, the screen can't display the entire width of the document (for example, when the document is at a high zoom level or when the Clipboard or Research pane is open). Nonetheless, you won't use the horizontal scroll bar much, except perhaps when you're working with Word's drawing features.

On the far right of the status bar is a Zoom slider. Simply click the slider button and drag it to the left to decrease magnification (10% is as low as it goes), or drag to the right to increase magnification (up to 500%). To move to a different page in the document, select that page and then double-click the marker in the middle of the Zoom slider to return magnification to 100%.

Rolling Around with the Mouse Wheel

Newer mice, such as the Microsoft IntelliMouse, have a cool little wheel between the mouse buttons. You can roll the wheel forward or backward, or you can click it as if it were a third mouse button. Word supports the mouse wheel control in the following ways:

✦ You can scroll your document by rolling the wheel, which is equivalent to clicking the up or down arrow buttons in the scroll bar.

✦ You can *pan* the document by pressing and holding the wheel and then dragging the mouse up or down. When you do so, the document scrolls in the direction you slide the mouse. The farther you drag the mouse, the faster the document scrolls.

✦ You can *autoscroll* the document by clicking the mouse wheel once. The document starts to slowly scroll down and continues to scroll down until you click any mouse button (including the wheel) or press any key. (As with panning, you can increase the speed of autoscrolling by dragging the mouse. The farther you drag the mouse, the faster the document scrolls. You can also reverse the autoscroll direction by dragging the mouse up.)

✦ You can zoom in or out by holding down the Ctrl key while rotating the mouse wheel. For fun, hold down the Ctrl key and roll the mouse wheel back and forth to watch your document zoom in and out.

Using the Go To Command

Don't need directions, just want to get there? The Go To command allows you to move where you want when you want. Ironically, you have several ways to get to the Go To command:

✦ Click the Find button in the Editing group of the Home tab. Then select the Go To tab of the Find and Replace dialog box.

✦ Press F5.

✦ Press Ctrl+G.

The Find and Replace dialog box (more on this later) appears with the Go To tab selected, as shown in Figure 1-1.

Figure 1-1:
The Go To
tab of the
Find and
Replace
dialog box.

In the Go to What list box, the Page option is automatically selected because this is the most common use of this feature. Simply type the page number in the Enter Page Number text box and click Go To (the Next button changes to a Go To button the moment you type a page number) or press Enter. Click the Close button or press Esc to dismiss the Find and Replace dialog box.

Besides going to a specific page, you can also go forward or backward a certain number of pages. To go forward, type a plus sign followed by the number of pages you want to skip in the Enter Page Number text box. For example, to go 3 pages forward, type **+3**. To go backward, type a minus sign instead of a plus sign. For example, type **-20** to go backward 20 pages.

In addition, besides going to a specific page, the Go To command enables you to go to a particular section, line, or any of several types of goodies that might reside in your document, such as bookmarks, annotations, footnotes, and so on. To go to something other than a page, just change the setting of the Go to What list box.

Just Browsing

Just below the vertical scroll bar is a set of three buttons called the browse control. Normally the top and bottom double arrows allow you to scroll through your document one page at a time. However, by using the circular Select Browse Object button in the middle, you can train them to do your bidding.

Clicking the Select Browse Object button (or pressing Alt+Ctrl+Home) opens the Browse menu, shown in Figure 1-2.

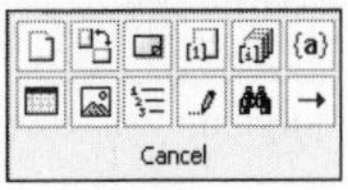

Figure 1-2:
The Select
Browse
Object
menu.

The first two buttons on the second row of this menu invoke the familiar Go To and Find commands. The ten remaining buttons change the unit by which Word browses the document when you click the double-up or double-down arrow control. Table 1-1 describes the function of each of the 12 buttons that appear on the Browse menu.

Table 1-1	Options on the Select Browse Object Menu
Button	*What It Does*
	Browse by Page
	Browse by Section
	Browse by Comment
	Browse by Footnote
	Browse by Endnote
	Browse by Fields
	Browse by Table
	Browse by Graphic
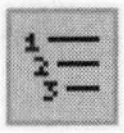	Browse by Heading (as indicated by standard heading styles)

(continued)

Table 1-1 *(continued)*

Button	What It Does
	Browse by Edits (works in conjunction with revision tracking)
	Find
	Go To

Going Back . . .

I can't tell you how many times I've pressed Ctrl+Z (Undo) to try to undo the effect of an errant navigation command. For example, I accidentally press Ctrl+End and find myself at the end of the document. Then I press Ctrl+Z thinking that takes me back to where I was. Unfortunately, Undo doesn't apply to navigation commands. So what happens instead is that the last editing operation I did gets undone. Sure, you can correct your mistake by pressing Ctrl+Y, the magic Redo command, to reinstate the editing undone by your inadvertent use of Ctrl+Z. But there's a better way.

The Go Back command is little known command that isn't accessible from the Ribbon. You can access this command only by using its keyboard shortcut, Shift+F5. Word remembers the last five revisions you made in your document, and each press of Shift+F5 returns the insertion point to one of those previous locations. So if you inadvertently use or misuse one of the navigation commands presented in this chapter and find yourself where you don't want to be, press Shift+F5 to go back to where you were.

When you first open a previously saved document, pressing Shift+F5 takes you to the location you were working when the document was last closed. Now *that's* a useful piece of computing!

Using Bookmarks

A Bookmark identifies a location or a selection of text that you name so you can call upon it as you would your faithful pup.

To create a Bookmark, follow these steps:

1. **Select the text or item to which you want to assign the Bookmark.**

You can select a specific point or you can select a selection of text.

2. **On the Insert tab in the Links group, click the Bookmark button or press Ctrl+Shift+F5.**

This opens the Bookmark dialog box, as shown in Figure 1-3.

3. **Enter a name for your selection in the Bookmark Name text box.**

Bookmark names may contain letters and numbers, but they must begin with a letter. No spaces or special characters are allowed. Use an underscore (_) to separate words in the Bookmark Name. If you try to use inappropriate characters, Word beeps at you and keeps the Add button grayed out until you change your wayward ways.

4. **Click Add.**

The Bookmark dialog box closes.

Figure 1-3:
The
Bookmark
dialog box.

To return to a place you have bookmarked, simply reopen the Bookmark dialog box by using a method from Step 2, select the location you want to travel to, and press Enter or click the Go To button. Note that you can sort the Bookmark Name list by name or location by using the Sort By radio buttons.

You can also use the Go To dialog box to find a Bookmark. Open the dialog box by clicking the Select Browse Object button or by clicking the Go To button on the Editing group of the Home tab. In the Enter Page Number text box, type the name of the Bookmark. You don't even need to change the Go to What option; Word is smart enough to figure out that you're looking for a Bookmark.

Deleting a Bookmark is as simple as opening the Bookmark dialog box, selecting the Bookmark to be deleted in the Bookmark Name list box, and clicking the Delete button or pressing Enter. *Note:* You cannot undo this action.

Using the Document Map

When you're working with a document that has a lot of headings, the Document Map feature is a quick way to navigate. This feature allows you to move from heading to heading at a click of the mouse button.

To open the Document Map pane, select the Document Map check box in the Show/Hide group on the View tab. As you can see in Figure 1-4, a separate pane opens to the left of the document's text with a list of all the headings. Simply click the heading you want to work with to have your insertion point moved there.

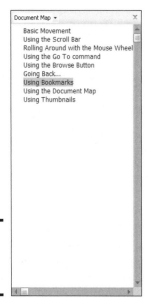

Figure 1-4:
The
Document
Map pane.

When you're done with the pane, you can close it by clicking the Close box in the corner of the pane or by deselecting the Document Map check box in the Show/Hide group on the View tab.

Using Thumbnails

Thumbnails are most useful when you're using graphics to navigate your way. To open the Thumbnails pane, select the Thumbnails check box in the Show/Hide group on the View tab.

As you can see in Figure 1-5, the Thumbnails pane displays a small image of each page in the document with a separate scroll bar for the pane. Click any image to go directly to that page.

Figure 1-5:
The
Thumbnails
pane.

After you open the Document Map or Thumbnails pane, you can switch between them by using the drop-down list at the top of the pane and selecting the other option. Also, notice in the Show/Hide group of the View tab that you can't have both check boxes selected at once.

To get rid of the Thumbnails, deselect the Thumbnails check box in the Show/Hide group on the View tab or click the Close box in the corner of the pane.

Chapter 2: Basic Text Formatting

*W*ord offers an unbelievable number of formatting options and some nifty new features to help your document appear shiny, new, and attractive. When a document looks nice, people are more inclined to think the information contained within is accurate and smart. (Unfortunately, sometimes looks can be deceiving.) So, to keep you from presenting a document that looks like your dog ate it, use the formatting techniques and tricks in this chapter.

Understanding Formatting

Digging right in, you can format three basic elements:

✦ **Characters:** Characters are the smallest element that you can format in Word. You can make characters bold, italic, or underlined; change their font size; and more. If you're deranged enough, you can format every character of your document differently. Doing so gives your documents a ransom-note appearance, which is something you probably want to avoid.

✦ **Paragraphs:** The next biggest element you can format in Word is a paragraph. You can format each paragraph so that it has its own tab stops, line spacing, extra space before or after the paragraph, indentation, alignment (left, right, centered, or justified), and more. All paragraphs in Word have a paragraph style, which includes some character formatting. So the only time you need to apply a character format is when you want your characters to vary from the paragraph's default character format, such as when you want to italicize or bold a word.

✦ **Sections:** Word also enables you to control the layout of sections. You can format each page by setting the top, bottom, left, and right margins, setting the number of columns and the size of each column, setting the paper size, controlling the placement of headers and footers, and more. You can format your document so that all pages have the same layout, or you can divide your document into *sections,* each with a different page layout. That's why Word refers to these formats as *section formats.*

A bit about sections

If you use more than one page layout in a document, the document is divided into two or more sections. Each section except the last one ends with a *section break,* which displays as a double line that spans the entire width of the page. Section breaks work much like paragraph marks: If you delete one, the text before the section break assumes the page layout of the section following the break.

Every document has at least one section, but you see section breaks only if you divide the document into two or more sections. Where's the section break for the last section of a document? There is none. The formatting information for the last section of a document is stored in the last paragraph mark in the document.

Not only are there many formatting options to apply, there are various ways to apply them from. You can use the tools in the Font and Paragraph groups on the Home tab on the Ribbon, keyboard shortcuts, or the Mini Toolbar. And if you still can't find what you're looking for, you can open up the Font dialog box.

You can apply formatting either before or after you type the text you want to format. To apply formatting before you type the text:

1. **Type text up to the point where you want to apply a format.**

2. **Turn on the special character formatting by using one of the keyboard shortcuts or buttons on the Ribbon listed in Table 2-1.**

3. **Type away.**

   Anything you type now assumes the format you applied in Step 2.

To apply a character format to text you already typed, follow these steps:

1. **Highlight the text you want to format.**

   To highlight a single word, double-click anywhere in the word. To highlight an entire paragraph, triple-click anywhere in the paragraph. If you want to select something specific that doesn't fall into one of those two categories, highlight the text that you want to format by clicking and dragging the mouse over it or by using the arrow keys to move the insertion point while holding down the Shift key.

If you enabled Word's Automatic Word Selection option, you don't have to double-click to select a word; Word automatically applies a formatting change to the entire word if the insertion point is anywhere in the word. To activate this option (or to deactivate it if it is already activated), choose Office➪Word Options to open the Word Options dialog box. Select the Advanced tab and then, under Editing Options, select the When Selecting, Automatically Select Entire Word check box. Click OK or press Enter to close the Word Options dialog box.

2. **Apply the format by using one of the keyboard shortcuts or buttons listed in Table 2-1.**

The effects of your formatting are immediately apparent.

3. **That is all.**

Disperse. There's nothing more to see here. Return to your homes.

Here are some other tidbits on character formatting:

CS: Please notice the double-underline in the following paragraph and make sure that it lays out properly.

✦ You can gang-tackle text with formats, if you want. For example, you can format text as ***bold italic double-underlined*** if you're really desperate for attention. (Can you hear the applause?)

✦ To remove *all* character formatting, highlight the text that you want to return to normal. Then select the Clear Formatting button in the Font group of the Home tab on the Ribbon or press Ctrl+spacebar.

✦ To remove a specific character format, such as bold or italic, but leave other character formats intact, highlight the text and press the keyboard shortcut, or click the button on the Ribbon for the format you want to remove.

Book II Chapter 2

Basic Text Formatting

Table 2-1	Character Formatting the Easy Way	
Toolbar Button	*Keyboard Shortcut*	*What It Does*
B	Ctrl+B	Bold
I	Ctrl+I	Italic

(continued)

Table 2-1 *(continued)*

Toolbar Button	Keyboard Shortcut	What It Does
U ▾	Ctrl+U	Underline (continuous)
	Ctrl+Shift+W	Word underline
	Ctrl+Shift+D	Double underline
Aa ▾	Ctrl+Shift+A	All caps
	Ctrl+Shift+K	Small caps
	Shift+F3	Toggle case
X₂	Ctrl+=	Subscript
x²	Ctrl+Shift+=	Superscript
Times New Roman ▾	Ctrl+Shift+F	Change font
12 ▾	Ctrl+Shift+P	Change point size
	Ctrl+]	Increase size one point
	Ctrl+[	Decrease size one point
A▴	Ctrl+Shift+>	Increase size to next available size
A▾	Ctrl+Shift+<	Decrease size to previous available size
	Ctrl+Shift+Q	Switch to Symbol font
	Ctrl+Shift+Z or Ctrl+spacebar	Remove character formatting

Formatting Text

The following sections show you how to apply various formats to characters. The easiest way is to use keyboard shortcuts (if you can remember them) or the various tools in the Font group on the Home tab on the Ribbon Table 2-1 is an overview of the Font group and those handy keyboard commands.

Setting the font and size

Okay, so you know you want to see your name in Goudy Stout, 28 point, bold, italicized, double underlined, green font. I want to show you how to do just that, starting with getting that Goudy Stout font and size.

When you start a new document, Word automagically selects Calibri size 11 font. Here's how you change the font and size:

1. **Select the text you would like to change or place the insertion point in the word that needs changing.**

2. **In the Font group on the Home tab on the Ribbon, select the Font drop-down list and scroll (or arrow down if you have time to burn) to Goudy Stout and select it.**

The Font drop-down list now says Goudy Stout.

As long as your text isn't hidden by the drop-down list, you can see what your text will look like after your changes thanks to Live Preview. Go ahead — keep moving your mouse over different fonts. I know you want to play with this feature. Done? Okay, let us now give thanks for Live Preview (which will probably prevent you from using Goudy Stout ever again after this example).

Note that the drop-down is divided into sections: Theme Fonts, Recently Used Fonts, and All Fonts. If you are regularly needing to swap between fonts, don't waste time scrolling to search, just check the Recently Used Fonts section.

3. **Select the Font Size drop-down list (which is next to the Font drop-down list) and then select 24, or select the text box and type 24.**

Yes, Live Preview is at work again here. I'm waiting. Go play.

If you just want to increase the font size, you can click the Grow Font button to the right of the Font Size drop-down list. Use the Shrink Font button next to it to, well, shrink the font.

If you don't particularly care for Calibri 11-point font, go ahead and change the default font for all new documents you create. Click the Font dialog box launcher in the bottom-right corner of the Font group on the Home tab. Select the options on the Font tab of the dialog box that you would like as part of your font and then click the Default button. If you're certain you want to change your font, click Yes in the window that appears asking whether you want this change to affect all new documents, thereby changing the NORMAL template. Otherwise, click No or Cancel.

Bold, italics, and other goodies

The second line of the Font group on the Home tab on the Ribbon is where you can start making things more interesting.

To apply bold, italic, underline, strikethrough, subscript, or superscript or to capitalize a character, use the fine buttons under the Font drop-down list.

Along with the default seven options on the Ribbon, the Font dialog box has options to further modify text. Double Strikethrough, Shadow, Emboss, Engrave, and the mysterious Hidden are the remaining options.

You can get to the Font dialog box by clicking the dialog box launcher in the Font group, in the lower-right corner.

Using the highlighter

Need to make something obvious? Afraid that Goudy Stout in green won't hold their attention? Highlight the information.

1. **Click the Text Highlight Color button in the Font group on the Home tab on the Ribbon.**

   You can select the drop-down list and select something other than the standard yellow to use from the color palette provided.

   The cursor is now an insertion pointer with a marker slanted across it.

2. **Click and drag in the document to select and highlight.**

   The mouse continues to act as a highlighter, enabling you to select multiple portions of text until you tell it to go away.

3. **Tell the highlighter to go away by clicking the drop-down list on the Text Highlight Color button and choosing Stop Highlighting.**

To remove highlighting, select the text involved and then select No Color from the Text Highlight Color drop-down list.

To avoid having the highlighter take over your mouse indefinitely, select the text you want highlighted before clicking the Text Highlight Color button.

Playing with text colors

The drop-down list attached to the Font Color button has three color palettes, one showing Theme Colors, one showing Standard Colors, and the last showing Recent Colors. (For a discussion of themes, see Chapter 3 of this minibook.)

If none of those colors are quite what you're looking for, select More Colors at the bottom to open the Colors dialog box. Here you have two tabs to choose from: Standard and Custom. Simply select a color block somewhere in either of the color palettes and click OK.

Using the Font dialog box

The character formatting options you're likely to use most — bold, italics, underlining, font, and point size — are all readily accessible in the Font group on the Home tab on the Ribbon or via keyboard shortcuts. Microsoft has now added some of the less-often-used options to the Ribbon, as well, such as the Strikethrough and Change Case options. Follow the steps in this section if for some reason you need to apply a here-to-for unmentioned formatting option such as one of the following:

✦ Double strikethrough

✦ Shadow

✦ Outline

✦ Emboss

✦ Engrave

✦ Character spacing

To apply one of the preceding formatting options, follow these steps:

1. **Highlight the text you want to format (or "to mangle with oddball formatting," as I like to say).**

2. **Open the Font dialog box by clicking the dialog box launcher at the bottom-right corner of the Font group or by pressing Ctrl+D.**

3. **Play with the options shown in Figure 2-1.**

   Fiddle with the various controls to set the Font, the Font Style (bold, italic, and so on), and the Size. Click the Effects you want (strikethrough, superscript, and so on). Use the drop-down lists to set the underline and color. Live Preview can't help you here.

4. **Click OK when you've had enough.**

   The dialog box vanishes, and your text magically transforms with the formats you selected.

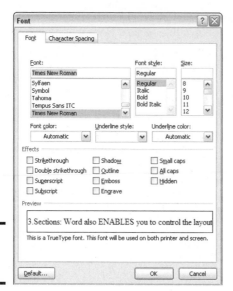

Figure 2-1:
The Font
dialog box.

I have a few more notes about using the Font dialog box:

✦ If you haven't yet typed the text you want to mangle, use the Font dialog box, select the formats you want, click OK, and then start typing. When you're done, press Ctrl+spacebar to resume normal type.

✦ Do you see the Character Spacing tab at the top of the Font dialog box? If you click the Character Spacing tab, you see options to control the spacing between characters, raise or lower characters from the baseline, and apply a spiffy desktop publishing feature called *kerning.* These options are in the realm of desktop publishing, so ignore them for now. If you can't wait, skip ahead to Book IV, Chapter 6 for information about using these options.

✦ You might be missing the Animation tab, which has left the software. However, don't despair. If you felt the need in the past to place your text on the go, and now open it with Word 2007, your content can still dance its jig.

✦ If you find yourself frequently using a formatting option that doesn't have a place on the Ribbon or a keyboard shortcut, you can create your own keyboard shortcut or add the icon to the Ribbon, which I describe in Book VIII, Chapter 1.

To get rid of all of your formatting and return your content to default settings, click the Clear Formatting button in the Font group on the Ribbon — which looks like a piece of paper above a white eraser.

Formatting Paragraphs

The Paragraph group on the Home tab on the Ribbon is shown in Figure 2-2 and is your first ally in formatting paragraphs.

Figure 2-2:
The
Paragraph
group on
the Ribbon.

To format a paragraph, first click anywhere in the paragraph that you want to format. (Where you click in the paragraph doesn't matter.) Then use one of the keyboard shortcuts or buttons on the Ribbon that I describe in the following sections. The effect of your formatting is immediately obvious.

To remove all paragraph formatting, press Ctrl+Q.

Justification

You can set the paragraph alignment to Align Left, Align Right, Center, or Justify by using the first four buttons at the bottom of the Paragraph group on the Home tab on the Ribbon. Table 2-2 shows the different ways you can align text using the Ribbon.

Table 2-2	Aligning Using the Ribbon	
Toolbar Button	*Keyboard Shortcut*	*What It Does*
	Ctrl+L	Left-aligns a paragraph
	Ctrl+E	Centers a paragraph
	Ctrl+R	Right-aligns a paragraph
	Ctrl+J	Justifies a paragraph

Line spacing

In the Paragraph group on the Home tab on the Ribbon, you find the Line Spacing button, which enables you to add space between the lines of text in a paragraph. By default, lines are single spaces, with slightly more than that below a paragraph. In the Line Spacing drop-down list (in the Paragraph group on the Home tab), you can select several options for the paragraph's line spacing. The ones you use most are Single, 1.5 Lines, and Double. Click the dialog box launcher to open the Paragraph dialog box, where you can select the following options from the Line Spacing drop-down list:

✦ **At Least** lets you specify a minimum measurement for the line spacing, such as "At Least 14 Points."

✦ **Exactly** lets you set an exact measurement, but I recommend avoiding it. You can get into trouble if you use 12-point type in a paragraph but set the line spacing to "Exactly 10 Points."

✦ **Multiple** lets you set some other line spacing, such as 3 lines.

The following keyboard shortcuts can help you format paragraph spacing more quickly:

Keyboard Shortcut	What It Does
Ctrl+1	Single-spaces paragraph
Ctrl+2	Double-spaces paragraph
Ctrl+5	Sets line space to 1.5

Paragraph formats are stored in the paragraph marker at the end of the paragraph. Don't make the mistake of spending hours polishing a paragraph's appearance and then deleting the paragraph marker to merge the text into the following paragraph. If you do, you lose all the formatting you so carefully applied. (If that happens, quickly press Ctrl+Z to undo the deletion.)

Creating simple bullet and number lists

If you're a lover of lists, I have good news and bad news. The good news is that I cover how to create bullet lists and number lists in this book! The bad news is that I don't cover that in this chapter. Instead, make your way to Book III, Chapter 3. Then cross that task off your to-do list.

Indenting

Some publications require that you indent the first line of each paragraph. Others require that you indent every line by moving them to the right — useful for nested paragraphs (a paragraph within a paragraph) or block quotes (a quote that is set off from the margins to give it more space on the sides). As with most formatting, your first line of defense is the Ribbon.

Place the insertion point somewhere in the paragraph you want nested and click the Increase Indent button in the Paragraph group on the Home tab. This it not a toggle button, so if you continue to press it again, you increase the indent.

Gone too far? To un-indent an indented paragraph, use the Decrease Indent button.

To indent both sides of a paragraph, summon the Paragraph dialog box (by clicking the dialog box launcher at the lower-left corner of the Paragraph Group) and set the left and right indents to the same value.

You can have Word automatically indent the first line of every paragraph you type, instead of trying to press the space bar exactly 8 times every time. Here's how:

1. **Open the Paragraph dialog box by using the dialog box launcher in the Paragraph group on the Home tab on the Ribbon.**

2. **In the Indentation area, select the First Line option from the Special drop-down list.**

3. **(Optional) If you so desire, change the amount in the By box.**

   The box automatically says 0.5" and can be changed by typing over the figure or using the spinner buttons to the right of the text.

4. **Click OK.**

To indent everything but the first line of a paragraph, select Hanging Indent from the drop-down list in Step 2.

Sorting

You know how it is: You're quickly dumping a list of information (which has turned into a 32-item list), and then you realized how much easier it would be to work from if it were in alphabetical order. Fortunately, you can do that to a one-level bulleted or numbered list. Follow these steps:

1. **Place the insertion point somewhere in the list and click the Sort button in the Paragraph group on the Home tab on the Ribbon.**

   This step opens the Sort Text dialog box shown in Figure 2-3. When the dialog box opens, the first drop-down list under Sort By has Paragraphs selected, and the Type drop-down list is set to Text — exactly what you're trying to do right now.

2. **Select either the Ascending or Descending option.**

3. **Click OK.**

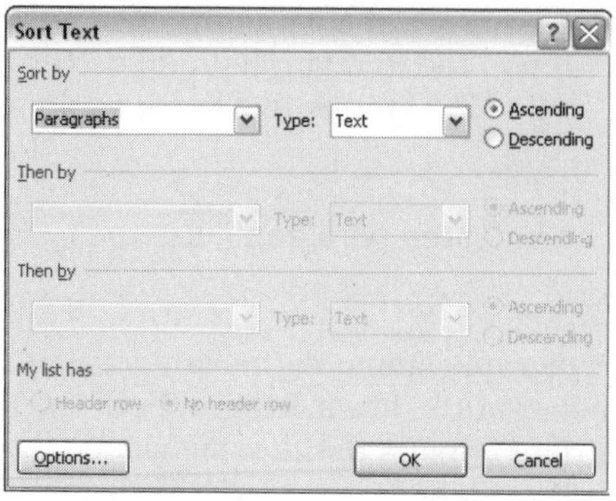

Sort Text   ? ✕

Sort by
Paragraphs ▼   Type: Text ▼   ● Ascending
                                  ○ Descending

Then by
           ▼   Type: Text ▼   ● Ascending
                                  ○ Descending

Then by
           ▼   Type: Text ▼   ● Ascending
                                  ○ Descending

My list has
○ Header row ● No header row

[Options...]   [OK]   [Cancel]

Figure 2-3:
The Sort
Text dialog
box.

The Sort Text dialog box also allows you sort tables, which I discuss in Book IV, Chapter 4.

Show paragraph marks

Paragraph formatting is contained with the paragraph mark at the end of the paragraph. The mark looks like a backwards letter P. If you want to permanently see the paragraph marks on your screen, follow these steps:

1. **Choose Office➪Word Options to get to the Word Options dialog box.**

2. **Click the Display tab.**

3. **Select the Paragraph Marks check box under the heading Always Show These Formatting Marks on the Screen.**

If you decide you don't want to see the paragraph marks, simply go back through the steps and deselect the check box.

To see paragraph marks and all other hidden formatting symbols, use the Show/Hide button in the Paragraph group on the Home tab on the Ribbon. This button acts as a toggle switch, allowing you display the symbols or not.

Using background colors

The Shading tab of the Borders and Shading dialog box lets you apply shading to a paragraph or a selection of text. Shading is a great way to draw attention to key parts of your document. For example, Figure 2-4 shows a document with a block of shaded text.

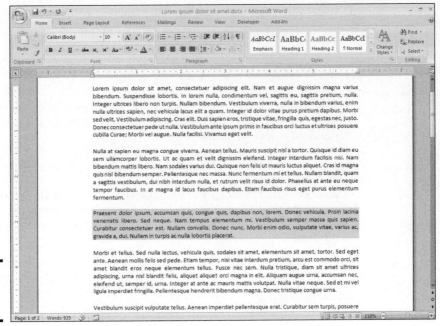

Figure 2-4:
A shaded
paragraph.

To apply shading to your text, follow these steps:

1. **Select the text you want to shade.**

You can select individual characters, a single word or group of words, or a single paragraph or even a group of paragraphs.

2. **Click the drop-down on the Shading button in the Paragraph group on the Home tab on the Ribbon.**

The color palette appears, as shown in Figure 2-5.

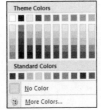

Figure 2-5:
The color
palette.

3. Select the color you want to shade the text with.

Your text now has a box of that color around it.

If you're picky and don't find the color you like, you can click the More Shading Colors button to bring up a dialog box that lists even more colors.

Notice that the first three columns of the Theme Colors palette list various shades of gray. The remaining columns list other theme colors. Standard colors are at the bottom.

Here are a few points to keep in mind when shading your text:

✦ Make sure that you can still read the shaded text. With darker shades, you might need to change the font color to keep the text readable. For more information about changing font colors, see Chapter 1 of this minibook.

✦ A common text effect is to create white text on a black background. To do that, first use the Shading drop-down in the Paragraph Group on the Home tab to set the background to black. Then use the Font Color button in the Font Group on the Home tab to set the font color to white.

✦ You must have a color printer to print colors other than black or gray.

Applying borders

The Paragraph group on the Home tab on the Ribbon has a handy Border button you can use to apply basic borders. You can click the button to apply the current border type to whatever text you select, or you can click the arrow next to the button to reveal a palette of border types, as shown in Figure 2-6.

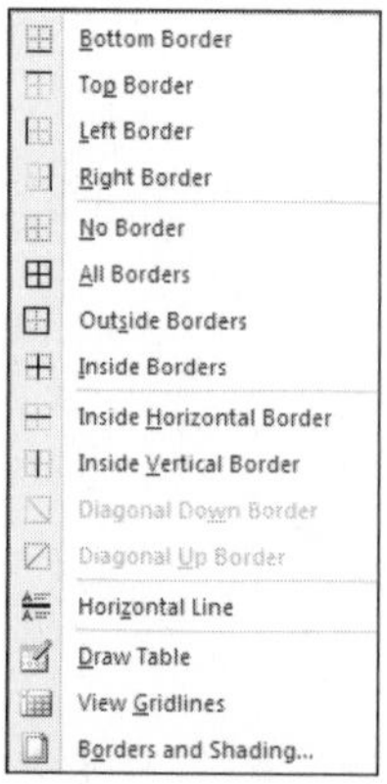

Figure 2-6:
Palette of
border
types.

Bottom Border
Top Border
Left Border
Right Border
No Border
All Borders
Outside Borders
Inside Borders
Inside Horizontal Border
Inside Vertical Border
Diagonal Down Border
Diagonal Up Border
Horizontal Line
Draw Table
View Gridlines
Borders and Shading...

If you want to draw a simple box around some text and choose a border, follow these simple steps:

1. **Select the text you want to draw a border around.**

You can select individual characters, a single word, a group of words, a single paragraph, or even a group of paragraphs.

If you don't select text at all, Word draws a border around the entire paragraph that the insertion point happens to be sitting in. As a result, if you want to draw a box around an entire paragraph, just click the anywhere in the paragraph and proceed to the next step.

2. **Click the down arrow on the Borders button in the Paragraph group in the Home tab on the Ribbon and select the Outside Borders option.**

The list disappears, and your text is bordered.

3. **(Optional) If you want to change the border's Style, Color, or Width, select the Borders and Shading option at the bottom of the Border buttons drop-down list. Otherwise skip to Step 5.**

This opens the Borders tab of the Borders and Shading dialog box.

4. **Make your selections in the Borders and Shading dialog box.**

- In addition to the Box border style, the Borders and Shading dialog box, as shown in Figure 2-7, offers two other preset border styles: Shadow and 3-D. You can experiment with these settings to see what effects they have.

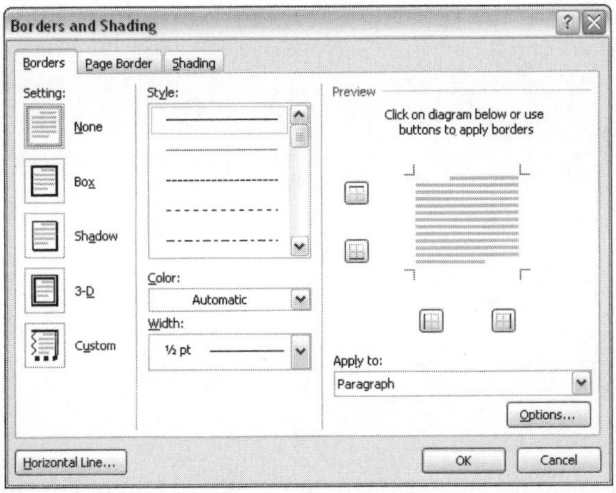

Figure 2-7:
The Borders and Shading dialog box.

- You can build a custom border one line at a time by clicking the buttons around the various edges of the paragraphs represented in the Preview area to indicate where you want a border to appear. These buttons control whether a border appears above, below, to the left, or to the right of the selection. If you select more than one paragraph, you also see a button that lets you add or remove lines between the paragraphs.

- The Style drop-down list lets you choose a fancy style for each line of the border. Various styles, such as double lines and dashed lines, are available. Note that you can change line styles as you apply individual borders, so that a paragraph can have a thin border at the top and a thick border at the bottom.

- The Color drop-down list lets you set the color for your border. You can select a Standard or Theme color that appears in the palette, or you can click More Colors at the bottom of the palette to bring up a dialog box that lets you select any color you want.

- The Width drop-down list lets you select a width for each segment of the border.

5. Click OK.

By default, the borders are placed one point from the top and bottom and four points from the left and right of the text they surround. If that placement is too tight for you, you can adjust it by clicking the Options button in the Borders and Shading dialog box. The Borders and Shading Options dialog box comes up, as shown in Figure 2-8.

Figure 2-8:
The Borders
and Shading
Options
dialog box.

If you select more than one adjacent paragraph of text and format them by using one of the preset border styles, all the paragraphs are contained within a single box, as shown in Figure 2-9.

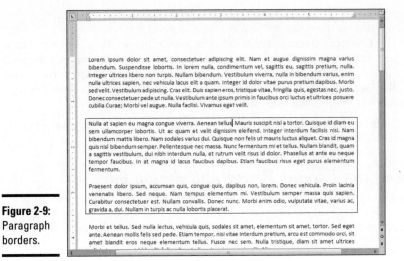

Figure 2-9:
Paragraph
borders.

If you want to box each paragraph separately, place an unboxed paragraph mark between each boxed paragraph simply by pressing Enter to add a blank line, as shown in Figure 2-10. These spacer paragraphs need not contain any text, and you might want to vary their Before or After spacing so that the boxed paragraphs are spaced the way you want.

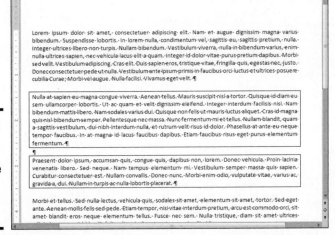

Figure 2-10:
Adjacent
paragraphs
showing the
unboxed
paragraph
marker.

Keep these things in mind when playing around with borders:

✦ The Border button applies borders to one or more edges of the selected text or paragraph. The Borders and Shading dialog box controls the style, color, and width of those borders. You have to summon the Borders and Shading dialog box by using the Borders and Shading option on the Borders drop-down list if you want to change those settings.

✦ Click the Border button once to apply a border. To remove a border, click the Border button again.

Using the Format Paragraph dialog box

If you find yourself in the unenviable pickle of needing to use a formatting option that's not on the Home tab and you can't remember its keyboard short-cut, you can always conjure up the Paragraph dialog box and pick and choose your paragraph formats from a palette of delightful formatting treasures.

Here's the procedure for using the Paragraph dialog box:

1. **Click anywhere in the paragraph that you want to format.**

Where you click in the paragraph doesn't matter as long as the insertion point is somewhere in the paragraph.

2. **Click the dialog box launcher on the Paragraph tab on the Ribbon.**

The Paragraph dialog box appears, shown in Figure 2-11.

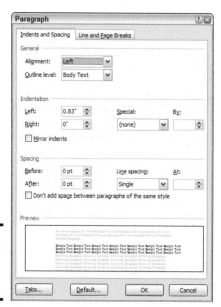

Figure 2-11:
The
Paragraph
dialog box.

3. **Play with the controls.**

You can set the paragraph alignment (Left, Right, Centered, or Justified) from the Alignment drop-down list. You can increase the Left or Right Indentation, or you can choose a First Line or Hanging indent from the Special drop-down list. You can also increase or decrease the amount of spacing before and after the paragraph and set the line spacing.

As you play with the controls, keep an eye on the Preview box to see the effect of your changes.

4. **Click OK when you're done.**

Presto change-o! You're done.

You can set left and right indentation as well as first line and hanging indents by playing with the ruler. See the section "Setting tabs by using the ruler," later in this chapter, for details.

Using the Format Painter

You can use the Format Painter to quickly copy character and paragraph formatting from one bit of text to another. The Format Painter works only if you already have some text formatted the way you like. Follow these steps to use the Format Painter:

1. **Highlight the text that has the format you want to copy.**

2. **Click the Format Painter button in the Clipboard Group on the Home tab on the Ribbon.**

   It's the button that looks like a paintbrush.

3. **Click and drag the cursor over the text you want to copy the format to.**

   Word formats the new text to look just like the already formatted text.

If you want to use the Format Painter to format two or more sections of text, highlight the text you want to use as your template and then double-click the Format Painter button. The Format Painter then continuously formats text that you highlight until you press a key, double-click in the document again, or click the Format Painter button again.

When you select text, a Mini Toolbar appears, and it looks like:

As you can see, the Mini Toolbar lets you quickly access many of the formatting commands discussed in this chapter: Font, Font Size, Bold, Italics, and many more.

All About Tabs

Word enables you to create seven types of tab stops: left, center, right, decimal, bar, first line indent, and hanging indent. You can set tab stops in one of two ways: by dropping them directly on the ruler or by ditzing around with the Tab dialog box. Dropping tabs directly on the ruler is far and away the easier method of the two. Get involved with the Tabs dialog box only when you want to use *leaders* (little rows of dots that run across the page).

Setting tabs by using the ruler

The easiest way to set tabs is to use the ruler. Here's the procedure for setting tabs with the ruler:

1. **If the ruler isn't visible, click the View Ruler button at the top of the vertical scroll bar.**

2. **Type some text that you want to line up with tab stops.**

   Type several paragraphs if you want. Press the Tab key once and only once between each column of information that you want lined up. Don't worry if everything doesn't line up at first. You can fix it later.

3. **Select the paragraph or paragraphs whose tabs you want to set.**

   If you're setting tabs for just one paragraph, click anywhere in the paragraph. If you're setting tabs for more than one paragraph, click and drag to select at least some text in each paragraph.

4. **Click on the ruler at each spot where you want a new tab stop.**

   Watch as the text you selected in Step 2 lines up under the tabs you create. Add one tab stop to the ruler for each column of information you want to align.

5. **Adjust.**

   Nothing works quite right the first time. If you dropped a tab at 1½ inches and want to move it to 1¾ inches, just click and drag the tab marker and slide it to the new location. When you release the mouse button, text in the currently selected paragraphs adjusts in the new tab position.

Here's more fascinating information about tabs:

✦ Default tab stops are placed every half inch. However, each time you create a new tab stop, any default tab stops to the left of the new tab stops are deleted. In other words, default tab stops exist only to the right of tab stops you create.

✦ To change the type of tab that's created when you click the ruler, click the Tab Alignment button at the far left edge of the ruler. Each time you click the button, the picture on the button changes to indicate the tab type, as shown in Table 2-2.

Table 2-2	Tab Types	
Tab Alignment Button	*Tab Type*	*Explanation*
	Left	Text left aligns at the tab stop. This is the default tab style.
	Center	Text centers over the tab stop.
	Right	Text right aligns at the tab stop.
	Decimal	Numbers align at the decimal point over the tab stop.
	Bar	A vertical bar appears at the tab location.
	First Line Indent	Sets the indentation for the first line of the paragraph.
	Hanging Indent	Creates a hanging indent.

Using the Tabs dialog box

If you have an unexplainable aversion to the ruler, you can set tab stops using the Tabs dialog box instead. Just follow these steps:

1. **Click the dialog box launcher in the Paragraph group of the Home tab on the Ribbon.**

The Paragraph dialog box appears, as shown earlier in Figure 2-11.

2. Click the Tabs button in the lower-left corner.

The Tabs dialog box opens, as shown in Figure 2-12.

Figure 2-12:
The Tabs
dialog box.

3. Type the position you want the new tab stop to appear in the Tab Stop Position field.

4. Select the Alignment option you want for the new tab stop (Left, Center, Right, Decimal, or Bar).

For more information about bar tabs, see the upcoming section, "Running a bar tab."

5. Select the tab leader type for the tab stop. If you don't want leaders, select 1 None.

I explain leaders later, in the section "Using tab leaders."

6. Click Set.

7. Repeat Steps 2 through 5 for any other tab stops you want to create.

8. Click OK to dismiss the Tabs dialog box.

You can quickly summon the Tabs dialog box by double-clicking the lower half of the ruler.

Removing all tabs

To remove a single tab stop by using the ruler, click the tab stop you want to remove and drag it straight down, off the ruler. When you release the mouse button, the tab stop is deleted.

To remove all tab stops, highlight the paragraphs you want to remove the tab stops from. Then do one of the following two actions:

✦ Use the dialog box launcher in the Paragraph group on the Home tab on the Ribbon to open the Paragraph dialog box. Then select the Tabs button to open the Tabs dialog box.

✦ Double-click the bottom half of the ruler to summon the Tabs dialog box.

Click the Clear All button to remove the tabs and click OK to return to the document.

Using tab leaders

A *tab leader* is a row of dots, dashes, or a solid line that precedes the tab, like what you often find on a restaurant menu. Dots and dashes are the leader type you use for lists; solid lines are typical for forms. Just look at the Table of Contents for this book for an excellent example of this type of tab leader.

The easiest way to create a tab leader is to first create the tab stop by dropping it on the ruler. Then open the Tabs dialog box double-clicking the bottom of the ruler to open Tabs dialog box, choose the tab stop you want the leader added to, and select a leader type (dots, dashes, or solid line). Then click OK and check the results.

If you want the tab leader to end at a certain location, create a left-aligned tab at that location by using the leader type of your choice. This technique is commonly used to create fill-in-the-blank forms. For example, the Figure 2-13 shows two left-aligned tab stops with solid-line leaders, one at 2.5 inches, the other at 5 inches.

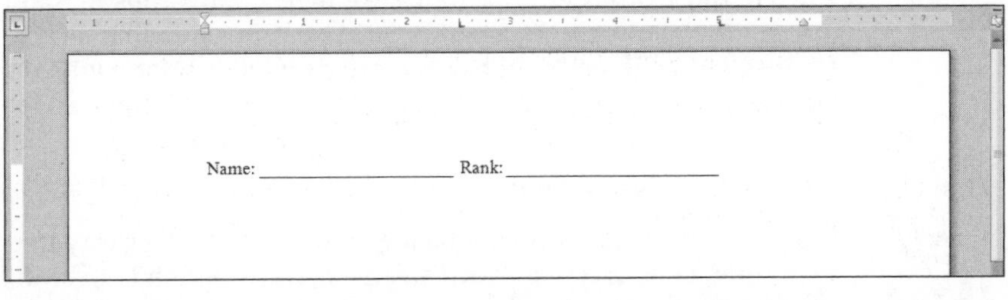

Figure 2-13:
Solid-line
leaders.

Name: _____ Rank: _____

If you're going to use dot or dash leaders to connect items in a list, you usually use right- or decimal-aligned tabs. For example, I formatted the document in Figure 2-14 with a single, right-aligned, dot-leader tab stop at 4.5 inches.

Figure 2-14:
Dot leaders.

```
Roland RS-50 ..................................................................$799.99
Novation KS-4...................................................................$999.99
Roland RD-700 ..............................................................$1,799.99
Yamaha S90 .........................................................................Call!
```

Running a bar tab

You must be 21 to use this feature in most states.

One of the more unusual things you can do with tabs is create vertical bars between columns of information, like the ones shown here:

Hawkeye	James T. Kirk	Gilligan
B.J.	Mr. Spock	The Skipper
Charles	Dr. McCoy	The Professor
Hot Lips	Mr. Chekov	Mary Ann
Radar	Mr. Sulu	Ginger
Col. Potter	Lt. Uhura	Mr. Howell
Father Mulcahy	Nurse Chapel	Mrs. Howell

Here, the vertical bars between the columns are actually special deviant versions of tab stops. Bar tabs aren't like regular tab stops in that the Tab key doesn't stop at them. As a result, you use only one tab character between each column. To set bar tabs, first create a left tab for each column. Then click the tab type button at the left of the ruler until the Bar Tab button appears. Then add a bar tab a little to the left of each of the left tabs you created.

Bar tabs are a crude way of making tables. A far better way to create tables with ruled lines is to use Word's Table feature, which I cover in Book IV, Chapter 4.

The Ten Commandments of Formatting

When Bill Gates came down from the mountain, he originally had 15 formatting commandments. But he dropped one of the three tablets, shattering it to pieces, so now we have but ten.

I. Thou shalt learn thy way around the Ribbon while continuing to use keyboard shortcuts.

The Ribbon displays many more handy tools in an easily accessible manner than ever before. However, keyboard shortcuts are rarely inadvisable. Don't bother memorizing the keyboard shortcuts for formats you rarely or never use. But do memorize the shortcuts for the formats you use frequently. Pressing Ctrl+B for bold is much faster than clicking the mouse button or contending with the Ribbon and dialog boxes. Make a short list of the shortcuts you want to memorize and tape it to your computer or somewhere within eyesight.

II. Thou shalt not press Enter at the end of each line.

You defeat the whole purpose of word processing if you press Enter at the end of each line you type. Let Word figure out where to break each line. Use Enter for the end of paragraphs.

III. Thou shalt not create empty paragraphs.

Don't press Enter twice to leave extra space between paragraphs. Instead, format the paragraph with 1½ or 2 blank lines before the first line.

IV. Thou shalt not use extraneous spaces.

On a typewriter, you're supposed to press the spacebar twice between sentences. With proportional fonts, use only one space following the period at the end of a sentence. Also, don't use spaces to align text in columns. Use tabs instead.

V. Thou shalt not use extraneous tabs.

Don't press Tab two or three times to move text across the page. Instead, press Tab once and then set a tab stop where you want to align the text.

Book II Chapter 2

Basic Text Formatting

VI. Thou shalt not underline when italics will do.

Underlining is for typewriters. Italics is for computers. You paid lots of hard-earned money for your computer, so you might as well get your money's worth.

VII. Thou shalt not use more than three fonts on a page.

Avoid the ransom note look at all costs. Use one font for your text, a second font for headings, and maybe a third font for emphasis. But no more than three fonts altogether, please.

VIII. Thou shalt not use Exact Line Spacing.

The Exact Line Spacing option (found by clicking the dialog box launcher on the Paragraph group on the Home tab) is a source of much trouble. Use Single, 1.5 lines, or Double instead.

IX. Thou shalt use the AutoCorrect feature.

The AutoCorrect feature can correct typos on the fly, as well as help with simple formatting chores such as making sure sentences start with capital letters and using "curly quotes" properly.

To further define this feature, choose Office➪Word Options to open the Word Options dialog box. Then click the Proofing tab and click the AutoCorrect Options button at the top of the dialog box. When the AutoCorrect dialog box appears, select the things you want Word to automatically correct; then click OK twice to close the two dialog boxes.

X. Thou shalt use styles.

The best way to deal with all this formatting nonsense is to put all the formatting you ever need into styles. Then you don't have to worry about line spacing, hanging indents, fonts and font sizes, or anything else. Just apply the correct style, and everything is taken care of. (I discuss styles in detail in Chapter 3 of this minibook. Aren't you lucky?)

Chapter 3: Working with Styles

In This Chapter

- ✔ Understanding why styles are important
- ✔ Formatting with styles by using the Styles gallery
- ✔ Changing the document look with style sets and themes
- ✔ Setting the look of new documents you create
- ✔ Exploring other ways of applying styles
- ✔ Finding and clearing the layers of formatting
- ✔ Setting advanced style features

Styles are what Tiggers like best. They're the secret to freeing yourself from the tyranny of using a sequence of formatting commands. With styles, you toil at formatting text until you get the look just right; then you provide a name by which Word remembers all the formatting you applied. From then on, you can apply the same formatting to other text simply by using the style. No more hunting and pecking your way through the various formatting commands, trying to recall how you got the paragraph to look so good.

If you're not yet using styles, I suggest you find out how to use them right away. Although the concept of styles might be confusing at first, they aren't really that hard to figure out. An hour or so invested in becoming familiar with how styles work pays off in many saved hours of unnecessary formatting time later.

Understanding Styles

The basic idea behind styles is to store all the formatting information for a paragraph under a single name. That way, you can quickly apply the saved formats to other paragraphs simply by referring to the style's name. For example, suppose you want to format headings with 16-point Arial Bold, with 18 points of space above the heading and 6 points below, and with a line drawn beneath the paragraph. You have to bounce the mouse all over the place to format this heading manually. But if you store the formats in a style, you can apply all the formats with a single click or a keyboard shortcut.

Styles can contain any or all of the following types of formatting:

✦ **Paragraph:** Includes left and right indentation, first line indentation and hanging indents, line spacing, before and after spacing, and text flow (widow/orphan control, keep with next, and so on).

✦ **Tabs:** Includes tab stop positions, tab types, leader tabs, and bar tabs.

✦ **Bullets or Numbering:** Enables you to set up numbered or bulleted lists. (See Book III, Chapter 3 for more information about bullets and numbers.)

✦ **Borders and Shading:** Includes borders and line styles as well as fill shades.

✦ **Font:** Includes the font name, style (regular, bold, italic, or bold italic), and special character attributes such as small caps or superscripts, the font color, and character spacing (including whether kerning is automatically done for some letter pairs).

✦ **Language:** Enables you to use an alternative dictionary for spelling and hyphenation or to tell Word to skip a paragraph specified with this style when the document is spell-checked.

With all these formats stored together under one name, you can imagine how much time styles can save you.

Styles are an integral part of the way Word works. Even if you think you don't use styles, you do: Word documents start off with several predefined styles, including the ubiquitous Normal style. The Normal style governs the default appearance of paragraphs in your document.

Here are some other benefits of using styles:

✦ **Changing the style definition changes all text using that style.** The real beauty of styles comes when you decide that all the headings in your 200-page report are too small. Without styles, you have to adjust the size of each heading separately. With styles, you simply change the style and — voilà! — all the paragraphs assigned to that style automatically adjust.

✦ **You can update the overall document look by changing the style set.** Styles let you take advantage of style sets, a new feature in Word 2007, that let you store collections of styles that you can swap with a single command. For example, you might have one set that defines all of your styles for a draft format (for example, double-spaced with the headers boxed with a border to make them stand out), another that is used for reviews (with single-spaced formatting but in a larger font), and finally one that formats the document into its final form. Word comes with a collection of style sets that let you change the overall look of your document easily — but only if you're using styles to format your text. For more information about style sets, see "Switching style sets and themes," later in this chapter.

✦ **Styles are part of the document.** Styles are stored along with your text in the document file. Thus, each document can have its own collection of styles, and styles with the same name can have different formatting characteristics in different documents. For example, a style named Bullet List might have ordinary round bullets in one document but check marks or pointy index fingers in another.

✦ **Styles can be defined in a template.** When you create a new document, the new document inherits its styles from the template you base the document on. For more information about templates, turn to Book I, Chapter 3.

✦ **Styles can be created by others for your use.** Suppose you don't know how to drop a line three points beneath the paragraph, and you don't want to learn how. No problemo. Just bribe a friendly Word guru into creating the style for you. After the style is created, you don't have to know how to use the formatting instructions contained in the style. All you have to know is how to apply the style, and that's as easy as clicking the mouse button.

✦ **Some Word features work better if you use styles.** Another benefit of using styles is that some Word features, most notably Table of Contents and Outline view, work best when you use styles for your headings and body text. Don't even attempt to use these features if you don't use styles.

For more information about Tables of Contents, see Book VI, Chapter 1. To find out more about Outline view, see Book II, Chapter 7.

The various controls discussed in this chapter contain three types of styles:

✦ **Character styles,** such as Emphasis, Strong, and Subtle Reference, which apply only to the selected text and can contain only font formatting and language information.

✦ **Linked styles,** such as Heading 1 and Title, which can apply either to the entire paragraph or to selected text.

✦ **Paragraph styles,** such as Quote, which can apply only to paragraphs — even if you select only part of the paragraph, the style is applied to the entire paragraph. Paragraph styles are identified by the special symbol (called a *pilcrow,* ¶) in front of the style name in the Styles gallery.

Word actually has five types of styles, but two of these are so important that they have their own galleries: table styles and list styles. The table styles are discussed in Book IV, Chapter 4, and list styles (which are used for numbering) are discussed in Book III, Chapter 3.

Applying Styles with the Styles Gallery

Sitting in the Styles group on the Home tab on the Ribbon is the Styles gallery. The Styles gallery contains the styles that the template designer has decided are the most useful for working with the document. Of course, it's your document, so you can add or remove styles as you like. The Styles gallery, shown in Figure 3-1, is the easiest way to work with styles.

Figure 3-1:
The Styles
gallery on
the Home
tab.

The More button

To apply a style to a paragraph, follow these steps:

1. **Click anywhere in the paragraph you want to format.**

For all styles except character styles, you don't have to select the entire paragraph; just move the insertion point anywhere in it.

2. **Choose the style you want from the Styles gallery.**

Click the More button next to the Styles gallery to reveal more styles, as shown in Figure 3-1. If the text you're formatting is covered by the gallery, thereby preventing the full benefit of Live Preview, use the arrows to scroll additional styles into view without expanding the gallery. Find the one you want and click it. The formatting contained in the style applies to the paragraph.

If the style you want to use isn't showing in the gallery, you can use the Styles pane to find it (see the section "Using the Styles pane" later in this chapter) or, if you know the name of the style, you can use the Apply Styles dialog box (see the section "Using the Apply Styles dialog box," later in this chapter).

To apply a style to two or more adjacent paragraphs, select a range of text that includes all the paragraphs you want formatted. Then choose the style. When you press Enter to create a new paragraph, the new paragraph normally assumes the same style as the preceding paragraph. See the section "Setting the style of the next paragraph," later in this chapter, for an important — and useful — exception.

As you work with your document, you might decide that you want to remove the style from a particular paragraph. The best way to remove the style and any formatting is to use the Clear Formatting button shown in the margin. Even though it's often used when working with styles, the Clear Formatting button prefers to hang out with the font formatting commands and can be found in the Font group rather than the Styles group. However, the Clear Formatting command on the bottom of the Styles gallery does the same thing (but you have to show the entire Styles gallery to get to this command).

The standard Styles gallery includes several character styles that are intended to be used to format text within your paragraphs. This includes three Emphasis styles, two Reference styles (for indicating text that refers to something such as a book title), and a style called Strong, which is used to provide strong emphasis. (The name Strong comes from HTML, where it usually means bold text and Emphasis usually means italic text.) The advantage to using the character styles becomes most obvious when you change themes or style sets and the character styles update so that your document keeps a consistent look.

Paragraphs always have a style associated with them (even if it's just the Normal style that Word applies automatically. You can layer a character style on top of the paragraph style if you want. For example, you can highlight text within a paragraph and assign it the Emphasis style to make it stand out from the rest of the text.

To apply a style just to a portion of text rather than entire paragraphs, follow these steps:

1. **Select the text you want to format.**

   When applying a character style, you can select text in more than one paragraph. When applying a linked style to selected text, all of the selected text must be in the same paragraph. You cannot apply a paragraph style to selected text.

2. **Select the style you want from the Styles gallery.**

   When you apply a character style, it sticks to the text that you've selected. If you move that text to a new paragraph, the character style remains on that text. To remove the character style, use the Clear Formatting button.

Here are some helpful hints to using styles effectively:

✦ The name of each style in the Styles gallery is formatted according to the style. This name gives you a hint of how your text will look before you apply the style. What's more, Live Preview shows you exactly what you're going to get.

✦ To quickly return a paragraph to Normal style, press Ctrl+Shift+N.

✦ To assign the built-in Heading 1, Heading 2, or Heading 3 styles, press Ctrl+Alt+1, Ctrl+Alt+2, or Ctrl+Alt+3.

✦ You can create keyboard shortcuts for any style that you create. See the section "Assigning shortcut keys," later in this chapter.

Finding Your Own Style

The styles included in the Styles gallery on the ones that Microsoft believes most people need for creating most types of documents. But perhaps you're not like most people and want some different ones.

Or perhaps you don't like the way the standard styles look. You might have already noticed that documents created with the default settings of Word 2007 have a dramatically different look from those created in Word 2003. That's because the definitions of standard styles including those for Normal paragraphs and for headings have changed.

Fear not! You're about to find out how to tailor the styles in the gallery to your needs, rather than what Microsoft started you off with.

Switching style sets and themes

Next to the Styles gallery is a button labeled Change Styles that reveals the hundreds of combinations of looks that are available for the Styles gallery. Clicking the Change Style button reveals controls for changing the three main elements that define the look of the Styles gallery. As shown in Figure 3-2, these are Style Set, Colors, and Fonts.

Figure 3-2:
The three choices on the Change Styles control.

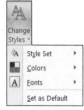

If your current document is saved in the Word 2003 format, you can't update the Font and Color aspects for your styles. To gain access to this powerful feature, you need to upgrade your document by selecting the Convert command from the Office menu.

The style sets in the Change Styles control update the definitions of the styles used in your document and the Styles gallery. Microsoft ships 11 style sets, but you can also create your own. Figure 3-3 shows the same document with two different style sets applied — the one on the right uses the Word 2007 set, and the one on the left uses the Modern set.

The Font and Color controls refine the current theme. A theme provides consistent formatting not only for the text in your document but also for objects that you might insert such as tables, charts, and SmartArt diagrams. Each theme has three components: fonts, colors, and effects. Effects are most important when working with charts and diagrams.

You can change the entire theme by using the controls on the Page Layout tab shown in Figure 3-4. The Font and Color controls are available both on the Change Styles control on the Home tab and in the Themes group on the Page Layout tab. PowerPoint and Excel share the same themes, making it easier to create a collection of documents with a very similar look.

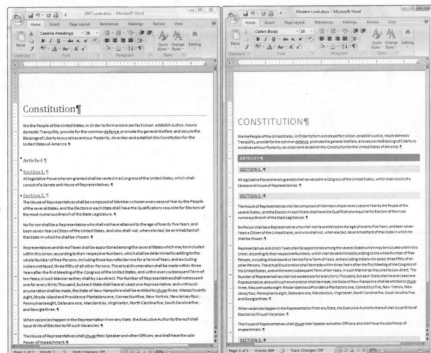

Figure 3-3:
The same document with the Word 2007 style set on the right and Modern on the left.

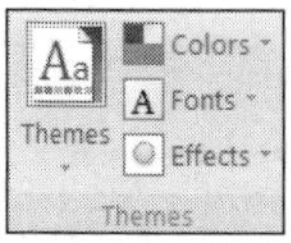

Figure 3-4:
The Themes
control on
the Page
Layout tab
lets you
change all
of the
settings
of the theme
at once.

To change the look of the styles in the Styles gallery and in your document, follow these steps:

1. **Make sure your document includes some text formatted with some of the styles in the Styles gallery.**

Generally, you want to have used Heading 1 and Heading 2 as well as the Normal style and perhaps some of the character styles. Although you can change the look of the styles in the Styles gallery without text in your document, it's much easier to see the various looks when you have styled text.

2. **Click the Change Styles button, point to the Style Set command, and then select one of the style sets from the list.**

As you move over the various style sets, the text in your document updates to preview the change. However, the styles in the Styles gallery don't change until you commit to your choice.

One of the major differences among the style sets is the spacing for the Normal paragraphs in your document. If you don't like the more open spacing of the Word 2007 defaults, you might prefer the Traditional set. If you want to create a document that is similar to the Word 2003 documents that you have, select the Word 2003 style set.

3. **Click the Themes button on the Page Layout tab and then select one of the themes from the list.**

When you move your cursor over the various themes, the text in your document updates with new fonts and colors. As with style sets, the styles in the Styles gallery update only after you commit to your selection.

4. **To fine-tune the look of the theme used in your document, click the Change Styles button, point to the Fonts command, and then select one of the font sets from the list.**

If you really want a document that looks like your old Word 2003 documents, select the Word 2003 style set and the Office Classic font set.

When you find a combination of style set and theme that you want to use for all of your documents, you can tell Word to use that for all new documents, as described in the section "Storing the look of your styles," later in this chapter.

Changing a style

You might or might not be able to teach an old dog a new trick, but you can teach Word to use your definitions for any of the styles that are in the Styles gallery. To do so, follow these steps:

1. **Apply the style you want to update to a paragraph in your document.**

You can just type a temporary paragraph, use it as a sample for the style, and then delete the paragraph. After the style is updated, the paragraph is no longer necessary for Word to remember the style definition.

2. **Make whatever formatting changes that you want to the formatting of the paragraph.**

If the style you're updating is a character style, Word ignores the paragraph formatting that you apply.

3. **Right-click the paragraph and select the Styles submenu, as shown in Figure 3-5.**

Book II
Chapter 3

Working with Styles

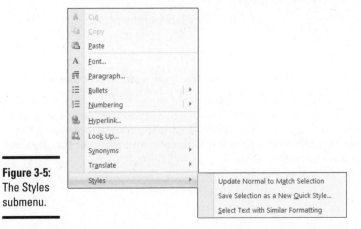

Figure 3-5: The Styles submenu.

If the menu that appears doesn't have the Styles submenu at the bottom, try clicking somewhere else in the paragraph. For example, if you click over an unrecognized word, you get the Spelling menu, which doesn't allow you to update the style definition.

4. Select Update *<style>* to Match Selection.

Well, it doesn't really say *<style>* in the command. Instead, the name of the style that you applied in Step 1 shows up here. Be sure to check that you're updating the right style — if the text that your cursor was over when you right-clicked in Step 3 has a character style applied, that character style is updated rather than the paragraph style.

You can also right-click the style either in the Styles gallery or the Styles pane to get to the command to update it to match the selection. With those methods, you can be certain that you're updating the style you want to change.

When Word goes to update the style, it uses the formatting from the start of the paragraph to update the character information stored in the style. So be sure that that part of the paragraph looks the way you want the style to look.

Because the Normal style is so important, Word offers another way to update Normal. One of the reasons that the Normal style is so important is that Word uses it for most of the paragraphs in your document. Another is that many other styles in your document use its settings as a base. The best method for updating the Normal style is to use the Default buttons found on the Font and Paragraph dialog boxes. For more information about working with these dialog boxes, see Chapter 2 in this minibook.

Creating your own style

You might find that the styles that are available in the Styles gallery aren't enough for you. And by golly, you want to add your own style! To do so, follow these steps:

1. Format a paragraph with the look that you want to store in a style.

You might want to look back at the list at the very start of the chapter (in the "Understanding Styles" section) to remind yourself of all of the things that you can store in a style. The most important ones are the character formatting, the paragraph indents, and whether the paragraph has a number or bullet.

In general, you want to make sure that the paragraph has the Normal style applied before you begin formatting it. If it has another style, that style will be used as the "Based on" style for the new style, as described in the section "Basing one style on another," later in this chapter.

2. **Right-click the paragraph and choose Styles⇨Save Selection as New Quick Style.**

   The dialog box shown in Figure 3-6 appears.

   Quick Style is the term Word uses to identify styles that appear in the Styles gallery.

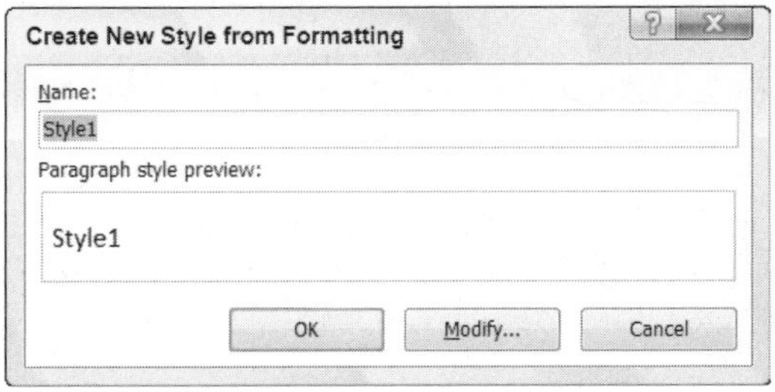

Create New Style from Formatting

Name:

Style1

Paragraph style preview:

Style1

[OK]   [Modify...]   [Cancel]

Figure 3-6:
Creating a
new style.

3. **Enter a name for the style and click OK.**

   The style now appears in the Styles gallery, near whichever style was previously applied to the paragraph (usually this is the Normal style, and the new style appears near the start of the Styles gallery).

Only linked styles can be created with this method. To create paragraph and character styles, you need to click the Modify button to open the dialog box shown in Figure 3-7. If you're changing an existing style, you can get to the same dialog box by right-clicking the style in either the Styles gallery or Styles pane. With the first approach, the dialog box is called Create New Style from Formatting, but if you open the dialog with the other steps, it's called Modify Style. It's the same dialog either way, so try not to worry too much about why Microsoft had to make this just a bit more confusing.

The Modify Style dialog box gives you complete control over the settings used in the style's definition. The controls within the "face" of the dialog box are the most commonly used, but you can use the Format button at the lower left to open additional dialog boxes with even more settings. All of the power comes with a price — the Modify Style dialog box is one of the most complex in Word. If you have to use it, try to find a friend to help you out.

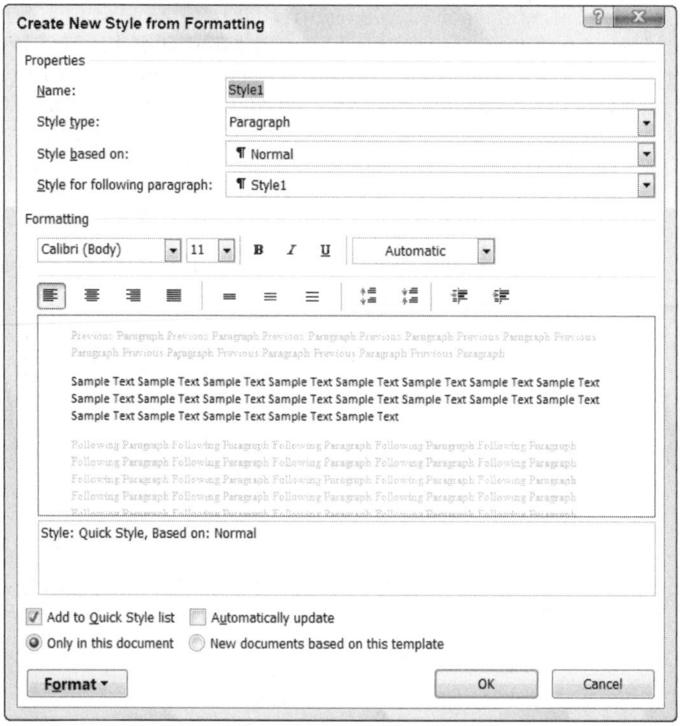

Create New Style from Formatting

Properties

Name: Style1

Style type: Paragraph

Style based on: ¶ Normal

Style for following paragraph: ¶ Style1

Formatting

Calibri (Body)   11   **B** *I* U   Automatic

Sample Text Sample Text

Style: Quick Style, Based on: Normal

☑ Add to Quick Style list   ☐ Automatically update
◉ Only in this document   ◯ New documents based on this template

Format ▾   OK   Cancel

Figure 3-7:
The Modify
Style dialog
box.

Adding and removing styles from the gallery

You might find that you never use some of the styles in the Styles gallery. You can remove any style from the gallery by right-clicking the style and choosing Remove from Quick Style Gallery.

To add a style back into the Styles gallery, you have to open the Styles pane (press Ctrl+Alt+Shift+S or click the dialog box launcher in the lower-left corner of the Styles group), locate the style, and then right-click the style. From the menu that appears, choose Add to Quick Style Gallery. The Styles pane is shown later in the chapter in Figure 3-8.

The other thing that you might want to do with the items in the Styles gallery is change their order. If you just want to list them alphabetically, you can open the Styles pane, click the Options link, set the Select How List Is Sorted drop-down list to Alphabetical, and click OK.

For more control over the order of the items in the Styles gallery and the Styles pane, you need to use the Styles Management dialog box — arguably the most complex dialog box in all of Word. You can open the Styles Management dialog box by clicking the middle button at the bottom of the Styles pane. The Recommend tab lets you specify the order in which styles should appear when the various styles lists are set to show in the Recommended order (set using the Options link on the Styles pane).

Storing the look of your styles

After you've gotten the Styles gallery looking exactly the way you want, you might be so happy with what you've done that you want any new document that you create to use those exact same settings. Not too surprisingly, Word offers an easy way to do that.

To set the styles that show in the Styles gallery for new documents, do the following:

1. **Update the Styles gallery to have the styles you want.**

   This might involve changing the style set, changing the theme, modifying the styles in the set, adding or removing styles, and even creating your own styles. (I cover all of these tasks earlier in this chapter.)

2. **Click the Change Styles button and then select the Set as Default command.**

   That's all there is to it. Go ahead. Try it. Press Ctrl+N and see whether your new document has the right settings. If not, check that the document that you're working with really has what you want to store.

   In some cases, the command name might have changed to identify a specific template. When that happens, it means that instead of updating the settings for all new documents created with Ctrl+N or any other method that starts with a plain blank document, you're changing the settings only for documents created with that template.

When you set the look for new documents, you don't create a separate style set or theme. Instead, you update the settings used in the Normal template. If you're working with a document and want to return to your customer defaults, use the Reset to Quick Styles from Template command on the Style Set menu and the Reset to Theme from Template on the Theme gallery.

You can also update and save just the contents of the Styles gallery as a style set. The command to store a style set is found on the Style Set menu, which you access by clicking the Change Styles button (in the Styles chunk of the Home tab right to the right edge of the Styles gallery) and then selecting Style Set. When you save a style set, Word prompts you to provide a name for the new style set. After you name and save the style set, it becomes available on the Style Set menu, and you can use it in any of your Word documents. You can save the current font, color, and effects setting as a theme by using the Save Current Theme command on the Theme gallery on the Page Layout tab. This command works in the same fashion as saving a style set, with the newly saved theme becoming available in the Theme gallery. One big difference between style sets and themes is that themes become available in PowerPoint and Excel as well as Word.

When you switch style sets, the styles in both sets are updated. Any style that is in use in your document but not in the new style set is left in the Styles gallery. Any style that is in the new style that wasn't showing previously is added.

Stepping Beyond the Styles Gallery

For most situations, the Styles gallery provides access to the styles you need and the commands to work with them. However, some situations require a larger list of styles, or you might want to work with your styles in ways not offered by the Styles gallery.

Using the Styles pane

One of the most common needs when working with styles is to be able to get to more styles than what can conveniently be displayed in the Styles gallery. For that, you can use the Styles pane shown in Figure 3-8 which you can open by clicking the More button at the bottom of the Styles gallery.

Instead of hunting through the Styles gallery to find which one is highlighted for the particular paragraph you are curious about, the Styles pane gives you the details on every style you have used in a document.

You apply a style from the Styles pane the same way that you do from the Styles gallery. To apply paragraph styles, place your cursor in the paragraph or select either the entire paragraph or parts of more than one paragraph and click on the style you want to apply. To apply character styles, select the text and then click on the style you want to apply.

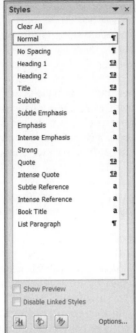

Book II
Chapter 3

Working
with Styles

Figure 3-8:
The Styles
pane.

You can control which styles appear in the Styles pane and how the styles are sorted for both the Styles pane and the Styles gallery by using the Options link. When you click the Options link, the Style Pane Options dialog box shown in Figure 3-9 appears.

Figure 3-9:
The Style
Pane
Options
dialog box.

The Styles pane is set to show as many styles as possible. If you make it wide enough, it even shows two or more columns of styles. As part of that, the style names are shown in the same font that's used for labels on the Ribbon. If you would rather see the styles formatted to preview the way that they format text, select the Show Preview option.

The icon at the right of the Styles pane identifies the style type for each style — character (the "a" character), paragraph (the pilcrow or paragraph mark, which also shows in the Styles gallery next to paragraph styles), or linked (with both an "a" and a pilcrow). I cover the difference among these three types of styles in the section "Understanding Styles," earlier in this chapter.

If you often end up applying linked styles to part of a paragraph when you meant to apply them to the entire paragraph, select the Disable Linked Styles option.

Microsoft certainly recommends that you set both the Select Styles to Show and Select How List Is Sorted drop-down menus to show the Recommended styles. The recommended setting for the Select Styles to Show is Recommended and for the Select How List Is Sorted is As Recommended. Maybe Microsoft is planning to trademark the word "recommended." The reason that these are the preferred settings in most cases is that they tell the controls that list styles to organize the information the way in which the template designer intended. However, you might have a different work style and want to change these settings. Most commonly, folks prefer setting Select styles to display a listing of all the styles in the current document, whether or not the template designer recommended each, and to sort the styles alphabetically.

Previous versions of Word kept track of the font and paragraph formatting that you had applied. Word 2003 displayed your applied formatting in the Styles and Formatting pane. With that information, you could treat the formatting as though it were a style. This is most useful for tasks such as selecting all text with that formatted and changing it. In Word 2007, if you want to display the same information, you need to click the Options link in the Styles pane and then select the Font formatting and Paragraph level formatting check boxes (under Select Formatting to Show as Styles).

Hovering over a style displays a description of the style's formatting. Right-clicking a style displays a menu, including an option to select all of the text using that style.

The three buttons at the bottom of the Styles pane provide you with the ability (from left to right) to create a new style using the Modify Style dialog box, to get more information about the current paragraph (see the section "Using the Style Inspector" later in this chapter, or open the scariest dialog box in Word — Manage Styles.

Using the Apply Styles dialog box

If you're the sort of user who prefers to keep your hands on the keyboard, you might prefer working with the Apply Styles dialog box shown in Figure 3-10. The advantage to using this approach is that you can display the dialog box by pressing Ctrl+Shift+S, typing the style name, and then pressing Enter to apply the style — all without moving your hands from the keyboard to your mouse.

Figure 3-10:
The Apply
Styles
dialog box.

As you type a style name, Word provides possible matches from the list of styles defined in the current document. If you don't like Word trying to guess what you're doing, you can turn this feature off by clearing the AutoComplete Style Names check box.

The Apply Styles dialog box also lets you create a new linked style by typing an unused name. If the style name you type isn't already defined, the Apply button becomes the New button. If you want to further refine the definition of the style before creating it, you can click the Modify button to open the Modify Style dialog box shown earlier in Figure 3-7.

If you've applied character or paragraph formatting and now want to clear that formatting and reapply the paragraph style, you can do this with the Apply Styles dialog box. Just type the style name for the paragraph and the Apply button becomes Reapply to let you know that clearing the formatting and reapplying the "pure" style.

The final control on the Apply Styles dialog box is the button with the double letter "A." Click this button to open the Styles pane.

Using the Style Inspector

As you work with styles, you might find yourself wondering which styles are applied to the current text. You might even want to know about any formatting that's hanging out in addition to the styles. To view these various levels of formatting, open the Styles pane and then click the Style Inspector button. This opens the Style Inspector dialog box, shown in Figure 3-11.

Figure 3-11:
The Style Inspector dialog box.

As described in the section "Understanding Styles" earlier in this chapter, all text gets some formatting from its paragraph style and might have additional paragraph formatting, formatting from a character style, and additional character formatting. The magic of the Style Inspector is that it reveals each of these levels of formatting and allows you to remove them one level at a time.

The large white box in the Paragraph Formatting section displays the current style for the paragraph. The button to the right resets the paragraph style to Normal. (Remember that all paragraphs in Word must have some paragraph style applied.)

Under that box but still in the Paragraph Formatting section is a list of any paragraph formatting that is applied to the entire paragraph. The button to the right clears all paragraph formatting that isn't part of the paragraph's style. Sometimes character formatting also appears here if applied to the entire paragraph; the button on the right doesn't clear this character formatting but resets it so that it shows correctly in the Text Level Formatting section.

The large box in the Text Level Formatting section reports the current character style. If the text has no character style applied, the text `Default Paragraph Font` is displayed. The button to the right clears the current character style.

As with the Paragraph Formatting section, any additional character formatting is shown in the box below. The button to the right clears the character formatting that comes from neither the paragraph nor character style.

To clear all formatting and reset the paragraph to the Normal style, you can use the Clear All button on the Style Inspector or the Clear Formatting button in the Font group on the Home tab.

Book II
Chapter 3

Working
with Styles

The Reveal Formatting pane provides much greater detail about the formatting applied to the currently selected text. You can open the Reveal Formatting pane by clicking the leftmost button in the group at the bottom of the Style Inspector dialog box or by pressing Shift+F1.

Using the Word 2003 Styles drop-down list

Previous versions of Word used a drop-down list on the Formatting toolbar to list the current style and to let you select which style to apply either by typing the style name (as you currently can do with the Apply Styles dialog box) or by selecting from a list. The Word 2007 Styles gallery and Styles pane both highlight the current style if it already appears in the list of styles currently displayed, but neither automatically scrolls to make that style visible. Therefore, it's often hard to tell at a glance what style is applied.

You can show the current style and provide yourself with an additional way of applying styles by adding the Word 2003 Styles drop-down list to your Quick Access toolbar (QAT) by doing the following:

1. **Open the Word Options dialog box from the Office menu.**

For more information about the Word Options dialog box, see Book I, Chapter 3.

2. **From the list of views on the right side of the dialog box, select Customize.**

The Customize tab of the Word Options dialog box is shown in Book VIII, Chapter 1.

3. **With the Popular Commands list showing, scroll down and select Style.**

Note that two commands have very similar names. You want the one that says Style, not Styles. The Styles entry adds a button to open the Styles pane.

4. Click the Add button to move the Style control into the list of commands on the QAT.

If you want, you can use the two arrows at the right of the dialog box to change the order of the commands on the QAT.

5. Click OK.

That's it. You can now see the current style with a quick glance at your QAT.

Better Living through Styles

Styles are one of the keys to using Word effectively. This list contains the best tips for simplifying your life by using styles right:

✦ **Always use styles.** This advice is kind of redundant, because with Word, you *have* to use styles. Whether you realize it or not, all paragraphs in Word are based on a style. If you don't use styles, the paragraphs are based on the utilitarian Normal style.

My point here is that for all but the simplest of documents, create and apply styles instead of applying direct formatting to your paragraphs. In the long run, using styles rather than direct formatting saves you a great deal of time and grief. You might curse the computer while you climb the steep-at-times learning curve that comes along with using styles, but when you get to the top, you'll say to yourself, "That wasn't so hard."

✦ **Use the built-in Heading 1, Heading 2, and Heading 3 styles for your headings.** Word has three predefined heading styles. If you don't like the way they look, redefine them. By using Heading 1, Heading 2, and Heading 3, you can work with your headings in Outline view (see Book II, Chapter 7) or create a Table of Contents (see Book VI, Chapter 1).

✦ **Whenever possible, create styles by example.** Just format a paragraph to have the look you want, right-click, and select Save Selection as a New Quick Style. Use the Modify Style dialog box only when you must.

✦ **Check out the style sets, themes, and templates that come with Word: Microsoft has already done a great deal of the hard work creating styles for you.** When you start to create a new document, check out the various templates that are available on Office Online to see whether any of them are suitable. If not, pick one that's close and modify it to suit your needs. For a bunch of information on using templates, check out Book I, Chapter 3.

✦ **Use keyboard shortcuts to assign styles quickly.** The second fastest way to assign styles is to use keyboard shortcuts. Assign a keyboard shortcut to each style that you use frequently. Don't bother with the ones you use infrequently, though. Remembering the keyboard shortcuts you use frequently is hard enough. For information about assigning keyboard shortcuts, see the section "Assigning shortcut keys," later in this chapter.

✦ **Base all text variants on the Normal style.** Most documents have several different types of paragraphs that are minor variations on normal text. For example, the bullet-list paragraphs in this book are variations of the book's normal-text paragraphs: They have the same typeface, point size, and line spacing, but the margins are different, and they have bullets. Paragraphs such as bulleted lists should be formatted with styles that are based on the Normal style. That way, if you decide to make a sweeping change, such as moving from 10- to 11-point type or switching from Times New Roman to Palatino, you can change the Normal style rather than changing each style individually. For more information, see the section "Basing one style on another," later in this chapter.

✦ **Use the Style for Following Paragraph field to automate your formatting.** The fastest way to assign styles is to have Word do it automatically. Set the Style for Following Paragraph field in the Modify Style or New Style dialog box. Then when you press Enter to create a new paragraph, Word automatically assigns the style. For more information, see the section "Setting the style of the next paragraph," later in this chapter.

✦ **Use Space Before or Space After, but not both.** When you create your paragraph styles, decide in advance whether you prefer to add extra space before or after the paragraphs. As much as possible, stick to your decision. If you have two adjacent paragraphs, the first with extra space after and the second with space before, you might end up with more space than you intend between the paragraphs.

Neat Things to Do with Styles

You can do much more with styles than creating and applying them. The sections that follow chronicle some of the more interesting things you can do with styles. Not only are they interesting, they're also somewhat more complex than the topics discussed already in this chapter. If you're not feeling very technical, you might want to just stop reading now.

Assigning shortcut keys

Word enables you to assign keyboard shortcuts to your favorite styles. Then you can apply those styles by simply pressing the keyboard shortcut. You can assign keyboard shortcuts in two ways. Because I'm in a talkative mood, I show you both (though one is in the sidebar called "The arcane shortcut key shortcut").

One way is to use the Styles pane. Follow these steps:

1. **Display the Styles pane.**

Press Ctrl+Shift+Alt+S or click the dialog box launcher in the lower-right corner of the Styles group on the Home tab.

2. **Point the cursor at the style you want to modify.**

Don't click the style; just point the cursor at it.

3. **Click the down arrow that appears next to the style and then choose Modify from the menu that appears.**

The Modify Style dialog box appears.

4. **Click the Format button and then choose Shortcut Key.**

The Customize Keyboard dialog box appears, ready for you to assign a keyboard shortcut for the style. (See Figure 3-12.)

Figure 3-12: The Customize Keyboard dialog box.

5. **Click in the Press New Shortcut Key text box and then press the key combination that you want to assign to the style.**

   When you press the keys, Word writes out the key combination for you. The plus sign indicates that the keys must be held down together.

6. **Verify that the shortcut isn't already in use.**

   If you choose a command already in use, then under the Current Keys box a very underwhelming line appears to tell you that it is Currently Assigned and which command is using it. You can then decide whether you want to find a different shortcut to use or remove it from the command that already has it.

7. **Click Assign to assign the keyboard shortcut.**

8. **Click Close; then click OK to get all the way out of there.**

The arcane shortcut key shortcut

You can assign a keyboard shortcut without bothering with the Styles pane. It involves an offbeat keyboard shortcut that turns the cursor into a weird-looking pretzel. Try this method sometime when you really want to impress your friends:

Long ago, Microsoft made an effort to make sure that all of the features in Word for the Macintosh were included in Word for Windows. One of the treasures that it included was an easy way to add shortcut keys to commands. You can tell that this came from the Macintosh world because the symbol that appears is from the Macintosh keyboard — it has never been on the keyboards used for most Windows machines.

1. **Press Ctrl+Alt+numeric plus.**

   That's the plus sign key on the numeric keypad, way over at the far right side of the keyboard.

Your cursor now looks like a pretzel. Avoid the temptation to douse it with mustard.

2. **Choose the style from the Styles gallery in the Styles group on the Home tab on the Ribbon or from the Styles pane.**

   Click the down arrow next to the Styles gallery; then click the style you want to assign a shortcut to. Word displays the Customize Keyboard dialog box, ready for you to type a shortcut. (See Figure 3-12.)

3. **Type the keyboard shortcut that you want to use in the Press New Shortcut Key text box.**

   For example, Ctrl+Alt+R.

4. **Click Assign to assign the shortcut to the style.**

5. **Click Close.**

   You're done.

Keep these tidbits in mind when using keyboard shortcuts for styles:

✦ To remove a keyboard assignment you previously assigned, select it in the Current Keys list in the Customize Keyboard dialog box; then click the Remove button.

✦ The predefined heading styles already have keyboard shortcuts associated with them:

Ctrl+Alt+1	Heading 1
Ctrl+Alt+2	Heading 2
Ctrl+Alt+3	Heading 3

✦ You can create keyboard shortcuts by using virtually any combination of keys on the keyboard. The shortcuts can utilize the Shift, Ctrl, and Alt keys, either alone or in combination. For example, you could assign Ctrl+K, Alt+K, Ctrl+Shift+K, Ctrl+Alt+K, or even Ctrl+Alt+Shift+K.

✦ You also can create prefix keyboard shortcuts, such as Ctrl+Shift+I, 1. To activate this shortcut, you must press Ctrl+Shift+I; then release those keys and press the 1 key. Using this approach, you can create one prefix key to access a group of styles. To enter this style of shortcut, press the combination of keys you want to use as the prefix and then the specific key you want to use for the style.

Basing one style on another

Suppose you create 20 different styles for various types of paragraphs in a complicated document, only to discover that your boss wants the entire document to have single-line spacing rather than the one-and-a-half lines you were told last week. Do you have to change all 20 styles to reflect the new spacing? Not if you set up your styles using *base styles*.

A base style is a style that provides formatting information for other styles. For example, suppose you have a style named Bullet List, and you want to create a similar style named Bullet List Last that you use for the last paragraph of a series of bulleted paragraphs. The only difference between Bullet List and Bullet List Last is that Bullet List Last has additional space after the paragraph. Otherwise, the styles are identical. Base styles enable you to do this. In this case, Bullet List Last consists of all the formatting from its base style, Bullet List, plus six points of space after.

A style *inherits* all the formats specified in its base style. If the base style changes, the changes are inherited, too. Any styles based on the style you change automatically reflect any changes you make to the base style.

However, a style can override the formats that it inherits from the base style. For example, if a style doesn't specify a point size, any paragraphs formatted with the style inherits the point size from the base style. However, if a style specifies a point size, the point size of the base style is ignored.

Thus, if all 20 of your paragraph styles are based on the Normal style, you can change the font for all 20 styles simply by changing the font for the Normal style. (The exception is any style based on Normal that specifies its own font to override the font picked up from the Normal style. In that case, the style retains its own font.)

Here's the procedure for creating a style that's based on another style:

1. **Choose the paragraph you want to format.**

2. **Apply the style that you want to use as the base style to the paragraph you selected.**

3. **Change the formatting of the paragraph.**

Add whatever extra formats you want applied to the new style. These formats are added to the base style's formats.

4. **Create the new style.**

The new style is based on the style originally applied to the paragraph.

You can also set the base style in the Create New Style from Formatting dialog box, which opens when you click the New Style button on the Styles pane. This dialog box is exactly the same as the dialog box shown earlier in Figure 3-7 except for the name change. Perhaps it's in the Witness Protection Program.

A style that serves as a base style may itself have a base style. For example, Bullet List Last may be based on Bullet List, which in turn may be based on Normal. In that case, the formats from Normal, Bullet List, and Bullet List Last are merged together whenever you apply the style.

Setting the style of the next paragraph

When you press Enter to create a new paragraph, the new paragraph normally assumes the same style as the previous paragraph. In some cases, you want to do exactly that. However, for some styles, the style of the following paragraph is almost always a different style. For example, a paragraph formatted with the Heading 1 style is rarely followed by another Heading 1 paragraph. Instead, a Heading 1 paragraph is usually followed by a Normal paragraph.

Instead of always changing the style assigned to a new paragraph in these situations, you can specify the style you want assigned to the next paragraph with the Modify Style dialog box. Then when you press Enter, the new paragraph is assigned the style you specified. This little trick can almost completely automate the chore of formatting your documents.

You can set the style for the following paragraph when you're creating a new style via the New Style button on the Styles pane. For existing styles, to set the Style for following paragraph, you need to use the Modify Style dialog box.

You can set the style for the following paragraph from the Create New Style from Formatting dialog box. You access the dialog box by summoning the Styles Window and then clicking the New Style button at the bottom left or the drop-down list next to the style you want to change and selecting the Modify option.

Examine the Style for Following Paragraph setting for each of your styles to see whether you can save yourself some work. Heading styles should specify Normal for the following paragraph, as should any other type of paragraph that usually occurs in singles. You might find other styles that should have this field set, too. For example, I have a Chapter Number style that specifies Chapter Title as Style for Following Paragraph.

Showing the Style area

Adding the Word 2003 Style drop-down list to the QAT provides a way of seeing the style of your current selection at a glance. But wouldn't it be cool to be able to see which paragraph style was assigned to each paragraph all at once? Well, I wouldn't have mentioned it if it wasn't possible. Figure 3-13 shows a document in Draft view with the Style area displayed.

To show the current paragraph style in the Style area, follow these steps:

1. **Make sure that you are in Draft view by checking the View tab.**

   If you're not in Draft view, switch to it by clicking the Draft button.

2. **Select Word Options from the Office menu to display the Word Options dialog box.**

3. **Select the Advanced option from the list on the left.**

4. **In the Display section of the very long list of advanced options, type the width that you want to use for the Style area in the text box labeled Style Area Pane Width in Draft and Outline Views.**

   Generally a width of an inch works well.

5. **Click OK.**

   The paragraph style for each paragraph now displays to the left of the text aligned with the first line of text in the paragraph.

To get rid of the Style area, follow the preceding steps but enter **0** for the width.

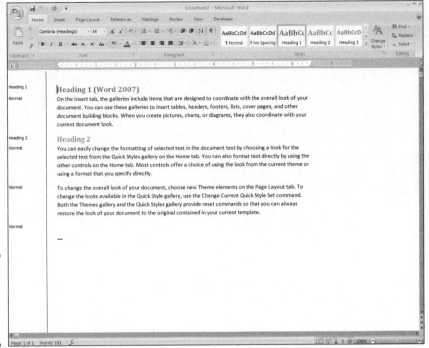

Figure 3-13:
A document
with the
Style area
displayed.

Storing styles in a template

The easiest way to store styles in a template is to open the template directly and edit the styles within it. You can also save any style you're modifying by selecting the New Documents Based on This Template option in the Modify Style dialog box and then clicking OK. If you want to save all of your style settings, do the following:

1. **Open the Styles pane by pressing Ctrl+Shift+Alt+S or using the dialog box launcher for the Styles group on the Home tab.**

2. **Click the Manage Styles button.**

   The Manage Styles dialog box appears. You may recall that this is the scariest dialog box in all of Word. It's so scary I won't even show a picture of it.

3. **Select the New Documents Based on This Template option.**

4. **Click OK.**

Styles stored in the template are available to any document that is created starting from that template. To make styles available for a variety of documents, consider storing them as a style set as described previously in the section "Storing the look of your styles."

Chapter 4: Editing Techniques

In This Chapter

✔ **Selecting and deleting text**

✔ **Moving text**

✔ **Using the Undo and Repeat commands**

✔ **Finding and replacing text**

*A*t its heart, Word is editing software. They call it processing software, but it doesn't process very much. It's for editing. It offers a lot of features that are involved with the editing of documents.

You would think that this is what the whole book is about. Not so fast, my friend — there is a special set of tools that relate directly to the technique of editing. That is what I cover here — the good, the bad, and the ugly of the editing tools of Microsoft Word.

Selecting Text

One of the most basic editing skills is selecting text. After you select some text, you can delete it, copy it, move it, apply formatting to it, change its capitalization, and do all sorts of other neat stuff to it.

The easiest way to select text is by clicking and dragging the mouse over the text you want to select. You can also use the following mouse actions to select text:

✦ Click at the start of the block of text, hold down Shift, and click at the end of the block. This action selects all the text between the points you click.

✦ To select a single word, double-click anywhere on the word. Click, click.

✦ To select an entire paragraph, triple-click anywhere on the paragraph. Click, click, click.

✦ To select an entire sentence, hold down Ctrl and click anywhere in the sentence.

✦ To select a column of text, hold down Alt, click and hold the mouse button, and drag. Drag the mouse left or right to increase or decrease the width of the column selected, and drag the mouse up or down to extend the column up or down. (This technique is especially useful if you arrange text into columns by using tabs and you want to rearrange the columns.)

Note that after you have selected text a mini formatting toolbar appears to the upper right of the cursor (see Figure 4-1), enabling you to quickly format a selection with some of the basic formatting tools discussed in Chapter 2 of this minibook.

Figure 4-1:
The mini formatting toolbar.

Using the invisible selection bar

Way off to the left of your text is an invisible, secret region of the Word screen that is officially called the *selection bar*. To find it, slide the mouse over toward the left edge of the screen until the cursor turns into a right-pointing arrow. When the cursor changes, say "Gotcha!" quickly so Word knows you're on to its game.

Here are a few selection tricks that use the selection bar:

✦ Click the selection bar once to select an entire line of text. Click.

✦ Double-click the selection bar to select an entire paragraph. Click, click.

✦ Triple-click the selection bar to select the entire document. Click, click, click.

✦ To select several paragraphs, double-click the selection bar to select the first paragraph, hold the mouse button down after the second click, and drag the mouse up or down the selection bar to select additional paragraphs.

Selecting with the keyboard

If you're allergic to the mouse, you can use the keyboard shortcuts summarized in Table 4-1 to select text.

Table 4-1	Keyboard Shortcuts for Selecting Text
Keyboard Shortcut	*What It Does*
Ctrl+A	Selects the entire document
Ctrl+NumPad5	Selects the entire document
Alt+NumPad5	Selects the entire table. (NumLock must be off for this shortcut to work.)
Shift	If you hold down the Shift key, the selection extends as you move the insertion point by using the arrow keys
F8	Places Word in Extend mode, which lets you extend the selection by using the arrow keys without holding down the Shift key
Ctrl+Shift+F8	Extends a column selection, similar to using the Alt key with the mouse

**Book II
Chapter 4**

Editing Techniques

After you press F8 to enter Extend mode, you can press it again to select the current word (like double-clicking). Press it a third time to select a sentence. Press it a fourth time to select the entire paragraph, and a fifth time to select the entire document.

To turn off Extend mode, press Esc.

Selecting cells in a table

If you create a table, you can use the following tricks to select individual cells, columns, or rows:

✦ Click in the cell that is your starting point. To select several cells, click and drag across the cells you want to select.

✦ To select an entire column, click the top gridline of the column. The cursor changes to a down arrow when it's in the right position to select the column. You can select several columns by dragging the mouse in this position.

✦ To select an entire row, click the selection bar to the left of the row. To select several rows, drag the mouse in the selection bar.

For the scoop on how to build a table, talk to a carpenter . . . or see Book IV, Chapter 4.

To delete a table or cells within a table, highlight the selection to be deleted and press Backspace. To delete all the text within a table or cells within a table, highlight the selection to be deleted and press Delete.

Deleting Text

Deleting text is one of the basics of good editing. Some people think they're such good writers that they shouldn't have to delete anything. Not me. I delete about half of what I write. And that's probably not enough.

Word has many ways to delete text. The most basic deletion technique is to delete characters one at a time by pressing one of these two keys:

✦ **Backspace:** Deletes the character to the *left* of the insertion point.

✦ **Delete:** Deletes the character to the *right* of the insertion point.

If you immediately catch a typing mistake, use the Backspace key to obliterate it, and then type the correct text. The Delete key is more appropriate when you discover your mistake a few moments after the fact. Then you can move the insertion point to the text in error, use the Delete key to erase the mistake, and then type the correct text.

You can also use the Backspace and Delete keys in combination with the Ctrl key to delete whole words. The same distinction between Backspace and Delete applies when you use the Ctrl key: Ctrl+Backspace deletes the previous word; Ctrl+Delete deletes the next word.

Note: Ctrl+Backspace and Ctrl+Delete work best when the insertion point is positioned between words. If the insertion point is in the middle of a word, Ctrl+Backspace and Ctrl+Delete delete only part of the word. Ctrl+Backspace deletes everything from the insertion point to the beginning of the word, and Ctrl+Delete deletes everything from the insertion point to the end of the word.

If you select text before you use the Backspace or Delete key, the forward and backward distinction between these two keys fades into the distance. With text selected, the Backspace and Delete keys simply delete the selected text. You can use this ability to delete large amounts of text with one blow. For example:

✦ **To delete a sentence,** hold down the Ctrl key and click in the sentence to select it, and then press Delete or Backspace.

✦ **To delete a paragraph,** triple-click the paragraph to select it, and then press Delete or Backspace.

✦ **To delete the entire document** (an act of extreme desperation, I would think), press Ctrl+A to select the entire document and then press Delete or Backspace.

If you become overzealous with the Delete or Backspace key, you can restore your smitten text by pressing Ctrl+Z to summon the Undo command. For more information, see the section "Undo and Repeat," later in this chapter.

Using the Clipboard

The Clipboard task pane is a nifty feature that lets you gather up to 24 different items of text or graphics from Word or any other Office application (such as Excel or PowerPoint), and then selectively paste them into your document. Figure 4-2 shows the Clipboard task pane in action.

Figure 4-2:
The
Clipboard
task pane.

You can summon the Clipboard task pane in a couple ways so that you can work with the items you add to the Clipboard:

✦ Click the dialog box launcher in the Clipboard group on the Home tab on the Ribbon.

✦ In the Clipboard task pane, click the Options button and then select the option labeled Show Office Clipboard When Ctrl+C Pressed Twice. Then you can press Ctrl+C twice to launch the task pane.

To paste an item from the Clipboard task pane, first click to mark the location in the document where you want to insert the item, and then click the item in the Clipboard that you want to insert.

If you like everything you copied to the Clipboard, you can paste it all into your document in one fell swoop by clicking the Paste All button. You find this button lurking near the top of the Clipboard task pane.

To remove an item from the Office Clipboard, click the Items drop-down list and choose Delete from the menu that appears. To clear out everything from the Clipboard, click the Clear All button that appears near the top of the Clipboard task pane.

For the Clipboard to collect items while it isn't displayed, you must open the Clipboard task pane, click the Options button, and then select the Collect Without Showing Office Clipboard option.

Dragging and Dropping

Drag-and-drop editing (or *dragon dropping*) helps you to move text from one location in a document to another by using only the mouse, without using the Clipboard. You simply highlight the text you want to move and use the mouse to drag the text to a new location. When you release the mouse button, the text is cut from its original location and pasted to the new location.

If you hold down the Ctrl key while dragging text, you can copy the text to the new location instead of moving it. In other words, the text is not deleted from its original location.

You can drag and drop text between two open documents, which is easier if both documents are visible on-screen. To ensure that both documents are visible, use the Arrange All button on the View tab on the Ribbon. To drag text from one open document to another without rearranging your windows, try this technique:

1. **Select the text you want to drag to another document.**

2. **Click and hold the mouse button.**

3. **While still holding down the mouse button, press Alt+Tab to switch to the document you want to drop the text into.**

   Note: Continue to hold the Alt key down and press Tab as many times as necessary to switch to the right document.

4. **While still holding down the mouse button, drag the text to the location where you want to drop it.**

5. **Release the mouse button to drop the text.**

By my reckoning, this way is more trouble than it is worth. I'd put my money on simple copy and paste (Ctrl+C and Ctrl+V) any day.

If you don't like this feature — and you may well find that you don't — you can disable it by choosing Office➪Word Options and then clicking the Advanced tab. Deselect the Allow Text to be Dragged and Dropped check box.

Undo and Repeat

The Undo command is one of the best ways to become a Word guru. Without the Undo command, you would be afraid of experimenting with Word for fear of losing your document. But with this command at hand, you can try anything you want, knowing that the worst that can happen is that you might have to use the Undo command to undo your mistake.

You can access the Undo command from the Quick Access toolbar, but Undo is useful enough that you should simply memorize its keyboard shortcut: Ctrl+Z. While you're at it, go ahead and memorize Ctrl+Y, the keyboard shortcut for an almost equally useful command: Repeat. The following minitable summarizes these shortcuts for your reference:

Keyboard Shortcut	*What It Does*
Ctrl+Z	Undoes the previous action.
Ctrl+Y	Repeats the previous action. If the previous action was Undo, Ctrl+Y redoes the undone action.

The Repeat command, as its name implies, repeats the last action. If you just used the Font dialog box (by using the dialog box launcher in the Font group on the Home tab on the Ribbon) to make a bevy of formatting changes all at once, select some other text that you want similarly formatted and then press Ctrl+Y. By using this Repeat command, you can apply the same formats to the other text.

The Repeat command repeats just about any action you can do in Word. But when the most recent command is Undo, the Repeat command becomes the Redo command: It redoes the action undone by the Undo command. Undo and Redo are a perfect combination for people who can't decide whether they like something.

Word keeps track of more than one recent action. In fact, you can undo hundreds of recent actions. I don't think undoing more than one or two at a time is a good idea, but who am I to second-guess what you do with Word? To undo more than one action at a time, click the drop-down list of the Quick Access toolbar's Undo button to reveal all the undoable actions. Drag the mouse to select the actions you want to undo, as shown in Figure 4-3. Then release the mouse button to undo them all. The Redo button on the Quick Access toolbar has a similar capability to redo multiple undone actions.

Figure 4-3:
The Undo
drop-down
list in action.

Finding and Replacing

The Find command enables you to locate specific text in your document. For example, you might remember that somewhere in your 200-page report you discussed the famous Bandersnatch, but you can't recall exactly where. So you fire up the Find command and ask it to find the first mention of Bandersnatch in your document.

You might then decide that whenever you mention the Bandersnatch, you should add the word *Frumious*. So you then summon the Replace command to replace all occurrences of "Bandersnatch" with "Frumious Bandersnatch."

Finding text

You can use the Find and Replace dialog box to find text anywhere in a document. Just follow these steps:

1. **Choose the Find button in the Editing group on the Home tab or press Ctrl+F to summon the Find and Replace dialog box.**

   Refer to Figure 4-4 for a glimpse of this dialog box.

2. **Type the text you want to find in the Find What field.**

   For example, type **Bandersnatch**.

3. **Click the Find Next button.**

   When Word finds the text, it highlights that text on-screen in gray. The Find dialog box remains on-screen so that you can click Find Next to find yet another occurrence of the text.

Figure 4-4:
The Find
and Replace
dialog box.

Here are a couple of hints to keep in mind:

✦ If you would like to highlight all the occurrences in yellow, click the Reading Highlight drop-down list and select Highlight All. To remove them, follow the same path to the Clear Highlighting Option.

✦ If Word doesn't find the search text, check your spelling. You might have spelled it wrong in the Find and Replace dialog box.

You can bail out of the Find and Replace dialog box at any time by clicking Close or pressing Esc.

Ctrl+F is the shortcut key for the Find command.

Changing the search direction

You can change the direction of Word's search by changing a setting in the Find and Replace dialog box. To expand the dialog box, click the More button and use the Search drop-down list in the Search Options sections to reveal what you see in Figure 4-5.

Three choices are available:

✦ **All:** Searches the entire document without regard to the position of the insertion point.

✦ **Down:** Starts the search at the position of the insertion point and searches forward toward the end of the document.

✦ **Up:** Searches backward from the insertion point, toward the beginning of the document.

Both the Down and Up options search until they reach the bottom or top of the document; then they ask whether you want to continue searching the rest of the document.

To hide the Search Options section, click the Less button (which was previously the More button).

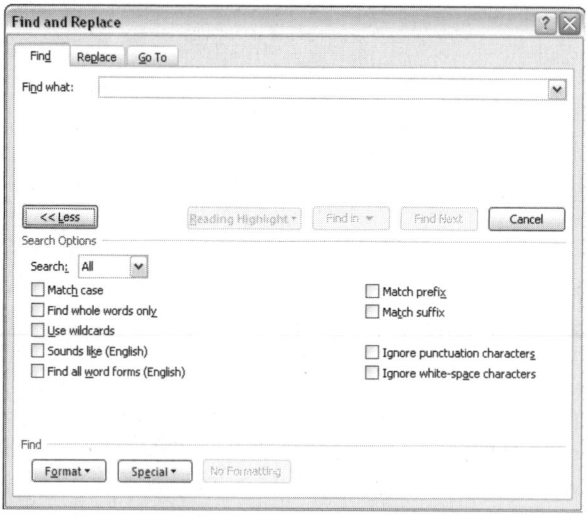

Figure 4-5:
The Find
and Replace
dialog box.

Refining your findings

The check boxes at the bottom of the expanded Find and Replace dialog box let you refine your searches in sometimes helpful ways, as described in the following sections.

Matching case

Select the Match Case check box before beginning the search if it matters whether the text appears in upper- or lowercase letters. This option is handy when you have, for example, a document about Mr. Mathers the math teacher.

Finding whole words

Speaking of Mr. Mathers the math teacher, select the Find Whole Words Only check box to find your text only when it appears as a whole word. If you want to find the text where you talk about Mr. Mathers the math teacher for example, type **mat** in the Find What text box and select the Find Whole Words Only check box. That way, the Find command looks for *mat* as a separate word and doesn't show you all the *mat*s in *Mathers* and *math*.

Using wildcards

Select the Use Wildcards check box if you want to include wildcard characters or other search operators in the Find What field. Table 4-2 summarizes the search operators you can use if you select this option.

Table 4-2	Advanced Search Operators for the Find Command
Operator	*What It Does*
?	Finds a single occurrence of any character. For example, f?t finds fat or fit.
*	Finds any combination of characters. For example, b*t finds any combination of characters that begins with b and ends with t, such as bat, bait, ballast, or bacteriologist.
#	Finds any numerical digit.
[abc]	Finds any one of the characters enclosed in the brackets. For example, b[ai]t finds bat or bit, but not bet or but.
[a-c]	Finds any character in the range of characters enclosed in the brackets. For example, b[a-e]t finds bat or bet, but not bit or but.
[!abc]	Finds any character except the ones enclosed in the brackets. For example, b[!ai]t finds bet or but, but not bat or bit.
@	Finds one or more occurrences of the preceding character. For example, 10@ finds 10, 100, or 1000.
{n}	Specifies the preceding character must be repeated exactly n times. For example, 10{2} finds 100, but not 10 or 1000.
{n,}	Specifies the preceding character must be repeated at least n times. For example, 10{2,} finds 100 or 1000, but not 10.
{n,m}	Specifies the preceding character must be repeated from n to m times. For example, 10{2,3} finds 100 or 1000, but not 10 or 10000.
<	Finds the following text only if it appears at the beginning of a word. For example, <pre finds predestined and prefabricated, but not appreciate or apprehend.
>	Finds the preceding text only if it appears at the end of a word. For example, ing> finds interesting and domineering, but not ingenious or ingest.

First word, short, sounds like . . .

Select the Sounds Like check box if you're not sure exactly how to spell the text for which you're searching. Word can search for words that are pronounced the same as the word you're searching for. For example, if you search for **your** with the Sounds Like option on, Word stops when it finds *you're.* Don't expect too much from this option, however. For example, if you typed **low** in the Find What field, you'd expect the option to find *Lowe* (well, *I* would anyway). But it doesn't.

Finding all word forms

If you select the Find All Word Forms check box, Word looks for alternative forms of most verbs. For example, if you search for **run**, Word finds *runs,* *running,* and *ran.* And the program is smart enough to know about certain oddball words such as go: If you search for **go**, Word finds not only *goes, going,* and *gone,* but also *went.* Searching for **be** finds *is, was, am, were, being,* and *been.*

Don't expect miracles, however. Find All Word Forms doesn't pick up every imaginable word form, especially where nouns are concerned. For example, a search for **introduction** doesn't pick up *introductory,* and **religion** doesn't catch *religious.* Find All Word Forms is more adept at finding alternative word forms for verbs than for nouns.

Ignorance is not bliss

Ignoring punctuation or white spaces *can* be bliss:

✦ The **Ignore Punctuation Characters** check box is useful to find out whether you were *online* or *on-line* at the click of the mouse.

✦ The **Ignore White-Space Characters** check box is useful to find out whether you typed *white-space* or *white space,* or *cell phone* or *cell-phone.*

Finding formats

To find specific types of formatting, click the Find button in the Editing group on the Home tab or press Ctrl+F, and then click the dialog box launcher to display the advanced search options; refer to Figure 4-5. Click the Format button and choose the type of format you want to search for from the pop-up menu. The following options are available:

✦ **Font:** Enables you to search for specific font formatting. You can search for specific fonts or for font formatting, such as bold, italics, font size, and so on.

✦ **Paragraph:** Enables you to search for specific paragraph formatting, such as indentation and alignment.

✦ **Tabs:** Enables you to search for paragraphs with specific tab settings.

✦ **Language:** Enables you to search for paragraphs formatted for a particular language.

✦ **Frame:** Enables you to search for specific frame formatting.

✦ **Style:** Enables you to search for paragraphs formatted with a particular style.

✦ **Highlight:** Enables you to search for highlighted text.

Make sure that the Find What field itself is blank; otherwise, the Find command searches for specific text formatted with the style you specify.

Finding special characters

You can also use the Find command to search for special characters such as em dashes or annotation marks. Call up the Find command (press Ctrl+F), click the More button to reveal the advanced Find options, and then click the Special button to reveal a list of special characters that you can search for, as shown in Figure 4-6. Select the character you want to search for and click Find Next to begin the search.

Paragraph Mark
Tab Character
Any Character
Any Digit
Any Letter
Caret Character
§ Section Character
¶ Paragraph Character
Column Break
Em Dash
En Dash
Endnote Mark
Field
Footnote Mark
Graphic
Manual Line Break
Manual Page Break
Nonbreaking Hyphen
Nonbreaking Space
Optional Hyphen
Section Break
White Space

Figure 4-6:
The Special
button drop-
down list.

When you select a special character, Word inserts a code into the Find What text box. If you know the code, you can bypass the Special button and its huge menu by typing the code directly into the Find What field. Table 4-3 summarizes the codes.

Table 4-3	**Search Codes for Special Characters**
Character	*Code*
Paragraph mark	^p
Tab character	^t
Comment mark	^a

(continued)

Table 4-3 *(continued)*

Character	Code
Any letter	^$
Section character	^%
Any character	^?
Any digit	^#
Paragraph character	^v
Caret character	^^
Column break	^n
Em dash	^+
En dash	^=
Endnote mark	^e
Field	^d
Footnote mark	^f
Graphic	^g
Manual line break	^l
Manual page break	^m
Nonbreaking hyphen	^~
Nonbreaking space	^s
Optional hyphen	^-
Section break	^b
White space	^w

Replacing text

You can use the Replace command in the Editing group on the Home tab to replace all occurrences of one bit of text with other text. The following steps show you the procedure:

1. **Choose the Replace command in the Editing group on the Home tab or press Ctrl+H.**

The Find and Replace dialog box appears with the Replace tab selected, as shown in Figure 4-7.

2. **Type the text you want to find in the Find What text box.**

For example, type **Bandersnatch**.

3. **Type the text you want to substitute for the Find What text in the Replace With text box.**

   For example, type **Frumious Bandersnatch**.

4. **Click the Find Next button.**

   When Word finds the text, it highlights that text on-screen.

5. **Click the Replace button to replace the text.**

6. **Repeat the Find Next and Replace sequence until you finish.**

Figure 4-7:
The Replace
tab of the
Find and
Replace
dialog box.

If you're absolutely positive that you want to replace all occurrences of your Find What text with the Replace With text, click the Replace All button. Taking this step automatically replaces all remaining occurrences of the text.

Replace All can be hazardous to the health of your document. You're bound to encounter at least one spot where you don't want the replacement to occur. Replacing the word **mitt** with **glove**, for example, changes *committee* to *comgloveee*. (Imagine the confusion *that* could cause.) So be cautious before you click that Replace All button and use the More options.

As for the Find command, you can click the More button to expand the dialog box so that additional options are visible, as shown earlier in Figure 4-5. You can then use the Match Case, Find Whole Words Only, Use Wildcards, Sounds Like, and Find All Word Forms options. The last option is even smart enough to properly replace alternative word forms with the correct version of the replacement text. For example, if you replace **run** with **walk**, Word replaces *running* with *walking* and *ran* with *walked*.

Because Word is not 100-percent confident in its capability to properly replace all alternative word forms, you get a warning message if you select the Find All Word Forms option and click Replace All. Find All Word Forms is tricky enough that you should verify each replacement.

Avoiding Overtype mode

Word has an evil editing feature called *Overtype mode.* When you're in Overtype mode, any text you type obliterates the text on-screen. For example, move the insertion point to the beginning of this paragraph, switch to Overtype mode, and type the letter G to change "Word" to "Gord." In Overtype mode, typing a character replaces the character to the right of the insertion point with the character you type. Fortunately, turning it on is no longer as easy as accidentally pressing the Insert key.

Now you have to enable the Insert key to toggle Overtype mode on and off by following the steps in this sidebar. Unless you like to unknowingly be in Overtype mode, obliterating all text in your path, you need to tell the status bar to let you know when Word is in Overtype or Insert Mode. So, if you're wishing to use Overtype mode, here's the info you need:

1. **Choose Office⇨Word Options and then click the Advanced tab.**

   This opens the Advanced tab of the Word Options dialog box.

2. **To enable the Insert key to be the Overtype toggle key, select the Use the Insert Key to Control Overtype Mode check box.**

3. **Click OK.**

4. **To turn on the status bar notification, right-click the status bar at the bottom of the window and choose Overtype from the menu that appears.**

Now the word Insert appears in your status bar. When you press the Insert key to use Overtype mode, the word Insert changes to Overtype, indicating that the Overtype mode is on.

Now, how to turn it off: Deselect the Use the Insert Key to Control Overtype Mode check box on the Advanced tab of the Word Options dialog box, which you can find using Step 1 of the preceding list.

If for some reason you want to use Overtype mode forever, use Step 1 of the preceding list to go to the Advanced tab of the Word Options dialog box, select the Use Overtype Mode check box, and obliterate any and all text in your way.

Chapter 5: All About AutoCorrect and AutoFormat

In This Chapter

✔ Using AutoCorrect

✔ Formatting with AutoFormat

✔ AutoFormatting as you type

✔ Inserting AutoText

*T*his chapter covers several advanced editing features of Word that you can access to modify by choosing Office➪Word Options to open the Word Options dialog box, clicking the Proofing tab, and then clicking the AutoCorrect Options button. These features include AutoCorrect itself as well as several similar features: Math AutoCorrect, AutoFormat As You Type, AutoFormat, and Smart Tags. Depending on the type of documents you create, these features may or may not prove invaluable.

Using AutoCorrect

AutoCorrect is a Word feature that monitors your typing, carefully watching for common typing mistakes and fixing them quicker than you can say "Bob's Your Uncle." For example, type **adn**, and AutoCorrect changes it to *and.* A misspelled **teh** becomes *the,* and **recieve** becomes *receive.* You get the idea. AutoCorrect has other features, as well: It corrects capitalization, including accidental use of the Caps Lock key, and it lets you insert special symbols.

If you don't like a change made by AutoCorrect, press Ctrl+Z or click the Undo button on the Quick Access toolbar to undo the change. Alternatively, you can play with the AutoCorrect Options button, as I describe in the following steps:

1. **When Word automatically makes a correction to your text, move the insertion point to the changed word.**

correct

Click in the word or use the arrow keys to move the insertion point to it. When you get to the changed word, a little blue rectangle appears beneath the modified text, as shown in the margin.

2. Point right at the blue rectangle until the insertion point changes to an arrow pointer.

The AutoCorrect Options button magically appears in place of the blue underline, as shown in the margin.

3. Click to reveal a menu.

The menu includes the following commands:

- *Undo Automatic Corrections That I Don't Want You to Do:* This option is the same as pressing Ctrl+Z or clicking the Undo button on the Quick Access toolbar. Because both of those alternatives are easier than hunting for the AutoCorrect Options menu, I doubt you'll use this command often.

- *Stop Doing That:* Well, this menu command doesn't actually say "Stop Doing That." Instead, it offers to stop making whatever type of AutoCorrect change you just made. For example, if AutoCorrect automatically capitalizes the first letter of a sentence, this command is called Stop Automatically Capitalizing the First Letter of a Sentence. You can choose this command to disable the particular AutoCorrect action that led you to find the AutoCorrect Options menu.

- *Control AutoCorrect Options:* Brings up the AutoCorrect Options dialog box so you can further customize your AutoCorrect options.

4. Choose the command you want to apply and be done with it.

If you find the AutoCorrect Options button to be more of an annoyance than a help, you can turn it off by choosing Office➪Word Options button and then clicking the Proofing tab. Next, click the Autocorrect Options button and then deselect the Show AutoCorrect Options Buttons check box.

Using AutoFormat

The AutoFormat feature as it was known in the past is no longer available. Word's AutoFormat feature cleans up your document and fixes common formatting problems. AutoFormat tries to deduce such things as which paragraphs in your document should be formatted as headings, which paragraphs should be bulleted or numbered lists, and so on. It doesn't always get it right, so you need to carefully review the changes that it makes.

You can, however, add the AutoFormat button to the Quick Access toolbar:

1. **Choose Office⟹Word Options.**

2. **Click the Customize tab.**

3. **In the Choose Commands From drop-down list, select All Commands.**

4. **Find AutoFormat in the All Commands list and then click Add.**

You can adjust the button's position on the toolbar by using the Up and Down arrows. Also, you can place separators between commands to help you organize your Quick Access toolbar.

After you have added the AutoFormat button to the Quick Access toolbar, you can use it by following these steps:

1. **Save your document.**

AutoFormat performs drastic surgery on your document, so you'd better save it first. That way, if you don't like what AutoFormat does, you have a saved copy to fall back on.

2. **Click the AutoFormat button on the Quick Access toolbar.**

The AutoFormat dialog box comes up, as shown in Figure 5-1.

3. **Click OK.**

AutoFormat reviews your entire document and makes whatever changes it deems necessary to spiff it up.

4. **Review the changes.**

Look over your document carefully to make sure you like the way it looks.

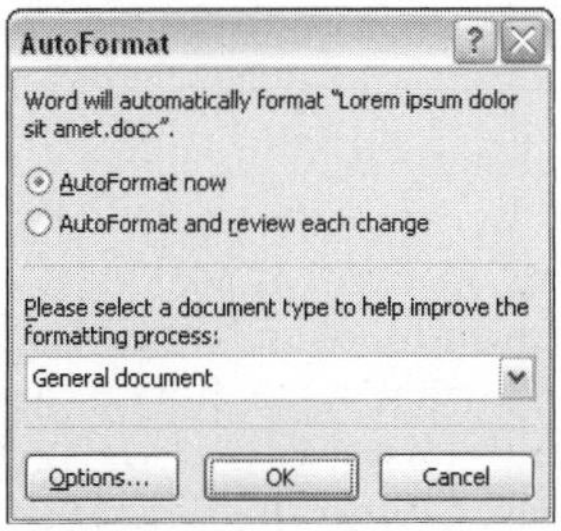

Figure 5-1:
The
AutoFormat
dialog box.

If AutoFormat makes a complete mess of your document, use the Undo command (click the Undo button on the Quick Access toolbar or press Ctrl+Z) to restore your document to its previous condition.

If you don't trust AutoFormat, select the AutoFormat and Review Each Change option in the AutoFormat dialog box. Then AutoFormat gives you an opportunity to review each change.

Setting AutoFormat options

You can control the changes made by AutoFormat by calling up the AutoCorrect dialog box, shown in Figure 5-2. To display this dialog box, choose Office➪Word Options and then click the Proofing tab. Then click the AutoCorrect Options button and select the AutoFormat tab. (Alternatively, if you've added the AutoFormat button to the Quick Access toolbar, you can choose it and then click the Options button.)

You can find most of the options on the AutoFormat tab or the AutoFormat As You Type tab of the AutoCorrect dialog box, which I describe in the next section. Because AutoFormat As You Type is a more interesting and useful feature, I describe the options in the next section rather than here.

Figure 5-2: AutoCorrect dialog box with the AutoCorrect tab selected.

Using AutoFormat As You Type

The Word AutoFormat As You Type feature automatically improves the formatting of documents written with little concern for appearance. This feature applies document formatting as you type, so it's closely related to the AutoCorrect feature. In fact, you find the options for controlling AutoFormat As You Type in the same window as the options for controlling AutoCorrect. Choose Office⇨Word Options and then click the Proofing tab. Then click the AutoCorrect Options button. (Alternatively, if you've added the AutoFormat button to the Quick Access toolbar, you can choose it and then click the Options button.)

Click the AutoFormat As You Type tab to display the options shown in Figure 5-3. I describe the options in detail in the following sections.

Figure 5-3: AutoCorrect dialog box with the AutoFormat As You Type tab selected.

Replace as you type

The first section of the AutoFormat As You Type tab is for items that are automatically replaced as you type them. These items work essentially the same as AutoCorrect items: When you type a particular bit of text, Word steps in and replaces the text with other, more appropriate text.

The following sections summarize the Replace As You Type options.

"Straight quotes" with "smart quotes"

This option tells Word to replace ordinary apostrophes and quotation marks automatically with curly apostrophes and quotes. The trick of quotes is figuring out whether to use the left or right variety of curly quote or apostrophe. The left quote appears to the left of quoted material; the right quote or apostrophe appears on the right. Word does its best to figure out which to use and usually gets it right. If a character immediately follows the apostrophe or quote, Word replaces it with a left quote or apostrophe. If a non-space character is immediately before the quote or apostrophe, Word replaces it with a right quote or apostrophe. Verdict: Thumbs up, with the following caveats:

The Smart Quotes feature works most of the time, but it bombs when you want to use a simple curly apostrophe. For example, try typing **Stop 'n Go**. You can't do it: Word insists on turning the apostrophe the other way 'round. (See, I did it again: Bet you can't!)

Okay, here's the secret to getting these apostrophes right: Simply type *two* apostrophes in a row. Word curls them both, the first one left, the second one right: ''. Now go back and delete the first one.

Another way to do it is to hold down Ctrl and press the apostrophe key twice. This trick omits a right apostrophe.

Smart Quotes is such a useful feature that you have little reason to turn it off. If you need to type an ordinary, non-curled apostrophe or quote once in awhile, just type the apostrophe or quote and press Ctrl+Z (Undo).

Ordinals (1st) with superscript

This option replaces ordinal numbers, such as 1st, 2nd, and 3rd, with properly formatted superscripts: 1st, 2nd, and 3rd. AutoCorrect can also accomplish ordinals, but the AutoFormat option is convenient. For most people, ordinals are one of the main reasons to use superscripts (the other being footnotes), so automatically converting them in this way is a real convenience.

Replace fractions (1/2) with fraction characters (½)

The standard Windows character set, which most fonts adhere to, includes three fraction characters: ½, ¼, and ¾. When you enable this option, Word automatically converts 1/2, 1/4, and 3/4 to their fraction equivalents.

Too bad the Windows character set doesn't include a few other fractions, at least 1/3 and 2/3. Sigh.

Two hyphens (--) with a dash (—)

This option does two things:

✦ It replaces two hyphens with a typographical dash called an *em dash,* so called because it is about as wide as a capital letter M. For example, — is an em dash.

✦ It replaces two hyphens preceded and followed by a space with an *en dash,* so called because it is about the width of a capital letter N. For example, June – July, Aug – Sep, and so on.

Internet and network paths with hyperlinks

This option watches for text that looks like an Internet address, such as `www.wiley.com` or `Gomez@Addams.com`, or network paths, such as `\\SERVER01\ADMIN`. It then formats these items as hyperlinks so that you can double-click them in Word to open the Web page or network location they point to in a browser window.

Apply as you type

The Apply As You Type section of the AutoFormat As You Type tab lets you select various formatting options that apply to text as you type. The following sections describe each of these options.

Automatic bulleted lists

If you start a paragraph with a character that resembles a bullet, such as an asterisk, a hyphen, an "o," or a >, followed by a space or tab, Word removes the bullet character and the space or tab and instead formats the paragraph as a bullet list. Automatic bullets are pretty convenient for users who haven't yet learned how to use the Bullets button in the Paragraph group on the Home tab on the Ribbon.

Automatic numbered lists

If you start a paragraph with a number followed by a period, space, parenthesis, or tab, Word removes the number and instead formats the paragraph as a numbered list. This option is okay for users who haven't yet learned how to use the Numbering button in the Paragraph group on the Home tab on the Ribbon, but it drives me batty. Usually, if I start a paragraph with a number followed by a tab, I'm creating a numbered list in a format that is too complicated for the Numbering button to handle, and I don't want to take the time to mess with Word's multilevel numbered list feature. For simple numbered lists, I always just click the Numbering button anyway.

Border lines

If you type three or more hyphens, underscores, or equal signs in a row and press Enter with the Border Lines option selected, Word deletes the characters and instead applies a border to the bottom of the paragraph. You get a thin line for dashes, a thick line for underscores, or a double line for equal signs. This feature is pretty neat.

Tables

This feature is the strangest of all the AutoFormat As You Type features. It automatically creates a table whenever you type a plus sign followed by one or more hyphens, another plus sign, and optionally another set of hyphens and plus signs. For example, to create a table with four columns, you could type this:

```
+---+---+---+---+
```

The number of hyphens you type between the plus signs determines the width of each column.

If you ask me, using the Table button in the Tables Group on the Insert tab is easier. You can look to Book IV, Chapter 4 for all of the delights regarding Tables.

Built-in heading styles

Whenever you type a line that starts with a capital letter, has no ending punctuation, and is at least 20 percent shorter than the maximum line length, Word makes the paragraph a heading if you select this option. Frankly, the rules for AutoFormatting headings as you type are too restrictive. What if the heading needs to be more than one line long? (Some do.) What if the heading ends with a question mark? What if you need to use two or more levels of headings? Memorizing the keyboard shortcuts for applying Word's built-in heading styles is much easier: Ctrl+Alt+1 for a Heading 1, Ctrl+Alt+2 for a Heading 2, and so on.

Automatically as you type

The last group of AutoFormat As You Type options applies the formatting described in the following sections.

Format beginning of list item like the one before it

This feature attempts to apply consistent formatting to the first portion of each item in a list. For example, if the first list item begins with boldface text and switches to normal after a colon, Word automatically applies that formatting to subsequent list items.

Set left- and first-indent with tabs and backspaces

When you select this feature, pressing the Tab key sets the indentation for paragraphs. For example, if you press Tab at the beginning of a new paragraph, Word automatically increases the paragraph's indentation by half an inch. Press Backspace to decrease the indentation by half an inch. If you press Tab when the insertion point is at the beginning of an existing paragraph, Word increases the first line indent by half an inch.

Personally, I'd rather use styles to set indentation so that it's consistent throughout the document. See Chapter 3 of this minibook for more on styles.

Define styles based on your formatting

This option automatically creates styles based on AutoFormat formatting. Normally, this option is turned off, and I recommend you leave it off. Styles are the best way to apply formatting consistently throughout your document, but you have much more control if you create and apply styles yourself rather than let Word automatically create them. Chapter 3 of this minibook tells you much more about styles.

Chapter 6: Spell-Checking and the Thesaurus

In This Chapter

✔ Spell-checking your document with the spell checker

✔ Correcting your grammar with the grammar checker

✔ Using the thesaurus

✔ Employing the dictionary

This chapter shows you how to tap into several Word features designed to help you improve your writing. The spell checker automatically detects and offers to correct spelling mistakes. The grammar checker can help you avoid embarrassing gaffs like using *it's* instead of *its* or *your* instead of *you're*. The thesaurus can help you find just the right word — that is, the correct, true, accurate, and precise word. And Word's research feature can help you look up words or topics in online dictionaries and encyclopedias.

Using the Spelling and Grammar Checker

I was voted "Worst Speler" in the sixth grade. Not that being "Worst Speler" qualifies me to run for president or anything, but it shows how much I appreciate computer spell checkers. Spelling makes no sense to me. Many years ago, I saw a program on public television called *The Story of English*. It made me feel better. Now at least I know whom to blame for all the peculiarities of English spelling: the Anglos, the Norms (including the guy from *Cheers*), and the Saxophones.

Fortunately, Word has a pretty decent spell checker. In fact, the spell checker in Word is so smart that it knows that you made a spelling mistake almost before you make it. The spell checker watches over your shoulder as you type and helps you to correct your spelling errors as you work.

By default, Word also checks for grammatical errors as you type. When it spots what it thinks is an error, it underlines the suspected text with a wavy green underline. You can right-click the underlined text to display a menu of suggested changes. If you choose Grammar from the menu that appears when you right-click the underlined text, the Grammar dialog box appears (see Figure 6-1).

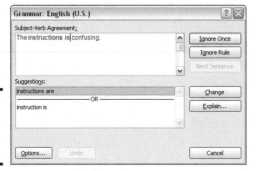

Figure 6-1:
The Grammar dialog box.

So, you can use the spelling and grammar checker in two basic ways. The first is to let it do its work as you type your document, pointing out and correcting mistakes as you make them. The second is to wait until you finish typing your document and then check it for spelling mistakes all at once. You can use whichever of these two techniques best fits your style. If you're an especially bad speler and grammerer, you might want to use both of them for good measure.

Checking spelling as you go

Word's on-the-fly spell checker watches over your shoulder as you type, politely pointing out spelling mistakes as you make them. The spell checker actually looks up every word you type in its dictionary to make sure you spelled it right. If you type something it can't find in its dictionary, the spell checker underlines the mistake with a wavy red line, as shown in Figure 6-2.

I tried to convince the good people at John Wiley & Sons to pop for an expensive four-color printing process for this book so you could actually see the red line in Figure 6-2. They informed me that they would be happy to oblige, but the added cost would be deducted from my royalty check. That's when I realized that you could probably just pretend that the wavy black line in Figure 6-2 is really a wavy red line.

Figure 6-2:
The wavy
red (truly it
is red) line.

> If you're an especially bad speler and grammerer you may want to use them both of them for good measure.

Word doesn't beep, chime, or yell at you when you misspell a word. As a result, unless you watch the screen as you type, you might not immediately notice a spelling error. Periodically checking the screen is a good idea, even if you're a 90-word-per-minute touch typist who never looks up.

In Figure 6-2, the word *Speler* is marked as misspelled. When you see the telltale wavy red line (trust me, it's red), you have some options:

✦ **Make the correction:** You can press Backspace to delete the word and then retype it with the correct spelling. After you do that, Word removes the wavy red underline.

✦ **Let Word help:** You can right-click the word to call up a menu that lists suggested spellings for the word. In most cases, Word makes guesses about what you meant to type and suggests correctly spelled words. For example, when you right-click *Speler,* the following suggestions appear:

> Speller
>
> Spellers
>
> Speer
>
> Spiller

To replace the misspelled word with the correct spelling, just choose the correctly spelled word from the menu.

The quick menu that appears when you right-click a misspelled word also shows the following commands:

✦ **Ignore All:** Sometimes, you want to misspell a word on purpose. For example, you might just happen to be writing a chapter about how to use the spell checker, and you want to misspell the word Speler on purpose. In that case, you want to just ignore the misspelling. To do that, right-click the word and choose Ignore All. Then the spell checker ignores the word throughout the document.

✦ **Add to Dictionary:** In some cases, the underlined word is spelled correctly after all; it just happens that Word's dictionary doesn't include it. Right-click the word and choose Add to Dictionary to add the word to Word's spelling dictionary. That way, Word won't flag the word as misspelled in the future.

✦ **AutoCorrect:** This command reveals a menu that lists the correct spelling suggestions for the misspelled word. When you select one of the suggestions, Word creates an AutoCorrect entry that automatically corrects this spelling error from now on. Choose this option only for words that you frequently misspell that aren't already in the AutoCorrect list.

If you accidentally use this feature and then you want to remove the AutoCorrect entry it creates, don't rely on the Undo command. The Undo command undoes the correction, but it won't remove the AutoCorrect entry. To remove the AutoCorrect entry, choose Office⇨Word Options and click the Proofing tab. Then click the AutoCorrect Options button, select the entry you want to remove from the list, and click Delete. Another way to get to the AutoCorrect Options dialog box is to right-click the wavy red line, select AutoCorrect, and then select AutoCorrect Options from the drop-down list.

✦ **Language:** This command lets you access the Language dialog box, shown in Figure 6-3. You can use this dialog box to specify the language dictionary that Word uses to check your spelling. You can also use it to suspend spell-checking for the entire paragraph.

The spell checker can't tell you when you use the wrong word if you spell it correctly. For example, you might type *dime navels* when you mean *dime novels.* Cheap literature may be a bad thing, but cheap citrus certainly is not.

Figure 6-3: The Language dialog box.

Checking for grammatical errors

By default, Word checks for grammatical errors as you type. When it spots what it thinks is an error, it underlines the suspected text with a wavy green underline. You can right-click the underlined text to display a menu of suggested changes. If you choose Grammar from the menu, the Grammar dialog box appears, as shown earlier in Figure 6-1.

Here you can ignore your mistake or ask the Grammar dialog box to help you understand the errors of your ways by clicking the Explain button. This action opens the Word Help dialog box, which attempts to instruct you to a better grammar way. You can also access this option when you right-click the underlined text by choosing About This Sentence.

Spell and grammar checking after the fact

If you prefer to ignore the constant nagging by Word about your spelling, you can always check your spelling and grammar the old-fashioned way: by running the spell checker after you finish your document. The spell checker works its way through your entire document, looking up every word in its massive list of correctly spelled words and bringing any misspelled words to your attention. It performs this task without giggling or snickering. As an added bonus, the spell checker even gives you the opportunity to tell it that you're right and it's wrong and that it should discern how to spell words the way you do.

The following steps show you how to check the spelling for an entire document:

1. **If the document you want to check isn't already open, open it.**

2. **Fire up the spelling and grammar checker.**

Click the Spelling & Grammar button in the Proofing group on the Review tab on the Ribbon, or press F7.

3. **Don't be startled if Word finds a spelling and/or grammatical error.**

If Word finds a spelling error, it displays the misspelled word along with a suggested correction, as shown in Figure 6-4.

If Word finds a grammatical error, it displays the error word along with a suggested correction, as shown in Figure 6-5.

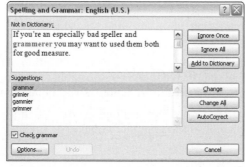

Figure 6-4:
The Spelling
and
Grammar
dialog box
on spelling.

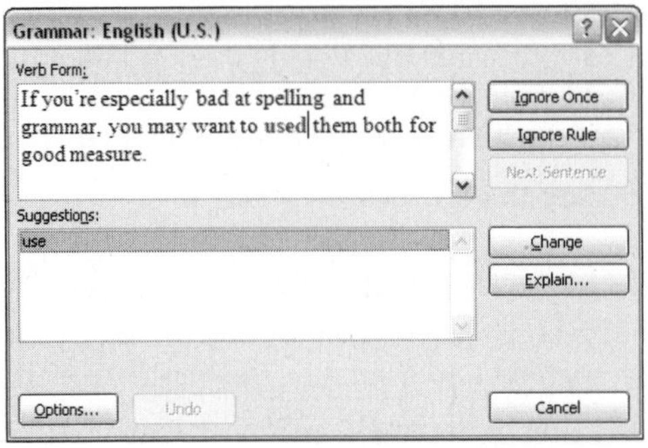

Figure 6-5:
The Spelling
and
Grammar
dialog box
on
grammar.

> Grammar: English (U.S.)
>
> Verb Form:
>
> If you're especially bad at spelling and
> grammar, you may want to used them both for
> good measure.
>
> Ignore Once
> Ignore Rule
> Next Sentence
>
> Suggestions:
>
> use
>
> Change
> Explain...
>
> Options...   Undo   Cancel

4. Select the correct spelling or laugh in Word's face.

If you agree that the word is misspelled, scan the list of corrections that Word offers and select the one that you like. Then click the Change button. Other options at your disposal include

- *Ignore Once:* Tells the Spelling and Grammar checker to ignore the alleged error. You click this button nine times out of ten (with the possible exception of Cancel).

- *Ignore Rule:* The grammar checker ignores the rule that caused it to flag the text. After Word incorrectly accuses you of using sentence fragments ten or twelve times in a row, you might want to click this button to make it stop.

- *Next Sentence:* Many times, the grammar checker reports multiple errors for a single sentence. You can often tell when the grammar checker isn't making heads or tails out of a sentence. For example, the grammar checker usually has trouble with headings, captions, and other bits of text that aren't complete sentences. Rather than wade through message after message for these non-sentences, you can click Next Sentence to direct the grammar checker to skip ahead to the next sentence.

- *Change:* This button allows you to edit the word or sentence directly in the Grammar dialog box and then record your change in the document.

- *Explain:* The grammar checker displays a description of the rule that caused the sentence to be flagged as a possible error. Some of the explanations are brief; others are elaborate grammar lessons.

- *Options:* Calls up the Word Options dialog box so that you can change the behavior of the grammar checker or spelling options.

- *Undo:* Undoes the last grammar checker action.

- *Cancel:* My favorite button in the Grammar dialog box.

5. Repeat Steps 4 and 5 until Word gives up.

6. Click OK when you see the following message:

    The spelling and grammar check is complete.

You're finished.

If Word detects a repeated word (that is, the same word occurring twice in a row), it displays a variation of the Spelling and Grammar dialog box that gives you two choices: Ignore Once or Delete. If you want to repeat the word, click Ignore. To delete the second occurrence of the repeated word, click Delete.

If Word can't come up with a suggestion or if none of its suggestions are correct, you can type your own correction directly into the box showing the text with the error and click the Change button. If the word that you type isn't in the dictionary, Word asks whether you're sure that you know what you're doing. Double-check and click OK if you really mean it.

If you get tired of Word always complaining about a word that's not in its standard dictionary, click Add to Dictionary to add the word to the custom dictionary. If you can't sleep at night until you know more about the custom dictionary, see the earlier section, "Checking spelling as you go."

The speller can't tell the difference between *your* and *you're, ours* and *hours, angel* and *angle,* and so on. In other words, if the word is in the dictionary, Word passes it by regardless of whether you used the word correctly. The Word spell checker, therefore, is no substitute for good, old-fashioned proofreading. Print your document, sit down with a cup of tea (or bourbon), and *read* it.

If you're interested only in checking the spelling of your document, after opening the Spelling and Grammar dialog box, select the Spelling & Grammar button in the Proofing group on the Review tab on the Ribbon, or press F7. Then deselect the Check Grammar check box in the lower-left corner of the dialog box.

Using the Thesaurus

One of the nifty Word features is a built-in thesaurus that can quickly show you synonyms for a word that you type. Using it is easy:

1. **Right-click a word that you typed and choose Synonyms from the menu that appears.**

   A menu listing synonyms for the word appears. (Sometimes Word throws an antonym into the list just to be contrary.)

2. **Click the word that you want to replace your word.**

   Word replaces the original word with your selection.

If you choose Thesaurus from the Synonyms menu, the Thesaurus section of the Research task pane appears with the synonyms listed, as shown in Figure 6-6. You can also summon this task pane by clicking the Thesaurus button in the Proofing group on the Review tab on the Ribbon. The Thesaurus task pane lets you look up words to find even more synonyms.

Figure 6-6:
The
Thesaurus
task pane.

For example, if you type **sometimes** in the Search For text box and click the Start Searching button (the arrow pointing to the right in the green square) or press Enter, the results of your search are displayed in the window below. One of your replacement options is *on occasion*. If you then select *on occasion,* a whole new list of words is presented. You can keep clicking words to find other synonyms as long as you like, until you're ready to get back to real work. Use the Back button above the results window to navigate back to a prior results pane. After you've gone Back, the Forward arrow becomes available. Use the drop-down lists attached to either button to quickly navigate to a specific results list.

As you mouse over the results list of synonyms, a drop-down button appears to the right of the word, and it allows you to Insert the word into your document, Copy it to the Clipboard, or Look Up the definition. If you want to show results from, say, a French thesaurus, use the drop-down list under the Search For text box to change what resources are used for your search.

Use the Research Options link at the bottom of the Research task pane to open the Research Options dialog box, which allows you to add or remove reference books and online resources by selecting or deselecting their check boxes.

Using Other Proofing Tools

In addition to the Spelling & Grammar button and the Thesaurus button, the Proofing group on the Review tab on the Ribbon contains more buttons to assist you:

✦ **Research:** This opens the Research task pane with the All Reference Books option selected. Simply enter your criteria in the Search For text box. Alternatively, you can highlight the text you're working with before you click the Research button.

✦ **Translate:** To translate text that you have highlighted or entered into the Search For text box into a specified language. Use the From and To drop-down lists to change the languages.

✦ **Translation ScreenTip:** Deselect the Turn Off Translation Tool Tip by selecting a language for the tip to translate to. Then hover the cursor over a word that you would like translated and wait for the ScreenTip to appear.

✦ **Set Language:** Want to change the language used to check the spelling and grammar of a particular portion of text? Select the text that you want to change the language for and then click this button to open the Language dialog box and do so.

✦ **Word Count:** To find out how many words are in a particular paragraph or sentence of your document, select the text you want counted and click this button. The Word Count dialog box opens to display all the vital statistics, as shown in Figure 6-7. That happens to be the vitals on this paragraph.

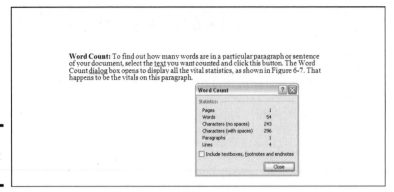

Figure 6-7:
Word Count
in action.

The status bar shows the total number of words in your document at all times. If you're solely interested in the number of words in a selection of text and not all the various vitals shown when using the Word Count button, select the text and take a glance at the status bar, which tells you how many words out of the entire document you have selected.

Chapter 7: Working with Outlines and Master Documents

In This Chapter

✔ Switching to Outline view

✔ Understanding Outline view

✔ Collapsing and expanding an outline

✔ Promoting and demoting paragraphs

✔ Editing in Outline view

✔ Printing an outline

✔ Working with master documents

Some writers have the outlining gene — others don't. Some writers manage to concoct at least a rudimentary outline only through an extraordinary act of self-will. Other writers spend days polishing the world's most perfect outline before they write a word. Their outlines are so good that they can write with their eyes closed after finishing the outline. Hmph. I fall somewhere in between. I spin a fairly decent outline up front, but I'm not compulsive about it. I rarely write with my eyes closed and usually revise the outline substantially as I go, sometimes beyond the point of recognition.

So here I discuss outlines and how to use them to your advantage. Next I discuss the concept of how to put all of the chapters of your great American novel all together in continuity and harmony with the Master Document feature.

Working with Outlines

Word has built-in outlining tools that are handy whether you like to create detailed outlines in advance or you just want to check occasionally on the overall structure of your document to see how it's evolving. I use it all the time, even though I'm not an outline fanatic. If you use Word to create reports, proposals, or other types of documents that have some sense of structure to them, you owe it to yourself to find out the basics of working with outlines.

Switching to Outline view

You have two ways to switch to Outline view. You can

✦ Click the Outline button in the Document Views group on the View tab on the Ribbon.

✦ Click the Outline button that is second from the right in the group of buttons next to the Zoom slider at the bottom right of the screen.

Either way you go about it, you have just summoned the Outlining tab, as shown in Figure 7-1, to a place of honor before the Home tab on the Ribbon.

Figure 7-1:
The
Outlining
tab.

Understanding Outline view

The key to understanding Word's Outline view is realizing that an outline is just another way of looking at a document. The outline is not a separate entity from the document. Instead, when you switch to Outline view, Word takes the headings from your document and presents them in the form of an outline. Any changes you make to your document while in Outline view automatically reflect in the document when you return to Print Layout view, and any changes you make in Print Layout view automatically appear when you switch to Outline view. The reason is because Print Layout and Outline view are merely two ways of displaying the contents of your document.

Note some important concepts about Outline view:

✦ The outline is made up of the headings and body text of the document. Any paragraph formatted with one of the built-in heading styles (Heading 1, Heading 2, Heading 3, and so on) is considered to be a heading; any other paragraph is considered body text.

✦ When you switch to Outline view, a new tab appears on the Ribbon, and the ruler (which isn't needed in Outline view) disappears. This tab, appropriately called the Outlining tab, contains buttons for performing routine outlining tasks. Refer to Figure 7-1 to see the Outlining tab and its groups; I list the buttons used for working with outlines in Table 7-1.

✦ When you first switch to Outline view, your document may not appear dramatically different than it does in Print Layout view. In the following sections, you see how Outline view enables you to view your document quite differently from the way you view it in Print Layout view.

✦ While in Outline view, you can type new text or edit existing text just as you do in Print Layout view. You can also apply character formatting, such as bold or italic, and you can apply styles to paragraphs. However, you can't apply direct paragraph formats, such as indentation, tab stops, alignment, and so on. To apply these types of formats, you must return to Print Layout view.

✦ Outline view has its own set of keyboard shortcuts (which I summarize in Table 7-2) to help you move things along.

Table 7-1	Buttons in the Outline Tools Group	
Button	*Button Name*	*What It Does*
	Promote to Heading 1	Promotes the selected text to Heading 1
	Promote	Promotes the selected text to the next higher heading level
Body Text	Outline Level	Sets the heading level of the selected text
	Demote	Demotes the selected text to the next lower heading level
	Demote to Body Text	Demotes the selected text to body text
	Move Up	Moves the selected text up in the outline
	Move Down	Moves the selected text down in the outline
	Expand	Expands the selection
	Collapse	Collapses the selection

(continued)

Table 7-1 *(continued)*

Button	Button Name	What It Does
Show Level	Show Level	Selects the level to be shown
Show First Line Only	Show First Line Only	Displays only the first line of each paragraph
Show Text Formatting	Show Text Formatting	Shows or hides text formatting

Table 7-2	Keyboard Shortcuts for Outline View
Keyboard Shortcut	*What It Does*
Ctrl+Alt+O	Switches to Outline view
Ctrl+Alt+N	Switches back to Draft view
Alt+Shift+A	Collapses or expands all text
Alt+Shift+- (hyphen)	Collapses the selection
Alt+Shift++ (plus)	Expands the selection
Alt+Shift+1	Collapses/expands to Heading 1
Alt+Shift+*(number)*	Collapses/expands to specified heading level
/ (on numeric keypad)	Hides/shows formatting
Shift+Tab	Promotes the selection
Alt+Shift+←	Promotes the selection
Tab	Demotes the selection
Ctrl+Shift+N	Demotes selection to body text
Alt+Shift+↑	Moves the selection up, similar to cutting and pasting it
Alt+Shift+↓	Moves the selection down, similar to cutting and pasting it

Showing and hiding formatting

Before you spend too much time working in Outline view, you may want to hide the formatting from the outline so that you can concentrate more closely on the document's structure. Hiding the formatting in Outline view doesn't actually remove the formatting from your text; it just temporarily hides it. The outline shown in Figure 7-2 has the formatting hidden.

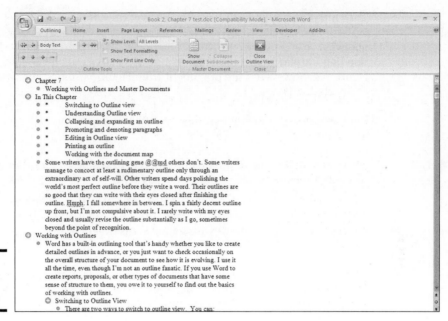

Figure 7-2:
Hidden
formatting.

 To show the text formatting in the outline, click the Show Text Formatting check box.

Keep these tips in mind when using the Show Text Formatting button:

✦ To remove formatting, deselect the Show Text Formatting check box.

✦ You don't need the formatting to distinguish among heading levels because the headings are indented for you. So I usually work in Outline view with formatting off.

✦ When you hide formatting, you're doing just that. You're not actually removing it. When you click the Show Text Formatting button again or return to Draft view, all the formatting that you so carefully applied to your document is restored.

Collapsing and expanding the outline

One of the main reasons for working in Outline view rather than in Draft view is so that you can get a handle on the overall structure of your document. The secret is in collapsing the outline so that the portions of your document you're not interested in are hidden.

The Outlining group includes a Show Level drop-down list that lets you collapse or expand the entire outline to a specific heading level. For example, if you want to see just the top-level headings (paragraphs formatted with the Heading 1 style), select Show Level 1 in the Show Level drop-down list. Figure 7-3 shows what the document from Figure 7-1 looks like when Level 1 is selected.

Here are some important features to note about working with collapsed text in Outline view:

✦ Notice that some of the headings have fuzzy lines under them. These fuzzy lines represent collapsed body text.

✦ Notice also that each heading has a large plus sign or minus sign next to it. Headings with plus signs have other headings or body text subordinate to them. Headings with minus signs do not.

You can double-click the plus and minus signs to show and hide text.

✦ If you're good with keyboard shortcuts, keep in mind that pressing Alt+Shift+A quickly toggles between Show Level 9 and Show All Levels. This handy shortcut quickly shows or hides all of the body text in an outline.

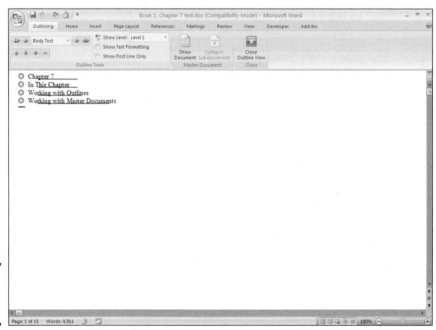

Figure 7-3:
Level 1 view
of outline.

Promoting and demoting paragraphs

To *promote* a paragraph means to move it up one level in the outline. If you promote a Heading 2, it becomes a Heading 1. You do this by placing the insertion point on the line you want to promote and clicking the Promote button in the Outlining Tools group on the Outlining contextual tab on the Ribbon. You can't promote a Heading 1 paragraph; it's already as high as it can get. If you promote a body text paragraph, it becomes a heading paragraph at the same level as the heading it is subordinate to. Thus, if you promote a body text paragraph that follows a Heading 2, the body text paragraph becomes a Heading 2.

To *demote* a paragraph is to move the paragraph down one level in the outline. You demote a paragraph by placing the insertion point on the line you want to promote and click the Demote button in the Outlining Tools group on the Outlining contextual tab on the Ribbon. If you demote a Heading 1, it becomes a Heading 2. Demote it again, and it becomes a Heading 3. You cannot demote a body text paragraph, but you can demote any heading to a body text paragraph.

**Book II
Chapter 7**

**Working
with Outlines and
Master Documents**

When you promote or demote headings, the body text paragraphs that fall under the heading always go along for the ride. You don't need to worry about losing a heading's body text. Whether or not subordinate headings get swept up in the move depends on how you handle the promotion or demotion.

Printing an outline

You can quickly print an outline of your document by following these steps:

1. **Switch to Outline view.**

2. **Collapse or expand the outline to show just the portion of the outline you want to print.**

3. **Click the Show Text Formatting button if you don't want the outline to include heading formats.**

4. **Click the Print button on the Quick Access toolbar.**

The outline prints.

A printed outline is no substitute for a Table of Contents. See Book VI, Chapter 1 for details on printing a Table of Contents — complete with page numbers.

Working with Master Documents

Suppose a great honor is bestowed upon you: serving as the moderator of this year's Neat Freaks Convention. As moderator, one of your jobs is assembling a little 1,200-page book titled *Neat Freaks '07: Proceedings of the Annual Neat Freaks Trade Show and Conference.* Notable Neat Freaks from all across the globe will present papers, and your job is to assemble all these documents into one huge book. Fortunately for you, the International Neat Freak Association (INFA) has adopted Word 2007 as its standard word processor, so each neat freak of note will send you a document on disk. All you have to do is combine the files into a single document and print it.

This job is definitely for Word's Master Document feature. It lets you create long documents by piecing them together from small documents. Master documents are all very confusing and worth figuring out only if you have to do this sort of thing often. If you find yourself needing to read this part of the chapter, I offer my sincerest condolences.

You probably shouldn't tackle master documents until you have a pretty good understanding of Word's Outline view because the Master Document feature is sort of an advanced form of outlining.

Understanding the master document

A *master document* contains special links to other documents, which are called *subdocuments*. If you're putting together a book that consists of 30 chapters, for example, you probably don't want to put the entire book into one document. Instead, you probably want to create a separate document for each chapter. That's all well and good, but what happens when you want to print the whole thing with page numbers that begin at page one and run through the end of the book rather than restart at page one at the beginning of each chapter? Or what if you want to print a Table of Contents for the book or create an index?

That's where master documents come in. With a master document, you create each chapter as a separate document. Then you create a master document for the entire book. In the master document, you create links to each of the chapters or subdocuments and format the text using the style definitions in the master document rather than from the individual documents. This method then provides consistent formatting for the entire final document. Then you can print the entire book, and Word takes care of numbering the pages for you. You can also create a Table of Contents or index in the master document, and the page numbers automatically adjust.

Word has a separate view for working with master documents, called — drum roll, please — *Master Document view.* Master Document view is a variation of Outline view. In Master Document view, little icons indicate the portions of the master documents that are subdocuments. You can double-click one of these icons to open a subdocument in a separate window to edit it.

For the most part, you use Master Document view to create a new master document, to change the order in which individual subdocuments appear in the master document, or to add or remove subdocuments. If all you want to do is edit one of the individual chapters in your book, you just open the chapter document as you normally do, without worrying about it being a subdocument in a master document.

If you open a master document and switch to Draft view or Print Layout view, Word treats the master document and all the subdocuments as though they're a part of one large document. You can scroll through the master document all the way to Chapter 12 and begin typing, for example, or you can choose Office➪Print to print the entire book, or you can use the Replace button in the Editing group on the Home tab on the Ribbon to replace all occurrences of *WordPerfect* with *Word* throughout the entire document.

You can assemble a master document in three ways:

✦ **From scratch:** If you know that you need a master document beforehand, you can create the master document and all the subdocuments from scratch. This technique results in a master document and a collection of empty subdocuments, which you can then call up and edit as you see fit. See the section, "Whipping up a master document," later in this chapter.

✦ **By breaking up:** If you get part of the way into a project and realize, "Hey! This document is way too long! I should have used a master document," it's not too late. You can bust a big document into several smaller subdocuments. See the section "Break it up!" later in this chapter.

✦ **By power of assembly:** If you already have a bunch of Word documents you want to assemble into a master document, you can create a master document by using the existing documents as the subdocuments. See the section "Putting an existing file into a master document," later in this chapter.

All this stuff about master documents is confusing, I'm sure, but it makes more sense when you begin to use them. (I promise.) Just to muddy the waters a little more, the following list shows you some additional things you need to know about master documents before I jump into the steps for creating and using them:

✦ In the master document, each subdocument is contained within its own section. Each subdocument, therefore, can have its own page layout, column arrangement, and any of the other niceties that go along with being in your own section.

✦ When you click Show Document in Master Document group on the Outlining tab on the Ribbon, the Master Document group expands to display additional buttons specially designed to work with master documents. Table 7-3 summarizes each button's function.

✦ Basing the master document and all the subdocuments on the same template is best. Otherwise, trying to figure out which styles, macros, and other template goodies are available is a nightmare.

Table 7-3	Buttons in the Master Document Group	
Button	*Name*	*What It Does*
Show Document	Show Document	Switches to Master Document view
Collapse Subdocument	Collapse/Expand Subdocuments	Acts as a toggle to collapse or expand a subdocument
Create	Create	Creates a new subdocument to be fleshed out later
Insert	Insert	Inserts an existing file as a subdocument
Unlink	Unlink	Deletes the link to the selected subdocument
Merge	Merge	Combines two subdocument files into one subdocument file
Split	Split	Splits a subdocument into two subdocuments
Lock Document	Lock Document	Locks or unlocks a subdocument

You can open a subdocument in two ways. The first way is to open the master document. Word displays any subdocuments contained in the master document as hyperlinks. To open a subdocument, all you have to do is

Ctrl+click the subdocument's hyperlink. Alternatively, you can ignore the master document and open the subdocument file the way you open any other Word document: by choosing Office➪Open to browse for the document.

If you have a network and more than one person is involved with the creation of your documents, Word keeps track of who owns which subdocument, based on the Author Name field of the subdocuments. Before you can edit a subdocument that someone else created, you must unlock it by clicking the Lock/Unlock Document button in the Master Document group on the Outlining tab on the Ribbon.

You can spread the master document and its subdocuments across different folders, and they can even live on different computers if you have a network. Life is much easier, however, if you create a separate folder for just the master document and all its subdocuments. If more than one person is working on the project, place this folder on a shared network hard drive so that everyone involved in the project can access it.

**Book II
Chapter 7**

Working
with Outlines and
Master Documents

Whipping up a master document

If none of the documents you want to combine by using a master document are created yet, the best way to begin is to create the master document and all its subdocuments at the same time. Then you can call up each subdocument individually to fill in the missing chapters of your book.

These steps show you the procedure for creating a master document and its subdocuments from scratch:

1. **Start Word if it isn't already open and choose Office➪New➪Document➪Create. Or press Ctrl+N.**

2. **On the View tab in the Document Views group, click the Outline button.**

   The Outline tab appears on the Ribbon. You can also get to Outline view by clicking the Outline button at the bottom right of the status bar (It is second to the left of the Zoom slider) or by pressing Ctrl+Alt+O.

3. **Click the Show Document button in the Master Document group on the Outlining tab.**

   The Master Document group of the Outlining tab expands.

4. **Create a Heading 1 paragraph for the title of the master document.**

   If you're creating a book, for example, type the book's title as a Heading 1 paragraph.

5. **Create a Heading 2 paragraph for each subdocument you want to create.**

If each subdocument represents a chapter, type the chapter titles as Heading 2 paragraphs.

Figure 7-4 shows an example of a master document with a Heading 1 paragraph for the master document title and a Heading 2 paragraph for each subdocument title.

6. **Select the Heading 2 paragraphs.**

Select them by dragging the mouse over them or by holding down the Shift key while you move the cursor with the arrow keys. Each Heading 2 paragraph you select converts to a separate subdocument in the next step. (Make sure you don't select the Heading 1 paragraph at the beginning of the document.)

Create
7. **Click the Create button in the Master Document group on the Outlining tab.**

Clicking this button tells Word to bust up the selected heading paragraphs into smaller subdocuments.

8. **Admire your handiwork.**

Figure 7-5 shows a document that's been busted up. Notice how Word draws a box around each subdocument and adds a little subdocument icon in the top-left corner of the box.

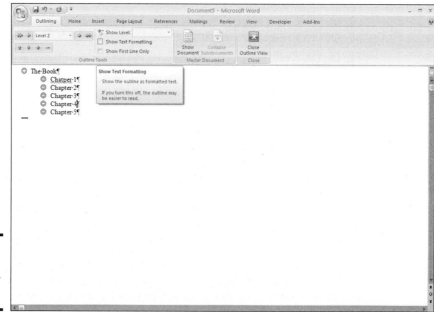

Figure 7-4:
The outline for a master document.

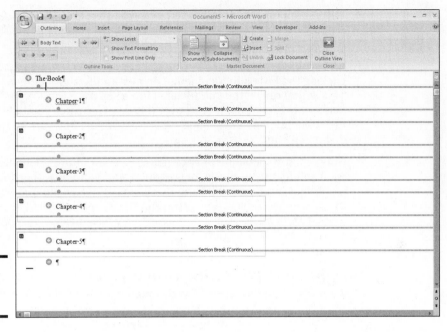

Figure 7-5:
All busted
up.

9. **Save the files by choosing Office⇨Save, by pressing Ctrl+S, or by clicking the Save button on the Quick Access toolbar.**

You have to provide the name and location of the master document. Word makes up names for all the subdocuments, using the first eight characters of the heading paragraph if possible.

10. **You're finished.**

Well, not quite. All you have is the outline of a book with a bunch of empty subdocuments. You still have to write the chapters!

Here are a few thoughts to keep in mind when you're creating a master document from scratch:

✦ You don't *have* to use the Heading 1 style for the master document title and Heading 2 for the subdocument titles. But doing so makes sense. Word examines the text you selected before you click the Create button to find the first Heading paragraph. Then it creates a separate subdocument for each paragraph in the selected text that's formatted with the same heading style as the first heading. If the first heading paragraph is formatted with the Heading 3 style, Word creates a separate subdocument for each Heading 3 paragraph. Most of the time, using Heading 1 for the master document title and Heading 2 for each subdocument title makes sense. Alternatively, you can use the Title style for the document and then have Heading 1 paragraphs for each subdocument.

✦ The subdocuments aren't saved until you save the master document. Then Word automatically saves all the subdocuments in the same directory as the master document.

✦ After you create subdocuments, you can edit a subdocument by double-clicking the little subdocument icon next to the subdocument heading. This action opens the subdocument in a separate window and leaves the master document open in its own window, too. After you finish editing the subdocument, save it and close the window to return to the master document window.

✦ Notice that the document shown in Figure 7-6 shows the contents of each subdocument in the master document window rather than just hyperlinks, as shown in Figure 7-6. When you close and reopen the document, the hyperlinks show instead of the actual subdocument text. Then, to edit a subdocument, press Ctrl while clicking the link to the subdocument you want to edit.

Putting an existing file into a master document

If you (or your buddies) have already created a bunch of smaller files that you want to combine into one larger publication, you can plug each file into a master document as a subdocument. Then you can create a Table of Contents or an index for the whole publication or print the publication with uninterrupted page numbers.

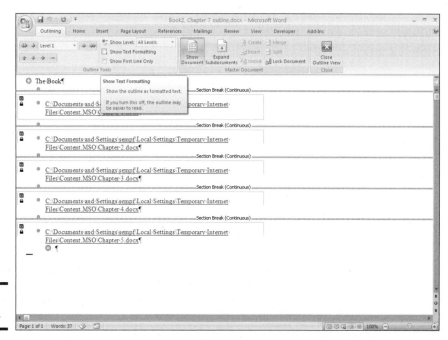

Figure 7-6:
Hyperlinks.

Follow these steps to create a master document and insert existing documents into it as subdocuments:

1. **(Optional) Using the My Computer window or Windows Explorer, copy the various files you need into a single folder.**

This step isn't strictly necessary; as creating a master document from subdocuments spread throughout your hard drive is acceptable. But life is simpler if the master document and all its subdocuments live together in harmony.

2. **Start Word if it isn't already open and then choose Office⇨New⇨Document⇨Create or press Ctrl+N.**

3. **On the View tab in the Document Views group, click the Outline button. Alternatively, press Ctrl+Alt+O.**

The Outline tab shows up on the Ribbon. You can also get to Outline view by clicking the Outline button at the bottom right of the status bar. It is second to the left of the Zoom slider.

4. **Click the Insert button in the Master Document group on the Outlining tab.**

An Insert Subdocument dialog box appears. This dialog box is identical to the Open dialog box except for its name.

5. **Find the file you want to insert as a subdocument, choose it, and click Open.**

The file is inserted into the master document as a subdocument. Word creates section breaks before and after it.

6. **Repeat Steps 4 and 5 for any other subdocuments you want to insert.**

7. **Save the master document by clicking the Save button on the Quick Access toolbar.**

8. **You're finished.**

Here are a few points to ponder when you insert subdocuments into a master document:

✦ Inserting a subdocument doesn't change the subdocument file's name or folder location.

✦ When you click the Insert Subdocument button, the subdocument is inserted at the position of the insertion point. Make sure that the insertion point is either at the beginning or end of the master document or between two previously inserted subdocuments. If the insertion point is within a subdocument when you click the Insert Subdocument button, the subdocument you select is inserted *within* the subdocument, not within the master document. If you're not careful, you can end up with subdocuments within subdocuments within subdocuments, kind of like those fancy Russian nesting dolls.

The contents of the subdocument file don't copy into the master document. Instead, a link to the subdocument file is created so that whenever you open the master document, you access the subdocument file also. You can still open the subdocument file separately, apart from the master document.

Break it up!

Sometimes a project just gets out of hand. It starts out as a half-page memo about where to keep spare pencils and ends up being a 300-page office-procedures manual. You obviously wouldn't use a master document for the half-page memo (unless you're really bored), but somewhere around page 100 you might wish that you had. No problem! Just bust up the big document into two or more subdocuments.

Follow these steps to break a large document into smaller subdocuments:

1. **Open the document.**

2. **On the View tab in the Document Views group, click the Outline button or press Ctrl+Alt+O to add the Outlining tab to the Ribbon.**

3. **Change the headings to make each section of text you want to become a subdocument begin with a Heading 2 style.**

The most logical thing is to format the document title as a Heading 1 and each subdocument as a Heading 2. You might have to use the Promote and Demote buttons to accomplish this task. The buttons are in the Outlining Tools group on the Outlining contextual tab on the Ribbon. Bother.

4. **Select the range of text you want to convert into subdocuments, beginning with the heading for the first subdocument and ending with the last paragraph of the last subdocument.**

5. **Click the Create button in the Master Document group on the Outlining tab on the Ribbon.**

Word breaks up the document into smaller subdocuments based on the heading paragraphs and inserts section breaks before and after each subdocument.

6. **Save your work by using one of the many options (Quick Access toolbar, Microsoft Office button, Ctrl+S, whatever).**

Word saves the master document and each of the subdocuments. Word retains the name of the original file for the master document and makes up names for the subdocuments, using the first eight characters of each subdocument's heading, if possible.

7. You're finished!

Celebrate by taking the rest of the day off.

 You can promote or demote all the headings in a document by selecting the entire document (press Ctrl+A) and then by clicking the Promote or Demote buttons in the Outlining Tools group on the Outlining tab on the Ribbon.

 One of the problems people run into with master/subdocument relationships is that they put section formatting into the master document. You really want all your content in the subdocuments and certainly no special formatting in the master document.

Numbering pages in subdocuments

When you use a master document, you can number all the pages of your publication consecutively. In other words, the first page of a subdocument is one greater than the last page of the subdocument that precedes it.

These steps show you the procedure:

1. Open the master document.

You can work in Print Layout view or Outline view, but you have to be working with the master document, not with an individual subdocument.

2. To add the page numbers to an existing header, select Edit Header from the drop-down list of the Header button in the Header & Footer group on the Insert tab on the Ribbon.

Word temporarily throws you into Page Layout view and adds the Header & Footer Tools Design contextual tab to the Ribbon.

To add page numbers to the footer, choose the Edit Footer option in the drop-down list of the Footer button in the Header & Footer group on the Insert tab on the Ribbon.

3. Format the header or footer to include a page number.

Add or change whatever text you want to include in the header or footer. To add a page number, click the Page Number button in the Header & Footer group (located on the Header & Footer Tools Design contextual tool) and use the options in the drop-down list. Chapter 1 of Book III describes headers and footers in detail.

4. Click the Close Header and Footer button in the Close group on the Header & Footer Tools Design contextual tool when you're happy with the header or footer.

Word returns you to Draft or Master Document view.

5. Print the master document and check the page numbers.

Pretty cool, eh?

If you want each subdocument to begin on a new page, add a page break to the Heading 2 style's Paragraph format (or whatever style you use for the title of each subdocument). You can find the Breaks drop-down list in the Page Setup group on the Page Layout tab on the Ribbon.

Book III

Formatting Pages

The 5th Wave   By Rich Tennant

"They won't let me through security until I remove the bullets from my Word document."

Contents at a Glance

Chapter 1: Basic Page Formatting and Sections

In This Chapter

✔ **Setting margins, page size, and other basic page formats**

✔ **Understanding the relationship between sections and page layout**

✔ **Creating section breaks**

✔ **Adding page numbers to your document pages**

✔ **Creating headers and footers**

C haracter and paragraph formatting determine how your text looks, but it's the page formatting that provides the container to hold all of your beautiful content. Tall pages, wide pages, pages with wide margins to make your four pages of text meet the teacher's requirement of five pages — you can set up all of these options with page formatting.

Word doesn't restrict you to using only one page format in a document. You can have as many different page formats as you want as long as you keep each in its own section. Each section can have its own page number and text that appears at the top of each page (a *header*) or the bottom (a *footer*). Sections can even have different margins or different paper sizes.

Of course, you don't have to have more than one section in a document; in fact, most often a document is just one big happy section all by itself. But that's okay, and the information in this chapter applies to one section just as well as to many. That includes such important tasks as setting up page margins, flipping pages from portrait to landscape orientation, and creating headers or footers at the top or bottom of each page.

Formatting the Page

The Page Layout tab on the Ribbon provides the controls for the various page layout formats. The Page Layout tab has five groups, but really only one of them has to do with the way that you arrange the available space on your page. It's the Page Setup group on the Page Layout tab that's most useful when you want to arrange how text fits on your page.

Actually, I also talk about the Page Background group in this chapter because it fits well with the rest of the material. But the Paragraph group is covered in Book II, Chapter 2; Themes are in Book II, Chapter 3; and the Arrange group is in Book IV.

Setting margins

The margins of your document determine the part of the pages that Word uses to position your text. For example, when you start typing on a page, the text starts at the top margin, and when you center text, it is centered between the left and right margins.

You can control whether the top and bottom margins are displayed in Print Layout view by double-clicking the lines that mark the top and bottom page boundaries. You can also change this setting by using the Show White Space between Pages option on the Display tab of the Word Options. (For more on views, turn to Chapter 2 of Book I.)

To change the margins of your page, select the Page Layout tab on the Ribbon and then click the Margins button to display the gallery shown in Figure 1-1. The choices in the gallery include the new standard settings for Word 2007 (1 inch on each of the four sides) as well as the old standard from Word 2003 (1.25 inches on the left and right).

Margins

	Normal			
	Top:	1"	Bottom:	1"
	Left:	1"	Right:	1"

	Narrow			
	Top:	0.5"	Bottom:	0.5"
	Left:	0.5"	Right:	0.5"

	Moderate			
	Top:	1"	Bottom:	1"
	Left:	0.75"	Right:	0.75"

	Wide			
	Top:	1"	Bottom:	1"
	Left:	2"	Right:	2"

	Mirrored			
	Top:	1"	Bottom:	1"
	Inside:	1.25"	Outside:	1"

	Office 2003 Default			
	Top:	1"	Bottom:	1"
	Left:	1.25"	Right:	1.25"

Custom Margins...

Figure 1-1:
The gallery of page margin choices.

Select one of the preset page margins to quickly set the top, bottom, left, and right margins of your page.

✦ If you want to get just a little more text onto your pages, select the **Moderate** option.

✦ The **Narrow** option lets you get more text on your page, but the margins are very small (only ½ inch).

✦ The **Wide** option leaves hardly any room for text.

✦ The **Mirrored** setting does two things: It makes your left and right pages behave differently and then sets the inner margin to be slightly wider than the outer (which is useful if you're going to be stapling your pages together along the inner edge).

Using Page Setup to control margins

If the choices on the gallery aren't enough for you, you can display the Margins tab of the Page Setup dialog box by selecting Custom Margins from the bottom of the gallery. Figure 1-2 shows the Margins tab of the Page Setup dialog box.

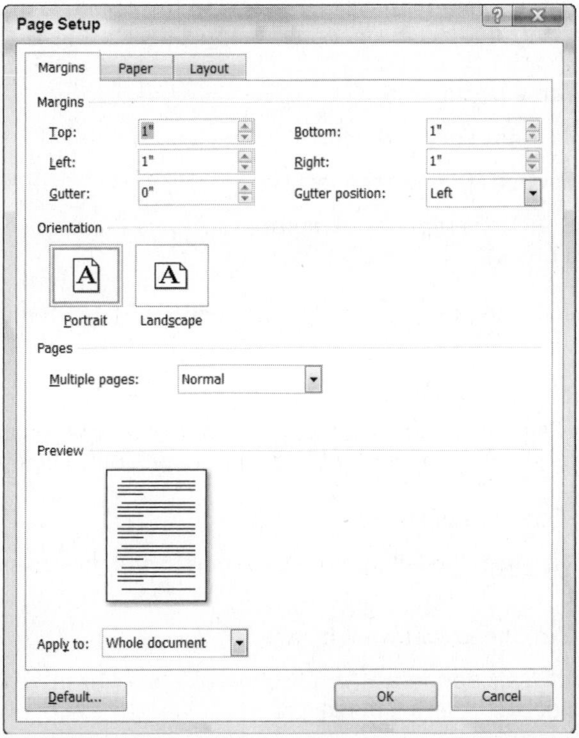

Figure 1-2:
The Margins tab of the Page Setup dialog box.

Normally, this dialog box contains the following options for setting margins:

✦ **Top:** Sets the distance from the top of the page to the first line of text. The default is 1".

✦ **Bottom:** Sets the distance from the bottom of the page to the last line of text. The default is 1".

✦ **Left:** Sets the distance from the left edge of the page to the start of the text. The default is 1".

✦ **Right:** Sets the distance from the right edge of the page to the end of the text. The default is 1".

✦ **Gutter:** Sets an additional amount of margin space for pages that are to be bound. The space is added to the left or top margin, depending on the setting of the Gutter Position option, unless you select Mirror Margins, Two Pages Per Sheet, or Book Fold for the Multiple Pages option.

When working with the gallery from the Ribbon, the margins that you set are applied to the current section (which is usually the same as your entire document). You can apply the settings to the entire document by selecting the document with Ctrl+A and then selecting from the gallery. The Page Setup dialog box gives you more precise control with the Apply To drop-down list. You use this control to decide whether to apply the settings.

✦ To the **Whole Document**

✦ From **This Point Forward** (which inserts a section break)

✦ To **This Section** (the current section)

✦ To **These Sections** (applies to multiple sections if you've selected across a section break)

For more on sections, see "Understanding Sections," later in this chapter.

Working with the Multiple Pages settings

The Multiple Pages drop-down list lets you control how pages are actually laid out on the sheets of paper that the printer spits out. The options are

✦ **Normal:** One page per sheet.

✦ **Mirror Margins:** The left and right margins switch places every other page.

✦ **2 Pages Per Sheet:** Just what it says.

✦ **Book Fold:** This option lets you print booklets — for more information, see the sidebar "Printing booklets."

If you select the Mirror Margins option from the Multiple Pages drop-down list, the Margins dialog box changes, as shown in Figure 1-3. The Left and Right options change to Inside and Outside, and the Gutter Position option becomes unavailable. This setting allows the margins for each page to alternate: On odd-numbered pages, the inside margin is on the left; on even-numbered pages, the inside margin is on the right. Any additional space provided for by the Gutter field is added to the inside margin.

Figure 1-3: The Margins tab with Mirror Margins selected.

Setting orientation

The Orientation button displays a gallery with two choices:

✦ **Portrait:** Orients the paper in an upright position, where the height is greater than the width.

✦ **Landscape:** Orients the paper sideways, so that the width is greater than the height. When you switch from Portrait to Landscape (and vice versa), the Height and Width values automatically swap.

Printing booklets

The Book Fold option in the Multiple Pages drop-down list on the Margins tab of the Page Setup dialog box (wow, that's a mouthful) lets you create booklets from pages you fold in half and staple in the middle. If you've ever assembled a booklet like that, you know that you can't just print the pages in order. Instead, the first sheet of paper must have the first and last page on one side, and the second and next-to-last page on the other. Each additional sheet has to have pages that alternate from the front of the booklet to the back of the booklet. The only sheet that has two consecutive pages side by side is the sheet that goes in the middle.

If you select the Book Fold option, Word automatically shuffles the pages correctly when you print your document so that they come out ready to fold in half and staple together. This option is an enormous timesaver if you want to create religious tracts, company songbooks, or any other kind of booklet.

If you don't have a fancy printer that can automatically print on both sides of the page, choose the Manual Duplex option in the Print dialog box when you print your booklet. Word prints the front side of each page of the booklet and then tells you to take the pages out and put them back into the printer's paper tray to print the backsides.

Choosing a paper size

The Size gallery contains a list of the available paper sizes for your computer and printer, which are probably more choices than you have paper in the house. Fortunately, the most commonly used size (Letter) is right at the top, and the slightly longer Legal paper is just an item away. Select the size of paper you want to use for the current section, and you're done with this gallery.

If you want greater control, select the More Paper Sizes option from the bottom of the gallery to display the Paper tab of the Page Setup dialog box, shown in Figure 1-4.

The Paper tab includes the following options for setting your paper size:

✦ **Paper Size:** Sets the paper size. The drop-down list allows you to pick from a variety of paper sizes, including Letter, Legal, and various other envelope sizes.

✦ **Width:** Sets the width of the paper. This field is automatically set when you choose a Paper Size. If you change the value of this field, the Paper Size field changes to Custom Size.

✦ **Height:** Sets the height of the paper. This field is also set automatically according to the Paper Size you select, and changing the height automatically changes Paper Size to Custom Size.

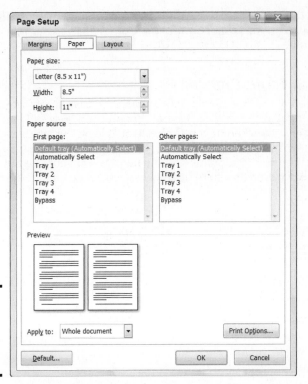

Book III
Chapter 1

Basic Page
Formatting
and Sections

Figure 1-4:
The Paper
tab of the
Page Setup
dialog box.

The Paper tab also has the following controls for telling your printer which paper to use for the pages in your document. This is very useful if your document is supposed to use letterhead for the first page and then regular paper for the rest of the document.

✦ **Paper Source — First Page:** Specifies which paper tray the printer uses for the first page of your document.

✦ **Paper Source — Other Pages:** Specifies which paper tray the printer uses for the second and subsequent pages of your document.

As with the other tabs in the Page Setup dialog box, you can use the Apply To control to decide which parts of your document are formatted with the new settings. For more on sections, see "Understanding Sections," later in this chapter.

In most cases, you use the same paper source for all your pages (both First Page and Other Pages). However, using a different paper for the first page of business letters is common.

The Paper tab also includes a Print Options button that brings up a dialog box filled with options that control how Word displays your text and works with the printer.

Choosing layout options

The third tab of the Page Setup dialog box is the Layout tab, which sounds more exciting than it really is. "Layout" conjures up hopes of an all-encompassing dialog box wherein you can control at least the major aspects of your document's layout. Alas, the lowly Layout tab should have been named "Leftovers" because it contains nothing but a few obscure layout options that apparently didn't seem to fit anywhere else. The Layout tab is shown in Figure 1-5.

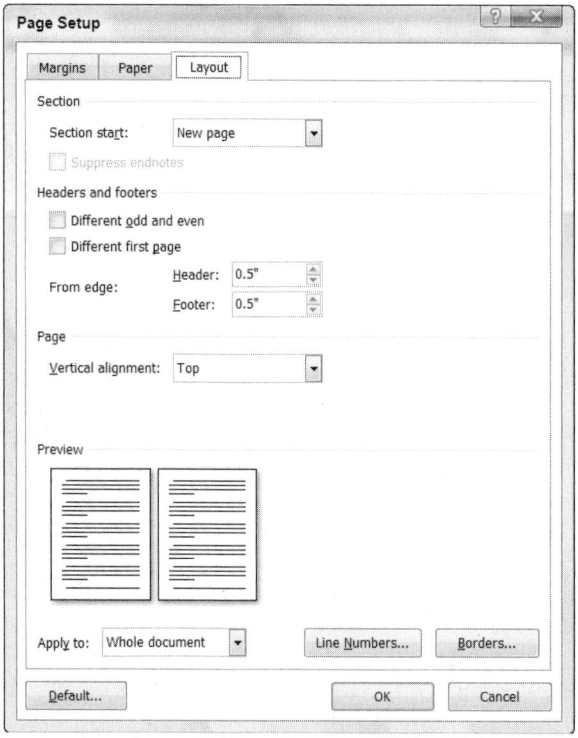

Figure 1-5: The Layout tab of the Page Setup dialog box.

Counting the lines of your document

The Line Numbers control must be the most important command on this tab because it has its own gallery control on the Ribbon. Line numbers are the numbers that appear in the margin of your document to count the lines (pretty obvious when you think about it). Figure 1-6 shows an example of a document with line numbers.

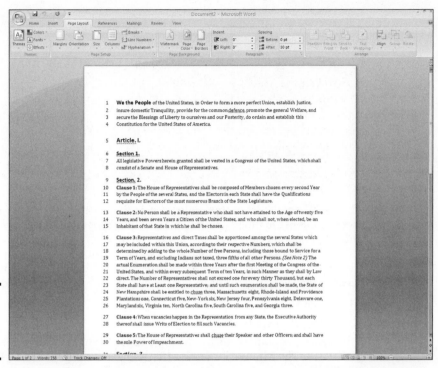

Figure 1-6:
A document with line numbers.

The Line Numbers gallery shown in Figure 1-7 lets you turn line numbering on or off for the current section and also to control when the numbering restarts. (The Continuous option means it never restarts until you move to another document.) This gallery is perhaps most useful because it includes the Suppress for Current Paragraph command, which lets you skip the current paragraph in the count.

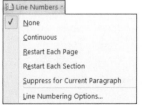

Figure 1-7:
The Line Numbers gallery.

The Line Numbering Options command calls up the Layout tab of the Page Setup dialog box, where you have to click the Line Numbers button to get to the dialog box shown in Figure 1-8. The Line Numbers dialog box gives you more control over how the line numbers are formatted. (Microsoft wanted to give you a little more exercise rather than opening the dialog box for you.)

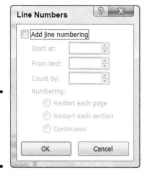

Figure 1-8:
The Line
Numbers
dialog box.

The most useful part of this dialog box is the setting to control which increment of lines is actually printed. (The values most commonly used here are 5 and 10.) Each line is still counted, but the numbers between the increment values are hidden. You can also set a starting value for the line numbers as well as the same options that are in the gallery — whether line numbering restarts for each page or section or is continuous for the entire document.

Formatting sections

The rest of the commands on the Page Layout tab don't have corresponding controls on the Ribbon. To work with them, you need to display the Layout tab. To display the Layout tab, you first need to display the Page Setup dialog box. You can do this by clicking the dialog box launcher (a little square control) at the end of the Page Setup group's label, as shown in Figure 1-9. Or you can just choose the Custom Margins command from the Margins menu and then click the Layout tab.

Figure 1-9:
The magic
spot for
launching
the Page
Setup
dialog box.

The dialog box launcher

The only other command on the Layout tab that relates to a button on the Ribbon is the one for controlling how sections start. The Breaks button on the Ribbon includes several different types of separators that you can insert into your text, including the standard page break (Ctrl+Enter), a column break, and the various forms of the section break. The Breaks gallery can be used to insert section breaks, but you need to use the Section Starts drop-down list on the Layout tab of the Page Setup dialog box to change a section once it is inserted.

The following commands (found on the Layout tab of the Page Setup dialog box shown in Figure 1-5) allow you to control section breaks and format your page in general:

✦ **Section Start:** This drop-down list offers essentially the same options that are available from the Breaks gallery in the Page Setup group on the Page Layout tab. It lets you change the section break type for the current section. For example, if you created the section and originally specified Odd Page but now you want to change it to New Page, you make the change with this option. (For more about different types of section breaks, see "Creating section breaks," later in this chapter.)

✦ **Vertical Alignment:** Top, Center, Justified, or Bottom. Top is the norm. Use Center if you want to center a title in the middle of the page and don't want to press Enter 10 or 12 times to center it. (I've never found a use for Justified or Bottom.)

✦ **Borders:** Brings up the Page Border tab of the Borders and Shading dialog box where you can add a border to each page of the document.

✦ **Different Odd and Even** and **Different First Page:** These two options let you set up different headers and footers for even and odd pages or for the first page in a section. This option is useful if you're printing on both sides of the page or if you don't want the header to appear on the first page. Go to the section "Working with Headers and Footers," later in this chapter for more on headers and footers.

✦ **Header:** Sets the distance from the top of the page to the header area. The default is 0.5".

✦ **Footer:** Sets the distance from the bottom of the page to the footer area. The default is 0.5".

Hyphenating Your Text

Word has the capability of automatically hyphenating words rather than breaking lines between words. Hyphenating words results in less empty space on each line, which is very important when using justified alignment or working with columns. You can set it up so that Word hyphenates your words as you type them, or you can wait until after you typed your text and then automatically hyphenate the document. Hyphenating as you type can slow Word down, especially if you don't have a blazingly fast computer. I suggest you type your document first and then hyphenate it.

Here's how:

1. **Type your text.**

   Don't worry about hyphens during this step.

2. **Select Automatic from the Hyphenation gallery, located in the Page Setup group on the Page Layout tab.**

   Word hyphenates the document.

3. **Check the results.**

   You might not be happy with Word's hyphenations. Always check the results and make any necessary corrections.

If you're not happy with the way Word hyphenated your document, you can click the Hyphenation Options command to get greater control over what Word is doing (at least about how it is hyphenating your document). Using the Hyphenation dialog box shown in Figure 1-10, you can control the following:

✦ **Deselect the Hyphenate Words in CAPS check box if you don't want words made entirely of capital letters to be hyphenated.** This is useful if your writing includes specialized jargon that appears in all capitals and shouldn't be hyphenated. For example, if you use terms like TECH-NOBABBLE VOCABULATOR, which must not under any circumstances be hyphenated, you'll love this option.

✦ **Adjust the Hyphenation Zone if you're picky.** This zone is the area within which Word tries to end each line. If necessary, Word hyphenates words that cross into this zone. If you make this zone larger, Word hyphenates more words, but sometimes that results in lines that look too spaced out (for justified text) or right margins that are too ragged (for left-aligned text).

✦ **Set the Limit Consecutive Hyphens To list box to 3 or 4.** Having two hyphens in a row isn't wrong, and three is okay once in a while. But Word's default setting for this field places no limit to the number of consecutive lines that Word can hyphenate. You don't want to see a page of 20 hyphenated lines, do you?

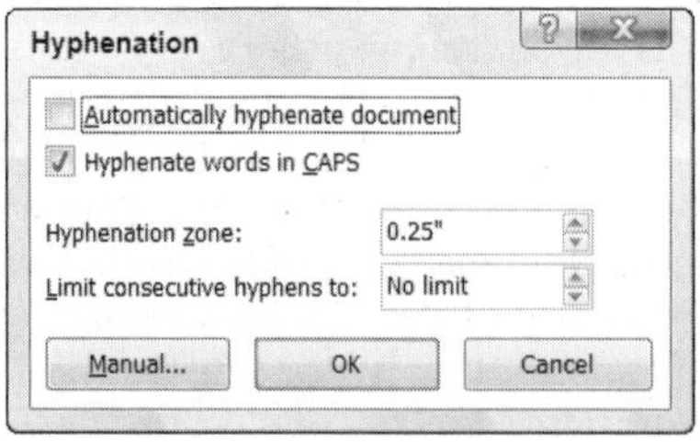

Figure 1-10:
The
Hyphenation
dialog box.

Here are some hyphenation pointers to keep in mind:

✦ Word uses its dictionary to determine where to hyphenate words. It probably spells better than you do. (I know it spells better than *I* do!)

✦ If you want to cause Word to hyphenate a word at a particular spot, place the cursor where you want the word hyphenated and press Ctrl+– (Ctrl and the hyphen sign). Pressing this shortcut creates an *optional hyphen,* which displays only when the word falls at the end of a line.

✦ Do *not* hyphenate a broken word at the end of a line simply by typing a hyphen. It might work for the time being, but if you later edit the text so that the hyphenated word no longer falls at the end of a line, the hyphen still appears, now in the middle of the line where it doesn't belong. Use Ctrl+– instead.

✦ Sometimes you want to use a hyphen in a compound word, but you don't want the word to be split up at the end of the line because it might look funny — for example, *G-Men.* In that case, use Ctrl+Shift+– to create the hyphen rather than the hyphen key alone. Word displays the hyphen but doesn't break the word at the hyphen.

✦ If you click the Manual button in the Hyphenation gallery, Word leads you through the entire document, asking you about each word it wants to hyphenate, which is tiresome beyond belief. Better to just hyphenate the document and then review it and remove any hyphens you don't like.

Inserting Page Numbers

Headers and footers, which I describe in detail in the next section, are for putting information at the top or bottom of each page. The most common type of information in a header or footer is the page number. If all you want to appear in your header or footer is a page number, you don't have to mess with headers and footers at all. Instead, just use the Page Numbers gallery from the Insert tab by following these steps:

1. **Click the Page Number button on the Insert tab.**

The Page Number gallery displays. It lets you decide where you want the page numbers to be.

2. **Set the position of the page numbers by selecting from the gallery.**

The choices are Bottom of Page, Top of Page, Page Margins, and Current Position. Each position displays a collection of preformatted page numbering. The display for the Bottom of Page is shown in Figure 1-11.

Book III
Chapter 1

Basic Page
Formatting
and Sections

Figure 1-11:
The choices
for
numbering
your pages
at the
bottom of
the page.

3. **Select the format that you want to use for your page numbers.**

   Word updates your document to have the selected page numbers.

   For greater control, you can click the Format Page Numbers command at the bottom of the gallery. The Page Number Format dialog box appears, as shown in Figure 1-12.

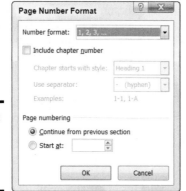

Figure 1-12:
The Page
Number
Format
dialog box.

This dialog box lets you control several aspects of page numbering. For starters, you can change the page number format by selecting an option from the Number Format drop-down list. You can choose normal Arabic numbering (1, 2, 3 . . .), upper- or lowercase letters (A, B, C . . . or a, b, c . . .), or upper- or lowercase Roman numbering (I, II, III . . . or i, ii, iii . . .).

You can select the Include Chapter Number option to create compound page numbers that include a number drawn from a heading paragraph, such as 1-1, 1-2, and so on. Follow these steps:

1. **Format the chapter headings by using one of Word's built-in heading styles.**

   In most cases, you should use the Heading 1 style.

2. **Choose a list format that numbers the headings. For more information about working with numbering, see Chapter 3 in this minibook.**

3. **Click the Page Number button on the Insert tab.**

   The Page Number gallery shows up.

4. **Select the Format Page Numbers command to summon the Page Number Format dialog box.**

5. **Select the Include Chapter Number check box and then indicate which style to use for the chapter titles and what character you want to use as a separator between the chapter number and the page number.**

   You can use a hyphen, period, colon, or dash as the separator.

6. **Click OK to return to the Page Numbers dialog box and then click OK to insert the page numbers into the document.**

The Page Number Format command also lets you set a starting page number for the document or section. Usually, you use Continue from Previous Section in the Page Numbering section of the Page Number Format dialog box so that page numbers are continuous throughout the document. However, if you created a separate section for front matter (such as a title page, Table of Contents, and so on), restarting the page numbers for the first chapter of the document at page 1 is customary.

Working with Headers and Footers

The Page Number command is great if all you want to appear at the top or bottom of a page is a plain, unadorned page number. Fortunately, Word provides two other galleries in the Header & Footer group (on the Insert tab) to give you more options. To add a header to the top of your pages, select from the Header gallery. To add a footer to the bottom of your pages, select from the Footer gallery. When you add a header or footer, Word activates the Header and Footer area and, on the Ribbon, displays the Header and Footer Tools tabs with the Design tab active. The body of your document remains visible but is dimmed to indicate that you cannot edit it. See Figure 1-13.

 You can activate the header or footer area by double-clicking over the header or footer. Be careful that you don't double-click between the pages in Print Layout view (see Chapter 2 of Book I for more on views), or else you'll hide the space between the pages rather than activating the header or footer area.

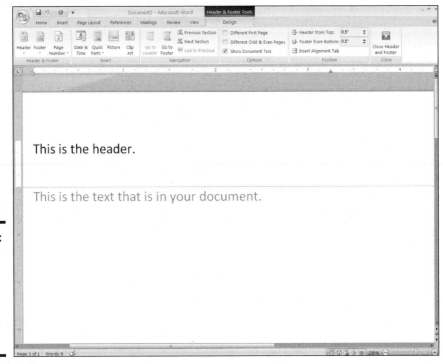

Figure 1-13:
Your
document
text dims
while you
work with
the header
or footer.

The Design tab under Header and Footer Tools provides the same three galleries that are in the Header & Footer group of the Insert tab along with commands for creating your own headers or footers. Table 1-1 describes the function of the buttons on this Design tab.

Table 1-1	The Headers and Footers Design Tab Buttons
Button	*What It Does*
Header	Lets you insert a variety of predefined headers.
Footer	Lets you insert a variety of predefined footers.
Page Number	Lets you insert a variety of predefined page numbers, which can be in the header or footer.
Date & Time	Lets you insert a marker to be replaced with the current date or time or both.

Button	What It Does
Quick Parts ▾	Lets you insert document properties or fields.
Picture	Lets you insert a picture.
Clip Art	Lets you insert ClipArt.
Go to Header	Switches from the footer to the header area.
Go to Footer	Switches from the header to the footer area.
Previous Section	If the document has more than one section, moves to the header for the previous section.
Next Section	If the document has more than one section, moves to the header for the next section.
Link to Previous	Makes this header or footer identical to the one in the preceding section.
Different First Page	Lets you have a different header and footer on the first page. You can also set this on the Layout tab of the Page Setup dialog box.
Different Odd & Even Pages	Lets you have a different header and footer on even and odd pages. You can also set this on the Layout tab of the Page Setup dialog box.
☑ Show Document Text	Controls whether the document text is shown dimmed or not at all.
Header from Top: 0.5" ↕	Sets the position of the start of the header area. You can also set this on the Layout tab of the Page Setup dialog box.
Footer from Bottom: 0.5" ↕	Sets the position of the end of the footer area. You can also set this on the Layout tab of the Page Setup dialog box.
Insert Alignment Tab	Inserts a special tab character that aligns the text that follows it relative to the margins. Unlike tabs that rely on tab stops to determine their positions, these alignment tabs change position as the margin changes. This is most useful for positioning things at the right margin. With a traditional tab and a tab stop, if you changed the margin, you'd also have to move the tab stop. But with an alignment tab, the position automatically updates.
Close Header and Footer	Returns the focus to the document so that the document text is shown normally and the header and footer are dimmed.

**Book III
Chapter 1**

**Basic Page
Formatting
and Sections**

Adding a button to show headers

If you create a lot of documents that have headers and footers, you might want a more convenient way to access them. Unfortunately, Word's standard setup doesn't have a Header and Footer button, but you can create one yourself easily enough. Just follow these steps:

1. **Choose Office⇨Word Options and click the Customize entry.**

   The Customize view of your options displays.

2. **In the Categories list, make sure Popular Commands is selected.**

3. **Select the Edit Header command.**

   It should be right there at the top.

4. **Click the Add button.**

   This adds the button to those showing on your Quick Access toolbar. You can use the up and down arrows on the right side of the list to change the order in which the buttons appear.

5. **Click OK to dismiss the Word Options dialog box.**

   The Edit Header is added to the Quick Access toolbar, making it very easy to find.

You can type anything you want in the header or footer areas, and you can apply any type of formatting you want. By default, Word creates a centered tab stop set dead in the middle of the page and a right-aligned tab stop at the right margin. As a result, you can use the Tab key to create a header that has some text flush against the left margin, some more text centered on the page, and still more text flush against the right margin.

You can often spruce up the appearance of the page by adding a border line beneath the header or above the footer. Just use the Borders and Shading gallery on the Home tab.

Understanding Sections

Sections are the basis of Word's page layout formatting. Most documents consist of only a single section, so all the pages in the document receive the same formatting. If some pages require different formatting, you can break up the document into two or more sections, each with its own page format.

Sections control the following formatting information:

✦ The size of the paper

✦ The left, right, top, and bottom margins

✦ The orientation of the paper; that is, whether the document is printed *portrait* (the height is bigger than the width) or *landscape* (the width is the larger measurement)

✦ The number and spacing of columns

✦ Header and footer information, including the positioning of the header or footer as well as its appearance

✦ Footnotes and endnotes, again including the positioning and appearance of the footnotes and endnotes

✦ Page numbering

✦ Line numbering

One of the most confusing aspects of working with sections is that a single page can contain more than one section. For example, a page might start off with a single-column layout, then switch to two columns, and then switch back to a single column. Such a page has three sections.

Unfortunately, Word doesn't include one convenient command that allows you to set all these formats from one location. In fact, you don't even set most of the section formats from the same tab. Instead, section formatting is scattered about the Word tabs:

✦ **The Page Layout tab:** The commands on this tab let you set basic page formatting information such as margins, the position of headers and footers, and paper size and orientation. It's also where you find the Breaks gallery that lets you insert new sections. You can set the number of columns and the size and spacing for each column. (For more information about columns, see Chapter 2 of this minibook.)

✦ **The Header & Footer group on the Insert tab:** These commands let you add a page number to your pages or add even more complex headers or footers. All settings relating to headers or footers can be set independently for each section.

The Design tab (under Header and Footer Tools) also relates to sections and lets you vary the page numbering style and to set the starting page number for the section.

✦ **The Reference tab:** These commands let you create footnotes or endnotes and control their appearance and position. (I cover this topic in Book VI, Chapter 2.)

All documents contain at least one section. In documents with only one section, the section formatting information is stored in the last paragraph mark of the document, along with the last paragraph's paragraph formats. If a document contains two or more sections, the end of each section (except the last section) is indicated by a section break, which is shown in Figure 1-14. To see the section break, you must be viewing the paragraph marks; use the Show/Hide Paragraphs button on the Home tab to change whether these marks are showing.

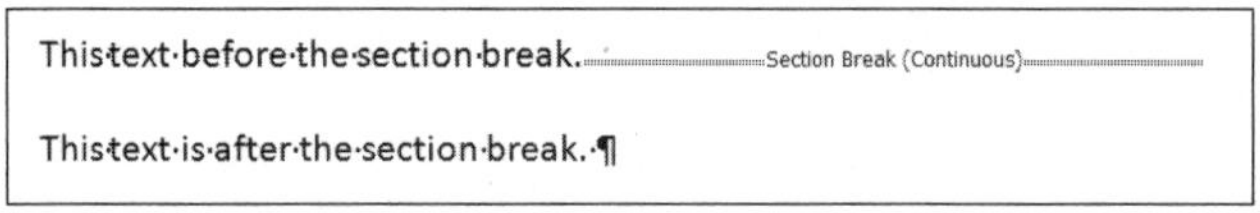

Figure 1-14:
The end of
the first
page has a
section
mark
showing.

This·text·before·the·section·break.————Section Break (Continuous)————

This·text·is·after·the·section·break.·¶

The section break contains the section formatting information just as a paragraph mark contains paragraph formatting. As a result, if you delete a section break, the sections before and after the break combine and use the formatting information from the section that followed the break. The text in parentheses shows you how the start of the section is set (Continuous, Next Page, Even Page, or Odd Page).

The one thing that the commands relating to sections usually have in common is an Apply To drop-down list. The settings on the drop-down list let you decide which sections within the document get the formatting that you've selected. The choices are

✦ **Whole Document:** The formatting is applied to the entire document, including any existing sections.

✦ **This Point Forward:** Word adds a section break at the cursor position and applies the formatting to the new section. Thus, text that follows the cursor is formatted but text that comes before it is not. If your document already contains sections, the formatting is applied only from the current point to the end of the current section.

✦ **This Section:** This option is available only if your document has more than one section and your current selection is entirely within the same section; compare this with the following option. The changes are applied only to the current section.

✦ **These Sections:** This option is available only if your document has more than one section and your current selection is in more than one section; compare this to the previous option. The changes are applied to all of the sections that include any part of the selection. So if your selection is from the middle of your first section to the middle of the third section, the changes are applied to the first, second, and third sections because a part of each was included in the selection. (Isn't it annoying how close section and selection sound when trying to understand this?)

✦ **Selected Text:** This option is available only if you selected some text before setting the formatting. When you select this option, a section break is inserted both before and after the selected text.

Creating section breaks

You can create a new section in several ways. One is to use the Breaks gallery from the Page Layout tab on the Ribbon. This method allows you to create a new section that inherits the formatting of the previous section. You can then make whatever formatting changes you want to the new section. To create a new section in this manner, follow these steps:

1. **Position the cursor at the spot where you want the new section to begin.**

2. **Click the Break button on the Page Layout tab.**

   The Breaks gallery appears, as shown in Figure 1-15.

3. **Select one of the four section break types:**

   • *Next Page:* Creates a new section that begins at the top of the following page.

   • *Continuous:* Creates a new section that begins on the next line of the same page. This type of section break is commonly used when changing the number of columns on a page.

   • *Even Page:* Creates a new section that begins on the next even-numbered page.

   • *Odd Page:* Creates a new section that begins on the next odd-numbered page.

Book III
Chapter 1

Basic Page Formatting and Sections

You can also use the Breaks gallery to create a page break or a column break. A page break simply skips the text to the top of the next page without starting a new section. A column break skips to the top of the next column. For more information about column breaks, see Chapter 2 of this minibook.

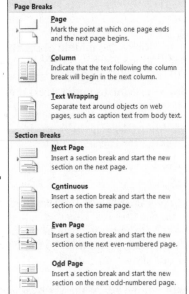

Figure 1-15:
The Breaks gallery with the sections breaks in the bottom portion.

Creating sections with different page numbers

Many documents require sections that have different page number formats. For example, many documents require that the first page or two — a cover page and perhaps an inside title page — have no page numbers at all. Then a section of front matter begins, including a Table of Contents, an acknowledgments page, and perhaps a preface, forward, or introduction, which can be numbered with roman numerals (i, ii, and so on). Then the body of the document begins, numbered with Arabic numerals starting with 1.

To create a document of this sort, you must use sections to format groups of pages with different numbering schemes. You don't have to perform a special action for the first group of pages — the ones with no page numbers.

To create the proper page numbering for the front matter, follow these steps:

1. **Place the cursor at the beginning of the front matter.**

If you already inserted a page break so that the first page of the front matter begins at the top of a new page, delete the page break. In the next step, you insert a section break that causes the front matter to start atop a new page.

2. Click the Break button on the Insert tab to display the Breaks gallery.

3. Choose Next Page.

4. Click OK to insert the break.

5. (Optional) Choose Edit Footer from the Footer gallery on the Insert tab if you want the page numbers at the bottom of the page.

   Use Edit Header from the Header gallery if you want the numbers at the top of the page.

6. Click the Link to Previous button to detach the footer from the previous section's footer.

7. Open the Page Number gallery by clicking the Page Number button on the Insert tab.

8. Select the formatting that you want to use from the Page Number gallery.

   If you're working with the footer, you should select from the Bottom of Page gallery. If you're working with the header, select from the Top of Page gallery.

9. Select the Format Page Number command from the Page Number gallery.

   The Page Number Format dialog box appears. (Refer to Figure 1-12.)

10. For the front matter, choose the Roman numeral number format (i, ii, iii . . .) in the Number Format list box.

11. Select Start At 1.

12. Click OK.

    The Page Number Format dialog box disappears.

You can follow a similar procedure to begin a new section of page numbering for the body of the document, using Arabic numerals rather than Roman numerals.

Chapter 2: Formatting Fancy Pages

In This Chapter

✔ **Creating columns**

✔ **Adjusting column width**

✔ **Forcing a column break**

✔ **Adding a cover page**

✔ **Inserting backgrounds to your document**

✔ **Adding a page border**

If you use Word to create newsletters, brochures, and other stuff for which you really should be using a desktop-publishing program like Adobe PageMaker, you'll be happy to know that Word enables you to create beautiful two- or three-column layouts. (Actually, you can create as many as 12 columns on a page, but unless you're using *really* wide paper, that's not such a good idea.)

Word refers to two- and three-column layouts as *newspaper-style columns*, but that's just a bit misleading. To implement a true newspaper-style column feature, Word would have to edit your prose automatically as you type it so that it focused on bad news and added a distinct left- or right-wing slant to your text.

This chapter jumps head first into setting up newspaper-style columns in Word, so get ready to slice your page into columns of text.

Creating Columns

When you create multiple columns, the column layout applies to the entire section. If the entire document consists of but one section, the column layout applies to the entire document. If you want part of the document to have one column and another part to have two or three columns, you have to create two or more sections to accommodate the different column layouts. (Chapter 1 in this minibook talks about working with sections.)

Creating columns the easy way

Here is the easiest way to create multiple columns in your document:

1. **Click the Columns button on the Page Layout tab on the Ribbon.**

The drop-down list shown in Figure 2-1 appears.

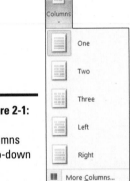

Figure 2-1:
The
Columns
drop-down
list.

2. **Click and drag the mouse to pick the number of columns you want.**

If you want more than three columns, drop everything. Take a nice long walk to clear your head of such nonsense. If you still want four or more columns when you return, use the Number of Columns control to set the number of columns you want.

3. **Let go.**

Voilà! The document is formatted with the number of columns you chose.

When you create a multicolumn layout, Word makes sure that you're using Print Layout view so that the columns are visible side by side on-screen. If you switch to Draft view (on the View tab, click the Draft command), the text is formatted according to the width of the column, but the columns don't display side by side on-screen.

Did you choke when you saw what your document looked like in columns? You can revert to single-column mode by pressing Ctrl+Z (the magic Undo command) or by using the Columns button to set the layout to one column.

For a quick glimpse of how the columns appear when printed, choose Office⇨Print⇨Print Preview. When you've seen enough, click the Close Print Preview button on the Print Preview tab to return to your document.

The Columns button enables you to set the number of columns, but it doesn't enable you to control the size of each column or the amount of space between columns. To do these latter actions, you need to use the Columns command, described next.

Creating columns the hard way

For more control over the appearance of columns, use the Columns command. Grab a cup of coffee and follow these steps:

1. **Move the insertion point to the location in the document where you want the columns to begin.**

   If you want to apply columns to the entire document, where you put the insertion point doesn't matter.

2. **Click the Columns button on the Page Layout tab, but rather than picking one of the easy preset selections from the drop-down menu, choose the More Columns command at the bottom of the menu.**

   You're greeted with the Columns dialog box, shown in Figure 2-2.

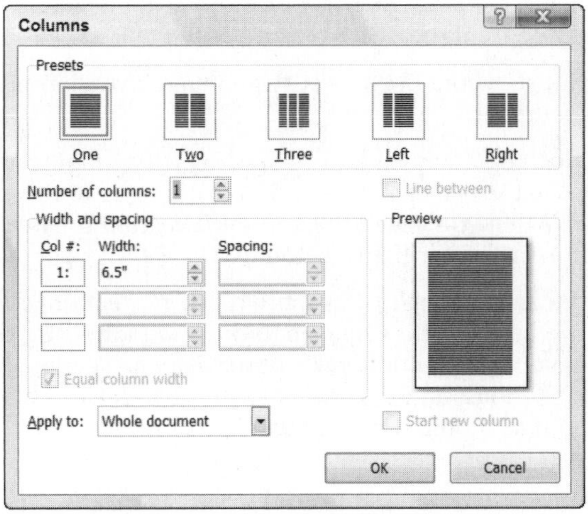

Figure 2-2: The Columns dialog box.

3. **Click one of the five preset column layouts.**

   These are the same choices you saw on the drop-down menu. If you want even more columns, you can tell Word how many to create by entering a number in the Number of Columns control.

4. **Change the Width or Spacing fields if you must.**

If you want to change the width of the columns, change the Width field. To change the amount of space between columns, change the Spacing field.

Word wants to make all the columns the same width, so when you change one, Word insists on changing all the others. If you want to make Word stop doing that, deselect the Equal Column Width check box.

5. Click the Line Between button if you want a line between the columns.

This is the line between the stuff you read, not the stuff you read between the lines.

6. Periodically peer at the preview box to see whether you like the column layout.

7. Here's the tricky part: You have to decide which parts of your document get turned into columns.

- If you choose *This Point Forward,* Word adds a section break at the cursor position and applies the column layout to the new section. Thus, text that follows the cursor is formatted in columns, but text that comes before it is not. When you have more than one section, however, the behavior of This Point Forward changes a bit — it formats only up until the next section break.

- If you choose *Whole Document,* the column layout applies to the entire document.

- If you selected some text before opening the Columns dialog box, you can use the *Selected Text* option to change the columns for just that text. When you select this option, a section break is inserted both before and after the selected text.

- If your document already has more than one section, choosing *This Section* applies the changes to the text in the current section. (If you have text selection from more than one section, the option is Selected Sections, and the text in all of the sections changes.) For more about sections, see Chapter 1 in this book.

8. Click OK.

Excellent!

Here are some things to remember as you twiddle with the Columns dialog box:

✦ If you select the Equal Column Width check box, Word balances the columns evenly. If you deselect this check box, you can create columns of uneven width.

✦ Using the Apply To: This Point Forward option is the way to create a headline or title that spans the width of two or three columns. Start by creating the headline, using a large font and centering it. Position the cursor at the end of the heading and then use Columns command to create a two- or three-column layout. Set the Select Apply To field to This Point Forward to throw the columns into a new section so that the headline remains in a single column.

Adjusting the Column Width

If you don't like the width of columns you create, you can change them at any time. You have two ways to change column width:

✦ Call up the Columns command from the Page Layout tab and play with the Width and Spacing fields.

✦ Click and drag the *column marker,* the box-like separator between columns on the ruler. If you selected the Equal Column Width check box in the Columns dialog box, all the column markers move in concert to preserve the equal column widths. Otherwise, you can adjust the column markers individually.

Some things to remember when you adjust column width:

Book III
Chapter 2

✦ Even if you use unequal column widths, try to keep the gap between the columns the same widths. Otherwise, you create an unbalanced look.

✦ When adjusting column width by dragging the column marker, hold down the Alt key before clicking. Doing so causes Word to display measurements that show the width of each column and the size of the space between columns.

Formatting Fancy Pages

✦ Any formatting applied to paragraphs in columns is still in effect. If you gave a paragraph a left indent of ½ inch, the paragraph is indented ½ inch from the left column margin. This indentation reduces the column width.

Forcing a Column Break

Left to its own devices, Word decides when to jump text from the bottom of one column up to the top of the next column. Sometimes, however, you want to intervene and insert a column break of your own.

Using linked text boxes to create columns

Word offers an alternative to the Columns command for creating complex multicolumn layouts: linked text boxes. A linked text box is a drawing object that contains text. You can link a series of text boxes together so that if the first text box isn't large enough to contain all the text, the text spills over to the second text box. If the second text box isn't large enough to show all the text, Word adds a third text box to the link. Turn to Book IV, Chapter 5 if you want to know more about using text boxes.

Follow these steps to force a column break:

1. **Place the insertion point where you want the new column to begin.**

2. **Press Ctrl+Shift+Enter.**

Or use the Break command from the Page Layout tab, which gives you a variety of breaks to choose from. (Fortunately, none of them are painful or require a cast.)

In Draft view, a column break is indicated in the text by a solid line running all the way across the screen. In Page Layout view, the column break is obvious when you see the text jump to the next column.

Don't try to create two or three columns of equal length by inserting column breaks where you think the bottom of each column should fall. Instead, insert a continuous section break at the end of the last column. A continuous section break balances all the columns in the section so that they're of equal length and then starts a new section without forcing a page break. To insert a continuous section break, click the Break command on the Page Layout tab and then select Continuous.

Adding a Cover Page

Many documents have an attractive first page that includes the document title and perhaps the author's name. That information is frequently repeated in the header or footer on each page. Word 2007 provides a very easy way of adding a cover page.

To add a cover page to your document, follow these steps:

1. **Click the Cover Page button on the Insert tab.**

The Cover Page gallery shown in Figure 2-3 appears.

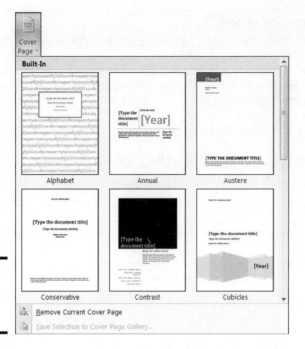

Figure 2-3:
The Cover
Page
gallery.

2. **Click the cover page that you want to add to your document.**

Word knows to put the cover page at the start of your document. If you want it to go somewhere else, right-click the cover page in the gallery and select the location you want from the menu that appears.

Most of the cover pages have areas where you can type the title of your document and the author's name. If you complete this information on the title page, the headers and footers that include the title, author name, or both also display the correct information. Many cover pages also have areas for the subtitle and an abstract.

Creating a Background

Word provides several commands for adding a background to your document. Your background might be a watermark (a faint image behind the text of your document), a background color, a background image, or a border around your text. Watermarks are commonly added to printed documents to provide a reminder to the reader about the status of the document (such as confidential or draft). Backgrounds are most often used online because you can use colored paper in your printer rather than use lots of ink to color the paper.

Adding a watermark

Watermarks are most useful for printed documents because they aren't displayed in the Web Layout view. And although a watermark can let the reader know that the document is confidential, it's not as good at protection as the features discussed in Book V, Chapter 3. The same watermark must be used for all pages in your document.

To add a watermark, follow these steps:

1. **Click the Watermark button on the Page Layout tab.**

The watermark gallery shown in Figure 2-4 appears.

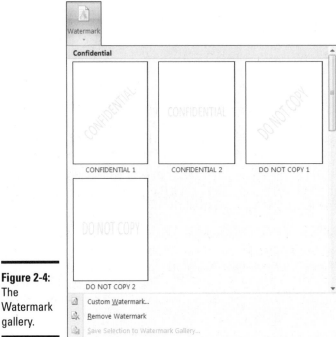

Figure 2-4:
The
Watermark
gallery.

2. **Click one of the watermarks to insert it or select Custom Watermark from the bottom of the gallery.**

If you elect to add a custom watermark, the Printed Watermark dialog box shown in Figure 2-5 appears. You can select a picture to be used for the watermark by selecting the Picture Watermark option and then using the Select Picture button to find the file that contains the image you want to use. For most images, you want to leave the Washout option selected, which makes the image look faded and therefore makes the text on top of the image easier to read.

Figure 2-5:
The Printed
Watermark
dialog box.

You can add text to your watermark by selecting the Text Watermark option in the Printed Watermark dialog box. You can then use the controls to select the language for the watermark and the text to be used. You can format the text by using the remaining controls, including deciding whether the text should be diagonal or horizontal.

To remove a watermark from your document, select the Remove Watermark command from the bottom of the Watermark gallery.

Adding a background

Page backgrounds are intended to be used primarily for online documents. By default, Word doesn't print the page background, so if you want the background to print, you need to go to the Display tab of the Word Options dialog box and select the Print Background Colors and Images option.

To add a solid color as a background to your entire document, select a color from the Page Color control on the Page Layout tab on the Ribbon.

To add a gradient, pattern, texture, or picture, select the Fill Effects command from the bottom of the Page Color control. The Fill Effects dialog box puts in an appearance on your screen. Each tab of the Fill Effects dialog box allows you to add a different type of background. Both the Texture tab and the Picture tab let you select an image file to use for the background. The Texture tab repeats the picture to fill the entire background, whereas the Picture tab centers the image.

Note that a document can have only one background for all pages in the document.

Adding a page border

Unlike watermarks and backgrounds, page borders are actually assigned to the section. This means that different sections in your document can have different borders. For more information about sections, see Chapter 1 in this minibook.

To add a page border, follow these steps:

1. **Click the Page Border button on the Page Layout tab.**

The Borders and Shading dialog box opens to the Page Border tab, as shown in Figure 2-6.

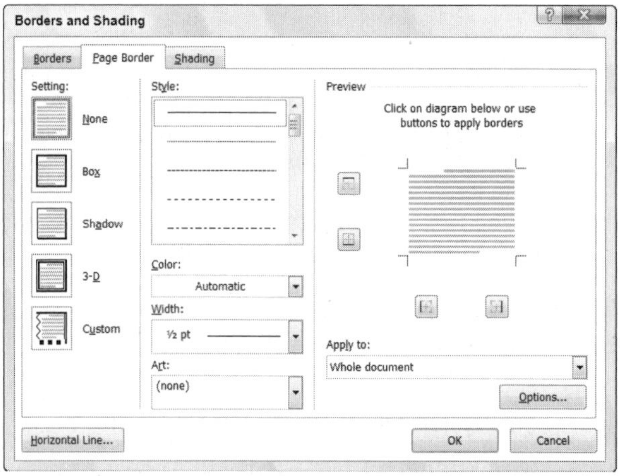

Figure 2-6:
The Page Border tab of the Borders and Shading dialog box.

2. **Select either a line or art to use as the border.**

You can select either a Style and Color for the line by using the top two drop-down lists in the center of the dialog box or a repeated image from the Art drop-down list at the bottom of the dialog box.

3. **Select the border width.**

Keep in mind that the border needs to fit within the margin of the page and that you want some space between the border and your text.

4. **Decide which sides of the page will have the border.**

You can use the preset Box, Shadow, or 3-D options on the left of the dialog box or select the Custom option on the left and use the controls on the right to select the sides that have the border.

5. If you want different sections to have different borders, use the Apply To drop-down list.

For more on working with sections, see Chapter 1 of this minibook.

6. Click OK.

The border displays only in Print Layout view and in Print Preview view.

To remove the border from a section, use the same steps but select the None option in Step 4.

Although it's possible for the same document to have a watermark, a page background, and a page border, that's generally appropriate only for something like a certificate or award.

Book III
Chapter 2

Formatting Fancy Pages

Chapter 3: Creating Lists

In This Chapter

✔ **Creating bulleted lists or numbered lists the easy way**

✔ **Using different bullets and number formats**

✔ **Creating your own bullets and number formats**

✔ **Formatting a list**

✔ **Working with lists that have more than one level**

*B*ullets and numbered lists are great ways to add emphasis to a series of important points or to add a sense of order to items that fall into a natural sequence. Glance through this book to see what I mean. It's loaded with bulleted and numbered lists.

In Word, you can add a bullet or a line number to each paragraph. The bullet or number is a part of the paragraph format, and Word adds the bullet character or the number so that you don't have to. Word even keeps the numbers in a numbered list in sequence, so if you add or delete a paragraph or rearrange paragraphs in the list, the numbers reorder automatically.

Several of the examples in this chapter walk through the steps for using bullets, but almost anything that you can do with bullets can also be done with number formats, and the steps are the same.

Creating a List Automatically

Word's AutoFormat feature can create bulleted and numbered lists automatically whenever Word determines that you're trying to create a bullet or numbered list. In previous versions, this feature was a somewhat hit-and-miss proposition, but it seems to be working much better in Word 2007. I suggest giving it a try and then deciding whether you'd prefer another approach (such as using the buttons, as I describe a bit later in the chapter).

One minor thing that has changed from previous versions of Word is that Word recognizes your list as soon as you type a space or a tab. No more waiting around for the end of the paragraph. Talk about your instant gratification.

✦ Word automatically formats text as a bulleted list whenever you begin a paragraph with a character that it matches to one of its rules. You can use any of the special characters shown in Table 3-1 to start a list.

Table 3-1	The Codes Word Recognizes for Bullets
This	*Gives You This*
*	<Insert character 183 from the Symbol font>
>	<Insert character 216 from the Wingdings font>
->	<Insert character 168 from the Symbol font>
<>	<Insert character 232 from the Wingdings font>
-	<Insert a hyphen from the current font>

✦ Word automatically formats text as a numbered list whenever you type a number followed by a period, hyphen, right parenthesis, or greater-than sign (>) and a space or tab. Word also starts a lettered list if you type the letter A (either upper- or lowercase) followed by a period, hyphen, right parenthesis, or greater-than sign and a space or tab or a list numbered with roman numerals if you type the letter I (either upper- or lowercase) followed by a period, hyphen, right parenthesis, or greater-than sign and a space or tab.

If you want to have a paragraph in the middle of your list that doesn't have a bullet on it but lines up with the text of the list items, just press Backspace once to remove the bullet or number. If you want the text to line up with the bullets or numbers, press Backspace again.

If you don't want this automatic formatting to occur, call up the Word Options dialog box by choosing Office⇨Word Options and then select the Proofing view. Click the AutoCorrect Options button, click the AutoFormat as You Type tab and deselect the Automatic Bulleted Lists and Automatic Numbered Lists options.

Creating a List the Button Way

Aside from creating lists automatically, nothing is easier than clicking a button, and that's about all you have to do to create a simple bulleted or numbered list. With the click of a button, you can create a bulleted list like this one:

✦ Cheery disposition

✦ Rosy cheeks

✦ No warts

✦ Plays games, all sorts

Click another button, and you transform the whole thing into a numbered list:

1. Cheery disposition

2. Rosy cheeks

3. No warts

4. Plays games, all sorts

One of the advantages to using the buttons to create your lists is that the buttons remember the last format that you used. So if you use a fancy bullet in one part of your document, when you apply bullets by clicking the button elsewhere in your document, the same bullet is applied. But the buttons have only a short-term memory — if the insertion point is next to or within a list, the format of that list is used. Otherwise, the last format you applied is used.

Creating a bulleted list

To create a bulleted list, follow this procedure:

1. **Type the first item of your list.**

Don't press Enter yet.

2. **Click the Bullet button on the Home tab.**

A bullet is added to the paragraph.

3. **Press Enter to begin the next item.**

A new paragraph with a bullet is created.

4. **Type the rest of the list.**

Press Enter after you type each item of the list. Word automatically adds bullets to each new paragraph.

5. **When you're done, press Enter twice.**

Pressing Enter the second time removes the bullet for the last item of the list.

When you create a bulleted list this way, Word uses a default bullet character (normally a small dot) and creates a ¼-inch hanging indent. (If the paragraphs already have hanging indents, the original indentation settings are preserved.) To discover how to use oddball bullets, find the section "Using a different bullet or number format," later in this chapter.

Book III
Chapter 3

Creating Lists

Here are a few additional tricks for bulleting your lists:

✦ To add more items to the bulleted list, position the insertion point at the end of one of the bulleted paragraphs and press Enter. Because the bullet is part of the paragraph format, it is carried over to the new paragraph.

✦ You can add bullets to existing text. Just select the paragraph or paragraphs you want to riddle with bullets, and then click the Bullet button.

✦ You can remove bullets as easily as you add them. The Bullet button works like a toggle: Press it once to add bullets; press it again to remove them. To remove bullets from an entire list, select all the paragraphs in the list and click the Bullet button.

✦ Ever notice how the good guys never run out of bullets in the movies? Well, try not to be like the good guys. The old notion of the six-shooter is a pretty good one. Placing more than six bullets in a row pushes the limits of just about any reader's patience. (Of course, I routinely disregard that advice throughout this book, but what are you going to do, shoot me?)

✦ Oh, and by the way, you probably shouldn't leave one bullet standing by itself. Bullets are used to mark items in a list, and you need more than one item to make a list. ("Army of One" is a good slogan for the military, but "List of One" is a lousy slogan for this chapter.)

Creating a numbered list

To create a numbered list, follow this procedure:

1. **Type the first item of your list.**

Don't press Enter yet.

2. **Click the Numbering button on the Home tab.**

A number is added to the paragraph.

3. **Press Enter to begin the next item.**

A new paragraph with the next number in sequence is created.

4. **Type the rest of the list.**

Press Enter after you type each item of the list. Word automatically adds numbers to each new paragraph.

5. **When you're done, press Enter twice.**

Pressing Enter the second time removes the number for the last item of the list.

When you use the Numbering button to create a numbered list, Word uses a default numbering format and establishes a ¼-inch hanging indent for each paragraph. (If the paragraphs are already formatted with hanging indents, the original indentation settings are kept.) You can use all sorts of crazy numbering schemes if you want; to find out how, skip ahead to the section "Creating Crazy Numbering Schemes."

If you want to have a paragraph in the middle of your list that doesn't have a number on it but lines up with the text of the numbered items, put the insertion point at the beginning of the paragraph and just press Backspace once to remove the number. If you want the text to line up with the numbers, press Backspace again.

Word is really cool about keeping the list in order. If you add or delete a paragraph in the middle of the list, Word renumbers the paragraphs to preserve the order. If you add a paragraph to the end of the list, Word assigns the next number in sequence to the new paragraph.

You can also apply numbering to existing text. Just select the paragraph or paragraphs you want to number and then click the Numbering button on the Home tab.

The Numbering button works like a toggle: Click it once to add numbers to paragraphs; click it again to remove them. To remove numbering from a numbered paragraph, select the paragraph and click the Numbering button. To remove numbering from an entire list, select all the paragraphs in the list and click the Numbering button.

Using a different bullet or number format

One of the nifty additions to Word 2007 is the little arrows next to the Bullets and Numbering buttons. Well, the little arrows really aren't that neat, but the galleries that they reveal are pretty cool. When you click the arrow next to the Bullets button, the gallery shown in Figure 3-1 is revealed.

Figure 3-1:
The Bullet Library shows your collection of bullets.

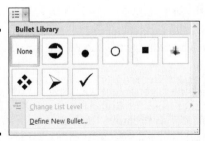

The Bullet Library portion of the gallery lets you store a collection of your favorite bullets. You can store up to a couple hundred, but most people don't really use more than a few dozen. Don't be greedy.

After you've started working with bullets in your document, some additional sections appear in the gallery. The Document Bullets section (shown in Figure 3-2) lists all the bullets in all the documents that are currently open. The Recently Used Bullets at the top part of the gallery shows you the last few bullets that you've applied by using the button.

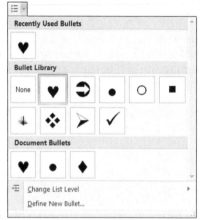

Figure 3-2: The Bullet Library can include recently used bullets and bullets from other opened documents.

What's great is that you can add a bullet from either of these sections to your Bullet Library by following these steps:

1. **Display the Bullet gallery by clicking the arrow next to the Bullet button.**

You should now see the bullet you want to add. If not, find a document that already uses that bullet and try again.

2. **Right-click the bullet you want to add to your Bullet Library and choose Add to Library.**

That's all you need to do. The bullet is now available for all of your documents.

Of course, if you get tired of a bullet, you might want to throw it out of the Bullet Library. To remove a bullet from the Bullet Library, right-click it and choose Remove. Note that this doesn't remove the bullet from the lists in your document.

If Word offered this feature only for the bullets, the numbers would sulk and refuse to work. If you select the arrow next to the Numbering button, you discover that the same type of gallery exists for numbers, as shown in Figure 3-3. And what's even better is that everything I just described for bullets works for numbers as well.

Figure 3-3:
The
Numbering
Library
shows your
collection of
number
formats.

Formatting a List

Two of the most interesting ways that you can format a list are by changing the font formatting used for the list character (the bullet or number format) and by changing the indent of the list. When you click a bullet used in a list, the bullets for all of the paragraphs in that list are highlighted in a soft gray, as shown in Figure 3-4.

Figure 3-4:
Clicking one
bullet
selects all
of those
in the list.

> • → Three·Little·Pigs
> • → Little·Red·Riding·Hood
> • → Little·House·on·the·Prairie

The same technique works for selecting all the numbers in a numbered list. And although the following steps describe working with a bulleted list, you can do the exact same thing with a numbered list.

With the bullets selected, you can use any of the font formatting controls on the Home tab to change the formatting of the character used as the bullet symbol. Using this technique, you can change the size or color for any individual list without creating your own bullet. However, if you want to use that format frequently, you might want to have that bullet in your Bullet Library, which is described in the next section, "Creating Deviant Bullets."

You can also change the position of the bullet and the text in the list by doing the following:

1. **Click one of the bullets in the list to make sure the entire list is selected.**

   It's very important to select the list rather than one or more of the items in the list. If you select the paragraph before performing these steps, only the selected paragraph changes, rather than the entire list.

2. **Right-click one of the bullets in the list and choose Adjust List Indents.**

   The Adjust List Indents dialog box shown in Figure 3-5 displays.

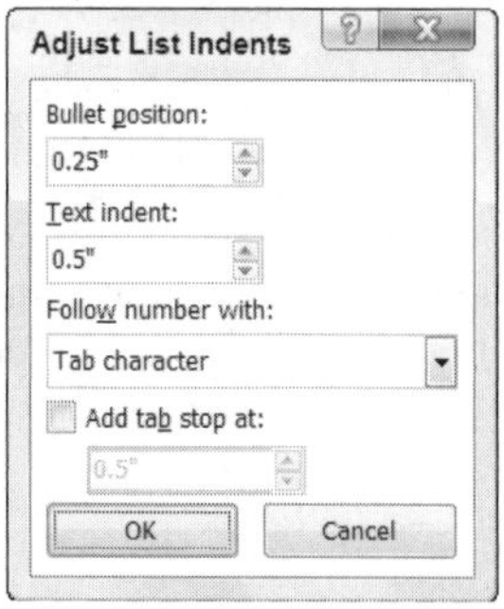

Figure 3-5:
The Adjust
List Indents
dialog box.

Adjust List Indents

Bullet position:
0.25"

Text indent:
0.5"

Follow number with:
Tab character

☐ Add tab stop at:
0.5"

OK   Cancel

3. **Change the value of the Text Indent option to control where the text is positioned.**

   By default, Word positions the text at a ½-inch indent.

4. **Change the Bullet position to control how far the bullet is from the left margin.**

    The greater this value is, the closer the bullet will be to the text.

5. **If you're creating lists where you want the bullet to be part of the text rather than separated with a tab, change the option selected in the Follow Number With drop-down list.**

    Just try to ignore the fact that the option says "Number" when you're working with bullets. Even Microsoft makes mistakes.

6. **If you want to have a tab included on each line in the list, select the Add Tab Stop At option.**

    The primary reason to do this is to match the way in which lists were created in previous versions of Word. When this option is active, you can specify the location of the tab stop that will be inserted.

7. **Click OK.**

    Check that your list is now neatly lined up where you want it. If not, you need to make further adjustments by following these steps again.

You can do all of the same things with a numbered list. The only difference is that rather than clicking a bullet, you click the number.

Word 2007 now uses a special paragraph style for formatting lists. This style, named List Paragraph, determines the starting font formatting used for the text in your list as well as the spacing between lines in the paragraph and between paragraphs. See Book II, Chapter 3 for more information about modifying the formatting used by a style.

**Book III
Chapter 3**

Creating Lists

Creating Deviant Bullets

If you don't like any of the choices available in your Bullet Library and want to create a new one of your very own, here's how:

1. **Click the arrow next to the Bullet button on the Home tab.**

    Behold! The Bullet gallery appears.

2. **Select the Define New Bullet command from the bottom of the Bullet gallery.**

    The Define New Bullet dialog box appears, as shown in Figure 3-6.

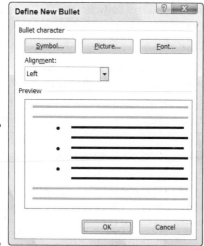

Figure 3-6:
The Define New Bullet dialog box lets you format your own bullets.

3. **If you want to use a character for the bullet, click the Symbol button.**

The Symbol dialog box shown in Figure 3-7 appears.

Figure 3-7:
The Symbol dialog box is where you pick what to use for your bullet.

4. **Pick the bullet character you want; then click OK.**

You can change the characters displayed by choosing a different font from the Symbols From list box. Find the character you want to use, click it, and then click OK.

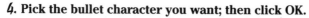

5. **(Optional) If you want to control the color or size of the character you're using, click the Font button to select your formatting.**

   The formatting that you apply appears when the bullet is used for normal text.

6. **OK your way back to the document.**

   Keep clicking OK until you get back to your document so that you can see the results of your bullet formatting efforts. Note that the bullet you just created is automatically added to your Bullet Library.

Keep these points in mind when changing your bullets:

✦ If the characters in the Symbol dialog box seem too small to read, fear not. When you click one of them, Word blows it up about four times the normal size so that you can see it.

✦ The Wingdings font (which comes with Windows) is filled with great bullet characters: pointing fingers, smiley faces, grumpy faces, thumbs up, thumbs down, peace signs for folks who were at Woodstock, time bombs, and a skull and crossbones. ("Yo ho, yo ho, a pirate's life for me!" I love that song more than Johnny Depp does!)

If you want to use a picture for a bullet rather than a symbol, when you're defining your bullet, click the Picture button rather than the Symbol button in Step 2, select the image you want to use, and then click OK. Figure 3-8 shows the Picture Bullet dialog box, which helps you choose a nice picture to use for your bullets. You cannot apply font formatting to picture bullets.

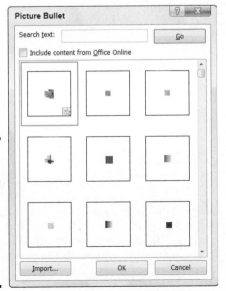

Figure 3-8:
The Picture Bullet dialog box is where you can pick an image to use for your bullet.

Creating Crazy Numbering Schemes

Most people like to count 1, 2, 3, and so on. But some people count A, B, C, or maybe I, II, III, like a Roman. Not to fear. With Word, you can count just about any way you like.

Follow these prudent steps to create your own crazy numbering schemes:

1. Click the arrow next to the Bullet button on the Home tab.

The Bullet gallery appears. It dutifully awaits your command.

2. Select the Define New Number Format command from the bottom of the Bullet gallery.

The Define New Number Format dialog box appears, as shown in Figure 3-9.

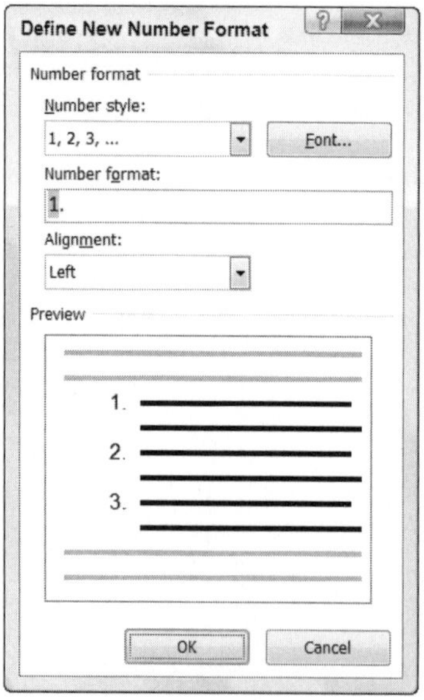

Figure 3-9: The Define New Number Format dialog box.

3. Modify the numbering scheme to suit your fancy.

You can change the number format and change the alignment of the numbers within the list. You can also type text to include before or after the number or both. The most common type of text that is included with a number is punctuation following the number. So when you want a number format to look like "1)", the closing parenthesis is included as text after the number — you just type it directly into the Number Format text box. A common type of text included before a number is a label such as Chapter or Section, particularly when the numbering is used with the heading styles, as described later in this chapter in the section "Numbering your headings."

By default, Word aligns most numbered lists to the left of the number (so that when 10 appears under 9, the 1 is lined up under the 9). If you want your 10 to line up under your 9 with the 0 under the 9, select the Right option in the Alignment drop-down list. Figure 3-10 shows an example of a list with the numbers right-aligned.

1.   Partridge
2.   Turtle·Doves
3.   French·Hens
4.   Calling·Birds
5.   Golden·Rings
6.   Geese
7.   Swans
8.   Maids
9.   Ladies
10.   Lords
11.   Pipers
12.   Drummers

Figure 3-10:
A list with numbers that are right-aligned.

If you want to specify a different font for the numbers, click the Font button when the Customize Numbered List dialog box appears. The font applies not only to the number, but also to any text that appears before or after the number.

4. Click OK.

Happy numbering! The number format is now stored in your Numbering Library.

Keep these points in mind when using numbered lists:

✦ Besides normal number formats (like 1, 2, 3 or A, B, C), you can specify One, Two, Three; 1st, 2nd, 3rd; or even First, Second, Third as the number format. Believe it or not, these oddball formats work even with unreasonably long lists. Try it and see for yourself: Word knows how to spell one-thousand one-hundred eighty-seventh. It also knows that the Roman numeral equivalent is MCLXXXVII. Isn't that amazing?

✦ You can add text that appears before or after the number by typing the text into the Number Format text box. Note that the number itself is shown in the Number Format text box with a gray background.

Breaking and Continuing a Numbered List

The menu that you get when you right-click a number in a numbered list includes two options that are useful in two situations:

✦ **Restart at 1:** Use this option when you want to begin a new numbered list, even if the paragraph comes in the middle of an existing numbered list. You can also use this option to work with two or more numbered lists that are adjacent to one another.

✦ **Continue Numbering:** Use this option when you want to insert a non-numbered paragraph in the middle of a numbered list, but you want the list numbering to continue in sequence across the unnumbered paragraph.

Here are a couple troubleshooting tips:

✦ If you're trying to create a new numbered list but the number for the first paragraph in the list refuses to start at 1, right-click the number and select Restart at 1 command.

✦ On the other hand, if a paragraph in the middle of a list insists on starting with the number 1, try selecting the Continue Numbering option.

The Set Numbering Value command also lets you do both of these tasks and lets you set a starting value for the list if you want it to start at a value other than 1. Such lists are useful in some cases, but be very careful. It's easy to set a starting value and then forget and wonder why it now has such strange numbering.

Working with Lists with Two or More Levels

Not all lists are simple one-level lists like the ones I've been describing. In some cases, you want to have a second level with a different format. Figure 3-11 shows an example of such a list.

Some people go completely crazy making lists with three or four levels. Word doesn't mind because it's able to manage lists with up to nine levels. Beyond that, you're on your own.

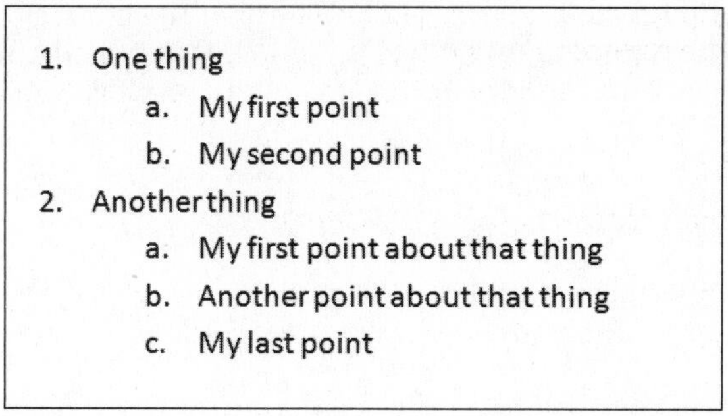

1. One thing
    a. My first point
    b. My second point
2. Another thing
    a. My first point about that thing
    b. Another point about that thing
    c. My last point

Figure 3-11:
A list with
two levels.

To create a list at an indent level, you can just press Tab at the start of the paragraph. If you're on the first item of your list, the indent position for the list changes so there is more white space to the left of the list. But if you're within a list, each time you press Tab, the numbering moves to the next level of the list. If you're more of a button person, you can use the Increase Indent button on the Home tab.

To move an item up a level in the list (for example, moving from the second level to the first level) while creating a list, you can press Enter. However, this shortcut works only before you start typing text on the line. After you've created the paragraph, you can use Shift+Tab at the start of the paragraph or the Decrease Indent button on the Home tab.

When you're at the end of a list, pressing Enter removes the number and returns the insertion point to the left margin. If you want to remove the number but not change the position of the text (at any level), press Backspace.

Changing the Look of a List with Many Levels

You can create compulsive outline lists that can satisfy even the most rigid anthropology professor by using Word's numbering feature. I wouldn't wish this task on anyone, but if you must create these types of lists, this feature is a godsend.

Right next door to the traditional Bullet and Numbering buttons on the Home tab is a new button called Multilevel List. When you click the Multilevel List button, the gallery shown in Figure 3-12 appears.

When the gallery displays, all the paragraphs associated with the current list are selected. This selection is similar to the one that you get when you click a bullet or number, but it extends to all levels within the list. You can select one of the entries on the gallery to change the formatting of the entire list.

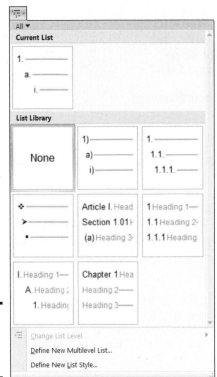

Figure 3-12:
The Multilevel List gallery.

If you hover the cursor over one of the entries in the List Library section for the Multilevel List gallery, a sample showing all nine levels of the list is displayed.

The entries on the Multilevel List gallery of are two types: traditional, old-fashioned multilevel lists and new, improved list styles. The differences between the two are that list styles have names and can be modified. Traditional multilevel lists can't be modified, so to change a list you have to create a new multilevel list and replace the old one you were using. The problem with that approach is that your document can become cluttered with unused list definitions. But the advantage to multilevel lists is that they can be added to your List Library and are available for any document you create; List Styles get their own section of the Multilevel List gallery and have to be copied from document to document.

Crafting your own multilevel list

But what do you do if there isn't a multilevel list that you like? Well, just like with bullets and numbers for single-level lists, you can create your own. Here's an outline of the procedure for creating a multilevel list.

1. **Click the Define New Multilevel List link at the bottom of the Multilevel List gallery.**

The Define New Multilevel List dialog box appears, as shown in Figure 3-13. This dialog box enables you to customize each level of an outline list.

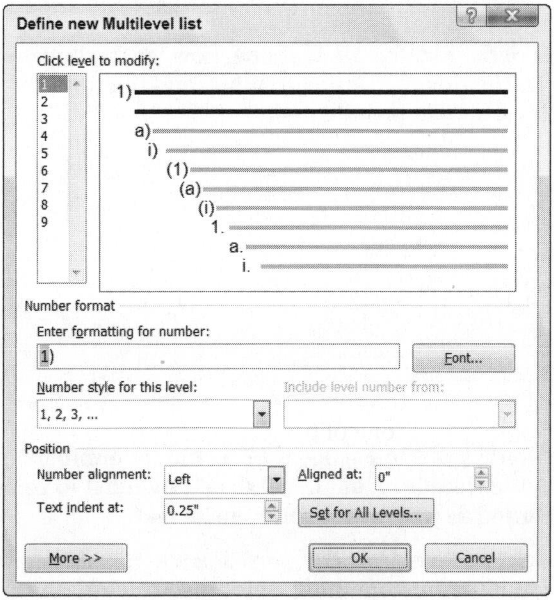

Figure 3-13: The Define New Multilevel List dialog box.

Book III Chapter 3

Creating Lists

2. **Select the level that you want to work with.**

It's easiest to start with the first level and work your way down. You can select other levels by clicking either the number or the preview of that number level in the Click Level to Modify section of the dialog box.

3. **Select the numbering format that you want to use for that level.**

When working with a number format, you can add text, such as punctuation, to be used with the number by typing in the Enter Formatting for the Number text box.

Most multilevel lists involve numbers so that dialog box is set up to make adding number formats easier. You can add bullets to a level by selecting one of the Bullet options from the bottom of the Number Style for This Level drop-down list. You can even define your own bullet or use a picture bullet with the New Bullet and New Picture commands at the very end of the menu.

4. **Adjust the formatting to be used for the level, including adding any text, setting the font, and setting the indent position for the list.**

   For more information, see the section "Formatting a List," earlier in this chapter.

If you want all of the levels to be indented equally with the bullet or number the same distance from the text, click the Set for All Levels button to display the dialog box shown in Figure 3-14. You can specify the position of the text for the first line, how far the bullet should be away from the left indent for the first line, and then by how much each additional level should be indented.

Figure 3-14:
The Set for
All Levels
dialog box.

Set for All Levels		? X
Bullet/Number position for first level:	0"	
Text position for first level:	0.25"	
Additional indent for each level:	0.25"	
OK	Cancel	

5. **(Optional) If you want to use legal or technical numbers (such as 1-1), use the Include Number from Level drop-down list to select which level is included as part of the number format.**

   When you select a level from the drop-down list, a placeholder representing the numbering from that level is inserted into the Enter Formatting for the Number text box. You want to make sure your insertion point is where you want the placeholder inserted before selecting a level (usually at the start of the number format). You probably want to add punctuation between the placeholders for the current level and any other levels you've included.

   This command is available only for levels 2 through 9.

6. **Repeat Steps 2 through 5 for each level.**

   You don't need to define all nine levels.

7. Click OK.

Your new list is now part of your List Library and ready to go.

Defining a List Style follows a similar process but starts with the Define New List Style command. The major differences are that the Define List Style dialog box shown in Figure 3-15 allows you to give the list style a name and has only some of the controls shown in the Define Multilevel List dialog box. To get to the entire set of controls used for defining multilevel lists, click the Format button in the lower-left corner of the New Style dialog box and then select Numbering. You can modify an existing list style by right-clicking it and choosing Modify from the menu. Remember that a list style that you create doesn't become part of your List Library.

Book III
Chapter 3

Creating Lists

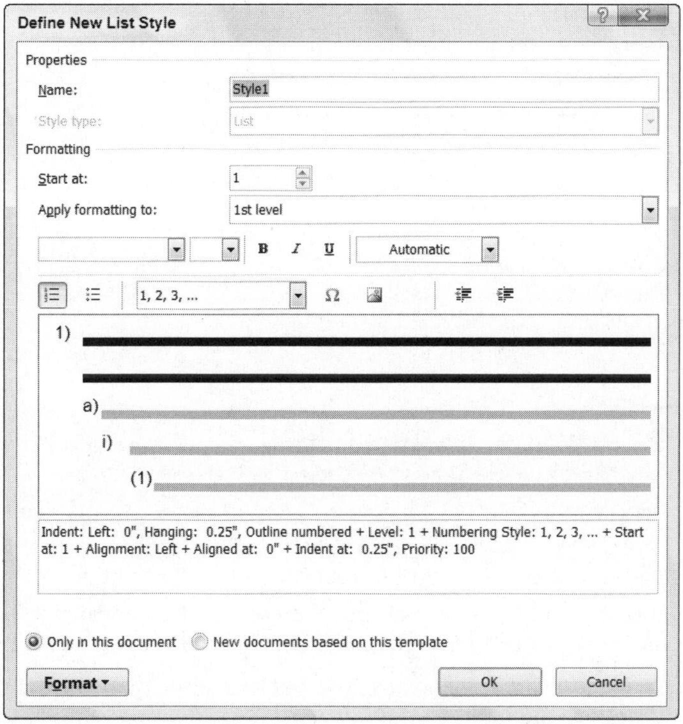

Figure 3-15:
The Define
New List
Style dialog
box.

Numbering your headings

If you want to add numbers to a document's headings, you can do so by creating a multilevel list that uses the standard heading styles. Then when you apply heading styles to your document's headings, the heading paragraphs number automatically according to the numbering scheme you created.

Here's the procedure for adding heading styles to a multilevel list:

1. Create the list by using the steps described previously in the section "Crafting your own multilevel list" but don't close the Define New Multilevel List dialog box.

If you prefer, you can add the heading for each level as you define it, but it's somewhat easier to separate the task of creating the numbering levels from associating them with the headings.

2. Click the More button to expand the dialog box to the version shown in Figure 3-16.

Try not to be scared. This is one of the most complex dialog boxes in all of Word, if not the universe.

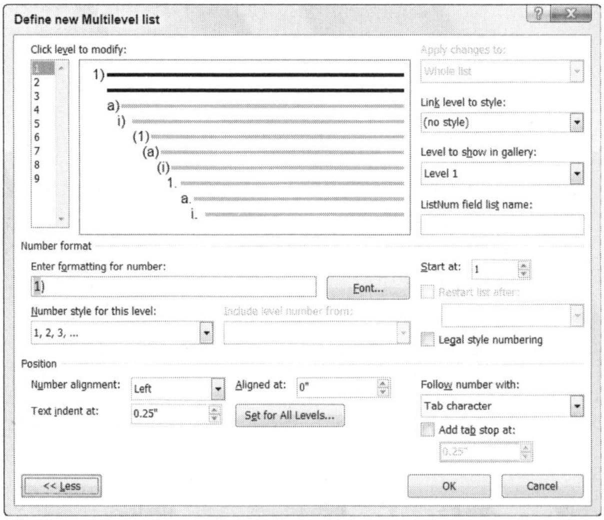

Figure 3-16:
The complete Define New Multilevel List dialog box.

3. Select a level of your list and then select the heading style you want to associate with it from the Link Level to Style drop-down list.

You can actually associate the level with any style, but the heading styles are the most commonly used.

4. Repeat for each level in your list.

You don't have to assign Heading 1 to level 1 and Heading 2 to level 2 and so on, but it sure makes the most sense.

5. **Adjust any other advanced settings you'd like to work with.**

   Actually, most of these have already been discussed and aren't that difficult. They're hidden from normal use because they aren't needed most of the time.

6. **Click OK.**

   The multilevel list now appears in your List Library, and the heading styles in your document have now been updated to use that numbering pattern. As you apply heading styles, Word automatically applies the number formatting.

   You can also change an existing list to use this formatting by selecting it from the List Library.

Heading numbering always applies to all the paragraphs in a document formatted with a given heading style. As a result, you can't selectively apply it to some heading paragraphs but not to others.

Using Fields to Create Sequence Numbers

Word's numbered lists are great when you have a series of consecutive paragraphs that need sequence numbers. But many documents have lists spread out through the entire document. For example, every chapter in this book has figures numbered consecutively starting with 1. Word's numbered list feature can't help you with this type of list.

Fortunately, Word's field codes feature has a special field called seq that's designed just for this purpose. I refer you ahead to Book VIII, Chapter 3, where you can find detailed information about this and other Word field codes.

Book IV

Inserting Bits and Pieces

The 5th Wave   By Rich Tennant

"I love the way Word justifies the text in my resume. Now if I can just get it to justify my asking salary."

Contents at a Glance

Chapter 1: Drawing Shapes on Your Document

In This Chapter

- ✔ Using the Word drawing tools
- ✔ Using predefined shapes
- ✔ Drawing polygons or curved lines
- ✔ Changing colors and line types
- ✔ Creating 3-D objects
- ✔ Flipping and rotating objects
- ✔ Understanding layers and groups
- ✔ Using advanced techniques

> *Chim-chiminey, chim-chiminey, chim-chim cheroo, I draws what I likes and I likes what I drew. . . .*

Art time! Get your crayons and glue and don an old paint shirt. You're going to cut out some simple shapes and paste them into your document so that people either think that you're a wonderful artist or scoff at you for not using clip art.

This chapter covers the drawing features of Word 2007. One of the best things about Word is its array of cool drawing tools. Once upon a time, Word had but rudimentary drawing tools — the equivalent of a box of crayons — but Word now has powerful drawing tools that are sufficient for all but the most sophisticated aspiring artist.

Some General Drawing Tips

Before getting into the specifics of using each Word drawing tool, in the following sections I describe a handful of general tips for drawing pictures.

Zoom in

When you work with the Word drawing tools, you might want to increase the zoom factor so that you can draw with greater precision. I often work at 200, 300, or even 400 or 500 percent when I'm drawing. To change the zoom factor, use the Zoom Slider located in the bottom-right corner of the screen.

Before you change the zoom factor to edit an object, select the object that you want to edit. This way, Word zooms in on that area of the page. If you don't select an object before you zoom in, you might need to scroll around to find the right location.

Save frequently

Drawing is tedious work. You don't want to spend two hours working on a particularly important drawing only to lose it all just because a comet strikes your building or an errant Scud lands in your backyard. You can prevent catastrophic loss from incidents such as these by pressing Ctrl+S or by frequently clicking the Save button as you work. And always wear protective eyewear.

Don't forget Ctrl+Z

In my opinion, Ctrl+Z — the ubiquitous Undo command — is the most important keyboard shortcut in any Windows program, and Word is no exception. Remember that you're never more than one keystroke away from erasing a boo-boo. If you do something silly, like forgetting to group a complex picture before trying to move it (see "Drawing a Complicated Picture," later in this chapter), you can always press Ctrl+Z to undo your last action. Ctrl+Z is my favorite and most frequently used Word key combination. (For left-handed mouse users, Alt+Backspace does the same thing.) And if you aren't ready to climb shrieking on a chair at the first sign of a mouse, try clicking the handy Undo button on the Quick Access toolbar.

Drawing Simple Objects

The basic element of every drawing is an *object*. To draw an object, first call up the Insert tab on the Ribbon. Then click the Shapes button to reveal the Shapes gallery, shown in Figure 1-1.

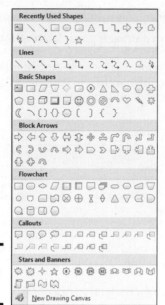

Figure 1-1:
The Shapes
gallery.

You find detailed instructions for drawing with the more important tools in the following sections. Before I get to that, though, I want to give you some pointers to keep in mind:

✦ **Choose a location:** Before you draw an object, move to the page on which you want to draw the object.

✦ **Fix your mistakes:** You can delete the object that you just drew by pressing the Delete key.

✦ **Hold down the Shift key:** If you hold down the Shift key while drawing a shape, Word forces the shape to be "regular." That is, rectangles are squares, ellipses are circles, and lines are either horizontal or vertical.

Drawing straight lines

You can use the Line button to draw straight lines on your pages. Here's the procedure:

1. **Click the Shapes button in the Shapes group of the Insert tab, then click the Line button.**

2. **Point the cursor to where you want the line to start.**

3. Click and drag the cursor to where you want the line to end.

4. Release the mouse button when you reach your destination.

After you've drawn the shape, the Ribbon displays the Drawing Tools tab, as shown in Figure 1-2. You can then use the controls in the Shape Styles group to change the fill, outline, and effects applied to the line.

Figure 1-2:
The
Drawing
Tools tab.

After you draw a line, you can adjust it by clicking it and then dragging the handles that appear on each end of the line.

Remember that you can force a line to be perfectly horizontal, vertical, or 45 degrees by holding down the Shift key while you draw. If you hold the Shift key and drag diagonally while you draw the line, the line will be constrained to perfect 45-degree angles.

Drawing rectangles, squares, ovals, and circles

To draw a rectangle, follow these steps:

1. On the Insert tab, click the Shapes button (in the Shapes group), and then click the Rectangle button.

2. Point the cursor so that one corner of the rectangle is positioned where you want the object to be.

3. Click and drag to where you want the opposite corner of the rectangle to be positioned.

4. Release the mouse button.

The steps for drawing an oval are the same as the steps for drawing a rectangle except that you click the Oval button rather than the Rectangle button. To draw a square or perfectly round circle, select the Rectangle button or the Oval button, respectively, but hold down the Shift key while you draw.

You can adjust the size or shape of a rectangle or circle by clicking it and dragging any of its love handles.

Creating Other Shapes

Rectangles and circles aren't the only two shapes that Word can draw automatically. The Shapes gallery includes many other types of shapes you can draw, such as pentagons, stars, and flowchart symbols. (To get to the Shapes gallery, click the Shapes button in the Shapes group of the Insert tab.)

The Shapes gallery organizes shapes into the following categories:

✦ **Recently Used Shapes:** The top section of the gallery lists the 24 shapes you've used most recently. The shapes found in this section change each time you draw a new shape. (When you first start to use Word, this section of the gallery is empty. But it fills up as you add shapes to your documents.)

✦ **Lines:** Straight lines, curved lines, lines with arrowheads, scribbly lines, and free-form shapes that can become polygons if you want. The free-form shape is useful enough to merit its own section, "Drawing a Polygon or Free-Form Shape," which immediately follows this section.

✦ **Basic Shapes:** Squares, rectangles, triangles, crosses, happy faces, lightning bolts, hearts, clouds, and more.

✦ **Block Arrows:** Fat arrows pointing in various directions.

✦ **Flowchart:** Various flowcharting symbols.

✦ **Callouts:** Text boxes and speech bubbles like those used in comic strips.

✦ **Stars and Banner:** Shapes that add sparkle to your presentations.

The following steps explain how to draw a shape:

1. **Click the More button in the Shapes group of the Insert tab.**

The Shapes gallery appears.

2. **Select the shape you want to insert.**

The shape is inserted, and the gallery disappears.

3. **Click the page where you want the shape to appear and then drag the shape to the desired size.**

Hold down the Shift key while drawing the Shape to create a regular shape.

When you release the mouse button, the Shape object takes on the current fill color and line style.

4. (Optional) Start typing if you want the shape to contain text.

After you've typed your text, you can use Word's formatting features to change its typeface, size, color, and so on.

In addition to the standard resizing handles, many shape buttons have an extra handle shaped like a yellow diamond; this handle enables you to adjust some aspect of the object's shape. For example, the block arrows have a handle that enables you to increase or decrease the size of the arrowhead. The location of these handles varies depending on the shape you're working with. Figure 1-3 shows how you can use these extra handles to vary the proportions and other aspects of six different shapes. For each of the six shapes, the first object shows how the shape is initially drawn; the other two objects drawn with each shape show how you can change the shape by dragging the extra handle.

Drawing a Polygon or Free-Form Shape

Mr. Arnold, my seventh-grade math teacher, taught me that a *polygon* is a shape that has many sides and has nothing to do with having more than one spouse (one is certainly enough for most people). Triangles, squares, and rectangles are polygons, but so are hexagons and pentagons, and any unusual shapes whose sides all consist of straight lines. Politicians are continually inventing new polygons when they revise the boundaries of congressional districts.

Figure 1-3:
Variations
on basic
shapes.

One of the most useful shapes in the Shapes gallery is the Freeform Shape tool. It's designed to create polygons, with a twist: Not all the sides have to be straight lines. The Freeform Shape tool lets you build a shape whose sides are a mixture of straight lines and free-form curves. Figure 1-4 shows three examples of shapes that I created with the Freeform Shape tool.

Follow these steps to create a polygon or free-form shape:

1. **Click the Shapes button in the Shapes group of the Insert tab to reveal the Shapes gallery, and then click the Freeform Shape tool (shown in the margin).**

This reveals the Shapes gallery, which was shown back in Figure 1-1.

2. **Click where you want to position the first corner of the object.**

3. **Click where you want to position the second corner of the object.**

4. **Keep clicking wherever you want to position a corner.**

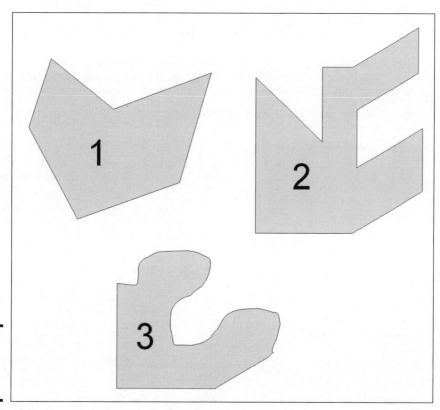

Figure 1-4:
Three free-form shapes.

5. **(Optional) To draw a free-form side on the shape, hold down the mouse button when you click a corner and then drag to draw the free-form shape. When you get to the end of the free-form side, release the mouse button.**

    You can then click again to add more corners. Shape 3 in Figure 1-6 has one free-form side.

6. **To finish the shape, click near the first corner — the one that you created in Step 3.**

    You don't have to be exact: If you click anywhere near the first corner that you put down, Word assumes that the shape is finished.

You're finished!

You can reshape a polygon or free-form shape by double-clicking it and then dragging any of the love handles that appear on the corners.

Flowcharting, 1970s style

I remember when I took my first computer programming class. The year was 1976. I had to buy a plastic template with flowcharting symbols cut into it so that I could learn how to draw proper flowcharts for my COBOL programs.

The 2007 edition of Microsoft Word has flowcharting symbols — a very good thing. Now I can throw away that old plastic template. You never know when you might need one of these symbols, just for old time's sake:

Card		Most modern computer users have never even seen one of these. They were considered old-fashioned 25 years ago.
Punched Tape		I used a computer that worked with punched tape once. The paper tape always broke, but I could easily mend it with Scotch tape.
Tape		Few PCs have reel-to-reel tape drives. But if you want to see one, tune into the SCI FI channel late at night.
Delay		Back in the 1970s, computers were so fast that sometimes you had to program in a delay so that the users wouldn't get spoiled.
Summing Junction		This popular TV series was a spin-off from *Petticoat Junction*.

If you hold down the Shift key while you draw a polygon, the sides are constrained to 45-degree angles. Shape 2 in Figure 1-5 was drawn in this manner. How about a constitutional amendment requiring Congress to use the Shift key when it redraws congressional boundaries?

You also can use the Freeform Shape tool to draw a multisegmented line, called an *open shape*. To draw an open shape, you can follow the steps in this section, except that you skip Step 6. Instead, double-click or press Esc when the line is done.

Drawing a Curved Line or Shape

Another useful tool is the Curve tool, which enables you to draw curved lines or shapes. Figure 1-5 shows several examples of curved lines and shapes drawn with the Curve tool.

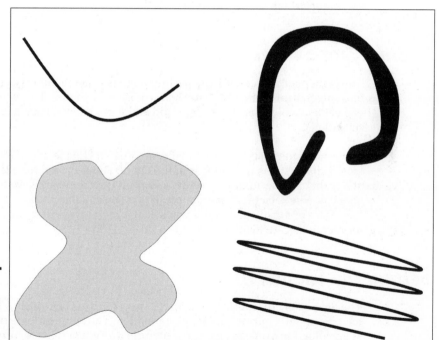

Figure 1-5:
Examples of curved lines and shapes.

Here is the procedure for drawing a curved line or shape:

1. **Click Shapes in the Shapes section of the Insert tab and then choose the Curve tool (shown in the margin).**

   You can find the Shapes gallery in the Shapes group on the Insert menu.

2. **Click where you want the curved line or shape to begin.**

3. **Click where you want the first turn in the curve to appear.**

   The straight line turns to a curved line, bent around the point where you clicked. As you move the mouse, the bend of the curve changes.

4. **Click to add turns to the curve.**

   Each time you click, you add a new bend to the line. Keep clicking until the line is as twisty as you want.

5. **To finish a line, double-click where you want the end of the curved line to appear. To create a closed shape, double-click over the starting point, which you created in Step 3.**

Styling Your Shapes

The center section of the Drawing Tools tab is called Shape Styles. This tab lets you control various stylistic features of your shapes. For example, you can set a fill color, set the outline, and add more effects, such as shadows or reflections.

You can set these styles individually, or you can choose one of the preselected shape styles that appear in the Shape Styles group. Note that the styles that appear in the Shape Styles group vary depending on the type of shape you've selected. For example, if you select a line, various predefined line styles are displayed. But if you select a rectangle, the styles appropriate for rectangles are displayed.

Setting the Shape Fill

The Shape Fill control (in the Shape Styles group of the Drawing Tools tab) enables you to control how shapes are filled. The simplest type of fill is a solid color. But you can also use a picture, a gradient fill, a texture, or a pattern to fill the shape. Figure 1-6 shows examples of these types of fills, and the following sections explain how to apply them.

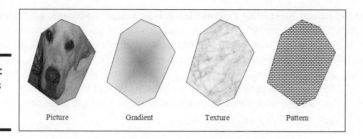

Figure 1-6:
Four types
of fill
effects.

Picture   Gradient   Texture   Pattern

Filling an object with a solid color

The easiest type of fill is a simple solid color. You can set a solid color by clicking the Shape Fill button and then choosing one of the colors that appears on the resulting menu. The Shape Fill menu includes two groups of colors:

✦ Colors that are a part of the current document theme

✦ Basic colors such as red, blue, yellow, and green

If you want to use a color that isn't visible on the menu, click More Fill Colors; clicking this option displays the Colors dialog box shown in Figure 1-7, which resembles a tie-dyed version of Chinese checkers. You can choose any color you want from this dialog box.

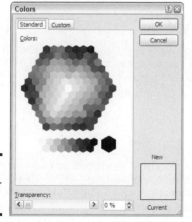

Figure 1-7:
Choose your
color.

The Standard tab of the Colors dialog box shown in Figure 1-8 shows 127 popular colors, plus white, black, and shades of gray. If you want to use a color that doesn't appear in the dialog box, click the Custom tab. This step summons the custom color controls, shown in Figure 1-8. Here, you can construct any of the 16 million colors theoretically possible with Word. You need a Ph.D. in physics to figure out how to adjust the Red, Green, and Blue controls, though. Play here if you want, but be careful. You can create some really ugly colors if you aren't careful.

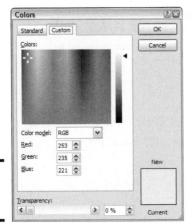

Figure 1-8:
Even more
colors!

Filling an object with a picture

If you choose Picture from the Shape Fill menu (click the Shape Fill button on the Drawing Tools tab on the Ribbon), the dialog box shown in Figure 1-9 appears. This dialog box allows you to select a picture to be used as a drawing object's fill. Just click the Select Picture button to bring up a dialog box that lets you rummage through your computer's hard drive to find a suitable picture.

Making the gradient

A *gradient fill* is a fill effect that smoothly blends two or more colors. Gradient effects can be subtle or bold, depending on how similar the blended colors are. For example, if you blend a bright shade of yellow into a not-so-bright shade of yellow, the effect is subtle. But if you blend a bright shade of yellow into a bright shade of red, the effect is bold.

Figure 1-9:
Filling an
object with
a picture.

To apply a gradient fill, click the Shape Fill button and choose Gradient. This reveals a gallery of gradient options, as shown in Figure 1-10. Then you can select the gradient you want to use.

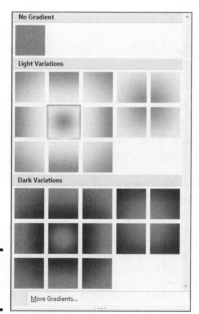

Figure 1-10:
Creating a
gradient fill.

**Book IV
Chapter 1**

**Drawing Shapes on
Your Document**

If none of the gradient fills in the gallery suits your fancy, you can create a custom gradient fill by clicking More Gradients. This action summons the dialog box shown in Figure 1-11. You can then customize the gradient fill to your liking. As you can see, you can choose single- or two-color gradients, and you can control the amount of transparency and the direction of the gradient.

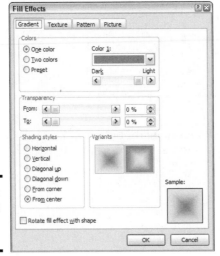

Figure 1-11:
Customizing a gradient fill.

Applying a texture

A *texture* is a photo-quality bitmap image designed so that it can be repeated throughout without any noticeable tiling. Textures let you create objects that look like they're made of wood, stone, parchment, and so on.

To apply a texture, click the Shape Fill button and choose Texture. The gallery is revealed, as shown in Figure 1-12. Here you can choose one of several textures to give your illustration a polished Formica look.

For more texture choices, click the More Textures option at the bottom of the gallery. This brings up the dialog box shown in Figure 1-13. Here you can choose one of the textures provided with Word, or you can click the Other Texture button to bring up a dialog box that lets you open an image file of your own to use as a texture.

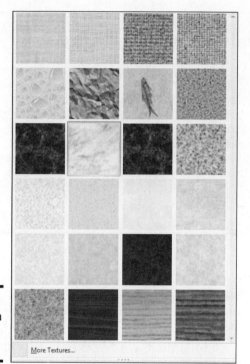

Figure 1-12:
The Formica gallery (just kidding).

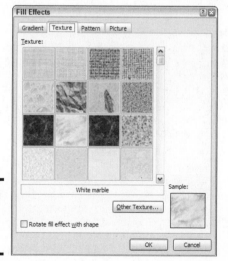

Figure 1-13:
Choosing a custom texture.

The problem with patterns

My only beef with Word's pattern fill feature is that you can't control the scale of the pattern. No matter how large or small the object being filled, the pattern always remains the same size. And, in general, the patterns are too small. In fact, the brick pattern is so small that when you print it, you almost have to use a magnifying glass to see the individual bricks.

What's even weirder is that the patterns all display the same size on-screen regardless of the zoom factor. For example, if you draw a 1-inch rectangle and fill it with bricks, each row of bricks has about 12 bricks in it. If you zoom in to 200 percent, the bricks don't get bigger. Instead, each row now has 24 bricks. Likewise, if you zoom down to 50 percent, each row now has 6 bricks. When I print the rectangle on my HP psc750 printer, each row has 18 bricks!

Using a pattern

If you choose Pattern from the Shape Fill menu, you can select a pattern from the dialog box shown in Figure 1-14. This dialog box lists 48 different patterns and lets you specify your choice of foreground and background colors.

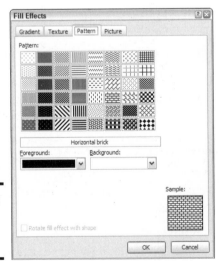

Figure 1-14: Filling an object with a pattern.

My personal favorites are the patterns that resemble bricks and cobblestones.

Note: You can change the background and foreground colors used to draw the pattern. You can create a nice brick pattern by setting the foreground color to a light gray and the background color to a deep red.

Setting the Shape Outline

The Shape Outline control (on the Drawing Tools Format tab) enables you to change the style of line objects or the border for solid shape objects. You can change the following settings for the outline:

+ **Color:** Sets the color used for the outline.

+ **Weight:** Sets the thickness of the line.

+ **Dashes:** The dashing pattern used for the lines that outline the object. The default uses a solid line, but different patterns are available to create dashed lines.

+ **Arrows:** Lines can have an arrowhead at either or both ends. Arrowheads are used mostly on line and arc objects.

+ **Pattern:** The outline of an object can use a pattern in the same way that the fill can have a pattern. Using a pattern for the outline lets you create interesting types of dashed lines.

Applying a Shadow

To apply a shadow effect to an object, select the object and use the buttons that appear in the Shadow Effects group of the Drawing Tools tab on the Ribbon. These buttons, listed in Table 1-1, let you turn the shadow on or off and nudge the shadow left, right, up, or down. You might have to click the nudge buttons several times to create the shadow effect you want.

Table 1-1	Buttons in the Shadow Effects Group	
Drawing Tool	*What It's Called*	*What It Does*
	Shadow On/Off	Turns the object's shadow on or off
	Nudge Shadow Up	Moves the shadow up a bit

(continued)

Table 1-1 *(continued)*

Drawing Tool	What It's Called	What It Does
	Nudge Shadow Down	Moves the shadow down a bit
	Nudge Shadow Left	Moves the shadow left a bit
	Nudge Shadow Right	Moves the shadow right a bit

You can also apply a predefined shadow type by clicking the Shadow Effects button in the Shadow Effects group. Clicking the button displays the gallery shown in Figure 1-15. As you can see, this gallery includes various types of perspective shadows. In addition, it includes a Shadow Color button, which lets you change the shadow's color.

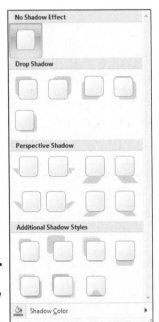

Figure 1-15:
The Shadow gallery.

Adding 3-D Effects

The 3-D controls are among the coolest buttons you can find anywhere on the Ribbon. These buttons let you transform dull and lifeless flat objects into exciting, breathtaking three-dimensional objects. Figure 1-16 shows how you can use the 3-D controls to transform several shapes into 3-D objects. In each case, the object on the left is a simple shape, and the three objects to the right of the simple shape are three-dimensional versions of the same shape.

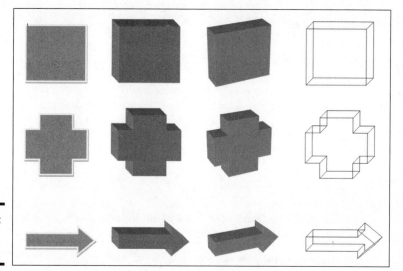

Figure 1-16: 3-D effects are cool.

To apply a 3-D effect to a shape, first create the shape as I describe earlier in this chapter. Then select the shape and click the 3-D Effects button in the 3-D Effects group of the Drawing Tools Format tab. This reveals a gallery of 3-D effect choices, as shown in Figure 1-17.

Book IV Chapter 1

Drawing Shapes on Your Document

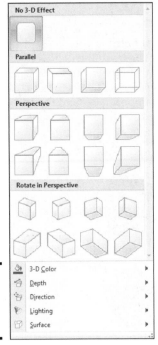

Figure 1-17:
The 3-D
Effects
gallery.

Besides the predefined 3-D effects listed in the gallery, you can also call up the following additional menus:

+ **Color:** Lets you set the color used for the 3-D effect

+ **Depth:** Lets you set the depth of the 3-D effect

+ **Direction:** Lets you set the direction used to create the 3-D effect

+ **Lighting:** Lets you move the light-source used to illuminate the 3-D object

+ **Surface:** Lets you choose one of several effects used to render the 3-D surfaces

The Drawing Tools Format tab also includes several buttons that let you tweak the 3-D effect after you've applied it. Table 1-2 lists these buttons.

Table 1-2	Buttons on the 3-D Effects Group	
Drawing Tool	*What It's Called*	*What It Does*
▓/▪	3-D On/Off	Turns the 3-D feature on or off

Drawing Tool	What It's Called	What It Does
	Tilt Left	Rotates the object left
	Tilt Right	Rotates the object right
	Tilt Up	Rotates the object up
	Tilt Down	Rotates the object down

Flipping and Rotating Objects

To *flip* an object means to create a mirror image of it. To *rotate* an object means to turn it from its center. Word lets you flip objects horizontally or vertically, rotate objects in 90-degree increments, or freely rotate an object to any angle.

Rotation works for text boxes and Shape text. Thus, you can use rotation to create vertical text or text skewed to any angle you want. However, flipping an object doesn't affect the object's text.

Flipping an object

Word enables you to flip an object vertically or horizontally to create a mirror image of the object. To flip an object, follow these steps:

1. **Choose the object that you want to flip.**

2. **On the Drawing Tools Format tab, click the Rotate button in the Arrange group, and then choose Flip Horizontal or Flip Vertical.**

Rotating an object 90 degrees

You can rotate an object in 90-degree increments by following these steps:

1. **Choose the object that you want to rotate.**

2. **On the Drawing Tools Format tab, click the Rotate button in the Arrange group, and then choose Rotate Right or Rotate Left.**

3. **To rotate the object 180 degrees, click the appropriate Rotate button again.**

Using the rotate handle

Remember how all the bad guys' hideouts were slanted in the old *Batman* TV show? The rotate handle lets you give your drawings that same kind of slant. With the rotate handle, you can rotate an object to any arbitrary angle just by dragging it with the mouse.

The rotate handle is the green handle that appears above the object, connected to the object by a line, as shown in Figure 1-18. You can rotate an object to any angle simply by dragging the rotate handle either clockwise or counterclockwise.

Figure 1-18:
The rotate handle lets you rotate an object to any arbitrary angle.

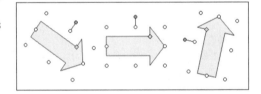

The following steps show you how to use the rotate handle:

1. **Click the object that you want to rotate.**

2. **Drag the rotate handle in the direction that you want to rotate the object.**

   As you drag, an outline of the object rotates around. When you get the object's outline to the angle you want, release the mouse button, and the object is redrawn at the new angle.

To restrict the rotation angle to 15-degree increments, hold the Shift key while dragging around the rotation handle.

Drawing a Complicated Picture

When you add more than one object to a page, you might run into several problems. What happens when the objects overlap? How do you line up objects so that they don't look like they were thrown at the page from a moving car? And how do you keep together objects that belong together?

This section shows you how to use Word features to handle overlapped objects and how to align and group objects. If you're interested in a description of how to use these features together to draw a picture, check out the sidebar titled "Don't let me tell you how I drew that funny face!" at the end of this chapter.

Changing layers

Whenever you have more than one object on a page, the potential exists for objects to overlap one another. Like most drawing programs, Word handles this problem by *layering* objects like a stack of plates. The first object that you draw is at the bottom of the stack, the second object is on top of the first, the third is atop the second, and so on. If two objects overlap, the one that's at the highest layer wins; objects below it are partially covered. So far, so good — but what if you don't remember to draw the objects in the correct order? What if you draw a shape that you want to tuck behind a shape that you've already drawn, or what if you want to bring an existing shape to the top of the pecking order? No problem. Word enables you to change the stacking order by moving objects toward the front or back so that they overlap just the way you want.

Word's layers aren't nearly as powerful as layers in programs like Adobe Illustrator or AutoCAD. All they really do is set the stacking order when objects are placed on top of one another.

The Drawing Tools tab provides two controls that let you move an object forward or backward in the layer order:

✦ **Bring to Front:** Brings the chosen object to the top of the stack. Note that this button has a down arrow next to it. If you click this down arrow, you reveal a menu with two commands: Bring to Front and Bring Forward. The Bring Forward command moves the object just one step closer to the top of the heap.

✦ **Send to Back:** Sends the chosen object to the back of the stack. Again, this button has a down arrow next to it. You can click this down arrow to access the Send Backward command, which sends the object one level down in the layer order.

Layering problems are most obvious when objects have a fill color. If an object has no fill color, objects behind it are allowed to show through. In such cases, the layering doesn't affect the appearance of the final drawing much, because the lack of fill allows all of the objects to be visible.

To bring an object to the top of another, you might have to use the Bring Forward command several times. The reason is that even though the two objects appear to be adjacent, other objects might occupy the layers between them.

Line 'em up

Nothing looks more amateur than objects dropped randomly on a page with no apparent concern for how they line up with each other. The Drawing Tools tab includes an Align button that brings up a menu with the following commands:

+ Align Left
+ Align Center
+ Align Right
+ Align Top
+ Align Middle
+ Align Bottom
+ Distribute Horizontally
+ Distribute Vertically

The first three commands align items horizontally; the next three align items vertically. The last two commands distribute the objects evenly either horizontally or vertically. Select the items that you want to distribute, click the Draw button, choose Align or Distribute, and then choose Distribute Horizontally or Distribute Vertically.

Using the grids and guides

To help you create well-ordered pages, Word lets you display a grid of evenly spaced lines over the page. These lines aren't actually a part of the page, so your audience won't see them when you give your presentation. They exist simply to make the task of lining things up a bit easier.

To display the grid or change its size, click the Align button on the Drawing Tools tab and then choose Grid Settings. The Drawing Grid dialog box, shown in Figure 1-19, is summoned.

To activate the grid, select the Snap Objects to Grid check box and then adjust the grid spacing to your satisfaction. If you want to actually see the grid on the screen, select the Display Gridlines on Screen check box.

Group therapy

A *group* is a collection of objects that Word treats as though it were one object. Using groups properly is one key to putting simple shapes together to make complex pictures without becoming so frustrated that you have to join a therapy group. ("Hello, my name is Doug, and Word drives me crazy.")

Figure 1-19:
The
Drawing
Grid dialog
box.

To create a group, follow these steps:

***1.* Choose all objects that you want to include in the group.**

Hold down the Shift key and click each of the items, or hold down the mouse button and drag the resulting rectangle around all the items you want to select.

***2.* Right-click one of the selected objects and then choose Group⇨Group from the menu that appears.**

You can also find the Group command in the Drawing Tools tab, but it's much easier to find by right-clicking.

To take a group apart so that Word treats the objects as individuals again, follow these steps:

***1.* Right-click the group you want to break up.**

***2.* Choose Group⇨Ungroup.**

If you create a group and then ungroup it so that you can work on its elements individually, you can easily regroup the objects. These steps show you how:

***1.* Right-click one of the objects that was in the original group.**

***2.* Choose Group⇨Regroup.**

Word remembers which objects were in the group and automatically includes them.

**Book IV
Chapter 1**

**Drawing Shapes on
Your Document**

Word enables you to create groups of groups. This capability is useful for complex pictures because it enables you to work on one part of the picture, group it, and then work on the next part of the picture without worrying about accidentally disturbing the part that you've already grouped. After you have several such groups, select them and group them. You can create groups of groups of groups and so on, *ad nauseam*.

Don't let me tell you how I drew that funny face!

In case you're interested, you can follow the bouncing ball to see how I created the goofy face that appears in a few figures in this chapter. By studying this creature, you can get an idea of how you use layers, groups, and alignment to create complicated pictures, as shown in these steps:

1. **Draw the face shape by using the Oval tool.**

   I filled the face with pale yellow.

2. **Draw the eyes by using the Oval tool.**

   To draw the eyes, I started by using the Oval tool to draw an oval for the left eye, which I filled with white. Next, I pressed Ctrl+D to make a duplicate of the oval. Then I dragged the duplicate eye to the right side of the face. Next, I used the Oval tool again to draw a little pupil inside the left eye, which I filled with black. I then duplicated the pupil and dragged the duplicate over to the right eye. Finally, I used the Curve Shape tool to draw the eyebrows.

3. **Draw the ears by using the Oval tool.**

   The only trick with the ears is using the Send to Back command (in the Arrange group) to send the ears behind the face where they belong.

4. **Draw the nose by using the Oval tool.**

   The nose is actually two ovals. The first is the center part of the nose: It's a tall but narrow oval. The other oval forms the nostrils, which are almost round. I used the Send Backward command on the nostrils to place them behind the first oval.

5. **Draw the mouth by using the Curve Shape tool.**

6. **Draw the body by using the Freeform Shape tool.**

   When the body was drawn, I used Send to Back to send it behind the face. Then, I used a pattern as the fill for the body to create a lovely striped shirt.

Oh, I almost forgot. The last step is to choose all the objects that make up the face (by dragging and clicking a dotted-line square around the entire picture) and group them by using the Group button, found in the Arrange section of the Drawing Tools Format tab. That way, I don't have to worry about accidentally dismembering my little friend.

Chapter 2: Inserting Pictures and Clip Art

In This Chapter

✔ Using free pictures

✔ Finding a picture you like

✔ Moving, sizing, cropping, and stretching pictures

✔ Adding special effects such as borders, shadows, and reflections

✔ Wrapping text around your pictures

✔ More!

Face it: Most of us weren't born with even an ounce of artistic ability. Some day (soon, I hope), the genetic researchers combing through the billions and billions of genes strung out on those twisty DNA helixes will discover the Artist Gene. Then, in spite of protests from the da Vincis, Van Goghs, and Monets among us (who fear that their NEA grants will be threatened), doctors will splice the little gene into our DNA strands so that we can all be artists. Of course, this procedure won't be without its side effects: Some will develop an insatiable craving for croissants, and others will inexplicably develop French accents and whack off their ears. But artists we shall be.

Until then, we have to rely on clip art, pictures we've found on the Internet, or pictures that we scanned into the computer with a scanner or took with a digital camera.

Exploring the Many Types of Pictures

The world is awash with many different picture file formats. Fortunately, Word works with almost all these formats. The following sections describe the two basic types of pictures that you can work with in Word: bitmap pictures and vector drawings.

Bitmap pictures

A *bitmap picture* is a collection of small dots that compose an image. Bitmap pictures are most often used for photographs and for icons and other buttons used on Web pages. You can create your own bitmap pictures with a scanner, a digital camera, or a picture-drawing program such as Adobe Photoshop. You can even create crude bitmap pictures with Microsoft Paint, which is the free painting program that comes with Windows.

The dots that make up a bitmap picture are called *pixels.* The number of pixels in a given picture depends on two factors: the picture's resolution and its size. *Resolution* refers to the number of pixels per inch, measured in *dpi* (for *dots per inch*). Most computer monitors (and projectors) display 72 dpi in their standard resolution. At this resolution, a 1-inch square picture requires 5,184 pixels (72 x 72). Photographs that will be printed on an inkjet or laser printer usually have a much higher resolution, usually at least 300 pixels per inch or more. At 300 dpi, a 4-x-6-inch photograph requires more than 2 million pixels.

The amount of color information stored for the picture — also referred to as the picture's *color depth* — affects how many bytes of computer memory the picture requires. The color depth determines how many different colors the picture can contain. Most pictures have one of two color depths: 256 colors or 16.7 million colors. Most simple charts, diagrams, cartoons, and other types of clip art look fine with 256 colors. Photographs usually use 16.7 million colors.

Pictures with 16.7 million colors are also known as *True Color* pictures or *24-bit color* pictures. There's also a 32-bit color version of True Color, but the additional bits aren't used for extra color. Instead, the extra 8 bits are called the *alpha channel* and are used for other purposes, such as transparency control.

A typical 4-x-6-inch photograph, which has more than 2 million pixels at 300 dpi, requires about 2MB to store with 256 colors. With True Color, the size of this typical picture jumps to a whopping 6.4MB. Fortunately, bitmap pictures can be compressed to reduce their size without noticeably distorting the image. Depending on the actual contents of the picture, a 6MB picture might be reduced to 250KB or less.

Bitmap picture files usually have filename extensions such as `.bmp`, `.gif`, `.jpg`, `.png`, or `.pcx`. Table 2-1 lists the bitmap file formats that Word supports.

If you have a choice in the matter, I recommend you use JPEG format images for photographs that you want to include in Word documents because JPEG's built-in compression saves hard drive space. (The JPEG compression method looses some detail in the image, but the loss of detail isn't usually apparent.)

Table 2-1	Word's Bitmap Picture File Formats
Format	*What It Is*
BMP	Garden variety Windows bitmap file, used by Windows Paint and many other programs
GIF	Graphics Interchange Format, a format commonly used for small Internet pictures
JPEG	JPEG, a common format for photographs that includes built-in compression. JPEG images sometimes use the extension JPG instead of JPEG, and there are variants of this format that use the extensions JFEF, and JPE
PCD	Kodak Photo CD format
PCT	Macintosh PICT files
PCX	A variant type of bitmap file
PNG	Portable Network Graphics file, an image format designed for Internet graphics
TGA	Targa files
TIFF	Tagged Image Format file, another bitmap program most often used for high-quality photographs

Victor, give me a vector

Besides bitmap pictures, you can also use vector drawings in Word. A *vector drawing* is a picture file that contains a detailed definition of each shape that makes up the image. Vector drawings are usually created with high-powered drawing programs such as Adobe Illustrator.

Word supports all the most popular vector drawing formats, as described in Table 2-2.

Table 2-2	Word's Vector File Formats
Format	*What It Is*
CDR	Format for CorelDRAW, a popular, upper-crust drawing program
CGM	Computer Graphics Metafiles
DRW	Format for Micrografx Designer or Micrografx Draw, two popular ooh-aah drawing programs
EMF	An Enhanced Windows MetaFile picture
EPS	Encapsulated PostScript, a format used by some high-end drawing programs
WMF	Windows MetaFile, a format that many programs recognize
WPG	A WordPerfect drawing

Using Clip Art

Whether you buy Word by itself or get it as part of Microsoft Office, you also get a collection of thousands of pictures, sound clips, and motion clips that you can pop directly into your documents.

Word lets you access clip art through a special Clip Art task pane, where you can search for clip art by keyword. The Clip Art task pane makes finding just the right picture to embellish your document easy.

The first time you access the clip art, a dialog box appears, offering to search your entire hard drive and create a catalog of all the pictures it contains. I suggest that you accept this offer so that you can use the Clip Art task pane to access your own picture files in addition to the clip art files that come with Word.

Be prepared to spend a few minutes waiting for this initial search to finish. This would be a good time to take a walk.

If you don't like the pictures that come with Word, you can scour the Internet for pictures to use. Beware, though, that copyright restrictions usually apply to pictures you find on the Internet. You can't legally point your browser to an Internet site, download any old picture, and use it in your documents without permission from the picture's copyright owner. For more information about finding clip art pictures on the Internet, see the section "Getting clip art from the Internet," later in this chapter.

Inserting Pictures

The following sections show you how to insert clip art and other pictures into your documents.

Inserting clip art

The following steps explain how to drop clip art into your document:

1. **Move to the page on which you want to plaster the clip art.**

2. **Click the Insert tab on the Ribbon, then click the Clip Art button in the Illustrations group.**

   After a brief moment's hesitation, the Clip Art task pane pops up in all its splendor, as shown in Figure 2-1.

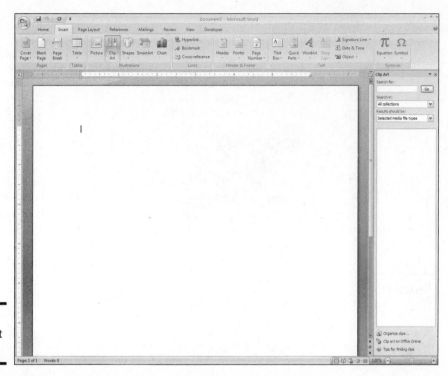

Figure 2-1:
The Clip Art
task pane.

3. **Type a keyword in the Search Text box and then click the Search button.**

For example, to search for pictures of animals, type **animal** in the Search text box and then click Search. Word then searches through the Clip Organizer to locate clip art that depicts animals, and then it displays thumbnails of the pictures it finds in the Clip Art task pane.

4. **Click the picture that you want to use.**

The picture is inserted on the current page, as shown in Figure 2-2. Notice that a special Ribbon Format tab with tools for working with pictures has appeared. This Format tab appears whenever you select a picture object.

5. **If you're finished inserting pictures, click the Clip Art task pane's Close button (the X in the upper-right corner of the task pane).**

The task pane vanishes.

You probably want to move the picture and change its size. To find out how, see the section "Sizing and stretching a picture," later in this chapter.

Book IV Chapter 2

Inserting Pictures
and Clip Art

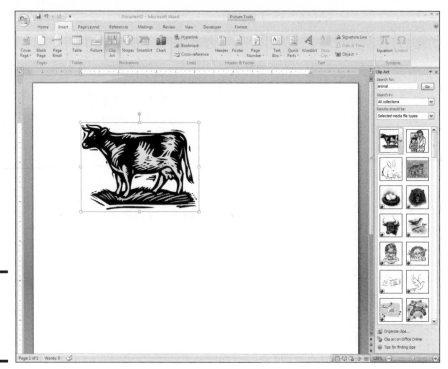

Figure 2-2:
Word
inserts the
picture on
the page.

If you find a clip art picture you like, you can find other pictures that are drawn in a similar style by right-clicking the picture in the Clip Art task pane (or by clicking the down arrow on the right side of the picture) and then choosing Find Similar Style.

Getting clip art from the Internet

As if the vast collection of clip art that comes with Office and Word isn't enough, Microsoft also maintains a clip art library on the Internet that you can use. Assuming you have a working Internet connection, you can access this additional clip art library by clicking the Clip Art on Office Online link at the bottom of the Clip Art task pane. A separate Internet Explorer window opens, which you can then use to search for additional clip art images. See Figure 2-3.

If you find a clip art image that you want, you can mark it for later download. Then, after you've found all the images you want to download, you can choose an option to download the images directly into Clip Organizer. You can then call up the images by using the Clip Art task pane as described earlier in this chapter, in the section "Using Clip Art."

Figure 2-3:
Getting clip
art from the
Internet.

Inserting a Picture from a File

If you happen to already have an image file on your computer that you want to insert into a document, Word lets you insert the file. These steps show you how:

1. **Move to the page on which you want to splash a picture.**

2. **Open the Insert tab on the Ribbon and then click the Picture button in the Illustrations group.**

This summons the Insert Picture dialog box, shown in Figure 2-4.

3. **Dig through the bottom of your hard drive until you find the file that you want.**

The picture you want might be anywhere. Fortunately, the Insert Picture dialog box has all the controls you need to search high and low until you find the file. Just click the icons at the left side of the box or click the Look In text box, and you're halfway there.

4. **Click the file and then click Insert.**

You're done! Figure 2-5 shows how a picture appears when it has been inserted on a page.

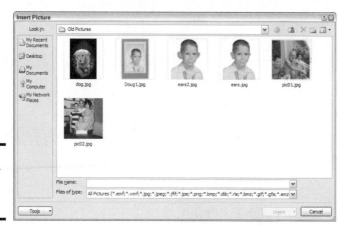

Figure 2-4:
The Insert
Picture
dialog box.

As you can see in Figure 2-5, Word scales your pictures so they fill as much
of the page as possible. You need to resize the picture if you want it to be
smaller. Just select the picture and then drag one of the size handles in the
corner of the picture.

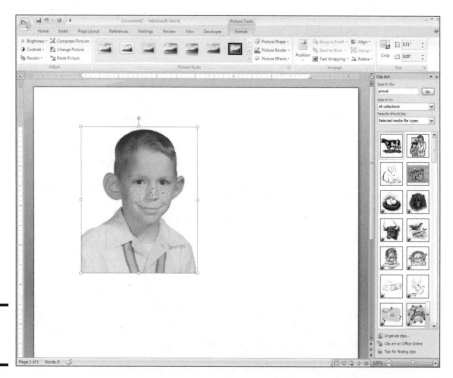

Figure 2-5:
Check out
that smile.

You also can paste a picture directly into Word by way of the Clipboard. Anything that you can copy to the Clipboard you can paste into Word. For example, you can doodle a sketch in Paintbrush, copy it, and then zap over to Word and paste it. Voilà — instant picture!

Playing with Your Pictures

After you get a picture into Word, you'll have an irresistible urge to play with it. You'll want to make it bigger, make it smaller, make it taller, make it skinnier, move it here, move it there, make it brighter, make it darker, and so on. With luck, you'll be able to play with the picture the entire afternoon, and everyone will think you're working really hard.

Sizing and stretching a picture

In most cases, you need to resize your picture after you insert it. To do so, click the picture to select it. Notice the eight handles that appear around the picture. You can drag any or all of these handles to resize the picture. When you click one of the corner handles, the proportion of the picture stays the same as you change its size. When you drag one of the edge handles (top, bottom, left, or right) to change the size of the picture in just one dimension, you distort the picture's outlook as you go.

Stretching a picture by dragging one of the edge handles can dramatically change the picture's appearance. For example, you can stretch an object vertically to make it look tall and thin or horizontally to make it look short and fat. I usually like to stretch pictures of myself vertically.

Cropping a picture

Sometimes, you want to cut off the edges of a picture so that you can include just part of the picture in your document. For example, you might have a picture of two people, only one of whom you like. You can use Word's cropping feature to cut off the other person.

To crop a picture, select the picture and click the Crop button located near the right side of the Format tab on the Ribbon, in the Size group. The selection handles change to special crop marks. You can then drag the crop marks around to cut off part of the picture. When you're satisfied, just click outside of the picture.

If you decide later that you don't like the cropping, you can right-click the picture and choose Format Picture from the menu that appears. Then click the Reset button.

Applying a picture border

You can apply a border to a picture by choosing the Picture Border button in the Picture Styles group on the Format tab. This action reveals the Picture Border menu, which lets you choose the border color, weight (the width of the border lines), and the pattern of dashes you want to use.

Adding Style to Your Pictures

Word enables you to draw attention to your pictures by adding stylistic features such as borders, shadows, and reflections. Figure 2-6 shows a page with several copies of a picture, each with a different style applied.

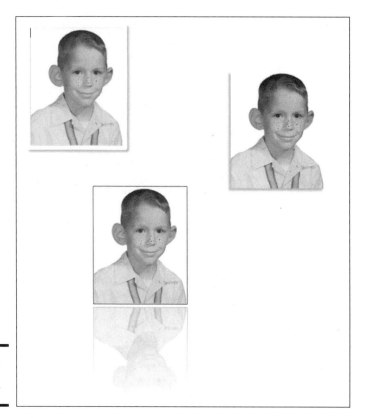

Figure 2-6:
Pictures
with style.

To add a style effect to a picture, select the picture. Word automatically selects the Drawing Tools Format tab on the Ribbon. Then simply select the picture style you want to apply.

Word comes with 28 predefined picture styles, shown in the gallery in Figure 2-7. You can summon this gallery by clicking the More button that appears to the right of the style buttons in the Drawing Tools Format tab. Each of these styles is simply a combination of three types of formatting you can apply to pictures: Shape, Border, and Effects. If you want, you can apply these formats individually as described in the following sections.

Figure 2-7:
The Picture
Style
gallery.

Applying a Picture Shape

A *picture shape* is a shape that is used to crop a picture. For example, if you choose a circle as the shape, the picture will be cropped to a circle. Figure 2-8 shows six pictures of my dog with various shapes applied to it.

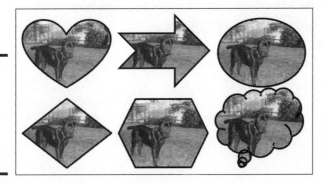

Figure 2-8:
Pictures
with
different
types of
shapes
applied.

To apply a shape to a picture, follow these steps:

1. **Select the picture you want to apply the shape to. Then select the Picture Tools Format tab if it isn't automatically selected.**

2. **Click the Picture Shape button in the Picture Styles group.**

This summons the Picture Shape gallery, as shown in Figure 2-9.

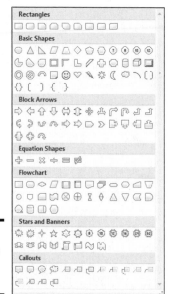

Figure 2-9:
The Picture
Shape
gallery.

3. **Click the shape you want to apply to the picture.**

The picture is cropped by the shape you select, and the Gallery disappears.

4. **If the shape has a yellow adjustment handle, drag it to adjust the shape.**

Many of the shapes have handles that let you adjust one or more aspects of the shape. If the shape you selected has one or more of these handles, you can further refine your picture by dragging the handle until you're satisfied with the result.

Applying Picture Effects

The Picture Effects button in the Picture Styles group of the Format tab lets you apply several interesting types of effects to your pictures. When you click this button, a menu with the following effect options is displayed:

✦ **Shadow:** Applies a shadow to the picture. You can select one of several pre-defined shadow effects or call up a dialog box that lets you customize the shadow.

✦ **Reflection:** Creates a reflected image of the picture beneath the original picture.

✦ **Glow:** Adds a glowing effect around the edges of the picture.

✦ **Soft Edges:** Softens the edges of the picture.

✦ **3-D Rotation:** Rotates the picture in a way that creates a three-dimensional effect.

The best way to figure out how to use these effects is to experiment with them to see how they work.

Adjusting the Color and Such

The Picture Tools group on the Format tab includes several additional controls that let you manipulate pictures in fun ways:

✦ **Brightness:** Lets you change the image brightness.

✦ **Contrast:** Lets you change the image contrast.

✦ **Recolor:** Changes the color tone of the picture. You can also use this control to set a transparent background color for the image.

✦ **Compress Pictures:** Instructs Word to compress the images so that they take up less disk space. In most cases, this doesn't noticeably diminish the quality of the pictures.

✦ **Change Picture:** Lets you pick a different picture.

✦ **Reset Picture:** Removes any formatting you've applied to the picture, including sizing, cropping, shapes, borders, effects, colorizations, and so on.

Wrapping Text Around Your Picture

When you first insert a picture, Word places it in line with the text, just like the figures in this book. Any text that appears before or after the picture is lined up with the bottom of the picture; no text appears alongside the picture. For example, have a look at the text in the top half of Figure 2-10. Here, I inserted the picture of a cute little kid right before the first word of the paragraph.

In many cases, you want the text to wrap around the picture. The text in the bottom half of Figure 2-10 shows one way to do this. *Tight wrapping* causes the text to hug as close to the picture as possible. To switch to tight wrapping, select the picture, click the Text Wrapping button in the Arrange group on the Format tab, and choose Tight from the menu that appears.

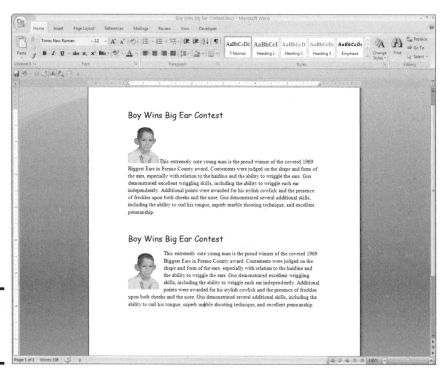

Figure 2-10: Wrapping text around a picture.

The Text Wrapping button includes several options:

✦ **In Line with Text:** The default wrapping option, and the one you're least likely to use. It places the picture inline with your text. The height of the line on which the picture appears is adjusted to match the height of the picture. In most cases, this wrapping doesn't look right.

✦ **Square:** Wraps the text squarely around the picture.

✦ **Tight:** Word figures out where the actual edges of the picture are and snuggles the text up as closely as possible.

✦ **Behind Text:** This option allows the text to spill right over the top of the picture, as if the picture weren't even there. The picture appears behind the text.

✦ **In Front of Text:** This option places the picture on top of the text. The picture might obscure some of the text, so use this option only if that's what you want.

✦ **Top and Bottom:** This option places text above and below the picture, but doesn't allow any text to appear beside the picture.

✦ **Through:** This option is kind of like the Tight option, but it results in an even tighter fit. If Word finds any blank spaces within the picture, it fills the space with text.

✦ **Edit Wrap Points:** This option lets you design your own wrapping shape around your picture by dragging little handles on a wrapping outline.

When you choose Tight wrapping (or any other type of wrapping besides In Line with Text), the picture becomes a free-floating object and is no longer tied to a specific position within the text. You can drag the picture around to any location you want. You can even put it right in the middle of a paragraph, and Word wraps the text around both sides. See Figure 2-11 for an example. Here, I set the wrapping style to Tight, and then I dragged the picture to the middle of the paragraph.

Figure 2-11:
Plopping a
picture into
the middle
of a
paragraph.

Boy Wins Big Ear Contest

This extremely cute young man Biggest Ears in Fresno County shape and form of the ears, and the ability to wriggle the wriggling skills, including the independently. Additional cowlick and the presence of nose. Gus demonstrated is the proud winner of the coveted 1969 award. Contestants were judged on the especially with relation to the hairline ears. Gus demonstrated excellent ability to wriggle each ear points were awarded for his stylish freckles upon both cheeks and the several additional skills, including the ability to curl his tongue, superb marble shooting technique, and excellent penmanship.

One other thing you need to know about how pictures work in Word is the idea of *anchors*. An anchor is a location in the document's text that is associated with the picture. By default, pictures move with text based on their anchors. For example, if you insert a picture and then back up a bit and type some additional text before the picture, the picture moves with the text. If that's not what you want, right-click the picture and choose Text Wrapping➪Advanced Layout Options. Then, deselect the Move With Text option on the Picture Position tab of the Advanced Layout dialog box that appears.

Chapter 3: Creating Charts and Diagrams

In This Chapter

✔ Adding a chart to your document

✔ Getting data from other programs

✔ Changing a chart's layout and style

✔ Getting smart about SmartArt

✔ Creating a diagram or an organization chart

*O*ne of the best ways to prove a point is with numbers, and one of the best ways to present numbers is in a chart. With Word, adding a chart to your document is easy. And getting the chart to look the way you want is usually easy, too. Getting things to look the way you want them to may take a little bit of pointing and clicking, but what you end up with works and looks great. This chapter shows you how.

In addition to good old-fashioned charts, Microsoft Word lets you create special types of diagrams called *SmartArt.* I discuss standard charts first in this chapter. Then you get to dive into SmartArt diagrams as well as organization charts.

Understanding Charts

If you've never attempted to add a chart to a Word document, the process can be a little confusing. A *chart* is simply a series of numbers rendered as a graph. You can supply the numbers yourself, or you can copy them from a separate file, such as an Excel spreadsheet. You can create all kinds of different charts, ranging from simple bar charts and pie charts to exotic doughnut charts and radar charts. Very cool, but a little confusing to the uninitiated.

The following list details some of the jargon that you have to contend with when you're working with charts:

✦ **Graph or chart:** Same thing. These terms are used interchangeably. A graph or chart is nothing more than a bunch of numbers turned into a picture. After all, a picture is worth a thousand numbers.

✦ **Microsoft Graph:** A program that was used in earlier versions of Word to create charts. Microsoft Graph isn't used anymore. For more information, refer to the sidebar, "Whatever happened to Microsoft Graph?"

✦ **Chart type:** Word supports several chart types: bar charts, column charts, pie charts, line charts, scatter charts, area charts, radar charts, Dunkin' Donut charts, and others. You can even create cone charts that look like something that fell off a Fembot in an Austin Powers movie. Different types of charts are better suited to displaying different types of data.

✦ **Chart layout:** A predefined combination of chart elements such as headings and legends that lets you easily create a common type of chart.

✦ **Chart style:** A predefined combination of formatting elements that controls the visual appearance of a chart.

✦ **Datasheet:** The origin of the numbers that you're using as the data for a chart. After all, a chart is nothing more than a bunch of numbers made into a picture. Those numbers come from the datasheet. In previous versions of Word, the datasheet was a mini-spreadsheet that resembled Excel. For Word 2007, Microsoft finally decided to give up on the mini-spreadsheet. Now the datasheet is actually an Excel spreadsheet. Thus, when you create a chart, Word automatically starts Excel (if it isn't already running) and uses Excel to hold the numbers in the datasheet.

✦ **Series:** A collection of related numbers. For example, a chart of quarterly sales by region might have a series for each region. Each series has four sales totals, one for each quarter. Each series is usually represented by a row on the datasheet, but you can change the datasheet so that each column represents a series. Most chart types can plot more than one series. Pie charts can plot only one series at a time, however. The name of each series can be displayed in a legend.

✦ **Axes:** The lines on the edges of a chart. The *X-axis* is the line along the bottom of the chart; the *Y-axis* is the line along the left edge of the chart. The X-axis usually indicates categories. Actual data values are plotted along the Y-axis. Microsoft Graph automatically provides labels for the X- and Y-axes, but you can change them.

✦ **Legend:** A box used to identify the various series plotted on the chart. Word can create a legend automatically if you want one.

Whatever happened to Microsoft Graph?

If you've worked with previous versions of Word, you might have been frustrated by the fact that charts were created by an external program called Microsoft Graph. In Word 2007, Microsoft has finally eliminated the separate Graph program. Instead, Word now relies on Microsoft Excel 2007 to create its charts.

Why the change? Microsoft did a little research and found out that half of all the charts inserted into Word documents were actually created in Excel anyway. The main reason people did that was that the data to be charted typically existed already in an Excel workbook. Rather than copy the data into Word and then create a chart, it was actually easier to create the chart in Excel and copy it into Word.

Microsoft Graph still exists, but Word uses it only in two cases:

✔ **When you open a document that contains a chart created with a previous version:** In this case, Word uses Microsoft Graph to display the graph.

✔ **When Excel 2007 is not present on your computer:** In this case, Word reverts to the old way of doing charts.

Incidentally, Word 2007 uses Excel to create its charts, too. So with Office 2007, charting is now identical whether you use Excel, Word, or PowerPoint.

The most interesting thing to know about charting in Word 2007 is that chart tools are closely integrated with Excel 2007. When you insert a chart in Word, Excel is automatically started, and the data that you chart is placed in an Excel workbook. However, that Excel workbook isn't stored as a separate document. Instead, the chart and the datasheet workbook are stored within the Word document. If you don't have Excel 2007, don't worry. You can still create charts in Word. (See the sidebar "Whatever happened to Microsoft Graph?" if you're interested in more information.)

Adding a Chart to Your Document

The following procedure shows how to insert a chart on a page:

1. **Move the insertion point to the spot where you want the chart to appear.**

2. **Click the Insert tab and then click the Chart button in the Illustrations group.**

   The Create Chart dialog box, shown in Figure 3-1, is summoned.

Book IV Chapter 3

Creating Charts and Diagrams

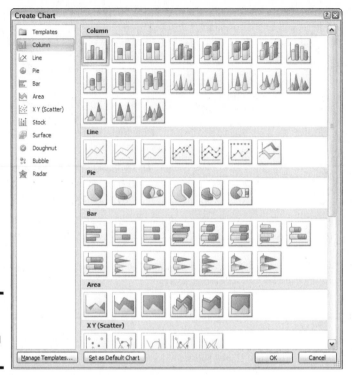

Figure 3-1:
The Create
Chart dialog
box.

3. **Select the type of chart you want to create.**

You can select any of the following chart types:

- **Column:** Data is displayed as vertical columns. The columns can be displayed side by side or stacked, and you can pick various shapes for the columns including simple bars, 3-D blocks, cylinders, cones, and pyramids.

- **Line:** The data is shown as individual points linked by various types of lines.

- **Pie:** The data is displayed as slices in a circular pie.

- **Bar:** The same as a column chart, except the columns are laid out horizontally instead of vertically.

- **Area:** Similar to a line chart, except that the areas beneath the lines are shaded in.

- **X Y (Scatter):** Plots individual points using two values to represent the X, Y coordinates.

- **Stock:** Plots high/low/close values.

- **Surface:** Similar to a line chart but represents the data as a three-dimensional surface.

- **Doughnut:** Similar to a pie chart, but with a hole in the middle.

- **Bubble:** Similar to a scatter chart, but uses a third value to determine the size of the bubble.

- **Radar:** Plots data relative to a central point rather than X- and Y-axes.

4. **Click OK.**

   Word whirs and grinds for a moment and then inserts the chart into the page, as shown in Figure 3-2. The reason for all the commotion is that in order to insert the chart, Word must find out whether Excel is already running. If not, Word launches Excel and rearranges your screen so that Word and Excel are displayed side by side, as you can see in the figure.

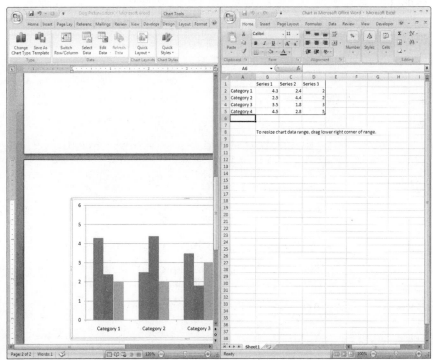

Figure 3-2:
A chart after it has been inserted into Word.

If Excel happens to be running already when you insert the chart, it won't be tiled alongside Word as shown in Figure 3-2. Instead, it will remain where it is — most likely maximized in its own full-screen window. You can press the Alt+Tab key combination to switch back and forth between Word and Excel.

5. **Change the sample data to something more realistic.**

   The data for the chart is shown in Excel, tiled alongside Word as you can see back in Figure 3-2. You need to change this worksheet to provide the data you want to chart. Notice that the chart itself changes to reflect the new data as soon as you return to Word (by clicking anywhere in the Word window).

   For more information, see the section "Working with Chart Data" later in this chapter.

6. **Customize the chart any way you want.**

   For example, you can change the chart layout or style, as described later in this chapter. Figure 3-3 shows a finished chart.

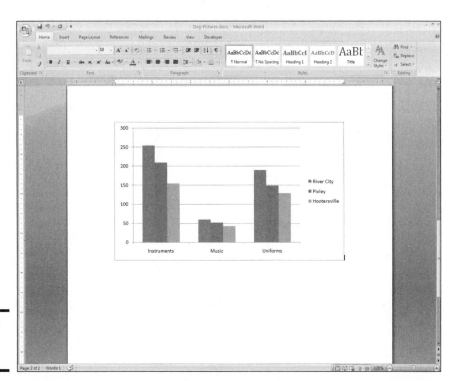

Figure 3-3:
A finished chart.

Pasting a Chart from Excel

If the data you want to chart already exists in an Excel workbook, the easiest way to chart it in Word is to first create the chart in Excel. Then copy the chart to the clipboard, switch over to Word, and paste the chart to the appropriate page. When you do so, the chart appears in Word exactly as it did in Excel.

When you paste an Excel chart into Word, a special smart tag icon appears next to the chart. You can click this smart tag to reveal a menu with the following choices:

✦ **Paste as Picture:** Converts the chart to a collection of Word shape objects, with no linkage to the original Excel chart or data.

✦ **Excel Chart:** This option creates a copy of the Excel data and stores it as a workbook object within your Word file. This effectively severs the chart in the Word document from the original workbook, so any changes you make to the data in the original workbook are not reflected in the Word chart (and vice versa).

✦ **Link to Excel Chart:** This option copies the chart into the Word document but creates a link to the data in the original Excel workbook. Any changes you make to the data in the original Excel workbook are reflected in the chart (and vice versa).

✦ **Keep Source Formatting:** This option keeps all of the formatting you applied in the original Excel chart. Thus, the Word chart looks exactly like the Excel chart.

✦ **Use Destination Theme:** This option reformats the chart according to the Document Theme used in the Word document. You get a chart that is formatted consistently with the rest of your document.

Changing the Chart Type

Word enables you to create 14 basic types of charts. Each type conveys information with a different emphasis. Sales data plotted in a column chart might emphasize the relative performance of different regions, for example, and the same data plotted as a line chart might emphasize an increase or decrease in sales over time. The type of chart that's best for your data depends on the nature of the data and which aspects of it that you want to emphasize.

Fortunately, Word doesn't force you to decide the final chart type up front. You can easily change the chart type at any time without changing the chart data. These steps show you how:

1. **Click the chart to select it.**

The Chart Tools Design tab appears on the Ribbon, as shown in Figure 3-4.

Figure 3-4:
The Chart
Tools
Design tab
on the
Ribbon.

2. **Click the Change Chart Type button in the Type group.**

Word displays a gallery of chart types.

3. **Click the chart type that you want.**

4. **Click OK, and you're done.**

Working with Chart Data

The data that provides the numbers plotted in a Word chart is stored in an Excel workbook. Depending on how you created the chart, this Excel workbook can either be a separate workbook document, or it can be embedded within your Word document. But either way, you work with Excel whenever you want to modify the chart data.

To change the data on which a chart is based, select the chart, and the Chart Tools Design tab appears on the Ribbon. Click this tab if it isn't already selected. The Chart Tools Design tab includes a group called Data, which provides four controls. These controls let you perform various tricks on the data, as described in the following sections.

Switching rows and columns

The first control in the Data group is called Switch Row/Column. It changes the orientation of your chart in a way that can be difficult to describe but easy to visualize. Look back at the chart in Figure 3-3. It's based on the following data:

	River City	*Pixley*	*Hooterville*
Instruments	255	210	155
Music	60	52	43
Uniforms	190	150	130

As you can see back in Figure 3-3, the rows are used to determine the data categories. Thus, the chart displays the data for Instruments, Music, and Uniforms along the horizontal axis.

If you click the Switch Row/Column button, the chart changes, as shown in Figure 3-5. Here, the chart categorizes the data by city, so sales for River City, Pixley, and Hooterville are shown along the horizontal axis.

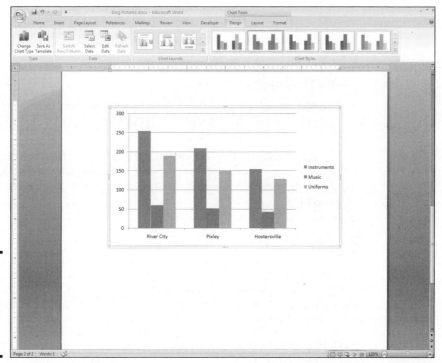

Figure 3-5:
Swapping the row/column orientation of a chart.

Changing the data selection

The Select Data button in the Data group of the Chart Tools lets you change the selection of data that your chart is based on. When you click this button, you're escorted to Excel, and the dialog box shown in Figure 3-6 is displayed.

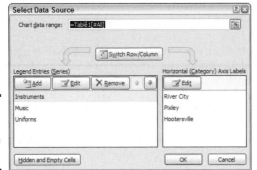

This dialog box lets you do three basic things:

✦ **You can change the range of data** that's used for the chart by using the Chart Data Range text box.

✦ **You can switch rows and columns** by clicking the Switch Row/Column button. This has the same effect as clicking the Switch Row/Column button on the Ribbon.

✦ **You can play with the individual ranges** that contain the data for each series. You can add a new series, edit the range used for an existing series, delete a series, or change the order in which the series are presented.

Editing the source data

To change the actual data values on which a chart is based, click the Edit Data button in the Chart Tools on the Ribbon. This launches Excel to display the chart data. You can then make any changes you want. After you return to Word (by clicking anywhere in the Word window), the chart is updated to reflect your changes.

Refreshing a chart

If a chart is linked to a separate Excel workbook, you can update the chart to reflect any changes that have been made to the underlying data. To do so, follow these steps:

1. **Click the chart to select it.**

Word adds the Chart Tools to the Ribbon.

2. **Click the Chart Tools Design tab if it isn't already selected.**

Refer to Figure 3-4 to see what this tab looks like.

3. **Click the Refresh Data button in the Data group.**

The chart is updated with the data from the underlying Excel workbook.

Changing the Chart Layout

A *chart layout* is a predefined combination of chart elements such as legends, titles, and so on. Microsoft studied thousands of charts and talked to chart experts to come up with galleries of the most common layouts for each chart type. For example, Figure 3-7 shows the Layout gallery for column charts.

Figure 3-7:
The Chart Layout gallery for column charts.

To change the layout for a chart, follow these steps:

1. **Click the chart to select it.**

Word adds the Chart Tools tab to the Ribbon.

2. **If it isn't already selected, click the Chart Tools Design tab on the Ribbon.**

Refer to Figure 3-4 to see what this tab looks like.

3. **Select the layout you want to use from the Chart Layouts group.**

The Chart Layouts group displays the most commonly used layouts for the chart type. If the layout you want to use isn't visible, you can click the More button (the down arrow found at bottom right of the chart layout icons) to display a gallery of all available layouts.

Changing the Chart Style

A *chart style* is a predefined combination of formatting elements such as colors and shape effects. Microsoft provides a large assortment of chart styles to choose from. For example, Figure 3-8 shows the Chart Style gallery for column charts.

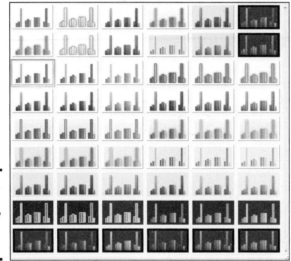

Figure 3-8:
The Chart Style gallery for column charts.

To change the style for a chart, follow these steps:

1. **Click the chart to select it.**

Word displays the Chart Tools tab on the Ribbon.

2. **If it isn't already open, click the Chart Tools Design tab on the Ribbon.**

See Figure 3-4 for a refresher.

3. **Select the style you want to use from the Chart Styles group.**

The Chart Styles group displays the most commonly used styles for the chart type. If the style you want to use isn't visible in this group, you can click the More button (the down arrow found at bottom right of the chart layout icons) to display a gallery of all available styles.

Using the Layout Tab to Embellish Your Chart

Word enables you to embellish a chart in many ways: You can add titles, labels, legends, and who knows what else. The easiest way to add these elements is by selecting a chart layout, as described previously in the section "Changing the Chart Layout." However, you can create your own unique chart layout by adding these elements individually.

To do that, select the chart and open the Chart Tools Layout tab. Figure 3-9 shows how this tab appears.

Figure 3-9: The Layout tab.

The Shapes group

The Shapes group on this tab lets you insert a picture, shape, or text box. For more information about working with these elements, see Chapter 1 of this minibook.

The Labels group

The Labels group on the Layout tab lets you add various types of labels to your chart:

✦ **Chart titles:** A chart title describes the chart's contents. It usually appears at the top of the chart, but you can drag it to any location you want.

✦ **Axis titles:** Axis titles describe the meaning of each chart axis. Most charts use two axes titles: the Primary Horizontal Axis Title and the Primary Vertical Axis Title.

✦ **Legends:** A *legend* identifies the data series that appears in the chart. When you click the Legend button, a menu with several choices for the placement of the legend appears. You can also choose More Legend Options to display the Format Legend dialog box, shown in Figure 3-10. From this dialog box, you can set the position of the legend as well as control various formatting options for the legend, such as the fill and border style.

Book IV Chapter 3

Creating Charts and Diagrams

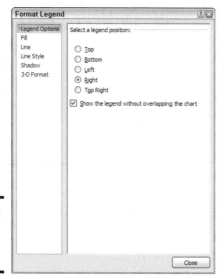

Figure 3-10:
The Format
Legend
dialog box.

Word enables you to create a legend, but you're on your own if you need a myth or fable.

✦ **Data Labels:** With data labels you can add labels to the data points on the chart. For maximum control over the data labels, choose More Data Label Options to display the dialog box shown in Figure 3-11.

Figure 3-11:
The Format
Data Labels
dialog box.

TIP

For most page types, data labels add unnecessary clutter without adding much useful information. Use labels only if you think that you must back up your chart with exact numbers.

✦ **Data Table:** The *data table* is a table that shows the data used to create a chart. Most charts do not include a data table, but you can add one if you think your audience will benefit from seeing the raw numbers. For example, Figure 3-12 shows a chart with a data table.

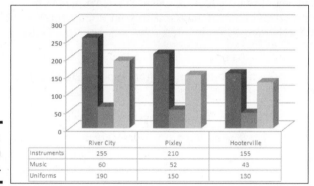

	River City	Pixley	Hooterville
Instruments	255	210	155
Music	60	52	43
Uniforms	190	150	130

Figure 3-12: A chart with a data table.

The Axes group

The Axes group on the Layout tab includes just two controls:

✦ **Axes:** Sometimes an axe is what you'd like to use to "fix" your computer. But in this case, *axes* refer to the X- and Y-axes on which chart data is plotted. The *X-axis* is the horizontal axis of the chart, and the *Y-axis* is the vertical axis. For 3-D charts, a third axis — *Z* — is also used. The Axes control lets you show or hide the labels used for each chart axis.

✦ **Gridlines:** *Gridlines* are light lines drawn behind a chart to make it easier to judge the position of each dot, bar, or line plotted by the chart. You can turn gridlines on or off via the Gridlines button.

The Background group

The Background group on the Layout tab includes the following useful controls for formatting various parts of the chart background:

✦ **Plot area:** This button lets you format the background of the main area of the chart.

✦ **Chart wall:** For chart formats that have a wall, this button lets you control the format of the wall.

✦ **Chart floor:** For chart formats that have a floor, this button lets you control the floor's format.

✦ **3-D View:** For charts that have a 3-D format, this button lets you control the rotation and other aspects of the 3-D display.

Understanding SmartArt

Word includes a nifty little feature called SmartArt, which lets you add several different types of useful diagrams to your document. With SmartArt, you can create List, Process, Cycle, Hierarchy, Relationship, Matrix, and Pyramid diagrams.

I give more information about the diagram types in Table 3-1.

Table 3-1	Types of Diagrams You Can Create	
Icon	*Diagram Type*	*Description*
List	List	Used to show a simple list. Some of the list diagrams show information that doesn't have any particular organization; others display information in a way that implies a sequential progression, such as steps in a task.
Process	Process	Used to show a process in which steps flow in a sequential fashion.
Cycle	Cycle	Used to show a process that repeats in a continuous cycle.
Hierarchy	Hierarchy	Shows hierarchical relationships, such as organization charts.
Relationship	Relationship	Used to show how items are conceptually related to one another. Included in this group are various types of radial and Venn diagrams.
Matrix	Matrix	Used to show four items arranged into quadrants.
Pyramid	Pyramid	Used to show how elements build upon one another to form a foundation.

The idea behind SmartArt diagrams is to represent bullet lists as a diagram of interconnected shapes. Although many different types of SmartArt diagrams are available, they all work the same way. The only real differences among the various SmartArt diagram types pertain to how they graphically represent the bullets.

For example, consider the following bullet list, which represents activities related to my day. The list is pretty vague, but it does structure activities in the order that they occur, which makes it a rough approximation of the *process* of going to work:

✦ Arrive

✦ Work

✦ Lunch

✦ More work

✦ Leave

Figure 3-13 shows this list represented by two different types of SmartArt. All I did to create both of these SmartArt diagrams was select the text, right-click, and choose Convert to SmartArt. The only difference between the two is the type of SmartArt diagram I selected.

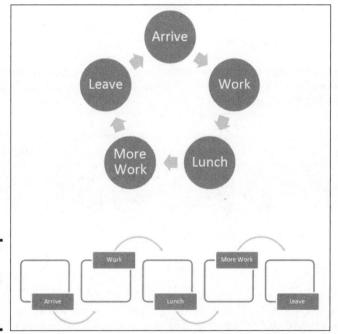

Figure 3-13: Two examples of SmartArt diagrams.

Book IV
Chapter 3

Creating Charts and Diagrams

Note that many of the SmartArt diagram types can display two or more outline levels in your bullet list. For example, suppose you have this list:

- ✦ Arrive
  - • Stop for coffee on the way
  - • Try not to be late
- ✦ Work
  - • Coffee break at 10:00
  - • Look smart!
- ✦ Lunch
  - • Best part of the day!
- ✦ More work
  - • Coffee break at 2:00
  - • Try to stay awake at 4:00
- ✦ Leave
  - • Leave early today?

Figure 3-14 shows how this list appears when formatted as a horizontal process chart. As you can see, the second-level bullets are incorporated as text within the diagram.

Figure 3-14:
Second-level text displayed in a horizontal process chart.

One of the most useful aspects of SmartArt is that you can easily change from one type of diagram to another. Thus, if you decide that a diagram doesn't convey the message you intend, you can try changing the diagram type to see whether the message is clearer.

Creating a SmartArt Diagram

The following steps outline the procedure for creating a SmartArt diagram:

1. **Move the insertion point to the spot where you want to create the SmartArt diagram.**

2. **Click the Insert tab on the Ribbon and then click SmartArt.**

   This summons the dialog box shown in Figure 3-15.

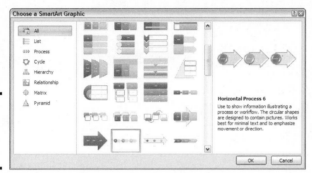

Figure 3-15: Creating a SmartArt diagram.

3. **Choose the SmartArt diagram type you want to insert.**

4. **Click OK.**

   The SmartArt diagram is inserted into the document, as shown in Figure 3-16.

5. **Type the bullet list items to use for the diagram.**

   Use the special dialog box provided for this purpose.

6. **Modify the diagram however you see fit.**

   For more information, see the section "Tweaking a SmartArt Diagram," later in this chapter.

7. **You're done!**

   Well, you're never really done. You can keep tweaking your diagram until the end of time to get it perfect. But at some point, you have to say, "enough is enough" and call it finished.

**Book IV
Chapter 3**

**Creating Charts
and Diagrams**

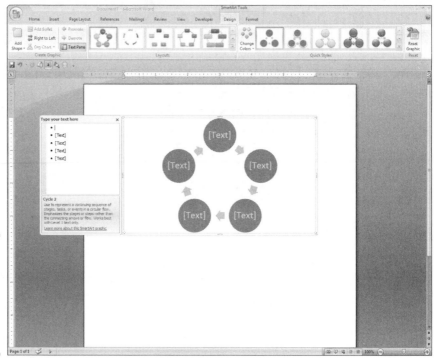

Figure 3-16:
A SmartArt diagram immediately after it has been inserted.

Tweaking a SmartArt Diagram

After you've created a SmartArt diagram, you can adjust its appearance in many ways. The easiest is to change the Quick Style that's applied to the diagram. A Quick Style is simply a collection of formatting elements such as colors and shape effects that are assigned to the various elements of a SmartArt diagram.

Microsoft provides a large assortment of Quick Styles to choose from. For example, Figure 3-17 shows the Quick Style gallery for pyramid diagrams.

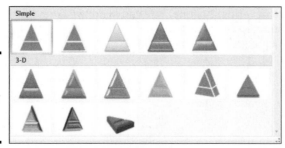

Figure 3-17:
The Quick Style gallery for pyramid diagrams.

Flowcharts, anyone?

One type of diagram that people often want to create with Word is a flowchart. Although SmartArt doesn't have an option for creating flowcharts, you can easily create flowcharts by using Word's shape objects. For example, take a look at the nearby flowchart, which I created with just a few minutes' work.

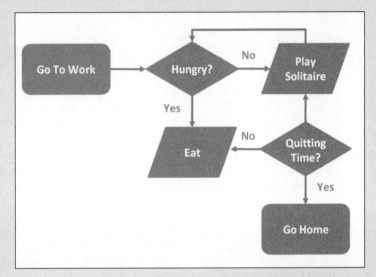

To create a flowchart like this, follow these basic steps:

1. **Draw each flowchart shape by using shapes.**

   See Chapter 1 of this minibook for more information about working with shapes.

2. **Enter text into each flowchart shape by clicking the shape and typing.**

   If necessary, adjust the text font and size.

3. **Connect the flowchart shapes by using shapes listed in the Connectors group of the shape gallery.**

   Connector shapes are special shapes that snap to other objects.

   First choose the type of connector that you want to use by clicking Shapes in the Insert tab, and then choose the connector from the Connectors menu. Click the first shape you want the connector to attach to, and then click the second shape. As you move the mouse around when you have selected a connector AutoShape, notice that connection handles appear on objects when you move the cursor within range. Move the cursor over to one of these connection handles and click to snap the connector to the object.

4. **Now adjust the alignment of your shapes.**

   Here's where the flowcharting AutoShapes really shine: The connectors stay attached to the shapes even when you move the shapes around! Pretty slick, eh?

To change the quick style for a SmartArt diagram, follow these steps:

1. **Click the diagram to select it.**

Word adds the SmartArt Tools tab to the Ribbon.

Figure 3-18 depicts the SmartArt Tools.

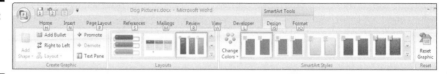

2. **Select the style you want to use from the Quick Styles group.**

The Quick Styles group displays the most commonly used styles for the diagram type. If the style you want to use isn't visible in this group, you can click the More button (the down arrow to the bottom right of the quick style icons) to display a gallery of all available styles.

Working with Organization Charts

Organization charts — you know, those box-and-line charts that show who reports to whom, where the buck stops, and who got the lateral arabesque — are an essential part of many documents.

The hierarchical SmartArt diagrams are ideal for creating organization charts. You can create diagrams that show bosses, subordinates, co-workers, and assistants. You can easily rearrange the chain of command and add new boxes or delete boxes. Figure 3-19 shows a finished organization chart.

This organization chart is based on the following bullet list:

✦ Doc

- Sneezy
- Grumpy
  - Sleepy
  - Happy
- Bashful

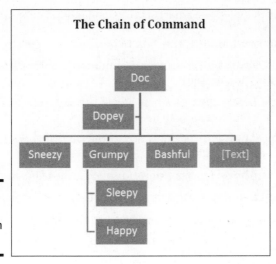

The Chain of Command

Figure 3-19:
A finished
organization
chart.

Notice that Dopey isn't in this list. That's because Dopey is in a special kind of box on the chart, called an *Assistant*. You find out how to add Assistant boxes later in this chapter.

Keep in mind that organization charts are useful for more than showing employee relationships. You also can use them to show any kind of hierarchical structure. For example, back when I wrote computer programs for a living, I used organization charts to plan the structure of my computer programs. They're also great for recording family genealogies, although they don't have any way to indicate that Aunt Milly hasn't spoken to Aunt Beatrice in 30 years.

Previous versions of Word used a clumsy program called Microsoft Organization Chart to handle organization charts. The new SmartArt feature is easier to use, though it isn't quite as adept at creating complicated charts as the old program was.

Adding boxes to a chart

You can add a box to an organization chart by calling up the Text pane and editing the text. Alternatively, you can use the controls in the SmartArt Tools on the Ribbon to add boxes. One nice feature that these controls provide is the ability to add an Assistant, which is a box that appears outside of the hierarchical chain of command.

Here are the steps:

1. **Click the box you want the new box to be below or next to.**

2. **Click the Add Shape button to reveal a menu of choices. Then select one of the following options:**

- **Add Shape Before:** Inserts a new box at the same level as the selected box, immediately to its left.

- **Add Shape After:** Inserts a new box at the same level as the selected box, immediately to its right.

- **Add Shape Above:** Inserts a new box above the selected box.

- **Add Shape Below:** Inserts a new box beneath the selected box.

- **Add Assistant:** Inserts a new box beneath the selected box, but the new box is connected with a special elbow connector to indicate that the box is an Assistant, and not a subordinate.

3. **Click the new box and then type whatever text you want to appear in the box.**

4. **If necessary, drag the box to adjust its location.**

Deleting chart boxes

To delete a box from an organization chart, select the box and press Delete. Word automatically adjusts the chart to compensate for the lost box.

When you delete a box from an organization chart, you should observe a moment of somber silence — or throw a party. It all depends on whose name was in the box, I suppose.

Changing the organization chart layout

Word lets you choose from four methods of arranging subordinates in an organization chart branch:

- ✦ **Standard:** Subordinate shapes are placed at the same level beneath the superior shape.

- ✦ **Both Hanging:** Subordinates are placed two per level beneath the superior with the connecting line between them.

✦ **Left Hanging:** Subordinates are stacked vertically beneath the superior, to the left of the connecting line.

✦ **Right Hanging:** Subordinates are stacked vertically beneath the superior, to the right of the connecting line.

You can set up a typical organization chart using all four of these layouts. For example, you could have the first layer of shapes beneath the top level use the Standard layout. Beneath the first shape on this layer you could add two shapes with the Both Hanging layout. You could then add two other shapes each having three subordinate shapes with the Left Hanging and Right Hanging layout.

To change the layout of a branch of your chart, first click the shape at the top of the branch and click the SmartArt Tools on the Ribbon. Then click the Org Chart button in the Create Graphic group and choose the layout type you want to use.

**Book IV
Chapter 3**

**Creating Charts
and Diagrams**

Chapter 4: Working with Tables

In This Chapter

✔ Setting up and using Word tables

✔ Formatting cells

✔ Editing table cells, columns, and rows

✔ Formatting table cells

✔ Using advanced table features

I couldn't figure out what to call this chapter: Setting the Table? Turning the Tables? Sliding Under the Table? Dancing on the Table? Tabling the Motion? The Periodic Table? Table for Two? So I gave up and decided to call it just "Working with Tables."

This chapter describes the ins and outs of formatting text and graphics into tables. Word's table feature is remarkably versatile, so figuring out how it works really pays off.

If you're going to sit at my table, you have to remember the same two rules of table manners I've been trying to teach my kids for years: No talking with your mouth open and no eating with your mouth full.

Understanding and Creating Tables

You can think of a *table* as a mini-spreadsheet within your Word document. It consists of *rows* and *columns,* with *cells* at the intersections of each row and column. Each cell can contain text or graphics, and you can format the table in any way you want. Figure 4-1 shows a simple Word table.

Figure 4-1:
A simple
table.

Survey Results			
Word Feature	Like It	Hate It	What is It?
Mail Merge	20%	50%	30%
Styles	25%	20%	55%
Templates	10%	5%	85%
Columns	35%	30%	35%
Tables	20%	70%	10%

Each cell can contain one or more paragraphs of text, and text automatically wraps within its cell. Whenever text wraps to a new line, Word automatically increases the height of the row, if necessary, to accommodate the new line of text. This situation is where the versatility of tables becomes apparent. I could create the table in Figure 4-1 by using tabs rather than the Table feature; in fact, creating the table by using tabs is probably easier. Consider the table in Figure 4-2, however. To create a table like this with tabs, you have to manually break the lines for each column, using the Tab key to separate columns from one another.

Figure 4-2:
A more complex table.

Feature	Advantages	Disadvantages
Tabs	Easy to set up for simple tables.	Difficult to use if the text must span several lines within a column.
Tables	Can apply any type of formatting within each cell. Text automatically wraps within cells.	More difficult to set up than simple tabs.

Figure 4-3 shows how this table appears in Word when it is being edited. Notice on the ruler how each table column has its own margins and indentation settings. (The ruler's indentation doohickeys are visible only for the column the insertion point is in; in this example, the first column is active.) Notice also that dotted gridlines appear around the table cells. These gridlines help you see the layout of the table as you edit the table. They don't appear when you print the table.

If you don't see gridlines when you work with tables, select the table and then, on the Layout tab on the Ribbon, click the Show Gridlines option (in the Table group).

If you elect to show paragraph marks in your document, each table cell displays a little box called the *end-of-cell marker*. You can think of these markers as the paragraph marks for cells. In fact, end-of-cell markers don't display unless you display paragraph marks also. If you don't see paragraph marks or end-of-cell markers in your documents, click the Show/Hide (¶) button on the Home tab.

A Word table can contain as many as 63 (narrow) columns. The number of rows is unlimited. When you create a table, Word adjusts the size of each column so that the table fits between the left and right margins. Each column is initially set to the same size, but you can adjust the size of individual columns later, and you can adjust the width of the entire table.

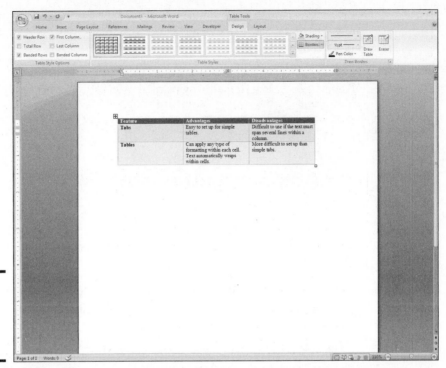

The following sections describe several methods for creating tables.

Creating a table using the Insert Table button

The Insert Table button, which resides on the Insert tab, is the fastest way to create a simple table. When you click this button, a drop-down grid appears, as shown in Figure 4-4. Drag the mouse down and across the grid until the correct number of columns and rows are selected and release the mouse button to create the table at the insertion point. (Naturally, you first need to place your insertion point where you want the table inserted.)

Using the Insert Table command

If you prefer the dialog-box approach to creating a table, you can use the Insert Table command instead. With this command, you pick an arbitrary number of rows and columns for your table. (The Insert Table button is limited to eight rows and ten columns.)

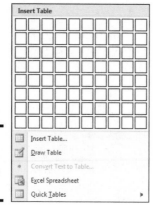

Figure 4-4:
Using the
Insert Table
button.

Follow these steps to create a formatted table by using the Insert Table command:

1. **Position the insertion point where you want to insert the new table.**

2. **Select the Insert tab, click the Insert Table button in the Tables group, and then choose the Insert Table command.**

The Insert Table dialog box appears, as shown in Figure 4-5.

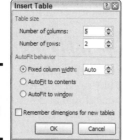

Figure 4-5:
The Insert
Table dialog
box.

3. **Adjust the number of rows and columns you want to create in the Number of Columns and Number of Rows fields.**

If you create the same type of table regularly, check the Remember Dimensions for New Tables check box.

4. **Click OK to insert the table.**

Drawing a table

The Draw Table command lets you draw complicated tables on-screen by using a simple set of drawing tools. This command is ideal for creating tables that aren't a simple grid of rows and columns, but rather a complex conglomeration in which some cells span more than one row and others span more than one column.

Here's the procedure for creating a table with the Draw Table tool:

1. **Select the Insert tab, click the Insert Table button in the Tables group, and then chose the Draw Table command.**

The cursor changes to a small pencil.

2. **Draw the overall shape of the table by dragging the pencil pointer to create a rectangular boundary for the table.**

When you release the mouse button, a table with a single cell is created, as shown in Figure 4-6. In addition, the Ribbon displays the Design tab under Table Tools.

Figure 4-6:
First draw a rectangle as the outline for the table.

3. Carve the table into smaller cells.

For example, to split the table into two rows, point the cursor somewhere along the left edge of the table and then click and drag a line across the table to the right edge. When you release the mouse button, the table splits into two rows.

You can continue to carve up the table into smaller and smaller cells. For each slice, point the cursor at one edge of where you want the new cell to begin and then click and drag to the other edge.

4. If you want to change the line size or style drawn for a particular segment, use the Line Style and Line Weight drop-down controls on the Design tab under Table Tools.

You can change the style of a line you've already drawn by tracing over the line with a new style.

5. If you make a mistake while drawing the table cells, click the Eraser (the one that looks like a table with an eraser in the corner) button and erase the mistaken line segment.

Click the Draw Table button if you want to draw additional segments after using the Eraser tool.

6. When you're done, click anywhere outside of the table.

Figure 4-7 shows a table carved up into several cells, with various types of line style and line weights.

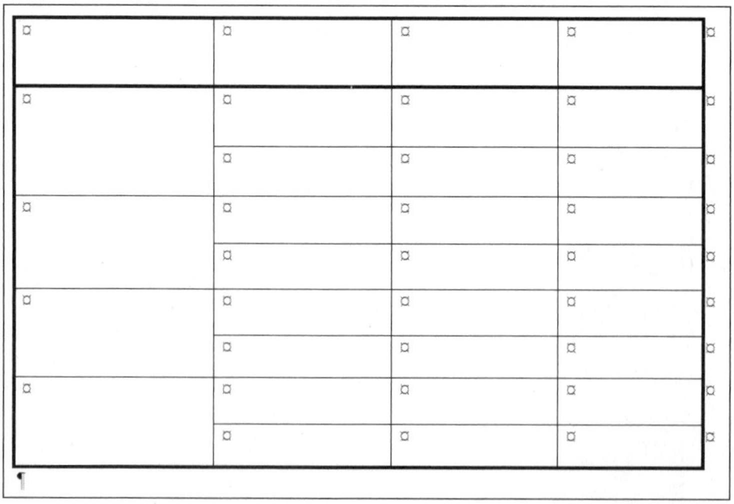

Figure 4-7:
A finished
table.

Using the Table Tools Tabs

When you work with tables, two tabs appear under Table Tools: Design and Layout. You find out how to use many of the tools on these tabs later in this chapter. Tables 4-1 and 4-2 present helpful summaries of the controls you can find on these tabs.

Table 4-1		The Design Tab
Control	*Name*	*What It Does*
☑ Header Row	Header Row	Applies different formatting to the first row of the table
☐ Total Row	Total Row	Applies different formatting to the last row of the table
☑ Banded Rows	Banded Rows	Alternates the shading of the rows
☑ First Column	First Column	Applies different formatting to the first column of the table
☐ Last Column	Last Column	Applies different formatting to the last column of the table
☐ Banded Columns	Banded Columns	Alternates the shading of the columns
Shading ▾	Shading	Applies shading to the table
Borders ▾	Borders	Applies borders to the table
Draw Table	Draw Table	Draws the outline of the table and then draws line segments to create new cells within a table
Eraser	Eraser	Erases line segments to remove cells from a table
▬▬▬ ▾	Line Style	Sets the line style for line segments drawn with the Draw Table tool
2 ¼ pt ▬▬ ▾	Line Weight	Sets the width of line segments drawn with the Draw Table tool
Pen Color ▾	Border Color	Sets the color of line segments drawn with the Draw Table tool

Table 4-2		**The Layout Tab**
Control	*Name*	*What It Does*
Select ▼	Select	A drop-down control that lets you select table cells, rows, or even the entire table
Show Gridlines	View Gridlines	Shows or hides the table gridlines
Properties	Properties	Displays the Table Properties dialog box
Delete	Delete	Delete rows, columns, cells, or the entire table
Insert Above	Insert Above	Inserts a row above the selection
Insert Below	Insert Below	Inserts a row below the selection
Insert Left	Insert Left	Inserts a column to the left of the selection
Insert Right	Insert Right	Inserts a column to the right of the selection
Merge Cells	Merge Cells	Merges selected adjacent cells to create one large cell
Split Cells	Split Cells	Splits a merged cell into separate cells
Split Table	Split Table	Splits the table into two tables
AutoFit	AutoFit	Adjusts the table layout to fit the page
Height 0.1"	Height	Sets the row height
Width 2.05"	Width	Sets the column width
Distribute Rows	Distribute Rows	Adjusts the height of the selected rows to distribute the rows evenly
Distribute Columns	Distribute Columns	Adjusts the width of the selected columns to distribute the columns evenly

Control	Name	What It Does
	Align Top Left	Sets the vertical alignment to Top and the horizontal alignment to Left
	Align Top Center	Sets the vertical alignment to Top and the horizontal alignment to Center
	Align Top Right	Sets the vertical alignment to Top and the horizontal alignment to Right
	Align Center Left	Sets the vertical alignment to Center and the horizontal alignment to Left
	Align Center	Sets the vertical and horizontal alignment to Center
	Align Center Right	Sets the vertical alignment to Center and the horizontal alignment to Right
	Align Bottom Left	Sets the vertical alignment to Bottom and the horizontal alignment to Left
	Align Bottom Center	Sets the vertical alignment to Bottom and the horizontal alignment to Center
	Align Bottom Right	Sets the vertical alignment to Bottom and the horizontal alignment to Right
Text Direction	Text Direction	Changes the direction of text in a cell
Cell Margins	Cell Margins	Sets the margins for individual cells
Sort	Sort	Sorts the selected cells
Repeat Heading Rows	Repeat Heading Rows	Repeats heading rows when the table spans multiple pages
Convert to Text	Convert to Text	Converts the table to text
Formula	Formula	Enters a calculated formula

**Book IV
Chapter 4**

**Working
with Tables**

Editing Tables

After you create a table, you may discover that you need to make a few changes. Don't just delete the whole table and start from scratch. As the following sections describe, you can follow a few procedures to perform basic table-editing tasks. In the following sections, you can find out how to select cells, add and delete rows and columns, and change column width.

As you experiment with the tables in your Word document, don't forget to do a little right-clicking. Just about everything you can do to a table cell is accessible on the shortcut menu that appears when you right-click the cell. Different combinations of commands appear depending on whether you select a single cell, a range of cells including an entire column or row, or an entire table.

Moving and selecting in tables

You can move from cell to cell in a table by using any of the keyboard shortcuts I list in Table 4-3.

Table 4-3	Keyboard Shortcuts for Moving Around in a Table
To Move to This Cell	*Use This Keyboard Shortcut*
Next cell in a row	Tab
Previous cell in a row	Shift+Tab
First cell in a row	Alt+Home
First cell in a column	Alt+Page Up
Last cell in a row	Alt+End
Last cell in a column	Alt+Page Down
Previous row	Up Arrow
Next row	Down Arrow

You can combine the keyboard shortcuts listed in Table 4-3 with the Shift key to extend the selection over a range of cells. In addition, you can select the entire table by placing the insertion point anywhere in the table and pressing Alt+Numeric 5 (the 5 on the numeric keypad, not the 5 key on the regular part of the keyboard).

You can also select various portions of a table by using the mouse actions listed in Table 4-4.

Table 4-4	Mouse Actions for Selecting Cells in a Table
To Select This	*Use This Mouse Action*
A single cell	Move the cursor over the left edge of the cell until the cursor becomes a right-pointing arrow and then click.
An entire row	Move the cursor just past the left edge of the leftmost cell in the row until the cursor changes to a right-pointing arrow and then click.
An entire column	Move the cursor just above the topmost cell in the row until the cursor changes to a down-pointing arrow and then click.
A range of cells	Drag the cursor across the rectangular area of cells you want to select.

Adding rows and columns

To add a new row or column to a table, you can use one of the Insert commands on the Layout tab under Table Tools.

To add new rows to a table, follow one of these procedures:

✦ **To insert a new row within the body of a table,** place the cursor inside the row adjacent to the place where you want the new row to be. Then click either Insert Above or Insert Below in the Rows & Columns group. The new row is inserted above or below the selected row.

✦ **To insert multiple rows,** select the number of rows you want to insert and then choose Insert Above or Insert Below in the Rows & Columns group.

✦ **To insert a new row at the bottom of the table,** move the insertion point to the last cell in the last row of the table and press the Tab key.

To add new columns to a table, follow one of these procedures:

✦ **To insert a new column within the body of the table,** click anywhere in the column where you want to insert the new column and choose either Insert Left or Insert Right in the Rows & Columns group. The new column inserts to the left or right of the selected column.

✦ **To insert several columns,** select the number of columns you want to insert and choose either Insert Left or Insert Right in the Rows & Columns group.

Inserting cells

Word also allows you to insert individual cells within a table. Start by high-lighting the cell or cells where you want to insert the new cells. Then click the dialog box launcher that appears at the bottom-right corner of the Rows & Columns group on the Layout tab under Table Tools. The Insert Cells dialog box appears, as shown in Figure 4-8.

Figure 4-8:
Inserting cells.

If you want to add new cells above the selected cells and shift the unselected cells in the same rows down, select the Shift Cells Down option. If you want to insert the new cells to the left of the selected cells, with extra cells being added to the affected rows, select the Shift Cells Right option. Then click OK.

Deleting cells

If you want to delete the contents of one or more cells, you can start by selecting the cells and pressing Delete. Unfortunately, even though the contents of the cells are deleted, the cells themselves remain in place. This may not be what you want.

To completely remove one or more rows or columns from the table, select the rows or columns you want to delete and click the Delete button on the Layout tab under Table Tools. This reveals a menu with the following choices:

✦ Delete cells

✦ Delete columns

✦ Delete rows

✦ Delete table

To completely remove a range of cells in the table, select the cells you want to remove. Then click the Delete button and choose Delete Cells from the menu that appears. The Delete Cells dialog box appears, as shown in Figure 4-9.

Select whether you want to shift the surrounding cells up or left to fill the void left by the deleted cells or to just delete entire rows or columns. Then click OK.

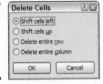

Figure 4-9:
The Delete
Cells dialog
box.

Adjusting column width

When Word creates a table, it initially makes each column the same width. Having equal columns isn't appropriate for many tables, however, because the data in each column is rarely uniform in size. For example, the first column of a table might contain the names of famous composers, and the second column might list their three most famous concertos. Obviously, the second column is wider than the first.

Fortunately, Word doesn't impose uniform column widths. You can manually adjust the width of each column individually, or you can let Word automatically adjust the width of each column based on the contents of the column.

To adjust the width of an individual column manually, you have a few options:

✦ **Drag the gridline to the right of the column to increase or decrease the column width.** Grabbing the gridline so that you can move it is a little tricky, but if you hold the mouse right over the line, the cursor changes into a double-beam thingy that indicates you've got the gridline.

✦ **Drag the column marker that appears on the ruler.**

Either way, the widths of the columns to the right of the one you adjust automatically adjust so that the width of the entire table remains the same.

If you hold down the Alt key while adjusting column width, the width of each column displays on the ruler. This can help you more precisely size the columns. (If the ruler isn't visible, you can display it by checking the Ruler option in the Show/Hide group on the View tab.)

✦ **Click the Properties button on the Layout tab to open the Table Properties dialog box.** Then click the Column tab, shown in Figure 4-10.

From this dialog box, you can set the width of each column to a precise measurement. The Table Properties dialog box shows the column width for one column at a time. Use the Previous Column and Next Column buttons to move from column to column.

**Book IV
Chapter 4**

**Working
with Tables**

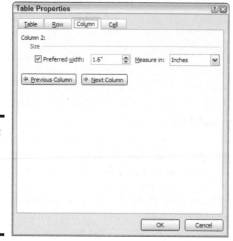

Figure 4-10:
Setting the
column
width with
the Table
Properties
dialog box.

Using the AutoFit command

The AutoFit command, found near the middle of the Layout tab, automatically adjusts the size of a table's columns and rows so that you don't have to mess with each column and row separately. The AutoFit command has three variations:

✦ **AutoFit Contents:** Adjusts the size of the cells based on their contents.

✦ **AutoFit Window:** Used for Web pages to resize the table so that it fits in the browser window.

✦ **Fixed Column Width:** Prevents the table from resizing itself as you type text in the cells.

Using Tabs in a Table

You can set tab stops for individual cells or a range of table cells. Tabs in tables work pretty much the way they do outside of tables, with two important exceptions:

✦ **To insert a tab character into a cell,** you must press Ctrl+Tab. Simply pressing the Tab key moves the cursor to the next cell without inserting a tab.

✦ **If you add a decimal tab to a table cell,** the text in the cell automatically aligns over the decimal tab. (A *decimal tab* is a tab that aligns numbers on the decimal point.) You don't have to press Ctrl+Tab to move the data to the tab stop.

Using Table Styles

You can apply many different formatting elements to tables. But the easiest way to format a table is to assign one of the predefined styles that appears on the Design tab under Table Tools. Several of the predefined styles appear directly on the Design tab. You can display the entire gallery by clicking the More button (the down arrow near the bottom right of the Table Styles group). See Figure 4-11.

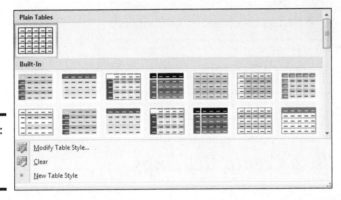

Figure 4-11: The Table Styles gallery.

The six check boxes on the left of the Table Tools Design tab govern which aspects of the table the style formatting is applied to. The options are

+ Header Row
+ Total Row
+ First Column
+ Last Column
+ Banded Columns
+ Banded Rows

To modify a table style that appears in the Table Styles gallery, click the Modify Table Style option. This brings up the Modify Style dialog box, shown in Figure 4-12. From this dialog box, you can change nearly every aspect of the table's formatting.

You can set the formatting for several different elements of the table by choosing the element you want to format from the Apply Formatting To drop-down list. This drop-down list lets you select various table elements.

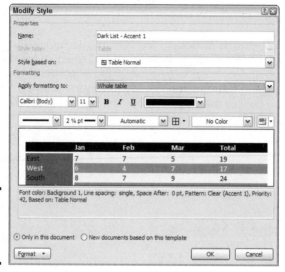

Figure 4-12:
The Modify
Style dialog
box.

Merging Cells to Create Headings

If your table requires a heading that spans more than one column, you can use the Merge Cells command, found on the Layout tab under Table Tools. For example, Figure 4-13 shows a table in which the cell that contains the heading "Survey Results" is merged so that it spans three columns.

Survey Results

Figure 4-13:
A table with
merged
cells.

	Survey Results		
Word Feature	**Like It**	**Hate It**	**What is It?**
Mail Merge	20%	50%	30%
Styles	25%	20%	55%
Templates	10%	5%	85%
Columns	35%	30%	35%
Tables	20%	70%	10%

To create a multicolumn heading, such as the one shown in Figure 4-13, follow these steps:

1. Create the table as usual.

For the heading that will span several columns, type the text into the cell above the first column you want the heading to span.

2. **Highlight the cells in the row where you want to create a multicolumn heading.**

3. **Click the Merge Cells button in the Merge group on the Layout tab.**

   The cells merge into one gigantic cell that spans several columns.

4. **If you want the heading centered over the cells, click the Center button on the Home tab or press Ctrl+E.**

If you want to separate cells you merged, select the merged cell and click the Split Cells button in the Merge group. When Word asks you how many columns to split the cell into, specify the number of columns the merged cell spans.

Designating Heading Rows that Repeat from Page to Page

If you have an unusually long table that spans more than one page, you can designate the top row or rows of the table to serve as heading rows, which repeat automatically at the top of each page. Select the row or rows you want to use for headings (include the top row of the table in the selection) and then click the Properties button (on the Layout tab under Table Tools) and select the Row tab. See Figure 4-14. Then select the Repeat as Header Row at the Top of Each Page option. Word duplicates the selected rows at the top of each page where the table appears.

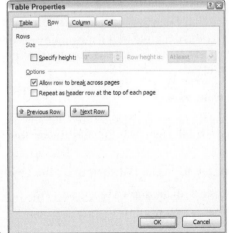

Figure 4-14:
The Row tab
of the Table
Properties
dialog box.

Splitting a Table

Suppose you create a large table and decide that you want to drop a paragraph of normal text right in the middle of the table, between two of the rows. In other words, you want to divide the table into two smaller tables. To do that, just select the row where you want to divide the table and click the Split Table button in the Merge group on the Layout tab. Word divides the table into two and inserts a blank paragraph between the two tables.

What about splitting a table vertically, creating two side-by-side tables? Unfortunately, you can't split a table vertically in Word. However, you can simulate two side-by-side tables by using an empty table column to create empty space between two separately bordered areas of the table, as shown in Figure 4-15. Here, what appears to be two tables is actually a single table: The space between them is an unused column with no borders or shading.

Figure 4-15: Creating the appearance of two side-by-side tables.

RED TEAM
Gilligan
Skipper
Professor
Ginger
Mary Ann
Mr. Howell
Mrs. Howell

BLUE TEAM
Hawkeye
B.J.
Col. Potter
Charles Emerson Winchester III
Radar
Klinger
Margaret

Sorting a Table

Some tables contain rows of data that should be presented in sequence. For example, you might want to show a table that lists employees in order by the employee's names. Fortunately, Word includes a Sort button that lets you do just that. Here's the procedure:

1. **Select the rows you want to sort.**

   For the best results, select entire rows and leave out any heading rows you don't want sorted. Usually, you want to sort the entire table except for headings.

2. **Click the Sort button, found in the Data group on the Layout tab.**

   The Sort dialog box comes up, as shown in Figure 4-16.

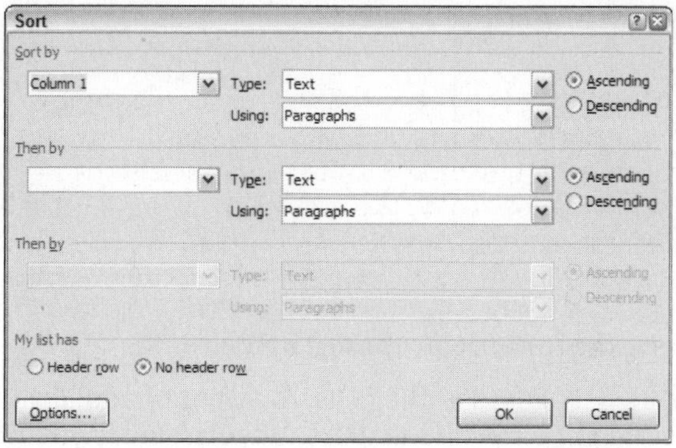

Figure 4-16:
The Sort
dialog box.

3. Set the column you want to use to sort the table and select the type of sort you want.

By default, the Sort dialog box sorts data into ascending sequence based on the first selected column. But you can pick a different column to sort by, or you can choose to sort in descending sequence, and you can tell Word whether the column contains text, numbers, or dates. You can also sort up to three columns. (This setting tells Word which columns to use to determine the sorted order. Keep in mind that Word keeps rows together when it sorts them.)

4. If your selection includes a heading row that you don't want sorted, select the Header Row option.

5. Click OK.

Using Table Formulas

If you can't afford a real spreadsheet program, you can use Word tables as sort of a poor-man's spreadsheet. Like a spreadsheet, Word tables let you enter data into rows, columns, and cells. It even lets you perform simple calculations on cells by using formulas similar to spreadsheet formulas.

The most common use for formulas in a Word table is to add up a row or column of cells. Here's the procedure:

1. Select the cell where you want the total to appear.

2. Click the Formula button, found in the Data group on the Layout tab.

The Formula dialog box displays, shown in Figure 4-17.

**Book IV
Chapter 4**

**Working
with Tables**

Figure 4-17:
The Formula
dialog box.

> Formula
>
> Formula:
> =SUM(ABOVE)*100
> Number format:
> 0.00%
> Paste function:
> [   ]   Paste bookmark:
>
> [OK]   [Cancel]

3. **Double-check the formula proposed by Word.**

   Word takes its best guess at the cells you want to add. If you insert a formula to the right of a row of numbers, Word assumes you want to add up
   the numbers to the left. If you place it beneath a column of numbers,
   Word assumes you want to add up the cells above.

4. **Click OK.**

5. **Double-check the results to make sure the numbers add correctly.**

   Yes, your computer does know how to add and subtract, but the formula
   might be set up to calculate the total differently than you expect.

Besides adding up a range of numbers, Word can perform a whole list of
other functions. Table 4-4 summarizes the most common of these functions.
In the Formula dialog box, you can use the Paste Function drop-down list to
select functions other than Sum.

Table 4-4	Formulas Most Commonly Used in Tables
Formula	*Explanation*
AVERAGE( )	The average of a list of cells
COUNT( )	The number of items in a list of cells
MAX( )	The largest value in a list of cells
MIN( )	The smallest value in a list of cells
PRODUCT( )	The product of a list of cells (that is, all the cell values multiplied together)
SUM( )	The sum of a list of cells

Just like formulas in a spreadsheet program (such as Excel), Word formulas
use a reference system to refer to individual table cells. Each column is
identified by a letter, starting with A for the first column, B for the second
column, and so on. After the letter comes the row number. Thus, the first cell

in the first row is A1, the third cell in the fourth row is C4, and so on. You can construct cell references in formulas as follows:

✦ A single cell reference, such as B3 or F7

✦ A range of cells, such as A2:A7 or B3:B13

✦ A series of individual cells, such as A3,B4,C5

✦ ABOVE or BELOW referring to all the cells in the column above or below the current cell

✦ LEFT or RIGHT, referring to all the cells in the row to the left or to the right of the current cell

You can also construct simple math expressions, like C3+C5*100. You can use any of the standard mathematical operators:

+	Addition
–	Subtraction
*	Multiplication
/	Division
%	Percent

You can also control the format of numbers that appear in formulas by editing the Number Format field in the Formula dialog box. The Number Format drop-down list includes several predefined formats. If you want, you can create your own number formats by using the characters listed in Table 4-5.

Table 4-5	Characters for Building Your Own Number Formats
Character	*Explanation*
0 (zero)	Displays a single digit of the result. If the result digit is zero, 0 displays. Use this setting to ensure that a minimum number of digits displays. For example, 00.00 displays the value 1.01 as 01.01.
#	Displays a single significant digit of the result, but doesn't display leading zeros.
x	Used as the rightmost digit on the right of the decimal point to round the result value at this digit. Use this setting in the right-most decimal position to display a rounded result.
. (decimal point)	The decimal point.
, (digit grouping symbol)	Separates series of three digits. For example, ##,##,0.00.

(continued)

Table 4-5 (continued)

Character	Explanation
– (minus sign)	Adds a minus sign to a negative result or adds a space if the result is positive or 0 (zero).
+ (plus sign)	Adds a plus sign to a positive result, a minus sign to a negative result, or a space if the result is 0 (zero).
%, $, *, and so on	Displays the specified character.
'text'	Adds text to the result. Encloses text in single quotation marks.

You can provide separate number formats for positive, negative, and zero values by separating the number formats with semicolons. For example, ##,##0.00;(##,##0.00) encloses negative numbers in parentheses, and ##,##0.00;(##,##0.00);n/a displays negative numbers in parentheses and zero values as "n/a."

Converting Text to a Table (And Vice-Versa)

If you have tabular information that you didn't originally enter as a table, you can use the Convert Text to Table command to convert the text to a table. Word automatically creates a table for you, making its best guess at how many rows and columns the table contains based on the format of the data you highlighted. This guess is especially useful if the information was originally created outside of Word (for example, as a simple text file that used tabs to align information into columns).

To convert text to a table, first highlight the text you want to convert. Then open the Insert tab, click the Table button in the Tables group, and choose Convert Text to Table from the menu that appears. The dialog box shown in Figure 4-18 displays.

Figure 4-18: Converting text to a table.

The main thing to pay attention to here is the character Word uses to determine what text goes into each cell: tabs, paragraph marks, commas, or any arbitrary character you want to use. Word usually deduces the proper character based on the text you highlight, but double-checking it is worth your time. If things don't work out as you expect, don't forget to use the Ctrl+Z to undo your misaligned table.

You can also convert an existing table to text. Select the table you want to convert and then click Convert to Text in the Data group on the Layout tab. This summons the dialog box shown in Figure 4-19.

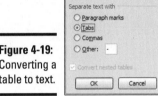

Figure 4-19:
Converting a
table to text.

Choose whether you want to use paragraph marks, tabs, commas, or some other character to separate the text for each table cell. Then click OK to convert the table to text.

Chapter 5: Inserting Fancy Text

In This Chapter

✔ **Creating text boxes**

✔ **Framing frames**

✔ **Using captions**

✔ **Inserting WordArt**

✔ **Employing callouts**

*B*et you thought that text was text and graphics were graphics. Wrong! This chapter describes several Word features that let you incorporate text into your drawings. For example, you can add captions to pictures. You can also add text to most shape objects. And you can use a special type of drawing object called *WordArt* to create fancy logos.

Have fun!

Using Text Boxes

A *text box* is a special type of shape designed to place text on your document without regard to the normal margins of the page. The most common use of text boxes is to add little bits of text to drawings. However, text boxes are also sometimes used to create interesting desktop-publishing effects, such as *pull quotes* or *sidebars*. For example, Figure 5-1 shows a document with a pull quote — a floating text box that highlights a quote from the document.

The following sections describe the ins and outs of working with text boxes.

Creating a text box

To create a text box, follow these steps:

1. **Click the Text Box button, located in the Text group on the Insert tab.**

2. **Choose Draw Text Box from the menu that appears.**

3. **Click where you want one corner of the text box to appear and drag to where you want the opposite corner.**

Drawing a text box is similar to drawing a rectangle.

4. Release the mouse button and then type your text.

The insertion pointer is automatically positioned in the text box, so you can immediately start typing text after you draw the text box.

Innocent Invertebrates Inadvertently Ingested

Save the Worms, a San Francisco-based invertebrate advocacy group, has published a report indicating that millions of children are unable to distinguish between Gummy Worm candies and the real thing.

"Many children," according to the report, "have become ill upon ingesting actual live worms. It is our contention that these children have been conditioned by the recent popularity of Gummy Worm candies that live worms are edible."

"While there have been no reports of deaths, there have been many reports of upset stomachs, nausea, and vomiting. And these are just the symptoms suffered by parents upon learning that their children have ingested worms! It is not known whether invertebrate ingestion poses any long-term health consequences."

"But it is not the kids we are worried about," says a spokesperson for Save the Worms. "The kids get what they deserve. It's the innocent worms that are being slaughtered which has us concerned. Just because a creature has no backbone doesn't mean it's OK for a six year old to have it for lunch."

The report warns that this behavior may soon be extended to slugs and small snakes.

Save the Worms has called for an all-out ban on

"The kids get what they deserve"

chewable imitation invertebrate products. Short of that, they insist that congress pass legislation requiring Gummy Worm manufacturers to affix a warning label to each worm, reading, "Warning: This is an imitation chewable worm product. Actual living worms should not be consumed."

In a published statement, the President has indicated that he is sympathetic to the "plight of innocent invertebrates inadvertently ingested by America's young people. This is a terrible national tragedy, one which I intend to do something about."

Figure 5-1:
A document with a text box.

The default wrapping style for a text box is In Front of Text. With this setting, the text box obscures any other text in the document that happens to fall behind the text box. In most cases, you want to change this setting to something more appropriate, such as Tight or Square. To do that, right-click inside the text box, choose the Format Text Box command, click the Layout tab, and change the Wrapping style. (For more information about what the different wrapping styles do, see Chapter 2 of this minibook.)

In Chapter 2 of this minibook, I also discuss shape objects. Well, shape boxes can also function as text boxes. If you want to add text to a shape, just click the shape and start typing. The text appears centered over the shape. (The only shapes that don't accept text are lines and connectors. But you probably guessed that.)

Formatting a text box

After your text box is in place, you want to apply some formatting. To start, you can format the text in the text box by highlighting the text and using the text formatting controls on the Home tab. For more information about formatting text, turn to Book II, Chapter 2.

You can format the text box itself by using any of the formatting controls on the Text Box Tools Format tab. These are the same controls that appear on the Format tab for any shape object. For more information, see Chapter 1 of this minibook.

By default, the text in a text box is indented a tenth of an inch from the left and right of the text box and five hundredths of an inch from the top and bottom. If you want to change this indentation (I often set it to zero), right-click the text box, choose Format Text Box, and click the Text Box tab, as shown in Figure 5-2. Here you can set the top, left, right, and bottom margins. In addition, you can set the following two options:

Figure 5-2:
The Text
Box tab of
the Format
Text Box
dialog box.

✦ **Word Wrap Text in AutoShape:** You almost always want to leave this option turned on. If you turn it off and the text box isn't wide enough, the text might get cut off.

✦ **Resize AutoShape to Fit Text:** This option automatically adjusts the size of the text box to fit the text you type in it. You usually leave this option turned off. You can always adjust the size of the text box manually by dragging any of the text box's corner handles.

Changing text direction

One of the most disappointing limitations of text boxes is that you can't freely rotate the text inside them. When you select a text box, no rotation handle appears, and the options under the Rotate button in the Format tab are disabled. Text boxes with rotation handles would be great so that you could spin the text to any angle, but Word is a word-processing program, not a desktop-publishing program. I guess the programmers at Microsoft figure that if you want to rotate text, you should buy Publisher instead.

But wait! You can rotate other types of shapes, can't you? And didn't I say a few pages back that you can add text to any shape object? Yes I did. But unfortunately, when you add text to a shape and then rotate the shape, the text stays put. That is to say, the text doesn't rotate with the shape. Sigh.

There is hope, however. Word provides a somewhat helpful Text Direction command that can rotate the text in a text box left or right 90 degrees. It doesn't let you rotate text to any arbitrary angle, but if you have a need to rotate text, 90 degrees is better than nothing.

To use the Text Direction command, simply select a text box and open the Text Box Tools Format tab on the Ribbon. The Text Direction button is found near the left edge of this tab. Each time you click this button, the text rotates 90 degrees. You might need to click the button two or three times to rotate the text to the angle you want.

You can still edit text after you rotate it. However, seeing letters crawl up or down the screen as you type them is a little disconcerting, unless you turn your head sideways. To save your neck, I suggest you enter the text for a text box *before* you rotate the text.

Using linked text boxes

If a text box isn't big enough to display all of its text, Word lets you continue the text into another text box. For example, you might use text boxes to create a sidebar that has text related to the main topic of your document. If the sidebar is particularly long, you can continue it in another text box.

Just follow these steps to create a set of nicely linked text boxes:

1. **Type the text you want to place in a series of text boxes.**

Linked text boxes work best if you first create the text they contain. You can even type the text in a separate document if you want.

2. **Create two or more text boxes to hold the text.**

Position the text boxes where you want them to appear in your document. They don't have to be on the same page.

3. **Select the text you typed in Step 1 and press Ctrl+C.**

The text copies to the Clipboard.

4. **Select the first text box and press Ctrl+V.**

The text from the Clipboard pastes into the first text box. The text box displays as much of the text as it can; the rest is hidden.

5. Right-click the text box and choose Create Text Box Link.

The cursor changes to a weird-looking coffee cup.

6. Click the second text box.

This action spills the coffee into the second text box. In other words, the text from the first text box continues into the second.

7. If you want to spill text into additional text boxes, repeat Steps 5 and 6.

You can link as many text boxes together as you want.

To remove a text box from a chain of linked text boxes, right-click the text box and choose Break Forward Link.

I've Been Framed!

Frames are an archaic but sometimes useful Word feature. At one time, frames were the only way to insert pictures into a Word document. And before the days of text boxes, you had to use frames if you wanted to put text in arbitrary locations on the page. But then along came text boxes, and frames are now hardly used at all.

Text boxes can do almost everything that frames can, and more. However, frames can do a few tricks that text boxes can't. In particular, frames can contain certain text elements that text boxes can't:

+ Footnotes and endnotes

+ Comments

+ Certain field codes — mostly those that number items in your document or build lists, such as AUTONUM, TOC, and TOA

Another major benefit of frames is that you can incorporate them into a style. In other words, you can create a style that places the paragraph it's applied to in a frame. (For more information, refer to Chapter 3 of Book 2.)

Creating a frame

Interestingly, Word doesn't provide a direct way to create a frame. Instead, you must first create a text box and then convert it to a frame. Here are the steps:

1. Create a text box.

The earlier section, "Creating a text box," covers how to do this.

2. Right-click the text box, choose Format Text Box, and click the Text Box tab.

Earlier in this chapter, Figure 5-2 shows this dialog box.

3. Click the Convert to Frame button.

A dialog box appears to let you know that some formatting will be lost. You're politely asked whether you want to continue.

4. Throw caution to the wind and click OK.

The text box converts to a frame, which looks exactly like a text box.

5. Congratulate yourself.

You're done. You can now include footnotes, comments, or weird field codes in the frame's text.

Formatting a frame

You can set some formatting options for a frame by right-clicking the frame and choosing the Format Frame command from the shortcut menu. The Frame dialog box comes up, as shown in Figure 5-3.

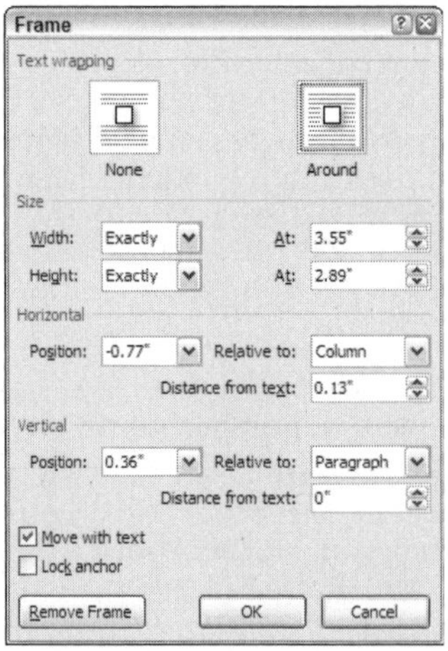

Figure 5-3:
The Frame dialog box.

Here's the lowdown on the various options in the Frame dialog box:

✦ **Text Wrapping:** Read this carefully: It's text *wrapping,* not text *warping.* (To warp your text, you must dig deeply into your own deviant sense of humor.) To wrap your text around a frame, click Around. To interrupt your text when the frame appears and resume it after the frame, click None.

Stop me, Smee, before I drop the anchor!

Every frame is *anchored* to a particular paragraph. When you move a frame around on the page, Word automatically picks up the frame's anchor and drops it on the nearest paragraph. The frame refers to this paragraph when you set the Frame dialog box's Vertical Relative To field to Paragraph.

If you don't want Word to change the paragraph that a frame is anchored to when you move the frame, select the Lock Anchor check box in the Frame dialog box. Then the frame anchor remains in the same paragraph even if you move the frame around the page.

Probably the most confusing aspect of working with anchors is that when the text that a shape is anchored to changes pages (because you add or delete text prior to the anchor), the shape itself can jump to the preceding or following page. When that happens, you can move the shape back to the original page if you want by cutting the shape from the page where it moved to and pasting it back on the original page.

You can actually see the anchors in Page Layout view if you click the Show/Hide button on the Home tab. When you select a frame, the paragraph it is anchored to has a little anchor next to it. You can change the anchor paragraph by dragging the anchor from paragraph to paragraph, and you can open the Frame dialog box by double-clicking the anchor. Shiver me timbers!

(Truth be told, text boxes and other drawing objects have anchors, too. Anchors are a behind-the-scenes thing for those types of objects. You have to worry about anchors only when you work with frames, and even then only if you want to mess with the Lock Anchor option.)

Frames have much more limited wrapping options than text boxes. That's one of the reasons to use text boxes instead of frames whenever you can.

✦ **Size:** Controls the Width and Height of the frame. You can leave both fields set to Auto to make Word figure out how big the frame needs to be. Or you can change either field to Exactly and then type a number in the corresponding At field to set the width or height precisely.

✦ **Horizontal:** Controls the horizontal left-to-right position of the frame. In the Position field, you can type a measurement, or you can choose Left, Right, Center, Inside, or Outside and allow Word to do the measuring for you. (Use Inside and Outside when even- and odd-numbered pages have different margins. Inside means left on a right-hand page and right on a left-hand page; outside means left on a left-hand page and right on a right-hand page.)

In the Relative To field, you can choose Page, Margin, or Column. This option tells Word where to measure from when applying the Position setting. For example, to place the frame flush left against the margin, set the Position field to Left and the Relative To field to Margin. To line it up against the right edge of the column, set the Position field to Right and the Relative To field to Column.

In the Distance from Text field, you tell Word how much empty space to leave between the right and left edges of the frame and any text that wraps around the frame. Increase this option if the text seems too crowded.

✦ **Vertical:** Sets the vertical, up-and-down position of the frame. You can type a number in the Position field or set it to Top, Bottom, or Center and let Word figure it out.

Set the Relative To field to Page, Margin, or Paragraph to control placement of the frame. For example, to set the frame down on the bottom margin, set the Position field to Bottom and the Relative To field to Margin. To place a frame one inch below a particular paragraph, set the Position field to 1" and the Relative To field to Paragraph.

✦ **Move with Text/Lock Anchor:** Select the Move with Text check box if you want the frame to travel along with the paragraph it's anchored to, and select Lock Anchor if you want to ensure that the anchor stays put. If extensive editing causes the anchor paragraph to move to the next page, the frame moves to the next page, too. If you want to force the frame to stay on the same page even if the anchor paragraph jumps pages, deselect the Move with Text check box. See the sidebar, "Stop me, Smee, before I drop the anchor!" if you're not sure what I mean by *the anchor paragraph.*

Adding Captions to Your Pictures

A *caption* is a bit of text that identifies a figure, table, chart, or other visual element you include in a document. Captions usually include a reference number (for example, Figure 58 or Table 293). Figure 5-4 shows a document with a captioned illustration.

If you want, you can create captions simply by creating a text box to hold the caption. (I cover text boxes earlier in this chapter.) But Word includes a Caption feature that automatically numbers your captions when you insert them, keeps the numbers in order, and lets you create a table of figures, tables, charts, or whatever when you're all done. You paid for this program, so you might as well know how to use as much of it as possible.

Figure 5-4:
A page with
a caption.

To add a caption to a picture, table, chart, or other graphic goodie, follow these steps:

1. **If you haven't done so already, insert the picture you want to apply the caption to.**

   For more information, see Chapter 2 of this minibook.

2. **Select the picture that you want the caption attached to.**

3. **Click the References tab on the Ribbon and then click the Insert Caption button.**

   You see the dialog box shown in Figure 5-5.

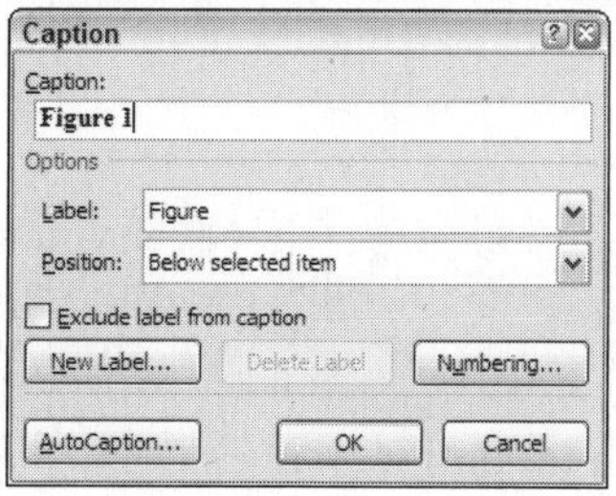

Figure 5-5:
The Caption
dialog box.

4. Type the caption.

Word starts the caption for you by providing the reference number. Type whatever text you want to describe the figure, table, chart, or whatever.

5. Change the Label field if it's incorrect.

Word keeps track of caption numbers for figures, tables, and equations separately. When you insert a caption, make sure the Label field is set to the type of caption you want to create.

6. Change the Position field if you want to change the positioning.

The two options are Above or Below the selected item.

7. Click OK.

Word inserts the caption.

Here are a few rapid-fire thoughts designed to inspire your use of captions:

✦ If you want to create captions for something other than figures, tables, and equations, click the New Label button and type a label for whatever you want to create captions for; say, for example, a limerick. Click OK, and from then on, Limerick appears as one of the Label types.

✦ When you create a caption, Word automatically applies the Caption style to the caption paragraph. You can control the format of all captions in a document by modifying the Caption style. (For more information about styles, see Chapter 3 of Book 2.)

✦ You can create a table of figures, tables, equations, or limericks by using the Insert Table of Figures command on the References tab on the Ribbon. (For more detailed information about this feature, see Book VI, Chapter 1.)

✦ At various and sundry times, caption numbers get out of sequence. Fear not! Word can put the caption numbers back into sequence when you print the document. If you're tired of looking at out-of-sequence numbers, press Ctrl+A to select the entire document and then press F9 to recompute the caption numbers.

✦ If you want Word to always create a caption whenever you insert a particular type of object into your document, click the AutoCaption button in the Caption dialog box. A dialog box lists all the various types of objects you can insert into a Word document. Select the ones you want to automatically create captions for and then click OK.

Creating Fancy Text with WordArt

WordArt is a nifty little feature that takes a snippet of ordinary text and transforms it into something that looks like you paid an ad agency an arm and a leg to design. Figure 5-6 is an example of what you can do with WordArt in just a couple of minutes.

Figure 5-6: You, too, can create fancy text effects like this by using WordArt.

Follow these steps to transform mundane text into something worth looking at:

1. **Click the WordArt button in the Insert group on the Insert tab.**

This step brings up the WordArt gallery, as shown in Figure 5-7.

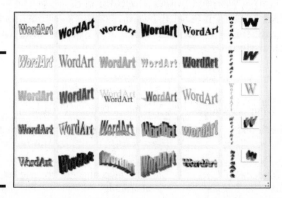

Figure 5-7: The WordArt gallery offers a choice of WordArt styles.

2. **Click the WordArt style that most closely resembles the WordArt that you want to create and then click OK.**

The Edit WordArt Text dialog box appears, as shown in Figure 5-8.

Figure 5-8:
The Edit
WordArt
Text dialog
box.

3. **Type the text that you want to use for your WordArt in the Text field and then click OK.**

The WordArt object appears along with the WordArt Tools on the Ribbon.

4. **Fool around with other WordArt controls in the Format tab under WordArt Tools on the Ribbon.**

When you create a WordArt object, the Ribbon displays the Format tab under WordArt Tools. Table 5-1 lists some of the key controls on this tab. Experiment with these controls as much as you want until you get the text to look just right.

Table 5-1	Buttons on the Format Tab	
Control	*What It's Called*	*What It Does*
Edit Text	Edit Text	Brings up the Edit WordArt Text dialog box
AV Spacing	Spacing	Lets you change the spacing between characters
Aa	Even Height	Makes each letter in the WordArt object the same height

Control	What It's Called	What It Does
	Vertical Text	Switches the text to a vertical format
	Alignment	Changes the text alignment
Change Shape	Change Shape	Lets you choose one of several 40 different shapes for the WordArt text

The WordArt Shape button is the key to creating fancy logos, such as text that wraps around circles. Figure 5-9 shows the menu that appears when you click this button. You need to experiment a bit with these shapes to see how they work. Note that some of them have two or three sections. For those shapes, enter the text you want to appear in each section of the shape on a separate line in the Edit WordArt Text dialog box.

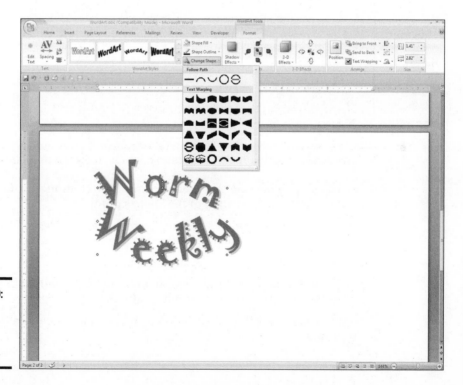

Figure 5-9:
The WordArt Shapes gallery.

Don't forget that, in the eyes of Word, a WordArt object is not text. Unlike a text box or frame, you can't edit it just by clicking it and typing. Instead, you have to edit the text from the Edit WordArt Text dialog box.

Drawing a Callout

A *callout* is a special type of AutoShape object that is like a text box but has a line or a series of bubbles connecting the callout to some other object, as shown in Figure 5-10. In the figure, the callouts illustrate the thoughts of the donkey.

Figure 5-10: The proper use of callouts.

Follow these steps to create callouts to contain your own thoughts:

1. **Call up the Insert tab and then click the More button (the down-facing arrow at the bottom right of the Shapes group).**

A gallery showing about a million different shapes appears. Within this gallery is a group of about 20 different callout styles.

2. **Select the callout type you want to use.**

3. **Click where you want the upper-left corner of the callout to appear and then drag out the shape of the callout.**

After you release the mouse button, a big one-inch-square callout box appears.

4. **Drag the little yellow dot that appears at the end of the connecting line (or bubbles, if you choose the *thought bubble* type of callout used in Figure 5-10) to the point where you want the callout to indicate.**

   As you drag the little yellow dot around, the shape of the callout changes.

5. **Click in the callout, and then type some callout text.**

   Word inserts the text into the callout. Presto! You're finished.

Keep the following points in mind when you work with callouts:

✦ Notice that if you drag a callout around the screen, the callout remains attached to the same point in your document. Cool!

✦ If the text doesn't fit inside the callout, try dragging the callout by one of its love handles to increase the size. Or right-click the callout and choose Format AutoShape from the menu that appears. Then click the Text Box tab and reduce the margins for the callout. Margins allow the text to creep closer to the inside boundaries of the callout.

✦ Try to think cheerful thoughts if you can.

Chapter 6: Other Things You Can Insert in Your Documents

In This Chapter

✔ Adding a cover page to your document

✔ Using drop caps

✔ Dealing with symbols

✔ Adding equations for fun and profit

*T*his chapter covers a variety of items that are found on the Insert tab on the Ribbon that aren't covered in other chapters. Here, you find out how to insert elements such as cover pages, drop caps, special symbols, and so on into your documents. Happy inserting!

Inserting a Cover Page

The Cover Page button provides a simple way to add a professionally designed cover page to a Word document. Figure 6-1 shows the type of cover page you can create with just a wave of your mouse. All you have to do to create a cover page like this is select the design and type the text.

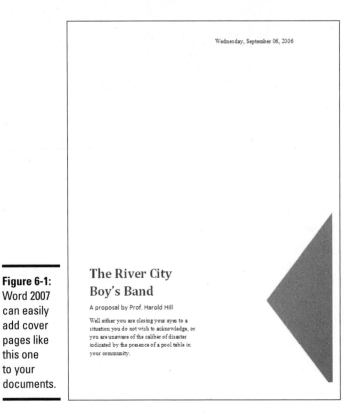

Wednesday, September 06, 2006

The River City
Boy's Band

A proposal by Prof. Harold Hill

Well either you are closing your eyes to a
situation you do not wish to acknowledge, or
you are unaware of the caliber of disaster
indicated by the presence of a pool table in
your community.

Figure 6-1:
Word 2007
can easily
add cover
pages like
this one
to your
documents.

To create a cover page, follow these steps:

1. **Don't worry about moving to the first page.**

Okay, I know this isn't really a step because it tells you *not* to do
something. But when I first saw the Cover Page feature, I wondered
whether you had to navigate your way to the beginning of the document to insert a cover page. It turns out you don't have to. No matter
where the insertion point is in the document, the cover page is
inserted at the beginning of the document, before the document's
first page.

2. **Open the Insert tab on the Ribbon and click the Cover Page button
(shown in the margin).**

The Cover Page gallery appears, as shown in Figure 6-2.

3. **Click the cover page style you want to use.**

   Word inserts the cover page at the beginning of the document. Initially, the cover page includes placeholder text for the document title, subtitle, and cover page copy.

4. **Type the title, subtitle, and cover page copy for the cover page.**

   If you don't want to include a subtitle or additional copy on the cover page, you can use the Delete key to delete those elements.

   That's all! You can now admire your beautiful cover page.

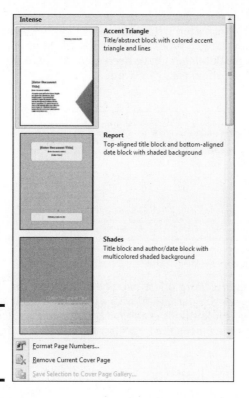

Figure 6-2:
The Cover
Page
gallery.

Here are a couple of additional points to ponder as you lie awake tonight marveling at this wonderful new feature:

✦ You can delete a cover page by clicking the Cover Page button and choosing the Remove Cover Page command.

✦ If you modify the design of the cover page, you can add your customized page to the Cover Page gallery by clicking the Cover Page button and choosing the Save Selection to Cover Page Gallery command. A dialog box appears, asking for a name and other descriptive information. Then your custom page is added to the gallery.

✦ You can insert a cover page somewhere in the middle of your document (say you want to start a section). Simply right-click the Cover Page in the gallery. This contextual menu reveals several other interesting options.

Inserting a Drop Cap

A *drop cap* is a specially formatted letter that appears at the beginning of a paragraph. Figure 6-3 shows two types of drop caps. Desktop publishing programs (such as Microsoft Publisher) have been able to create drop caps for years. You can also create them easily in Word.

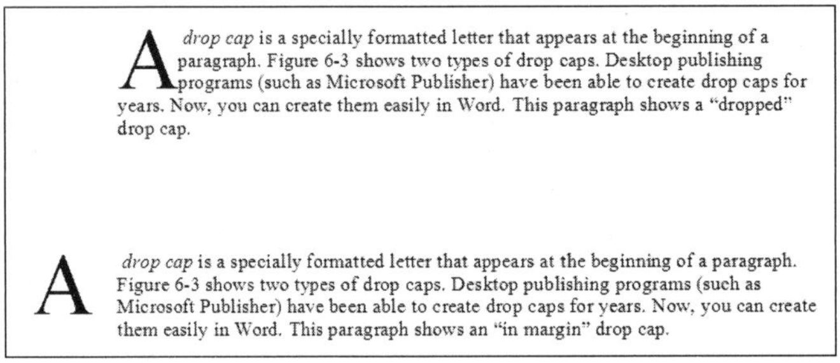

A drop cap is a specially formatted letter that appears at the beginning of a paragraph. Figure 6-3 shows two types of drop caps. Desktop publishing programs (such as Microsoft Publisher) have been able to create drop caps for years. Now, you can create them easily in Word. This paragraph shows a "dropped" drop cap.

Figure 6-3:
A drop cap.

A drop cap is a specially formatted letter that appears at the beginning of a paragraph. Figure 6-3 shows two types of drop caps. Desktop publishing programs (such as Microsoft Publisher) have been able to create drop caps for years. Now, you can create them easily in Word. This paragraph shows an "in margin" drop cap.

As you can see in the figure, Word offers two styles of drop caps. The first, and most common, begins the paragraph with a large letter that spills down into the text. Thus, the first few lines of the paragraph are displaced by the drop cap. The second style places the large first letter in the margin adjacent to the paragraph.

To create a drop cap, follow these steps:

1. **Type the paragraph as you normally would, without worrying about any special formatting for the first letter.**

When you use the Drop Cap command, the special formatting for the first letter will be taken care of.

2. Open the Insert tab on the Ribbon and click the Drop Cap button (shown in the margin).

A menu that lists the two drop cap styles appears.

3. Choose the drop cap style you want to use.

The first letter of the paragraph is converted to a frame that is properly positioned for the drop cap. (For more information about frames, refer to Chapter 5 of this minibook.)

4. Adjust the drop cap if you want to.

Because the drop cap is simply text placed inside a text box, you can use any of Word's formatting features to format the drop cap to your liking. Change the size, switch colors, or add a shadow if you want.

You're done!

If you want to remove the drop cap, click the Drop Cap button and choose None.

For greater control over the drop cap, click the Drop Cap button and choose Advanced. This brings up the dialog box shown in Figure 6-4, which lets you set several additional options for your drop cap. In particular, you can specify the number of lines to drop the first letter and the distance to displace the drop cap from the rest of the text.

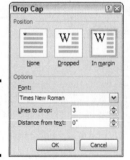

Figure 6-4:
The Drop
Cap dialog
box.

Inserting Symbols

The Insert tab's Symbol button (shown in the margin) lets you insert a special symbol into your document. The most commonly used symbols appear in a Symbol gallery that's displayed when you click this button. To insert one of these symbols, simply click the symbol you want to insert.

If the symbol you want to insert isn't in the gallery, choose the More Symbols command to bring up the dialog box shown in Figure 6-5. You can insert a symbol from this dialog box by double-clicking the symbol or by selecting the symbol and clicking Insert.

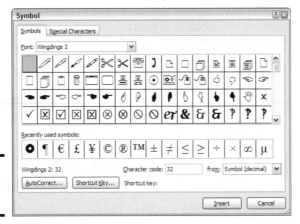

Figure 6-5:
The Symbol
dialog box.

You can also insert certain symbols by using the predefined keyboard shortcuts shown in Table 6-1.

Table 6-1	Keyboard Shortcuts for Special Symbols	
Symbol	*Name*	*Shortcut*
©	Copyright	Ctrl+Alt+C
®	Registered mark	Ctrl+Alt+R
™	Trademark	Ctrl+Alt+T
—	Em dash	Ctrl+Alt+- (the minus sign on the numeric keypad)
–	En dash	Ctrl+- (the minus sign on the numeric keypad)
...	Ellipsis	Ctrl+Alt+. (period)

The following things can aid you in your quest for special characters:

✦ You can add a keyboard shortcut to any special character by summoning the Symbol dialog box. Then click the Symbols tab or the Special Characters tab in the dialog box and click the Shortcut Key button.

✦ An *em dash* is a dash the width of the letter M. An *en dash* is as wide as a letter N. If you're using a dash as a punctuation mark — like this — use an em dash instead of two hyphens. The old double-hyphen treatment is a carryover from the days of manual typewriters. (Note that the AutoCorrect feature can insert these characters for you. Just type a pair of hyphens, and AutoCorrect automatically converts them to an em dash.)

✦ The minus sign required for the em dash and en dash shortcuts is the minus sign on the numeric keypad, way off to the far-right side of the keyboard. (This key would probably be Rush Limbaugh's favorite key if he used a PC, but he's a Mac fanatic.) The shortcut won't work if you use the hyphen that's between the zero (0) and the equal sign (=) at the top of the keyboard.

✦ Notice also that there's a Special Character tab that lets you select the most commonly used special symbols from a list.

Inserting an Equation

Steven Hawking wrote in the preface to his book, *A Brief History of Time,* that his editor warned him that every mathematical equation he included in the book would cut the book's sales in half. So he included just one: the classic $e=mc^2$. See how easy that equation was to type? The only trick was remembering how to format the little 2 in *superscript.*

My editor promised me that every equation I included in this book would double its sales, but I didn't believe him; not even for a nanosecond. But just in case, Figure 6-6 shows some examples of the equations you can create by using Word's handy-dandy Equation feature. You wouldn't even consider trying to create these equations by using ordinary text, but they took me only a few seconds to create by using Equation Editor. Aren't they cool? Tell all your friends about the cool equations you saw in this book so that they'll all rush out and buy copies for themselves. Or better yet, read this section to find out how to create your own knock-'em-dead equations, and then try to convince your friends that you understand what they mean.

$$(x + a)^n = \sum_{k=0}^{n} \binom{n}{k} x^k a^{n-k}$$

$$(1 + x)^n = 1 + \frac{nx}{1!} + \frac{n(n-1)x^2}{2!} + \cdots$$

$$f(x) = a_0 + \sum_{n=1}^{\infty} \left(a_n \cos \frac{n\pi x}{L} + b_n \sin \frac{n\pi x}{L} \right)$$

$$a^2 + b^2 = c^2$$

$$x = -b \pm \frac{\sqrt{b^2 - 4ac}}{2a}$$

$$e^x = 1 + \frac{x}{1!} + \frac{x^2}{2!} + \frac{x^3}{3!} + \cdots, \qquad -\infty < x < \infty$$

$$1s1i1n\,\alpha \pm \sin\beta = 2\sin\frac{1}{2}(\alpha \pm \beta)\,1c1o1s\frac{1}{2}(\alpha \mp \beta)$$

$$1c1o1s\,\alpha + 1c1o1s\,\beta = 2\cos\frac{1}{2}(\alpha + \beta)\cos\frac{1}{2}(\alpha - \beta)$$

Figure 6-6:
These eight equations probably won't affect the sales of this book one way or another.

π Equation ▾ To add an equation to a document, open the Insert tab on the Ribbon and click the Equation button (shown in the margin). This displays the Equation gallery, as shown in Figure 6-7. Pick the equation you want to use from this gallery, and Word inserts the equation into the document.

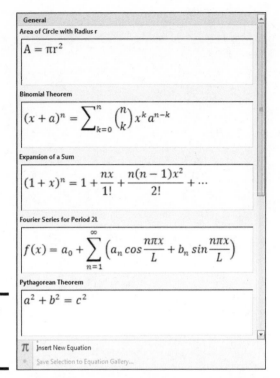

Figure 6-7:
The
Equation
gallery.

The Equation gallery includes several popular types of equations, but odds are good that the equation you actually need for your document isn't in the gallery. In that case, select an equation that's close to what you want and then modify it as needed. Or, if you prefer, choose New Equation to start an equation from scratch.

When you select an equation, a special Equation Tools tab appears on the Ribbon with tools that let you edit the equation. I leave it to you to experiment with the controls on this tab.

Note that the AutoCorrect feature also includes shortcuts for creating equations. Choose Office⇨Word Options. Then select the Proofing tab and click the AutoCorrect Options button. Then click the Math AutoCorrect tab. This displays a list of the equation shortcuts you can use. For example, you can type **\alpha** to insert a Greek letter alpha (α).

Book V

Publish or Perish

"Needlepoint my foot! These are Word fonts.
What I can't figure out is how you got the
pillow cases into your printer."

Contents at a Glance

Chapter 1: Blogging with Word

*H*aving a Web log, or *blog,* is the latest thing. You know that this thing has become mainstream when *The Washington Post* starts referencing blogs as critical sources. You know that this *thing* is here to stay when the most popular word-processing software in the world adds the capability to publish a Word document as a blog entry.

A blog is a diary of sorts that is published online and characterized by ease of editing, the ability of readers to add comments about entries, and syndication of some kind. Jorn Barger coined the phrase Web log in 1997, though people were making daily updates to their sites before then.

The world of blogging has three parts:

✦ The authoring software that you use to create the blog entry

✦ The hosting software that organizes the blogs, syndicates them, and provides for comments

✦ The reader software that consumes the syndication

In this chapter, I'm concerned with only the creation of blogs (hence the title of the chapter), but for that process to be any use to you, you need some understanding of blogging in general. Therefore, I throw tips and suggestions your way as I go. In the meantime, I recommend that you reference the Wikipedia entry on blog (`http://en.wikipedia.org/wiki/Blog`). I also suggest that you check our *Blogging For Dummies,* by Brad Hill (Wiley).

Introducing Word's Blogging Features

What Word provides is the ability to create a blog entry by using the word processor. Then you can move the entry seamlessly to your blog without having to copy and paste into a form, or directly upload a document, or even open your Web browser at all.

I don't get into a big discussion of what a blog is here, but for the record, Figure 1-1 shows what a typical blog looks like on the Web — just a Web page with diary entries.

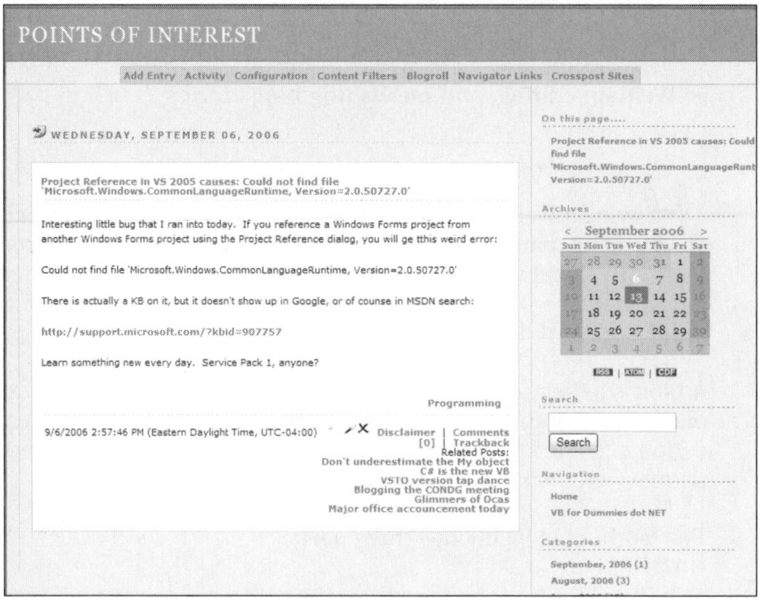

Figure 1-1:
A blog entry.

Word allows you to avoid what is usually a Web-based entry screen for your blog so that you can use the familiar Word interface instead. The blogging feature, in a sense, is all of Word.

Word provides all of this through the Publish command of the Office button (see Figure 1-2). This command starts a process that takes your blog entry and moves it to your blog. As part of that, the command transfers your document to HTML, uses the blog's Upload API to move the document, and sets it up for display.

To use Word's blogging features, you need a couple things:

✦ **Some content:** Content should be easy enough to come up with. If you have something at all to say, it's worth blogging about. i don't know you at all (though I hope that if we happen to meet you will introduce yourself), and I'm certain that what you have to say is better than most of what is out there.

✦ **A blog host:** Word is set up to use Windows Live Spaces, SharePoint, Blogger.com, and Telligent's Community Server. You can use another host, such as TypePad, or even a locally hosted solution like DasBlog.

Figure 1-2:
The Publish
command.

Of course, the best way to get the gist of working with Word's blogging features is to blog with Word. The following section shows you how to put together a blog entry.

Creating and Editing Blog Posts

Creating a blog post is remarkably easy. Just make a document. In fact, I have been using the Word file of this chapter as my test case for the blogging tools, and I am surprised at how well it handles it.

Working from a blank entry

Word seems to give you a couple of options on creation. You can start with an existing document or an empty one. The New command provides an option to create the new blog entry:

1. **Choose Office⇨New.**

The Create a New Word Document dialog box rears its head.

2. **Select New Blog Entry from the Create a New Word Document dialog box.**

A new Word document appears, as shown in Figure 1-3, ready for your blog entry.

Figure 1-3:
Selecting a
blank blog
entry.

Figure 1-3:
Selecting a
blank blog
entry.

If you create a new document using the New Blog Post template, Word creates an empty blog post for you as shown in Figure 1-4.

Figure 1-4:
The default
blogging
template.

You can start here and work from a blank document if you like. You might notice that the blog entry template has given you a neat Blog Post tab on the Ribbon with publishing specific features along with editing tools that every blogger needs:

✦ Publish

✦ Clipboard

✦ Basic Text

✦ Styles

✦ Properties

✦ Proofing

There is also an Insert tab that is specific to blogging, but I go over that later, in the section "Inserting Hyperlinks and Stuff." For now, I stick with formatting.

If you're starting with a blank entry, format it as you would any other Word document. Tabs, lines, color, whatever — it all works. You must understand some of the constraints of Web development, but the style gallery helps you out. (See Book II, Chapter 3 for the lowdown on styles.) Just stick with what Word is letting you do, and you'll be fine — no special knowledge necessary.

For an example, just take a sample bit of text with a few headings and mouse through the style sets that are provided as part of the blog entry template. Click the Change Styles control in the Styles group, choose Style Set, and take your pick of style sets, as shown in Figure 1-5.

Figure 1-5:
The style
sets for
blogs.

Although the styles are neat, Word offers a lot fewer wild options for blogs than it does for Office documents. That's because, frankly, you just can't do as much with a blog entry because it's going on the Web eventually. You just can't have a heading that is periwinkle and does the mashed potato on a blog entry without a lot of fireworks, which isn't the goal here.

Don't forget to fill out the Post Title field (see Figure 1-6). You're really filling out a form here, with two fields. The title goes in Post Title, and everything else is considered the entry.

Figure 1-6:
The Post
Title field.

New MSN Spaces Account

Follow the steps below to register a MSN Spaces account. Clicking ok will contact your provider and configure your account settings.

Step 1: Enable Email Publishing

In order to publish to your MSN Spaces account, you must first setup email publishing from the accout settings page on your MSN Spaces web site.

Show me how

Step 2: Enter Account Information

Space Name   sempftest

Secret Word   ******

☑ Remember Secret Word

Step 3: Specify Picture Upload Options

Automatically upload pictures to my picture storage location

⦿ Don't upload pictures in my blog post.

◯ Post images to the following location:

Tell me more about Picture Upload...

OK   Cancel

Editing your blog entries

You edit a blog post about the same way you edit any other document. You have access to the spelling dictionary, the Research tab, the thesaurus, and Language tab just like usual. You can't find those in the average Web-based blog-editing screen.

However, after you publish the blog entry (which you find out about later, in "Publishing Blog Posts"), your fate is sealed. If you want to edit the document, you have to do it by using the built-in tools of the blogging engine.

Why? Because the post mechanism moves the content of your post from the Word document into a database on the host side of things. After you have published, the data is disconnected from the Word document, and changes don't carry over.

Compare it to e-mailing a copy of a letter. If you make a document and e-mail it, and then make changes to the original document a month later, the person you mailed the original to a month ago won't see the changes. You have to e-mail a new document or ask the recipient to let you see the original so you can make changes. The same is true here.

Registering a Blog Account

You must have an existing blog account to use Word to publish to your blog. Word helps you register your account so that you can publish, but getting the blog is up to you.

Registering a new blog depends on a Web site that is subject to change. Some of the following instructions might change between the time I write them and the time you read this. Watch the page in front of you and check the Word documentation if you have a question.

I started with Windows Live Spaces because it is very straightforward, and I already had a Space set up for testing. Windows Live Spaces, like most blog hosts, requires a few pieces of information that you need to collect before you start:

✦ The name of the blog or a URL to post to

✦ A password

✦ A URL or online host to put pictures

Additionally, the blog must be set up for remote posting.

To use Spaces, you first need to turn on Post by E-mail, one of three ways that word can currently post to a blog. (The other ways are metaweblog API and FTP.) This requires a trip to your Space. The easiest way to get there is to click the MySpaces button on your Windows Live messenger as shown in Figure 1-7.

Figure 1-7:
Going to
your Space.

When you're at your Space, go to Options (the link is in the navigation at the upper right) and then click E-Mail Publishing in the navigation. Then you just need to select the Enable E-Mail Publishing check box, give the resulting form your e-mail address (where you'll be sending the post from), and enter a Secret Word (basically a password). See Figure 1-8.

Figure 1-8:
Setting up
e-mail
publishing.

After you set up your Spaces account, you need to fill out the form in Word. Follow these steps to get your Spaces account working with Word:

1. **In Word, click the Manage Accounts button in the Publish group of the Blog tab.**

The Manage Accounts dialog box appears.

2. **Click New to open the New Blog Account dialog box.**

3. **Select MSN Spaces.**

4. Click Next.

5. Type the name of your Space — not your title — in the Space Name dialog box.

The name of your Space is the word before the first dot in the URL for your Space. So if your Space's URL is `http://thebestblogever.spaces.live.com/`, the name is thebestblogever.

6. Type the Secret Word that you set up in the Secret Word field.

7. Click OK.

The finished form looks a lot like what's shown in Figure 1-9.

Figure 1-9:
Setting up a
new blog
account.

You're probably wondering about the picture upload process, which I clearly turned off. Microsoft says it will support metaweblog, SharePoint libraries, and one or two others by the time it goes to press, so check the documentation.

If you did everything right, Word lets you know. If you messed up, Word stops you from exiting the screen. Figure 1-10 shows the Blog Accounts list.

Figure 1-10:
The Blog
Accounts
list.

Publishing Blog Posts

When you have edited content and a blog account, you're ready to go. You can publish your blog entry by clicking on the Publish button on the Ribbon as shown in Figure 1-11.

Figure 1-11:
The Publish button.

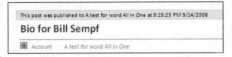

This post was published to A test for word All In One at 9:25:23 PM 9/14/2006

Bio for Bill Sempf

Account   A test for word All In One

If your blog host allows you to post to a draft, you can click the little arrow at the bottom of the Publish button and select Publish as Draft.

If you have some text highlighted and click the Publish button, just that highlighted text is made into the blog entry.

After clicking, a message appears on the document, informing you of the success or failure of the post (see Figure 1-12).

Figure 1-12:
The confirmation message.

Create a new Word Document

New Blank

Blank document   New blog entry   Blank template   My templates...   New from existing...

The post and all of my other tests are up at `http://sempftest.spaces.live.com`. The blog is presented in a component of Windows Live spaces called a *widget*.

Magic? I don't think so. I'm pretty sure that it just sent an e-mail from the Word application (which we know it can do) through to the Spaces site, and there is an existing protocol to handle that. It seems like it just magically happens though, doesn't it?

Figure 1-13:
The blog
widget on
my Space.

Inserting Hyperlinks and Stuff

Blogs get their own cool Insert tab on the Ribbon. At last count, you have
the option to add the following blog-ready items:

✦ Table

✦ Picture

✦ Clip Art

✦ Smart Art

✦ Chart

✦ Hyperlink

✦ WordArt

✦ Equation

✦ Symbol

None of this is new. You can find great instructions for using all of these elsewhere in this book. They're all great features.

Hyperlinks are especially useful when dealing with blog entries because of
the interlinking nature of blogs and Web pages in general.

The Insert Hyperlink dialog box is the same as it is when used in a regular Word document, but it brings special significance to a blog entry. The Browse Web button (the little magnifying glass with a globe in it) allows you to open a Web browser and surf away. The URL of whatever page you stop on appears in the Hyperlink field.

To use the Hyperlink function

1. **On the page, type some text that you want to appear as a link.**

2. **Select it with your mouse.**

3. **Click the Hyperlink button in the Link group of the Insert tab.**

The Insert Hyperlink button appears.

4. **Click the Browse The Web button.**

Your default browser opens.

5. **Browse to the site you want the text to link to in the browser.**

6. **Press Alt+Tab to return to Word.**

7. **Click the OK button in the Insert Hyperlink dialog box.**

When you publish the page, the hyperlink appears on the blog entry, with whatever style is set in the blog for hyperlinks (such as in blue underlined text).

Chapter 2: Working with SharePoint

In This Chapter

✓ Opening and editing documents

✓ Integrating Word and SharePoint

*P*ut down this book and walk over to your refrigerator. If your fridge is anything like mine, it has a calendar stuck to it, a few pictures, and several "essential" papers stuck to it with what might be spaghetti sauce. The items on your fridge might be different than the ones on mine, but certainly what's there is important to you and your family. Microsoft Word uses SharePoint the same way you use your fridge: It sticks important stuff on it so that it's easily accessible to anyone who needs it.

SharePoint is the Microsoft platform that enables members of a team to share projects, track the history of all the changes made to it, schedule meetings, and work together in other ways. SharePoint is essentially a Web application that runs off Windows Server (a version of Windows for large organizations), providing a number of services to Internet Explorer and Office users. Although it's designed for the workplace, really any collection of users on a network who are sharing documents can benefit from it, even users who don't have Office installed. SharePoint is highly customizable, so it is likely to function any way you want it to.

This chapter serves as a brief introduction to Microsoft's collaboration platform. For more SharePoint-related information, I recommend *SharePoint 2007 For Dummies,* by Vanessa Williams (Wiley). This is a well-thought-out and very readable book on a somewhat sophisticated topic. Give it a try.

Understanding How SharePoint Documents Are Organized

Out of the box, SharePoint offers a lot to groups. Its features are compartmentalized into *WebParts.* WebParts are separate groups of functions, and they come in several flavors, like

✦ **Libraries:** All documents, Forms, Wikis, and Pictures are categorized into libraries.

✦ **Communications:** Any communications functions, such as Announcements, Contacts, and Discussions, are in the Communications WebPart.

✦ **Tracking:** Any tools that help you track your projects and activities — Links, Calendars, Tasks, Projects, Issues, and Surveys — are located in the Tracking WebPart.

✦ **Custom Pages:** All your SharePoint Spreadsheets, Datagrids, Web pages, and Workspaces are located in the Custom Pages WebPart.

Integrating SharePoint with Office is not a trivial activity. This chapter helps you get your documents integrated with SharePoint, but getting SharePoint running is the responsibility of your network administrator.

Connecting Your Document to SharePoint

Your documents are only accessible to the people you're collaborating with if you make them that way. To make your document accessible to other SharePoint users, you need to create a *document workspace*. A document workspace is a special Library within a SharePoint site that contains documents like yours.

Creating document workspace is a pretty straightforward endeavor if you have SharePoint set up already. Follow these steps:

1. **Choose Office⇨Publish⇨Create a Document Workspace.**

The Document Management task pane appears.

2. **Add the Document Title as the Document Workspace Name to the Document Workspace module.**

3. **Type the URL for your SharePoint site in the Location for the New Workspace field.**

You can get this URL from your IT manager. Figure 2-1 shows how the Document Management pane might look when you're done.

Figure 2-1:
The
Document
Manage-
ment task
pane.

4. **Click the Create button.**

5. **You're asked to save the document; click OK.**

After this, you have a newly refurbished Document Management task pane, with views for Status, Users, Tasks, Documents, and Links related to this workspace. Creating the Workspace connects the task pane to the various parts of the Workspace.

Accessing the Document Workspace

The best way to get to your document is from SharePoint, which you can easily access with Internet Explorer. Even though you're using your Internet connection, this process is pretty similar to using Windows Explorer to get to a file on your hard drive or your network.

You can also often get to a SharePoint document that you recently created or edited from the Recently Used Documents list.

1. **Open Internet Explorer.**

2. **Go to the URL provided by your administrator.**

All SharePoint sites can be set up differently, though there is a default setup. On the SharePoint site, look for the Sites and Workspaces link. You see it in the upper-right corner of the workspace if you published a Word document to the workspace (I describe how to do share Word documents in the preceding section). Your document appears there in a document workspace, as in Figure 2-2.

In your document workspace, you can manage the users, tasks, and announcements surrounding your document or documents, as well as the document itself.

Figure 2-2:
The
document
workspace.

3. **Choose Edit in Microsoft Office Word from the context menu of the document workspace, as shown in Figure 2-2.**

   The context menu items are all the stuff you see on the Document Workspace tab in Word: Tasks, Links, Announcement, Users. It's all linked together.

4. **Edit the document as usual.**

5. **Save the document as usual.**

   When you save, it saves back to SharePoint.

Using a Document Library

After you open a document from SharePoint, you can access the document library features by choosing Office⇨Server Tasks.

When a book is checked out of the local library, no one else can access it. SharePoint's libraries work similarly. Only one person can access a document at a time and make changes to it. (If the file is checked out, everyone can look at a read-only version of the document or make changes to it that are saved on the user's local hard drive — but the version on SharePoint isn't affected.) The library controls who can access a file when, so that the document history can be managed and changes to it don't occur simultaneously. Simultaneous changes can be devastating to document management because two members of your team could cancel out each other's work. See Figure 2-3.

Figure 2-3:
The Server
Tasks menu.

This menu gives you access to three features:

+ **View Version History:** Among other things, SharePoint is a document change control system, and the first menu item is about seeing the history of changes that have been made to a document. Here you can view the various changes made to the document since it was added to SharePoint. You can even recover a previous version — no matter who made the changes.

+ **Document Management Information:** The Document Management window provides access to all the people, links, tasks, announcements, and course documents related to your workspace.

+ **View Workflow Tasks:** This feature helps you to manage the project flow around a document. You're actually able to route documents through an approval cycle by using SharePoint. For more information on this, check out *SharePoint 2007 For Dummies,* by Vanessa Williams (Wiley Publishing, Inc.).

Retrieving a document from a library

You can get a new document from the library, as you saw earlier in "Using a Document Library." In the workspace, all the documents are listed in the document module.

The document module lists all files as clickable hyperlinks.

However, the Document Management window can help you with that, too as shown in Figure 2-4.

Figure 2-4:
The
Documents
tab.

The Documents tab provides access to all the documents in the workspace. Click the context-sensitive menu to open the document, delete it from the workspace, or get alerts. The menu appears to the right of the document name. See Figure 2-5.

Figure 2-5:
The context-
sensitive
menu for a
document
in the
workspace
appears just
to the right
of the
document
name.

You can get the latest changes to the workspace by clicking the Get Updates button near the bottom of the document workspace.

Of course, you can also just click the document link to open the version of it saved locally (on your hard drive). The documents' names are all links, and the documents are accessible there.

Additionally, you have the option of finding the document in the Recent Documents list and opening it there. All documents are saved locally even if they're hosted remotely.

The moment you open a document from your local hard drive that is also saved at the SharePoint, Word prompts you to update the document so that the most up-to-date version is available to other users when you're finished. A warning appears when the document opens. If you're connected and can update the document, do so. If you have checked out the document, you don't have to update the file. If you do *not* have it checked out, you need to save your changes to a local file.

Adding a document to a library

You can find a few nice tools at the bottom of the Document Management window. From that window, you can add a document, add a folder for more documents, or ask for alerts when other add documents. Pretty comprehensive, no?

The Add New Document link acts as expected, giving you a dialog box with a Browse button where you can select a local document to add to the workspace. This is shown in Figure 2-6.

Figure 2-6:
The Add
New
Document
dialog box.

The Add New Folder link works about the same, but the Alerts link just takes you to the SharePoint site. Remember, these are just replications of the SharePoint commands put here for your convenience.

Customizing your experience

The document workspace is no stranger to the idea of providing options. You can edit a number of these options (see Figure 2-7), which are accessible from the Options button next to the Get Updates button.

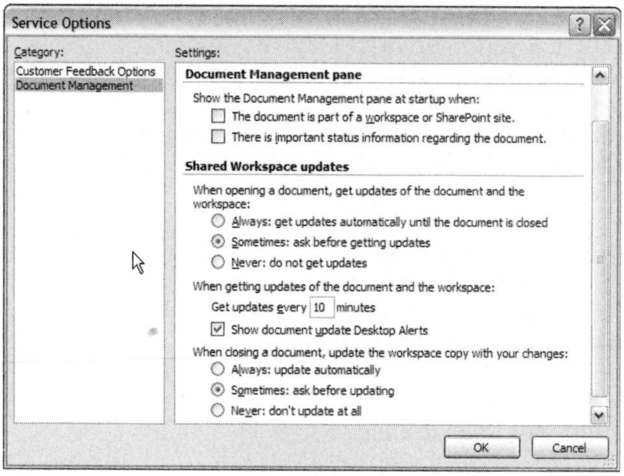

Figure 2-7:
Document
manage-
ment
options.

You can increase your exposure to the Management window if you use SharePoint a lot. If there are updates, you can have the workspace alert you right from Word! Just change the Shared Workspace Updates to the level of exposure you need.

Also, a few options here relate to timing. Updating changes can be important if you're on a slow connection or if you're in a hot workspace with documents that see frequent changes.

Chapter 3: Collaborating with the Review Tab

In This Chapter

✔ Commenting on text

✔ Tracking editorial changes

✔ Protecting documents

*I*n writing documents, one of the most significant things that an author has to perform is the Rite of Review, where people who are generally uninformed about the content of the document change it at will. The Review tab is all about making that process as painless as possible.

The importance of review is accentuated by the fact that it has a whole tab all to itself. Buttons for proofing, comment creation and management, change tracking, comparison, and protection all fall into this Review tab. The goal is to make the process of passing a document through a workflow easier for all involved.

Reviewing isn't new. Word 2003 was riddled with toolbars and commands for reviewing. In Word 2007, all of the reviewing features are combined into a single Review tab to make them easier to use.

In this chapter, I cover management of comments from your collaborators, tracking changes that others make to your documents, comparing two or more documents and protection.

Reviewing Documents

The document review process is something that most organizations don't do well. Word has a lot of tools that help you to move documents through any review process, but you must implement the tools as part of the process to be effective. For instance, a chain of editing for the company newsletter will be much more effective if the editors use the Word reviewing tools.

Reviewing the agreement

The key to reviewing tools is agreement. Not agreement on the content of the document per se; agreement on using the tools. Organizations can effectively route documents by using SharePoint and then manage changes by using comments and track changes, as long as people agree on using the tools. A good first start is to read this chapter and get your reviewers to do the same.

For editing, you can use two very effective tools:

✦ **Comments** are less intrusive; they allow reviewers to leave commentary in a document without changing the content. Think of comments as little notes that editors can place in documents. Using this tool is as easy as highlighting a word, sentence, or any object in a document and clicking the Add Comment button on the Ribbon. Comments are tracked by user (using the initials that were entered as part of the setup process) and are easy for the author to manage.

✦ **Track changes** is something that the author turns on and off, and it makes sort of a source document with overlaid changes. Editors can change documents while still allowing the author control over the content by using track changes. It's somewhat like editing a printed copy of the document. The author can accept or delete changes, and the author can use built-in tools to view and compare various versions of the document.

Usually comments and track changes are used in tandem. Comments are used to suggest changes in tone or content, whereas track changes are used for editorial changes or directly altering text. I recommend using both at the same time.

Working with Comments

Comments are little notes that reviewers can add to your document without disturbing the content. A reviewer can highlight a letter, a word, or a phrase — even an image or an object — and add a box with his or her initials, a color specific to his or her comments, and some text, as shown in Figure 3-1.

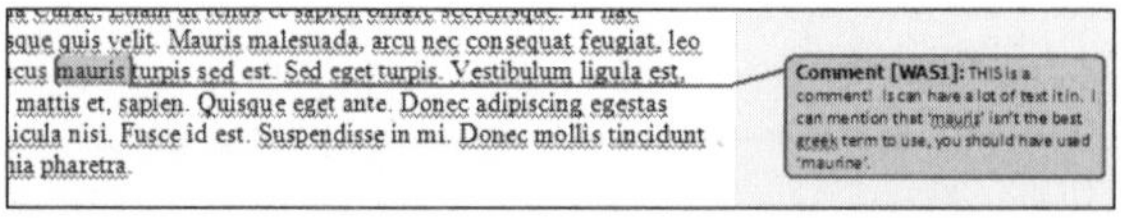

Figure 3-1:
A comment.

Comments are clear to read but aren't damaging to the document. They do print, and you can save them in a document. They don't upset your formatting, and they go all the way back to Word 97, so even if everyone isn't using the same version of Word, they're still useful.

Creating a comment

To create a comment, follow these steps:

1. **Highlight a letter, word, phrase, image, or object.**

2. **Press the New Comment button on the Reviewing tab, as shown in Figure 3-2.**

3. **Type the comment in the comment box that appears off to the right.**

4. **Click elsewhere in the document or continue reading.**

Figure 3-2:
The New
Comment
button.

To edit a comment, you can just click inside the comment box and start typing. Comments can't be added to the comment text, though if you click inside the comment text and add a new comment, it is added with the same text selected as the original comment. It's an effective way to make a comment about a comment.

Note that not only the initials of the reviewer are added — the comments are automatically numbered, as well. This numbering is excellent for tracking comments, but it's also rather depressing when you scroll to the bottom of the document and notice that your reviewer left you 134 comments to work through. (I hope you have some caffeine handy.)

Deleting a comment

Deleting is a simple, rather fun procedure. After you handle a comment, simply right-click it and choose Delete Comment from the contextual menu, as shown in Figure 3-3:

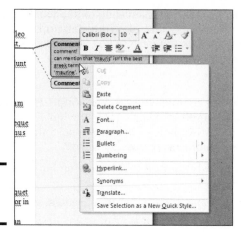

Figure 3-3:
Deleting a
comment.

You can, of course, also click a comment and choose the Delete Comment command, as shown in Figure 3-3, but what's the fun in that? For the record, when you click a comment to select it, the color becomes darker so you can see what you're deleting.

Additionally, you can use the Delete button on the Review tab on the Ribbon, as shown in Figure 3-4. A drop-down menu is available if you click the little black triangle under the Delete button, which allows you to delete all the viewable comments or delete all the comments.

Figure 3-4:
Using the
Ribbon to
delete
comments.

Viewing comments

At first blush, viewing a comment seems pretty straightforward. However, even something this simple has a few options.

The comments appear to the right of the text. If you can't see them, the view mode might be set improperly for viewing.

In the Tracking group on the Review tab on the Ribbon, you find a drop-down list that allows you to set the view mode. By default, it's set to Final Showing Markup, which allows you to see tracked changes. More importantly, it shows the comments. If the document is set to Final, the comments don't appear.

There's a lot more to viewing comments, however. For instance, you can move from one comment to another by using the Previous Comment and Next Comment buttons on the Ribbon — as long as the comments aren't hidden by the current view mode, as shown in Figure 3-5.

Word has four view modes:

✦ **Final Showing Markup:** This is the working mode for reviewing. If your document is in Print view, insertions appear inline, and deletions appear shown in balloons.

✦ **Final:** This view mode shows the document as it will be if you accept all changes.

✦ **Original Showing Markup:** If your document is in Print view, the deletions appear inline, and the insertions show up in balloons.

✦ **Original:** This mode shows the unchanged document, as it would be if you reject all changes.

Figure 3-5:
Pay attention to the view mode.

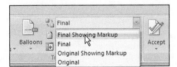

Why use these? Because you can then use the Delete button on the Ribbon or the Delete key on your keyboard to delete the comment. Also, clicking the Ribbon buttons moves the insertion point through the whole document from comment to comment, so that you can see the context.

If Word is in Draft view, comments appear differently, and the Previous and Next button become more important. The comments don't appear as notes in Draft view, they appear as the reviewer's initials in the document, and you have to mouse over them to see the comments, as shown in Figure 3-6.

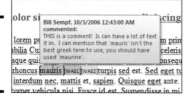

Figure 3-6:
Viewing a
comment in
Draft view.

In Normal view, comments also appear in the Reviewing pane. To access Summary view from a comment, right-click the comment and choose Edit Comment. This command takes you to the Review pane, allowing you as the author to change the content of the comments easily, as shown in Figure 3-7.

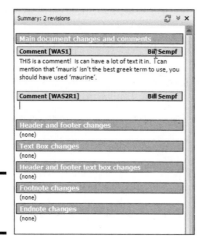

Figure 3-7:
Summary
panel.

Viewing comments inline or viewing them in the balloons is an option you can find on the Track Changes tab on the Ribbon. I discuss it more in the following section.

Tracking Changes

More intrusive than comments, track changes can sometimes be more effective. It allows an editor (or several editors) to alter a document while maintaining the integrity of the original.

If Word is in Print view, shown in Figure 3-8, the look of deleted text is very similar to comments; the added text works just like a draft model. You can get to Print view by clicking it in the View tab on the Ribbon.

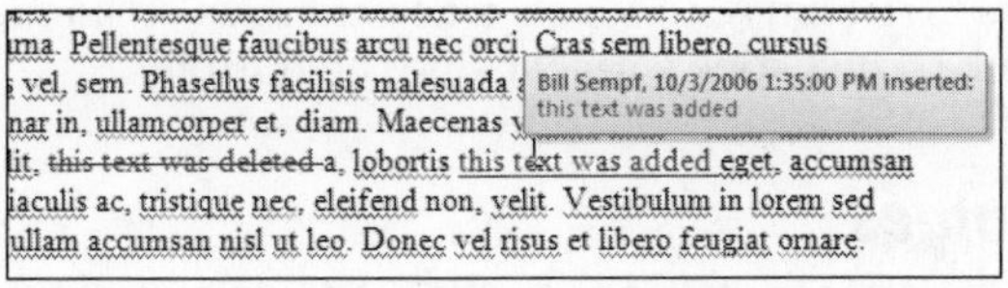

Figure 3-8:
Tracked
changes in
Print view.

If Word is in Draft view (see Figure 3-9), text added with track changes looks
the same as the text around it in terms of typeface and style, except it's
underlined, and the color is different. Text deleted with tracked changes is
marked with the strikethrough font, and the color is changed. Each editor's
changes have a different color.

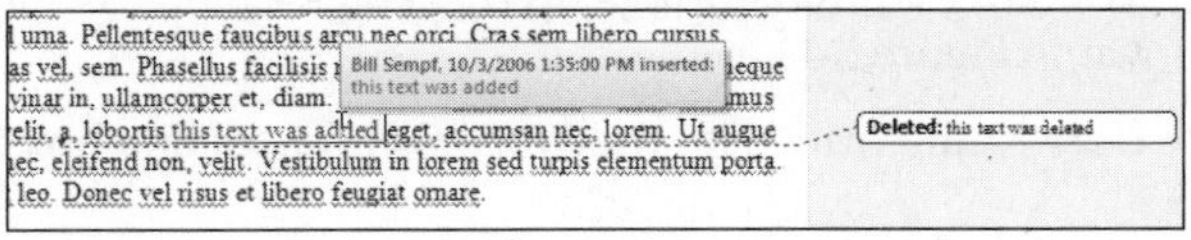

Figure 3-9:
Tracked
changes in
Draft view.

Notice that when you hover the mouse over the change, you see a box with
the editor's name, the time of the edit, and the edit itself.

All of the view options are, well, optional. I go over how to make changes in
the "Viewing changes" section later.

All of the track changes functions you will ever need can be found in the
Tracking group on the Reviewing tab on the Ribbon.

Turning track changes on and off

Track changes is like a light switch — it is on or off for the entire document.
You can use the Track Changes button, shown in Figure 3-10, on the Ribbon
to toggle the status of track changes.

Figure 3-10:
The Track
Changes
button.

You can also press Ctrl+Shift+E to toggle track changes on and off, as it says in the menu. I think I'll just stick with clicking the button.

Viewing changes

You have a lot of options for viewing changes. The default options, which I described in the previous section, are fine for most uses but sometimes you need to have a touch more control.

If you click the drop-down button (the little black triangle) under the Track Changes button, you see three options:

✦ **Track Changes** does the same thing as clicking the button above the menu.

✦ **Change Tracking Options** brings up the Track Changes Options dialog box, shown in Figure 3-11.

✦ **Change User Name** brings up the Word Options dialog box for you to change.

Figure 3-11: View options for tracking changes.

Most of the options in the Track Changes Options dialog box are self-explanatory. You have the opportunity to have shocking control over the exact color, placement and positioning of just about every part of the track changes feature.

More useful is the Balloons button in the Tracking group on the Ribbon. This button brings up a list that allows you to toggle viewing of changes between inline view (default for Draft) or balloons (default for Print) without changing the document view mode.

Additionally, you can view only comments and formatting changes in the balloons. That way, the edits show as edits (blue-lined in this case) like an editor would do to a paper document. Comments show as notes on the side of the document, which doesn't interact with readability.

Accepting or rejecting changes

Tracking changes isn't enough for the people at Microsoft — they even give you the ability to do something about the changes! Accepting or rejecting changes is part of the last step of reviewing: rewrite. After you as the author have received your marked up document, you can accept or reject changes made by others or yourself.

To accept or reject a change, right-click the change (either as a balloon or an inline change) and you'll see the Accept Change and Reject Change options in the contextual menu, as shown in Figure 3-12.

Figure 3-12:
The
Tracking
contextual
menu.

From here you can accept or reject the change. Accepting the change allows whatever the editor did to stand, permanently altering the document. Rejecting it removes it from the document completely.

Comments can't be accepted or rejected. They can only be deleted.

Another slick way to handle changes is with the Changes group of the Review tab on the Ribbon, shown in Figure 3-13. There you can click the Accept Change button when it's highlighted. You can also accept (or reject) all the changes in a document by clicking the drop-down list next to the buttons. This is great for showing your favorite editors what you really think of them!

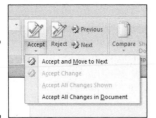

Figure 3-13:
The changes section.

Comparing Documents

Compare Documents is a rarely used and really cool feature that can help in those situations when reviewing wasn't used, and now you have two copies of the document. Simply put, you can pick two documents, and this feature marks all the differences for you. The dialog box with all of the options is shown in Figure 3-14.

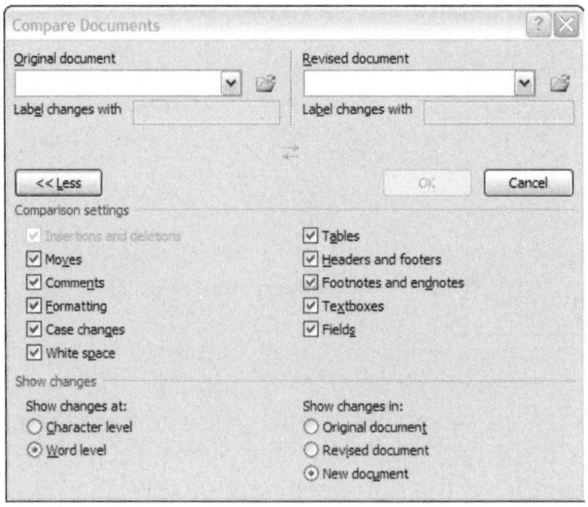

Figure 3-14:
The Compare Documents dialog box.

Say for the sake of argument that you have two different documents, and you need to see what is different about them. Here's what you do with them:

1. **Click the Compare button on the Ribbon to open the Compare Documents dialog box.**

2. **Use the Browse button (it looks like a little folder with an arrow on top of it) to select the original document in the Original Document field.**

3. **Use the Browse button next to Revised Document to find the document that was edited.**

4. **Pick the options that you want compared.**

You might have to click the More button to see this part of the dialog box.

5. **Click OK.**

There you have it. A full-blown comparison of the two documents in a new document suitable for printing. This is great not only for reviewing but also for source code, Web pages, and legal documents.

Protecting a Document

Throughout this chapter, I assume that you, the author, were accepting edits made by someone else, the editor. In reality, anyone can change a document, turn track changes on and off, delete comments, or accept and reject changes . . . that is, unless you have document protection enabled.

Document protection is a suite of tools that allows you to prevent the document from being used in unauthorized ways. For the purposes of reviewing, it makes sure you have the right to author, and someone else has the right to edit, and that's it.

The Protect Document button on the Ribbon gives you a quick three-step process by which to prevent people from mangling your writing:

✦ You can set the styles to a limited set by selecting the Limit Formatting to a Selection of Styles check box.

✦ You can allow only certain kinds of changes by a certain set of users by selecting the corresponding check box.

✦ You can enforce those restrictions with either your Windows Login or a document password after you click Start Enforcing Protection.

Book VI

Using Reference Features

The 5th Wave   By Rich Tennant

"I can tell a lot from your resume. You're well educated, detail oriented and own a really tiny printer."

Contents at a Glance

Chapter 1: Creating a Table of Contents or Table of Figures

In This Chapter

- Choosing the right format
- Creating a Table of Contents
- Using other styles to create a Table of Contents
- Creating a table of figures or other similar tables
- Updating a Table of Contents or table of figures

In the old days, creating a Table of Contents for a book, manual, or other long document was a two-step affair. First you created the Table of Contents, leaving blanks or Xs where the page numbers eventually went. Then after the pages of the document were in their final form, you browsed through the entire document, made a list of the page numbers for each chapter, and went back to the Table of Contents and changed all the Xs to the actual, correct page numbers.

Now, assuming that you format your document properly, creating a Table of Contents is a matter of clicking the mouse button a few times. Word assembles the Table of Contents for you by using the headings you cleverly placed throughout your document. And it takes care of the drudgery of counting pages and even adjusts the Table of Contents for you if you make changes to the document that affect page numbers in the table.

This chapter shows you all the ins and outs of making a Table of Contents. It also shows you how to create a table of figures or other types of similar tables.

The term Table of Contents is a little cumbersome to use over and over again throughout this chapter. Being a bit of a computer nerd myself, I kind of like using TLAs (three-letter acronyms). So I frequently use *TOC* to stand for Table of Contents in this chapter, if for no other reason than to save ink and paper.

Understanding Tables of Contents

A Table of Contents is simply a list of the headings that appear in a document, typically with the page number for each heading as shown in Figure 1-1. Word can create a TOC for you automatically based on the heading paragraphs in your document.

Contents

Contents 1

Understanding Tables of Contents 1

Creating a Table of Contents 5

Beyond Heading Styles 8

Creating a Table of Figures or Other Similar Tables 11

Updating Tables of Contents or Figures 14

Figure 1-1: A simple Table of Contents.

The Table of Contents feature is one of several Word features that depend on the proper use of styles for trouble-free operation. When you create a TOC, Word searches through your document and looks for heading paragraphs to include in the table. How on Earth does Word know which paragraphs are supposed to be headings? By looking at the style you assign to each paragraph: You format the heading paragraphs with heading styles, such as Heading 1, Heading 2, and so on.

If you plan to create a Table of Contents, make sure that you use heading styles to format your document's headings, especially those headings that you want to appear in the TOC. You should do this anyway, of course, because styles help you format your headings consistently.

Word provides three shortcut keys for applying heading styles:

Shortcut Key	***Description***
Ctrl+Alt+1	Heading 1
Ctrl+Alt+2	Heading 2
Ctrl+Alt+3	Heading 3

If you want, you can tell Word to use different styles to create a TOC. If you format your chapter titles with a Chapter Title style, for example, you can tell Word to include paragraphs formatted with the Chapter Title style in the TOC. For more information, see the section "Beyond Heading Styles," later in this chapter.

Creating a Table of Contents

If you assign heading styles to your document's headings, creating a Table of Contents is easy. Just follow these simple steps:

1. **Move the insertion point to the place where you want the Table of Contents to appear.**

The TOC generally appears on its own page near the beginning of a document. Press Ctrl+Enter to create a new page if necessary and then click to position the insertion point on the empty page.

2. **Open the References tab on the Ribbon and then click the Table of Contents button found in the Table of Contents group.**

A menu that lists several Table of Contents styles is displayed.

3. **Click the Table of Contents style you want to use.**

The TOC is added to the document, as shown in Figure 1-2. Note that the shaded frame that's drawn around the Table of Contents is visible only when you hover the cursor over the table. This frame doesn't appear when you print the document.

You're done!

Book VI
Chapter 1

Creating a Table of Contents or Table of Figures

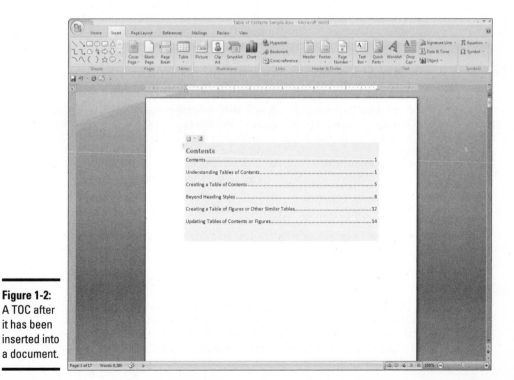

Figure 1-2:
A TOC after it has been inserted into a document.

If you don't like any of the predefined Tables of Contents, you can create a customized TOC by clicking the Table of Contents button and selecting Insert Table of Contents Field. This action summons the dialog box shown in Figure 1-3, from which you can manually choose the options for your table.

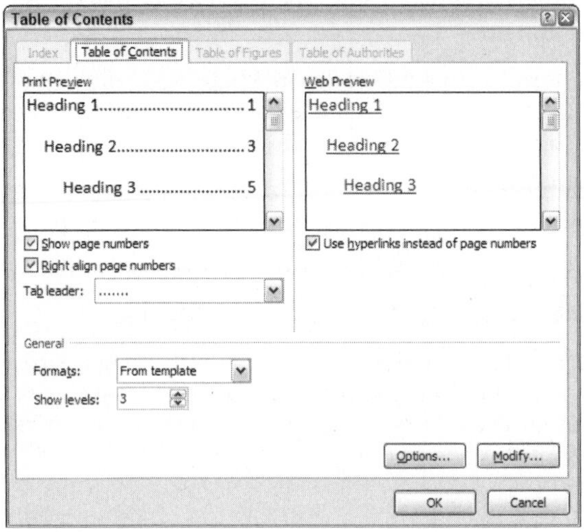

Figure 1-3:
The Table of Contents dialog box.

Among other things, the Table of Contents dialog box lets you select the following options:

✦ **Show Page Numbers:** Deselect this check box if you want the TOC to show the document's outline but not page numbers.

✦ **Right Align Page Numbers:** Deselect this check box if you want the page numbers placed right next to the corresponding text rather than at the right margin.

✦ **Tab Leader:** Use this drop-down list to change or remove the dotted line that connects each TOC entry to its page number.

✦ **Formats:** Use this drop-down list to select one of several predefined formats for the Table of Contents.

✦ **Show Levels:** Use this control to specify which heading levels to include in the table.

Here are some additional techniques to remember when you compile a TOC:

✦ You can make changes directly to a TOC by clicking in the table and typing. However, this is a bad idea because any changes you make are lost the next time you regenerate the Table of Contents. See the section "Updating a Table of Contents" for more information.

✦ Unfortunately, Word doesn't add Chapter 1 in front of the TOC entry for Chapter 1. If you want chapter numbers to appear in your TOC, you must include them in the paragraphs formatted with a style that is included in the TOC (such as Heading 1).

✦ To delete a TOC, select the entire table and press Delete. Or click the Table of Contents button on the References tab on the Ribbon. From the menu that appears, choose Remove Table of Contents.

✦ Word formats entries in a TOC with a set of standard styles named TOC 1, TOC 2, TOC 3, and so on. If you don't like any of the predefined formats in the Formats list in the Table of Contents dialog box (refer to Figure 1-3), select From Template from the list and click the Modify button. A special version of the Style dialog box, showing only the standard TOC styles, appears. You can then change the appearance of your table by modifying the various TOC styles.

Updating a Table of Contents

When you create a TOC, Word scans the entire document to determine which entries should go in the table and which page numbers should be used for each entry. However, after you create the TOC none of the changes you make to the document are reflected in the TOC. So if you create a TOC before you're done with the document, the TOC quickly becomes out of date.

To rebuild a TOC after you make changes, just click the Update Table button in the Table of Contents group of the References tab. The dialog box shown in Figure 1-4 appears. Here, you can choose whether to rebuild the entire table or just update the page numbers. Click OK to update the table.

Figure 1-4:
Updating a
Table of
Contents.

Here are a few other ways to update a Table of Contents:

✦ Select the table and press F9.

✦ Right-click the table and choose Update Field from the shortcut menu.

✦ Press Ctrl+A to select the entire document and then press F9. Doing this updates all of the Tables of Contents in the document, in case you have more than one.

Don't forget to save your file after you update the tables.

Adding Text

Sometimes you want a Table of Contents to include a bit of arbitrary text that hasn't been formatted with a heading style. To do so, just highlight the text you want to include in the table and click the Add Text button in the Table of Contents group on the References tab. A menu appears that allows you to select the level where you want the text to appear in the table.

After you've added the text, you need to update the table before the text will appear in the table. For more information, see the section "Updating a Table of Contents," earlier in this chapter.

Beyond Heading Styles

Using the standard heading styles to create a Table of Contents is convenient but not always exactly what you want to do. What if you created a document that consists of several chapters and you marked the title of each chapter with a Chapter Title style? Fortunately, Word lets you create a Table of Contents based on paragraphs formatted with any style you want, not just the standard heading styles.

To create a Table of Contents by using styles other than the standard heading styles, follow these steps:

1. **Click Table of Contents in the Table of Contents group on the References tab and then choose Insert Table of Contents Field.**

The Table of Contents dialog box appears. (Refer to Figure 1-3.)

2. Click the Options button.

The Table of Contents Options dialog box appears, as shown in Figure 1-5. This dialog box lists all the styles available in the document and lets you assign a Table of Contents level to each style.

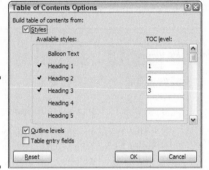

**Book VI
Chapter 1**

Creating a Table
of Contents or
Table of Figures

Figure 1-5:
The Table of
Contents
Options
dialog box.

3. Adjust the TOC level fields to reflect the styles you want to include in your Table of Contents.

The TOC level fields initially are set to include standard heading styles, but that's easy to change. To exclude a style from the Table of Contents, select the style's TOC level field and delete the number in the field. To add a style to the Table of Contents, choose the style's TOC level field and type the outline level you want that style to represent.

4. Click OK to return to the Table of Contents dialog box.

5. Click OK again to insert the Table of Contents.

Voilà! You're finished.

Keep in mind the following when using styles other than the standard style to create a Table of Contents:

✦ The initial settings for the TOC level fields reflect the Show Levels setting in the Table of Contents dialog box (refer to Figure 1-3). If you plan to exclude the standard heading levels from your Table of Contents, set the Show Levels drop-down list to 1 before calling up the Table of Contents Options dialog box. Then you have to clear only the TOC level field for the Heading 1 style.

✦ If you really mess up the Table of Contents options, you can click the Reset button to return everything to the default settings.

♦ No rule says that the styles you include in the Table of Contents all have to appear at different levels. Suppose that you want to include paragraphs formatted with the Chapter Title, Preface Title, Foreword Title, and Appendix Title styles in the Table of Contents at the top level. No problem. Just type **1** in the TOC level field for each of these styles in the Table of Contents Options dialog box.

TECHNICAL STUFF

Only a crazy person would use fields to create a Table of Contents

Because of styles, compiling a Table of Contents in Word is as easy as pie — as easy as popping a frozen pie in the oven, that is. The Table of Contents equivalent of baking a pie from scratch is using fields rather than styles to create the TOC. The only real reason to use fields is if you want the text that appears in the TOC to vary slightly from the document text on which you base the TOC. You might want to add "Chapter 1" in front of the title for Chapter 1, for example.

To create a TOC from fields rather than from styles, you first must insert special TC fields throughout your document wherever you want a TOC entry created. These TC fields are Word field codes that mark the text that will be assembled to create the table of contents. Here are the painful steps for inserting these fields:

1. **Place the insertion point where you want to insert the TC field.**

   For example, place a TC field at the start of each heading in the document.

2. **Click the Field button in the Quick Parts group of the Insert tab.**

   The Field dialog box appears.

3. **Select Index and Tables from the Categories list.**

4. **Select TC from the Field Names list.**

5. **In the Text Entry field, type the text that you want to include in the TOC in quotation marks immediately after the TC field code, as shown in this example:**

   ```
   Chapter 1: I Am Born
   ```

6. **Click OK or press Enter.**

The field is inserted in the document at the insertion point location. It looks something like this:

```
{ TC "Chapter 1: I Am Born" }
```

Word formats it as hidden text, so you might not be able to see it. If you can't, choose Office⇨Word Options⇨Display, click the View tab, select the Hidden Text check box, and then click OK.

After you insert all the TC fields, you create the TOC by choosing Table of Contents⇨Insert Table of Contents Field in the Table of Contents group on the References tab. Click the Options button and then check the Table Entry Fields check box in the Table of Contents Options dialog box. Click OK to return to the Table of Contents dialog box and then click OK again to compile the table.

Creating a Table of Figures or Other Similar Tables

Tables of Contents aren't the only kind of tables you can create with the References tab. You can also compile tables of figures, tables of tables, tables of equations, or other similar collectibles. Chapter 3 of this mini-book shows how to use this command to create an index, and Chapter 5 of this minibook shows how to create a table of authorities for legal documents.

The process for creating a table of figures is the same as the process for creating a table of tables or equations. Follow these steps to create any of these kinds of tables:

1. On the References tab in the Captions group, click the Insert Caption button.

Figure 1-6 shows the Caption dialog box.

2. Select the type of caption you want to create (Figure, Table, or Equation) in the Label field. Then type the caption in the Caption field. After you finish, click OK.

Figure 1-6:
The Caption dialog box.

Repeat Steps 1 and 2 for every caption you want to insert.

3. Move the insertion point to where you want to insert the table.

4. On the References tab in the Captions group, click the Insert Table of Figures button.

Figure 1-7 shows the resulting dialog box.

5. Select the type of table you want to create from the Caption Label drop-down list.

The Caption Label setting corresponds to the Label setting in the Caption dialog box. To create a table of all figure captions, for example, select Figure from the Caption Label drop-down list.

6. **Select the style you want from the Formats drop-down list.**

As you click the various formats, the Preview window shows how the resulting table appears.

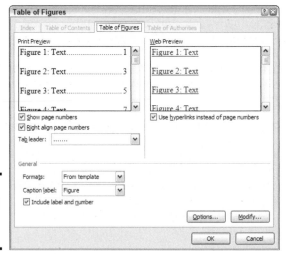

Figure 1-7:
The Table of
Figures
dialog box.

7. **Fiddle with the other controls to fine-tune the table's appearance.**

- *Show Page Numbers:* Deselect this check box if you want the table to list the captions but not page numbers.

- *Right Align Page Numbers:* Deselect this check box if you want the page numbers placed right next to the corresponding text rather than at the right margin.

- *Tab Leader:* Use this drop-down list to add or remove the dotted line that connects each table entry with its page number.

- *Formats:* Use this drop-down list to choose one of several predefined formats for the table of figures.

- *Caption Label:* Use this drop-down list to choose whether you build a table of figures, a table of equations, or a table of tables.

- *Include Label and Number:* Deselect this check box if you want the table to include the caption text (for example, "A Heffalump and a Woozle" or "Ratio of Red M&Ms") but not the number (for example, Figure 1 or Table 3).

8. Click OK.

The table is inserted into the document.

Word is set up to create captions and tables for equations, figures, and tables. If you want to create other types of captions and tables — for limericks or cartoons, for example — you can add items to the list of labels that appears in the Caption and Table of Figures dialog box. On the References tab in the Captions group click the Insert button. Then click the New Label button. Type a new label (such as Limerick or Cartoon) and click OK. Type the caption text and click OK to insert the first caption of the new type. Later, when you insert the Table of Figures, the label you created appears in the Caption Label list.

To delete a table of figures, select the entire table and press Delete.

The entries in a table of figures are formatted with a standard Table of Figures style. If you don't like any of the predefined formats in the Formats list in the Index and Tables dialog box, select From Template and click the Modify button. A special version of the Style dialog box appears, showing only the standard Table of Figures style. You can then change the appearance of your table by modifying the Table of Figures style.

Book VI Chapter 1

Creating a Table of Contents or Table of Figures

Chapter 2: Working with Footnotes and Endnotes

In This Chapter

✔ Adding footnotes

✔ Changing the appearance of footnotes

✔ Modifying the reference marks

✔ Changing the footnote separators

✔ Finding a footnote reference

Footnotes. Back when I was in college, typing them was a major pain in the derriere[1]. You had to count out the lines just right to make sure that you left enough room at the bottom of the page. And what could you do to deal with footnote references that fell right at the bottom of the page, too close to the margin to place the note on the same page?

Footnotes are one of the neatest features of word processors, at least if you're in college. After that, they're pretty useless appendages, unless you happen to work at the college, in which case the footnote feature becomes a source of resentment — just one among many examples of how easy kids have it today. Hmph.

Adding a Footnote

Using footnotes is a snap, unless you want to get fancy with them. Here's the down-and-dirty procedure for adding plain-vanilla footnotes:

1. **Put the insertion point where you want the little footnote reference number to appear in your text.**

2. **On the References tab in the Footnotes group, click the Insert Footnote button.**

   The footnote reference is added to the text, and the footnote itself is placed at the bottom of the page.

[1] Hind part; rear appendage; stern.

3. Type the footnote.

Figure 2-1 shows how a completed footnote looks.

You're done.

Word automatically numbers footnotes for you. Heck, that's the point. When you insert a footnote, Word adds a little footnote reference number in the text and pairs it with a number in the footnote itself. If you go back later and insert a new footnote in front of an existing one, Word automatically juggles the footnote numbers to keep everything in sync.

Here are a few tips for working with footnotes:

✦ For an extra-quick way to create a footnote, use the keyboard shortcut Ctrl+Alt+F. This keyboard shortcut means "Go directly to the footnote. Do not display the Footnote and Endnote dialog box; do not collect $200."

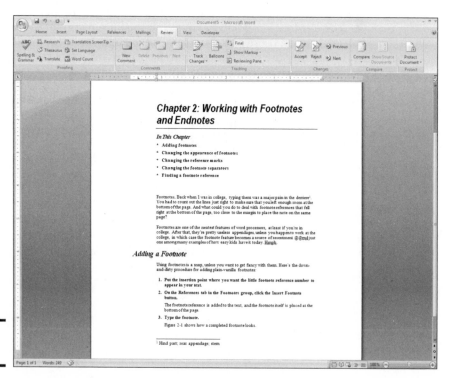

Figure 2-1:
A footnote.

♦ To create an *endnote* instead of a footnote, click the Add Endnote button instead of the Add Footnote button. *Endnotes* are similar to footnotes, but appear all together at the end of the page instead of at the bottom of each page.

♦ For more control over endnotes and footnotes, call up the Footnote and Endnote dialog box by clicking the dialog box launcher at the bottom right corner of the Footnotes group of the References tab. See Figure 2-2.

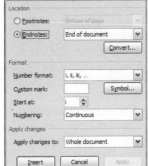

Figure 2-2:
The
Footnote
and Endnote
dialog box.

♦ If you start off with endnotes but then decide that you want to convert your endnotes to footnotes (or vice versa), fear not. Just call up the Footnote and Endnote dialog box and click the Convert button. This brings up the Convert Notes dialog box, shown in Figure 2-3. Then click OK to convert your footnotes to endnotes. Click Close to dismiss the Footnote and Endnote dialog box.

Figure 2-3:
The Convert
Notes dialog
box.

♦ To delete a footnote, select its footnote reference number in the text and press Delete.

Changing the Footnote Format

The formatting of footnotes is governed by the Footnote Text style. You can change the appearance of all the footnotes in your document by simply modifying the Footnote Text style. (Refer to Chapter 3 of Book 2 for information about modifying styles.)

Similarly, you can format footnote reference numbers by using the Footnote Reference style. This style is a character style, so it doesn't affect formatting for the entire paragraph.

The initial setting for footnote text is Normal + 10 point. Therefore, footnotes are formatted with the same font that's in your Normal paragraphs, except that they are 10 point regardless of the Normal text size. If you want your footnotes to appear in a different font or size than the rest of the document, change the font or size for the Footnote Text style.

The initial setting for footnote references is Default Character Format + Superscript. As a result, footnote reference numbers print using the same font as the rest of the text in the paragraph, except that the superscript attribute applies. If you want to see footnote references in a different font, all you have to do is change the Footnote Reference style.

Both footnote text and footnote references automatically apply when you create footnotes, so you shouldn't have any cause to apply these formats directly.

Changing the Reference Marks

Most footnotes are numbered 1, 2, 3, and so on, but Word enables you to change this standard numbering format to use letters, Roman numerals, or the special reference symbols *, †, ‡, and §.

Follow these steps to change reference marks:

1. **Summon the Footnote and Endnote dialog box by clicking the dialog box launcher in the bottom-right corner of the Footnote group on the References tab.**

The Footnote and Endnote dialog box is shown back in Figure 2-2.

2. **Select the Number Format you want.**

This list shows your choices:

   1, 2, 3 . . .

   a, b, c . . .

A, B, C . . .

i, ii, iii . . .

I, II, III . . .

*, †, ‡, § . . .

3. **Click Apply.**

All the footnotes in a section must use the same numbering scheme. You can't mix and match.

If you choose the special symbols *, †, ‡, and § for your reference marks, Word doubles them if necessary to create unique reference marks. The first four footnotes use the symbols singly. The mark for the fifth through eighth notes are **, ††, ‡‡, and §§. After that, the symbols are tripled.

To keep this doubling and tripling of symbols in check, select the Restart Each Page option in the Note Options dialog box. That way, the mark for the first note on each page is always an asterisk (*). Otherwise, you end up with reference marks like §§§§§§§§§§, which look really silly.

You can bypass Word's automatic footnote-numbering scheme at any time by entering any text you want to use for the mark in the Custom Mark text box in the Footnote and Endnote dialog box. For example, you can specify that an asterisk (*) mark all footnotes. If you want to enter a symbol that's not readily available from the keyboard, click the Symbol button and select the symbol you want from the resulting Symbol dialog box.

Finding a Footnote Reference

To quickly find the reference mark for a particular footnote or endnote, follow these steps:

1. **Click the Home tab, and in the Editing group, click the Go To button.**

   Or press Ctrl+G. A dialog box that isn't worthy of a separate figure here displays.

2. **In the Go To What list box, select Footnote or Endnote.**

3. **In the Enter Footnote Number text box, type the number of the footnote that you want to go to.**

   If the notes are numbered with reference symbols (*, †, ‡, and §), type the corresponding number (1, 2, 3, and so on).

4. **Click OK.**

   There it is.

Or, for an even easier method, click the Select Browse Object button located near the bottom of the scroll bar on the right edge of the document window. Then choose one of the following buttons from the pop-up menu that appears:

Browse by endnote

Browse by footnote

The double-headed up- and down-arrow buttons that appear above and below the Select Browse Object button change so that they go to the previous and next footnote or endnote, respectively.

Chapter 3: Indexing Your Masterpiece

In This Chapter

- ✔ Marking index entries
- ✔ Creating an index
- ✔ Updating an index
- ✔ Marking a range of pages
- ✔ Creating subentries
- ✔ Creating cross-references

*I*f all you ever use Word for is to create one- and two-page memos on mundane subjects, such as how to clean the coffee maker, you can skip this chapter. After all, you don't need an index for a two-page memo on coffee maker cleaning unless you work at the Pentagon. If, on the other hand, your memo turns into a 200-page policy manual on appliance maintenance, an index may well be in order.

As luck has it, Word just happens to have a most excellent indexing feature that can help you with the tedious task of indexing. It doesn't create the index for you automatically, but it does help you identify which words to include in the index, and, without too much complaining, Word compiles and formats the index from the words you mark.

Creating an index is a three-stage affair. First, you must mark all the words and phrases within your document that you want to appear in the index. Second, you go to the Index group on the References tab and click the Insert Index button to create the index. This command takes all the words and phrases you mark, sorts them in alphabetical order, and combines identical entries. Third, you carefully review the index, lament that Word didn't do a better job, and fix what you can.

I've indexed quite a few books in my day, and I have yet to find a word processor with an indexing feature that really does the trick. Word is no exception. It can gather your index entries for you, but it can't organize them or make sure that you create your index entries with any degree of consistency. It does a better job than any other word processor I've had the pleasure of working with, but you should still be prepared to do a ton of work yourself.

You can mark the words you want to include in an index in two ways: manually, marking each word one by one; or automatically, giving Word a list of words you want in the index and letting it mark the words in the document. First I show you the manual way and then, later in the chapter, I show you the automatic way (in the section, "Isn't There an Easier Way?").

Mark Those Index Entries

The first — and most important — task in creating an index is to mark the words or phrases you want to include in the index. The most common way to do that is to insert an index marker in the document at each occurrence of each item you want to appear in the index.

To mark index entries manually, follow these steps as long as you can stay awake:

1. **Open the document you want to index.**

2. **Select the word or phrase you want in the index by using the mouse or the keyboard.**

3. **Press the keyboard shortcut Alt+Shift+X.**

Alt+Shift+X is one of Word's more memorable keyboard shortcuts, to be sure. It opens the Mark Index Entry dialog box, shown in Figure 3-1.

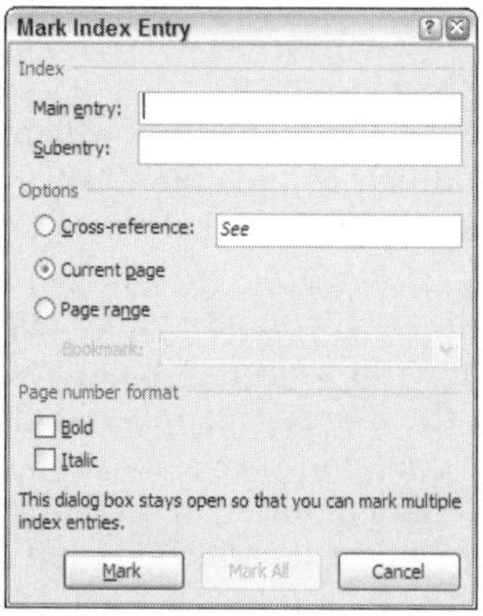

Figure 3-1: The Mark Index Entry dialog box.

4. **Double-check the content in the Main Entry field. If it's correct, click the Mark button. If not, correct it and then click Mark.**

The text doesn't have to appear in the index exactly as it appears in the document. You may highlight an abbreviation to include in the index, for example, but then edit the Main Entry field so that the full spelling of the word, rather than the abbreviation, appears in the index.

5. **To index an entry under a different word, type the alternative entry in the Main Entry field and click the Mark button again.**

   For example, you might want to create an entry for "mutt, mangy" in addition to "mangy mutt."

6. **Mark any additional index entries by highlighting them in the document and clicking the Mark button.**

   The Mark Index Entry dialog box works somewhat like the Spelling dialog box in the way that it stays on-screen so that you can efficiently mark additional index entries. So, while the Mark Index Entry dialog box remains visible, you can select the text for another index entry and then click Mark to mark it. You can keep indexing for as long as you have the energy.

7. **After you mark each of the index entries you want, click the Close button.**

The index entries are marked with special codes formatted as hidden text so that you can't normally see them and they don't print. They are there, however, waiting to be counted when you create the index.

Here are some timely tips for preparing your index entries:

✦ The most efficient way to create an index is after you write and edit your document. Set aside some time to work through the document with the Mark Index Entry dialog box. Don't bother to create index entries as you write your document; it just slows you down and distracts you from your primary task: writing.

✦ Another way to summon the Mark Index Entry dialog box is to open the References tab on the Ribbon and then click the Mark Entry button in the Index group. (This button is shown in the margin.)

✦ If you come across a word or phrase while marking index entries that you know occurs elsewhere in your document, click the Mark All button in the Mark Index Entry dialog box. By clicking the Mark All button, you create an index entry not only for the selected text, but also for any other occurrence of the selected text within the document.

✦ Each time you mark an index entry, Word activates the Show All Formatting Marks option, which reveals not only the hidden text used to mark index entries, but also other characters normally hidden from view, such as field codes, tab characters, optional hyphens, and so on. This behavior is normal, so don't be surprised when it happens. To return your display to normal, just click the Show/Hide button in the Paragraph group of the Home tab (shown in the margin).

✦ Index entries look something like this: { XE "mangy mutt" }, formatted as hidden text. You can edit the index entry text (the part between quotation marks) if you want to change an index entry after you create it.

Creating an Index

After you mark the index entries, the process of generating the index is relatively easy. Here are the steps:

1. **Move the insertion point to the place where you want the index to appear.**

   The index generally begins on a new page near the end of the document. Press Ctrl+Enter to create a new page if necessary, and click to position the insertion point on the empty page. You might want to add a heading, such as Index, at the top of the page.

   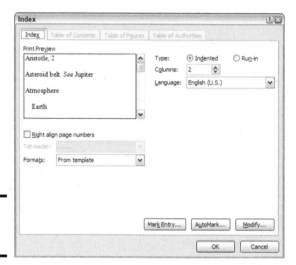
   Insert Index

2. **Open the References tab on the Ribbon and then click the Insert Index button found in the Index group. (This button is shown in the margin.)**

   The Index dialog box appears, as shown in Figure 3-2.

Figure 3-2:
The Index
dialog box.

3. **Select the index style that you want from the Formats drop-down list.**

   As you click the various formats, the Print Preview area shows how the resulting index will appear.

4. **Play with the other controls in the Index tab to fine-tune the index.**

   - *Type:* Lets you place index subentries on separate indented lines (Indented) or run together (Run-in).

   - *Columns:* Sets the number of columns you want in the index. Two is the norm.

- *Language:* If you have multiple language options installed in Word, you can select the language to use in this drop-down list.

- *Right Align Page Numbers:* Select this check box if you want the page numbers placed at the right edge of the index.

- *Tab Leader:* Changes or removes the dotted line that connects each index entry to its page number. You can remove the dotted line only when you select the Right Align Page Numbers option.

- *Formats:* Lets you choose one of several preset formats for the index. Or, you can specify From Template to use styles in the document's template to determine the formatting for the index.

5. Click OK.

The index is inserted into the document.

If you see the index's field code (`{ INDEX \r \h "A" \c "2" }`) rather than the index itself, right-click the index field code and choose Toggle Field Codes.

To delete an index, select the entire index and then press Delete.

The entries in an index format with a set of standard styles named Index 1, Index 2, Index 3, and so on. If you don't like any of the predefined formats listed in the Formats list in the Index and Tables dialog box, select From Template in the Formats drop-down list and then click the Modify button. A special version of the Style dialog box appears, listing only the standard Index styles. You can then change the appearance of your index by modifying the various Index styles.

Updating an Index

Whenever you edit your document, you run the risk of messing up the index. Even a slight change can push text from the bottom of one page to the top of the next and possibly invalidate the index. Fortunately, this section gives you several ways to keep your index up-to-date.

Choose Office➪Word Options to bring up the Word Options dialog box. Select the Display tab and then check the Update Fields Before Printing in the Printing Options section and click OK. Word automatically updates the index every time you print your document.

To update an index without printing the document, select the index and press F9. If you point to the index and right-click, the shortcut menu that appears includes an Update Field command. Using this command works the same as pressing F9.

Marking a Range of Pages

If a particular topic is discussed for several pages in your document, you might want to create an index entry that marks a range of pages (for example, 26–29) rather than each page individually (26, 27, 28, 29).

Unfortunately, the procedure for marking page ranges isn't as slick as it could be. You have to mess around with a Word doohickey called a book-mark. A *bookmark* is a name you can assign to a selection of text. You usually use bookmarks to mark locations in your document so that you can get back to them later, but they have all sorts of more interesting uses. Marking a range of pages for an index is just one.

To use a bookmark to create a range of pages in an index, follow these steps (this process gets tricky, so hang on to your hat):

1. **Highlight the entire range of text you want included in the index entry's page range.**

A long discussion of a single topic could go on for pages, so be prepared.

2. **Open the Insert tab on the Ribbon and click the Bookmark button, found in the Links group. (This button is shown in the margin.)**

The Bookmark dialog box appears, as shown in Figure 3-3.

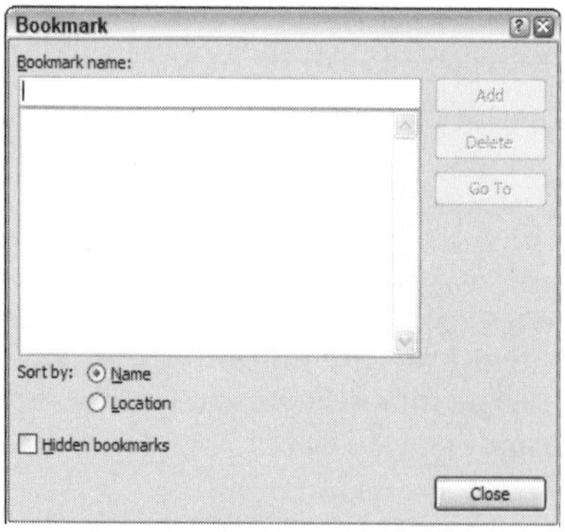

Figure 3-3:
The
Bookmark
dialog box.

3. **Type a bookmark name to identify the bookmark.**

Bookmark names can be as long as 40 characters and can be made up of any combination of letters and numbers. Spaces aren't allowed, but you can use an underscore to double as a space.

4. **Click Add to create the bookmark.**

5. **Position the insertion point at the beginning of the bookmark and press Alt+Shift+X.**

   The Mark Index Entry dialog box appears.

6. **Type the text you want to appear in the index in the Main Entry field.**

7. **Select the Page Range option.**

8. **Select the bookmark you just created from the Bookmark drop-down list box.**

   All the bookmarks in the current document appear in this drop-down list.

9. **Click the Mark button to create the index entry.**

After you create the bookmark and an index entry naming the bookmark, the index includes the range of page numbers for the entry.

The location of various bookmarks in your document can be indicated by large brackets in the text. To activate these brackets, open the Word Options dialog box by clicking the Office button, then clicking the Word Options button. Then, check the Show Bookmarks option in the Show Document Content section of the Advanced tab.

Make the bookmark name as close to identical to the index entry text as you can. Use underscore characters rather than spaces: master_document for master document, for example.

Book VI
Chapter 3

Indexing Your
Masterpiece

Creating Subentries

You include a *subentry* when a word is used for two different meanings or when a word serves as a category organizer for several related words. For example, you might want to create an index entry that looks like the following example:

crew

>   Kirk, James T., 15
>
>   McCoy, Leonard H., 16
>
>   Scott, Montgomery, 16
>
>   Spock, Mr., 17

Here, the index entries for Kirk, McCoy, Scott, and Spock are all subentries of the main entry: crew.

To create index subentries, you follow the procedure for marking index entries, which I explain earlier in this chapter. You type text for both the main entry and the subentry, however, in the Mark Index Entry dialog box. Each of the preceding index entries, for example, has crew for the Main Entry field and the individual crew member's name as the subentry.

You can create a subentry directly in the Main Entry field by typing the main entry, a colon, and the subentry. For example, type **crew:Kirk, James T.** to create *Kirk, James T.* as a subentry of *crew.*

See Also . . .

A cross-reference is one of those annoying messages signaling that you're about to embark on a wild goose chase:

crew, see cast.

To create a cross-reference, begin by marking an index entry as you normally do. On the Mark Index Entry dialog box, select the Cross-Reference option and then type some text in the accompanying text box. Word automatically merges the cross-reference with other index entries for the same text.

Isn't There an Easier Way?

Yet another way to create index entries is to use an *automark file,* which is simply a list of the words that you want Word to include in the index. Word then creates an index entry for each occurrence of each word in the list. Sounds like a great timesaver, eh? It is, sometimes. Provided you do a good job creating the automark file in the first place.

Here are the steps:

1. **Create a new document for the word list.**

2. **Type the list of words you want to index, each on its own line.**

For example:

Kirk

Spock

McCoy

Scotty

3. **(Optional) If you want the text in the index to be different from the text in the document, press the Tab key and then type the text exactly as you want it to appear in the index.**

   For example:

Kirk	Kirk, James T.
Spock	Spock, Mr.
McCoy	McCoy, Leonard H.
Scotty	Scott, Montgomery

   Note: You can have more than one line referring to the same index entry. For example:

McCoy	McCoy, Leonard H.
Bones	McCoy, Leonard H.

4. **Save the word list document by clicking the Save button on the Quick Access toolbar.**

5. **Close the word list document.**

6. **Open the document you want to index.**

7. **Click the Insert Index button in the Index group of the References tab.**

   The Index dialog box pushes its way to the front.

8. **Click the AutoMark button.**

   A dialog box similar to the File Open dialog box appears.

9. **Find the file you saved in Step 4, choose it, and click Open.**

10. **Hold your breath while Word adds the index entries.**

    If your word list or the document is long, adding the index may take a while. Be patient.

11. **Select the index and press F9 to update your index with the marks added in Step 10.**

    It's done.

After you create the automatic index entries, you probably want to work your way through the document by creating additional index entries.

Unfortunately, the AutoMark option doesn't account for running discussions of a single topic that span several pages. It results in index entries such as *Vogons, 14, 15, 16, 17, 18* that should read *Vogons, 14-18.* So you'll have to manually fix problems such as these.

When you use tabs to separate the keywords used to locate the items to index and the actual text you want inserted in the index for those items, keep in mind that the tab-stop positions in the word list document don't matter.

If you want, you can use Word's Table feature to create the word list. Create a two-column table and use the first column for the text to find in the document and the second column for the text to include in the index.

Word sometimes refers to the word list as a *concordance.* Just thought you'd want to know.

Chapter 4: Citations and Bibliographies

In This Chapter

✔ Creating reference citations

✔ Working with sources

✔ Creating a bibliography

*I*f you're a student or an academic, you're going to love the new Citations and Bibliography feature of Word 2007. This new feature lets you create a list of sources, add references to those sources throughout your document, and automatically generate a bibliography that lists all the sources referenced in the document.

Best of all, these tools can generate the references and the bibliography in one of ten different standard formats, including most commonly used formats such as MLA, APA, and Chicago as well as more obscure formats such as GOST and Turabian.

And — get this — if you copy a citation from a document that uses MLA and paste it into a document that uses Chicago, the citation will automatically be changed to Chicago! Where was this program when I was in college? Kids these days don't appreciate anything.

The bad news — or good news, if you're a teacher — is that Word still can't do your research for you. You still have to hunt through stacks and stacks of books to find the perfect source. But when you find it, Word will help you cite it in the correct format.

Creating References and Sources

The first time you create a reference from a particular source, you can create a citation and enter the source data so that Word will remember it for future use. To create a citation for a new source, follow these steps:

1. **Click at the location where you want to insert the citation.**

Usually, this location is at the end of the sentence that refers to the source.

2. **Use the Style drop-down list in the Citations & Bibliography group of the References tab to select the bibliography format. (This control is shown in the margin.)**

   You can select one of the following formats:

   • APA

   • Chicago

   • GB7714

   • GOST — Name Sort

   • GOST — Title Sort

   • ISO 690 — First element and date

   • ISO 690 — Numerical reference

   • MLA

   • SIST02

   • Turabian

   Wow! Can you believe there are so many formats? The most commonly used formats on college campuses in the United States are APA, Chicago, and MLA.

3. **Click Insert Citation button in Citations & Bibliography group of the References tab (shown in the margin).**

   This reveals a drop-down menu with the following options:

   • Add New Source

   • Add New Placeholder

   • Search Libraries

4. **Choose Add New Source.**

   The Create Source dialog box, shown in Figure 4-1, appears.

Figure 4-1:
The Create
Source
dialog box.

5. **Use the Type of Source drop-down list to select the source type.**

You can enter bibliographic information for the following types of sources:

- Book
- Book Section
- Journal Article
- Article in Periodical
- Conference Proceedings
- Report
- Web Site
- Document from Web Site
- Electronic Source
- Art
- Sound Recording
- Performance
- Film
- Interview
- Patent
- Case
- Miscellaneous

**Book VI
Chapter 4**

**Citations and
Bibliographies**

The fields that appear in the Create Source dialog box change depending on the source type you select. For example, the Create Source dialog box for a book includes fields for the book's author and publisher. For a film, fields for the performer's and director's names are included.

6. **Enter the bibliographic information into the dialog box.**

For a book, you need to enter the author, title, year, city, and publisher. You probably want to have the book with you to enter this information correctly.

You can select the Show All Bibliography Fields check box to expand the Create Source dialog box to include additional fields. For most bibliographies, the basic fields are sufficient so you can safely ignore this check box.

7. **Click OK.**

The source information is added to Word's database of bibliographic sources, and a reference to the source is added to the document.

You're done! At least for this source. If you have other references and sources, you need to repeat this procedure. And when you're ready, you need to create the bibliography as described in the section "Creating a Bibliography," later in this chapter.

Here are a few additional pointers for creating references and sources:

✦ After you have created a source, that source appears on the drop-down menu for the Insert Citation button. To create another reference to the same source, just click the Insert Citation button and choose the source you want to cite.

✦ If you want to create a reference but you don't yet know the details, click the Insert Citation button and choose Insert New Placeholder. Enter a name for the placeholder and click OK. You can then enter the details, as described in the section "Managing Your Sources," later in this chapter.

✦ The menu that appears when you click the Insert Citation button includes a Search Libraries link that opens the Research task pane. You can then use the various research sources available from the Research pane to locate references for your bibliography.

✦ When you insert a citation, the citation itself becomes an object that you can select and edit. When you select a citation, an arrow appears next to the citation; you can click this arrow to reveal a menu that lets you edit the citation itself or edit the source information. You can also delete the citation by selecting it and pressing Delete.

Creating a Bibliography

After you've marked all the citations in your document, you can easily create a bibliography that references the citations in the correct format. Here are the steps:

1. **Click at the location where you want to insert the bibliography.**

This is usually at the end of the document.

2. **Click the Bibliography button in the Citations & Bibliography group of the References tab (shown in the margin) and then choose Insert Bibliography.**

The bibliography is inserted. That's it!

The bibliography is formatted according to the style selected via the Style drop-down list in the Citations & Bibliography group of the References tab.

Managing Your Sources

Word keeps a list of all the sources you've created, not just for the current document, but for all documents. You can manage this list by clicking the Manage Sources button in the Citations & Bibliography group on the References tab. This brings up the dialog box shown in Figure 4-2.

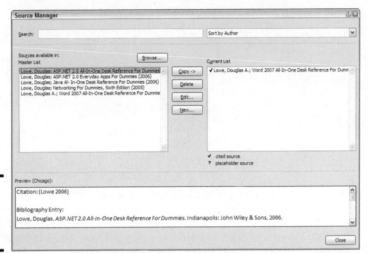

**Book VI
Chapter 4**

**Citations and
Bibliographies**

Figure 4-2:
The Source
Manager
dialog box.

As you can see, this dialog box presents two lists of sources. The list on the left is the Master List of all sources you have created, in any document. The list on the right is the list of sources to include in the bibliography for the current document. Any sources you have referenced in the current document are included in the Current List.

Here are a few interesting things you can do with this dialog box:

✦ You can add a source to the bibliography for the current document even if the source isn't referenced in the document. To do that, select the source in the Master List and click Copy.

✦ You can search for sources by using the Search text box.

✦ To edit the information for a source, select the source and click the Edit button.

✦ Click the New button to create a new source.

✦ The Browse button lets you open a different list.

Chapter 5: I Object! (To Tables of Authorities, That Is)

*I*nasmuch as you, hereinafter referred to as the *reader,* have deemed it necessary, appropriate, and befitting to create, prepare, and otherwise compile a table, list, or enumeration of various and sundry citations, references, and quotations from legal authorities and other sources, including, but not limited to, cases, statutes, rules, treatises, regulations, constitutional provisions, and other authorities occurring within and among documents, files, and other materials prepared with the word-processing software known as Microsoft Word 2007, hereinafter referred to as *Word,* now therefore and thereupon I, hereinafter referred to as *I,* agree to provide within this chapter a thorough and comprehensive description, discussion, and presentation of the techniques, methods, and procedures required to prepare such aforementioned tables, lists, or enumerations. In consideration hitherto, so let it be written, so let it be done.

In other words, this chapter shows you how to use Word's Table of Authorities feature. If you're a lawyer or legal secretary, you already know what a table of authorities is. If you aren't, turn to another chapter before it's too late.

Creating a table of authorities is much like creating an index (see Chapter 3 of this minibook). First you mark the citations where they appear within the document. Then you use Insert Table of Authorities button (in the Table of Authorities group on the References tab) to compile the table of authorities based on the citations you marked. If necessary, you can then edit the table or adjust its formatting. You can also update the table to make sure that all the entries are up-to-date.

Marking Citations

The first step in creating a table of authorities is reviewing the entire document and marking any citations you want to include in the table. Follow these steps:

1. Find a citation you want to mark.

Start at the beginning of the document and work through the whole thing, marking citations as you go. You can simply read through the document to find citations, or you can let Word find the citations for you.

2. Highlight the citation with the mouse or keyboard and press Alt+Shift+I.

The Mark Citation dialog box appears, as shown in Figure 5-1.

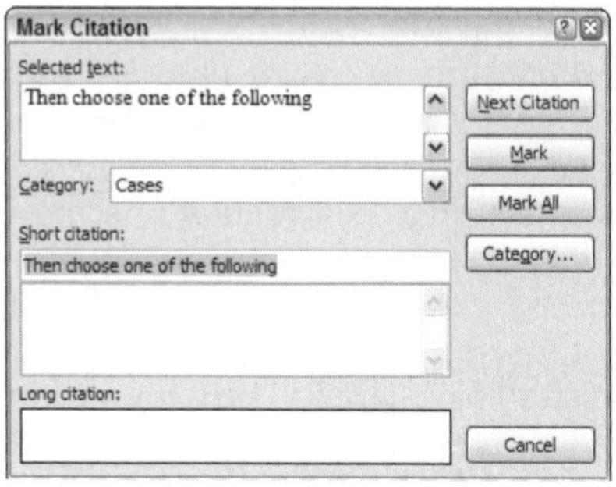

Figure 5-1:
The Mark
Citation
dialog box.

3. Edit the Selected Text field so that it is exactly the way you want the citation to appear in the table of authorities.

The Selected Text field initially contains the text that you selected when you pressed Alt+Shift+I. If the citation in the document isn't how you want it to appear in the table of authorities, click in the Selected Text field and type away. If you want to split the citation into two lines, just position the insertion point where you want the line to split and press Enter.

4. Edit the Short Citation field so that it exactly matches the way the short version of the citation is used in subsequent references throughout the document.

The first time you cite an authority, you must provide a complete citation (such as "Kringle v. New York, 28 NY 2d 312 (1938)"), but thereafter you use the short form ("Kringle v. New York"). Edit the Short Citation field to match the short form of the citation. That way, Word can automatically locate subsequent citations and mark them.

5. Select the type of authority being cited from the Category drop-down list.

Word comes equipped with several common categories: Cases, Statutes, Other Authorities, Rules, Treatises, Regulations, and Constitutional Provisions. You can also create your own categories.

6. Click the Mark button to mark the citation.

Word inserts a hidden field code to mark the citation. The Mark Citation dialog box stays open on-screen so that you can mark additional citations.

7. Click the Next Citation button to find the next citation.

The Next Citation button searches for the next citation in the document by looking for text that is commonly found in legal citations, such as *v.*

8. Highlight the complete text of the citation found by the Next Citation button.

The Next Citation button doesn't highlight the complete citation — only the text it finds that convinces it to stop because a citation is probably nearby. Use the mouse to select the citation in the document. (The Mark Citation dialog box patiently stays on-screen while you mark the citation.)

9. Repeat Steps 3 through 8 until you mark all the citations you can stand.

10. After you finish marking citations, click the Close button.

Word marks citations with field codes formatted as hidden text so that they are normally invisible. They jump to life, however, when you compile a table of authorities. See the next section, "Creating a Table of Authorities," for the steps.

Another way to summon the Mark Citation dialog box is to click the Mark Citation button (shown in the margin). You can find this button located in the Table of Authorities group of the References tab.

If the screen suddenly changes to Print Preview mode when you try to mark a citation, don't panic. You probably pressed Ctrl+Alt+I rather than Alt+Shift+I. Ctrl+Alt+I is the keyboard shortcut for toggling Print Preview on and off. These two keyboard shortcuts are perilously close to one another. If you press the wrong keys, just press Ctrl+Alt+I again to return to Normal view and then start over.

**Book VI
Chapter 5**

I Object! (To Tables of Authorities, That Is)

Every time you stumble onto a citation that you know occurs later in your document, click the Mark All button. The Mark All button creates a citation not only for the selected text, but also any subsequent occurrences of the citation.

 Each time you mark a citation, Word activates the Show All Formatting Marks option. To return your display to normal, click the Show/Hide button (shown in the margin) on the Paragraph group in the Home tab of the Ribbon.

The field codes for citations look like the following example:

```
{ TA \l "Kringle v. New York
28 NY 2d 312 (1938)" \s "Kringle v. New York" \c 1 }
```

The preceding codes are formatted as hidden text, so you don't normally see them. You can edit the long citation text (the part between quotes following \l) or the short citation text (the quoted text that follows \s) if you want to change a citation after you create it.

Creating a Table of Authorities

After you mark all the citations in your document, follow these steps to create the table of authorities:

1. **Move the insertion point to the place where you want the table of authorities to appear.**

You can place the table of authorities at the front or back of the document. If you want the table to appear on its own page, press Ctrl+Enter to create a page break. You might also want to type a heading, such as **Table of Authorities**.

2. **Click the insert Table of Authorities button in the Table of Authorities group on the References tab.**

The Table of Authorities dialog box appears, as shown in Figure 5-2.

3. **Pick the style you want from the Formats drop-down list.**

As you click the various formats, the Print Preview area shows how the resulting table of authorities appears.

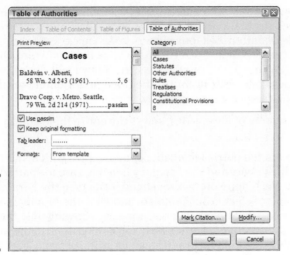

Book VI
Chapter 5

I Object! (To Tables
of Authorities,
That Is)

Figure 5-2:
The Table of
Authorities
dialog box.

4. Play with the other controls to fine-tune the table of authorities.

- *Use Passim:* Select this check box if you want Word to use the word *passim* when a citation occurs on five or more pages. (Passim is a Latin word that means either "scattered throughout," or "an ugly, overgrown, rat-like creature that hangs upside down by its tail.")

- *Keep Original Formatting:* Select this check box if you want the character formatting (such as underline and italics) that Word applies to the document's citation to carry over into the table of authorities.

- *Tab Leader:* Use this drop-down list to add or remove the dotted line that connects each table entry with its page number.

- *Formats:* Use this drop-down list to select one of several predefined formats for the table of authorities.

- *Category:* Use this list box to choose the citation category you want compiled. Usually you leave the category set to the default, All. If you want to compile a table of one category (cases, rules, regulations, and so on), select the category from the drop-down list.

5. Click OK.

The table of authorities is created.

Here are some things to remember when you compile a table of authorities:

✦ If the table of authorities looks like { TOA \h \c "1" \p }, call up the Word Options dialog box (choose Office button⇨Word Options), click the Advanced tab, and deselect the Show Field Codes Instead of Their Values check box (found in the Document Content group). Click OK, and the table appears correctly.

✦ To delete a table of authorities, select the entire table and then press Delete.

✦ Word formats the entries in a table of authorities with a standard Table of Authorities style, and the category headings are formatted with a TOA Heading style. If none of the predefined formats in the Formats list tickles your fancy, select From Template and click the Modify button. A special version of the Style dialog box appears, showing only the standard styles used in a table of authorities. You can customize the appearance of your table by modifying the Table of Authorities and TOA Heading styles.

Updating a Table of Authorities

If you edit a document after creating a table of authorities, the table might become out-of-date. To make sure that the table is up-to-date, use one of these techniques:

✦ **Use the Word Options dialog box.** In the Word Options dialog box (Office⇨Word Options), click the Display tab, then select the Update Fields Before Printing check box (found in the Printing Options section), and then click OK. Then the table of authorities automatically updates every time you print your document.

✦ **Press F9.** To update a table of authorities without printing the document, select the table and press F9.

✦ **Use the right-click context-sensitive menu.** If you point to a table of authorities and right-click, the shortcut menu that appears includes an Update Field command. Using the Update Field command works the same as pressing F9.

Adding Your Own Categories

Word comes with seven predefined table of authorities categories: Cases, Statutes, Other Authorities, Rules, Treatises, Regulations, and Constitutional Provisions. If these categories aren't sufficient for your needs, you can add your own. Word has room for up to 16 categories, and you can either add new categories or replace existing categories with new categories of your choosing.

To create your own categories:

1. **Call up the Mark Citation dialog box by pressing Alt+Shift+I. Then click the Category button.**

The Edit Category dialog box appears, as shown in Figure 5-3.

Figure 5-3:
Creating a custom category.

**Book VI
Chapter 5**

I Object! (To Tables
of Authorities,
That Is)

2. **If you want to replace a category, select it in the Category list. If you want to create a new category, scroll past the predefined categories and select one of the dummy categories numbered 8 through 16.**

3. **Type the name you want to use for the new category in the Replace With field and click the Replace button.**

When you add your own categories, they appear in the Category drop-down list box on the Mark Citation dialog box. Then you can assign citations to the new category as you mark them.

Note that the categories you create are stored on your computer, and not as part of the document. As a result, if you use custom categories, be sure to create them consistently on all the computers in your office.

Disclaimer of Warranties and Limit of Liability

The author, Doug Lowe, and the publisher, Wiley Publishing, Inc., make no representations or warranties with respect to the accuracy or completeness of the contents of this chapter and specifically disclaim any implied warranties or merchantability or fitness for any particular purpose and shall in no event be held liable for any loss of profit or any other commercial damage, including, but not limited to, such damages as losing a big case because of a key citation being omitted from a pleading or a brief; tripping, falling, or stumbling over this book; or the cost of medical treatment and/or hospitalization, pain and suffering, lost wages, or emotional anguish due to stress inflicted or sustained while using or attempting to use the Table of Authorities feature in the Word 2007 software program. Et cetera, et cetera, et cetera.

Book VII

Mailings

The 5th Wave   By Rich Tennant

@RICHTENNANT

"You want to know why I'm mad? I suggest you download my latest novel called, 'Why an Obsessive Control-Freak Husband Should Never Pick out Bathroom Tiles Without Asking His Wife First.'"

Contents at a Glance

Chapter 1: Creating Envelopes and Labels

In This Chapter

✔ Printing on envelopes

✔ Creating labels

✔ Printing return-address labels

✔ Creating a custom label for odd-sized labels

Word has a sophisticated mail-merge feature that you can use to print envelopes, labels, and personalized letters from a list of recipient names.

That's not what this chapter is about. If you want to find out how to do mail merges, skip ahead to Chapter 3 of this minibook.

In this chapter, I show you how to use a few relatively simple features of Word 2007: The Envelopes and Labels commands let you create a single envelope or label or an entire page full of labels that are all the same.

Printing an Envelope

Word includes a special Envelopes command that can quickly and professionally print a mailing address (and your return address) on an envelope so that you can stuff your letter into it. You can send the envelope directly to your printer without ever creating a document, or you can add an envelope to an existing document so that you can print your letter and envelope together.

To add an envelope to a letter you already created, open the letter (if it isn't already open) and follow these steps:

1. **Open the Mailings tab on the Ribbon and then click the Envelopes button in the Create group.**

   The Envelopes and Labels dialog box appears, as shown in Figure 1-1.

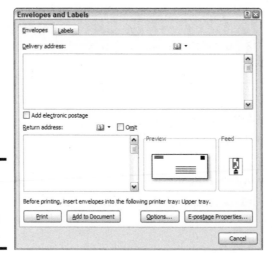

Figure 1-1:
The
Envelopes
and Labels
dialog box.

If the current document contains an address, Word sniffs it out and stuffs it into the Delivery Address field automatically. So you might not need to enter the address. Sometimes Word gets lost and can't find the address, so you have to type it in yourself.

If the Envelopes and Labels dialog box appears without the delivery address filled in, you can click Cancel to dismiss the dialog box. Then select the recipient's address in the letter and click the Envelopes button again. This time, the address is filled in.

2. **If you want your return address to print on the label, type it in the Return Address text box.**

3. **Click the Add to Document button to add the envelope to the letter.**

   The envelope is added to your document as a separate page that appears before the first page of your letter.

When you print the letter, the envelope prints first. So you have to be prepared to insert an envelope into the printer. The exact steps for inserting an envelope depend on your printer. But most printers prompt you to insert an envelope when it wants to print one. Be an obedient printer user and do as you're told.

To print your envelope directly without adding it to a document, click the Print button instead of the Add to Document button in Step 4.

If your envelope prints upside down, you might need to configure Word so that it knows how your printer handles envelopes. From the Envelopes and Labels dialog box, click the Options button. When the Envelope Options dialog box appears, click the Printing Options tab to reveal the printing options, as shown in Figure 1-2. Then select the Feed Method options that correspond to the way your printer accepts envelopes. Click OK to dismiss this dialog box when you're done. Word memorizes these options, so you have to set them only once.

Figure 1-2:
The Printing
Options tab
of the
Envelope
Options
dialog box.

Printing Labels

Word also lets you quickly print labels rather than envelopes. You can use labels in Word three ways:

✦ **You can print just one label.** You can even tell Word which label on a sheet of blank labels you should print. That way, you don't have to waste an entire sheet of labels just to print one label.

✦ **You can print an entire sheet of the same label.** This option is useful for printing return-address labels. I do this approximately once a year, when I send out a few hundred Christmas cards to my inner circle of close and dear friends.

✦ **You can print labels from a database.** This option is really a mail-merge topic, so you have to skip ahead to Chapters 3 and 4 of this minibook to find out more about how to do it.

Here are the steps for printing a full sheet of the same label:

1. **Get some labels.**

You find a huge assortment of labels at your handy office supply store. Pick whichever ones you like, but make sure you get labels that work with your printer.

Word works best with Avery labels, but you can buy a cheaper brand if you want. Most generic labels list the Avery equivalent on the package.

2. **Display the Mailings tab on the Ribbon and then click the Labels button in the Create group.**

The dialog box shown in Figure 1-3 appears.

Figure 1-3:
The Labels tab of the Envelopes and Labels dialog box.

3. **Type the address you want to print in the label in the Address text box.**

Naturally, if you're printing labels for something other than addresses (for example, name tags or file folders), you don't actually type an address here. Instead, type whatever you want to appear on each label in this text box.

4. **Make sure the right labels are selected.**

The label number appears in the lower-right corner of the dialog box. If this number doesn't match the number you're using, click the Options button and select the right label type from the Label Options dialog box, shown in Figure 1-4. Then click OK to return to the Envelopes and Labels dialog box.

Figure 1-4:
Selecting
the label
type.

5. **Click New Document.**

   A new document is created with an entire page of labels, all lined up in a nice table.

6. **(Optional) If you want to format the labels differently, press Ctrl+A to select the entire document and then apply any formatting you want to use.**

   For example, you might want to change the font and size to make your text fit better in the space available in the label.

7. **Insert a sheet of labels in the printer.**

   Be sure to insert the label with the correct orientation. If you're not sure, try this time-honored trick: Draw an arrow on a plain sheet of paper indicating the direction in which you feed the paper, and then test print the labels on that page. When the page comes out of the printer, make a note of whether labels print on the same side of the page as the arrow or on the opposite side. That helps you determine whether to insert the labels face up or face down. (Printing a test page on plain paper is a good idea before using a sheet of labels anyway.)

8. **Choose Office⇨Print to print the labels.**

   That's it; you're done.

To print a single label, select the Single Label option button before you click the New Document button in Step 5. Then use the Row and Column controls to specify which label on the page you want to print. For example, to print on the first label in the upper-left corner of a sheet of labels, choose Row 1 and Column 1.

To send the label or labels directly to the printer rather than to a document, click Print instead of New Document in Step 5.

Creating Custom Labels

If your labels don't appear in the list of predefined labels, you have to create a custom label format. To do so, select a label type that's close in size to the labels you want to create and click the New Label button in the Label Options dialog box. The Label Details dialog box appears, as shown in Figure 1-5.

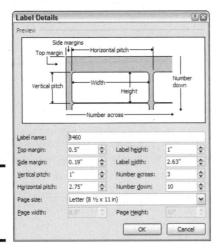

Figure 1-5:
The Label
Details
dialog box.

To set up your custom label, enter appropriate values for each of the fields in this dialog box:

+ **Label Name:** The name for your custom label type.

+ **Top Margin:** The distance between the top of the sheet and the top of the first label.

+ **Side Margin:** The distance between the left edge of the sheet and the left edge of the first margin.

+ **Vertical Pitch:** The distance between the top of one label and the top of the label beneath it.

+ **Horizontal Pitch:** The distance between the left edge of one label and the left edge of the label to its right.

+ **Label Height:** The height of each label.

+ **Label Width:** The width of each label.

✦ **Number Across:** The number of labels in each row.

✦ **Number Down:** The number of labels in each column.

✦ **Page Size:** The size of each sheet of labels, usually 8½ x 11 inches.

As you change these values, the diagram in the Preview window changes to reflect the settings you enter. When you're satisfied with the layout, click OK. Word asks whether you're sure you want to change the label format; click Yes to proceed.

Chapter 2: Faxing and E-Mailing Documents

In This Chapter

✔ **Faxing a document the old-fashioned way**

✔ **Faxing a document with an Internet fax service**

✔ **Sending a document via e-mail**

✔ **Sending a document as an e-mail attachment**

This chapter covers two features in Word that let you send documents to other people. First, you find out how to send a Word document as a fax to anyone who has a fax machine. Then you discover how to e-mail a Word document directly to anyone who has an e-mail address.

Given the choice, e-mailing a document is usually the better solution: The user who receives a document via fax gets a pile of paper, crudely printed on a low-resolution fax machine. But if you e-mail the document, the recipient gets an actual copy of your Word document file, which he or she can then save to disk, print, and perhaps even modify and send back. But the choice is yours.

Sending a Fax

Betcha didn't know that the first patent for a workable fax machine was issued in England in 1843, and that by the 1920s, AT&T offered a fax service that could send copies of photographs over telephone lines for use in newspapers.

Point being that faxing is a pretty old technology. And Word has supported document faxing almost from the very beginning. You can fax a Word document three basic ways:

✦ **Print and fax the document.** The easiest way is to print the document and then use a separate fax machine to actually send the fax. I know it doesn't sound very elegant, but if you send only occasional faxes and you have a fax machine at your disposal, this technique saves you the hassle of figuring out how to deal with Word's built-in faxing features.

✦ **Use a fax modem.** If you have a fax modem installed in your computer and the modem is plugged in to a telephone line, you can send the document to a fax recipient by printing the document, specifying "Fax" as the printer name. I describe this technique in the upcoming section, "Using a fax modem."

✦ **Use a fax service.** If you don't have a fax modem but do have a connection to the Internet, you can send a fax by using one of the many Internet-based faxing services. For more information, see the section "Using a fax service," later in this chapter.

Using a fax modem

To send a fax by using a built-in fax modem, you must properly install the modem in your computer and plug it in to a phone line. In addition, your computer must have Windows Fax Services installed.

If the Fax Services aren't installed, you can install them by choosing Start➪ Control Panel to open the Control Panel folder. Double-click the Add/Remove Programs icon and then click Add/Remove Windows Components. When the Windows Components Wizard appears, select Fax Services, click Next, and follow any other instructions Windows throws in your face.

To send a document by using your fax modem, follow these steps:

1. **Open the document you want to send.**

2. **Choose Office➪Print.**

The Print dialog box appears.

3. **Select Fax from the drop-down list of printers.**

This brings up the Send Fax Wizard. Note that the Send Fax Wizard is part of Windows, not a part of Office. Sending a fax by using this wizard is the same in any program.

4. **Complete the Send Fax Wizard.**

You're asked to enter the recipient's name and fax number, create a cover page, and indicate when you want the fax to be sent.

5. **When the wizard is finished, click Finish to send the fax.**

The fax is sent to the recipient.

Using a fax service

If you don't have a fax modem installed on your computer but do have an Internet connection, you can use an Internet faxing service to send a fax.

Unfortunately, these services aren't free. Fees range from $5 to $20 or more per month, depending on the features you sign up for. In addition, you must have Outlook installed on your computer to use a fax service.

To send a document via a fax service, choose Office➪Send➪Internet Fax. The first time you do this, a dialog box appears telling you that you have to first sign up for a faxing service. When you click OK, Word launches an Internet Explorer window that goes to a Microsoft Web page that lists Internet fax services. You can then follow the links to sign up for a service.

After you properly sign up, choosing Office➪Send➪Internet Fax adds a special header at the top of the document that lets you specify the subject and recipient information. Fill in this information and then click Send to send your fax.

Sending a Document Via E-Mail

If your computer is connected to a network or to the Internet, you can send a copy of the document you're working on to a friend or co-worker via e-mail by using Office➪Send➪Email. Here's the procedure:

1. **Open the document you want to send as an attachment.**

2. **Choose Office➪Send➪Email (as Attachment).**

The New Message dialog box opens, as shown in Figure 2-1.

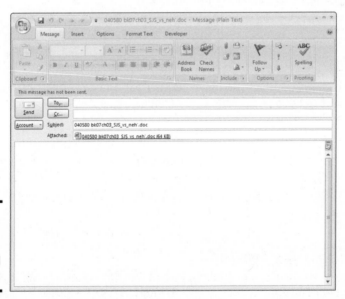

Figure 2-1:
Sending a
document
as an e-mail
attachment.

3. **Type the e-mail address of the person you want to send the document to in the To text box.**

   If you have the recipient's e-mail address on file in your address book, click the To button to summon the Address book. Then select the correct recipient and click OK to return to the New Message dialog box.

4. **Type a subject for your message in the Subject text box.**

5. **Type a message in the message area of the New Message dialog box.**

6. **Click the Send button to send the message.**

   Your message is sent on its way. Hopefully it receives a warm welcome.

Chapter 3: Using the Mail Merge Wizard

In This Chapter

✔ Understanding how mail merge works

✔ Getting started with the Mail Merge Wizard

✔ Following the Mail Merge Wizard's instructions

✔ Working with the Mailings tab

Mail merge. Just the sound of those two words is enough to drive even veteran Word users into a state of utter and complete panic. Just when you think that you've figured out enough about mail merge to put out a simple form letter, along comes Word with a bunch of additional mail-merge features. Arghhhh! What next?

This chapter shows you how to use Word's Mail Merge Wizard to perform basic mail merges. After you master the basics, you might also want to read the next chapter, which presents some more advanced mail-merge features that come in handy from time to time.

Understanding Mail Merge

Mail merge refers to the process of merging a file that contains a list of names and addresses with another file that contains a model letter to produce a bunch of personalized form letters. Suppose that you decide to do some volunteer work for the local public library, and the library decides to put you in charge of getting deadbeats to return long overdue books. A personalized letter is the ideal way to communicate your message to these good-for-nothings. And Word's mail-merge feature is ideal for preparing such a personalized letter.

The beauty of the whole thing is that you can keep the names and addresses in a separate file and use them over and over again. After all, you know these same people are probably going to have overdue books again soon.

Mail merge involves three basic steps:

1. **Create the *main document.***

The main document contains the letter you want to send. It includes the text printed for each letter, plus special *merge fields* that indicate exactly where to place in each letter the information from your mailing list, such as the recipient's name and address.

2. **Create the *data source.***

The data source is just a fancy name for the list of names and addresses that is used to create the form letters. The data source can be a Word document, in which case the information is stored in a table, with one row for each name and address. Individual fields, such as name, address, city, state, zip code, and so on, are stored in separate columns. Or, the data source can be a list of contacts maintained by Outlook, a database created by a program such as Access, or some other type of file. The data source must list the data in a consistent format.

3. ***Merge* the main document with the data source.**

This step creates a form letter for each row in the data source table. You can create the form letters as a separate document, with one letter on each page, or you can send the merged letters directly to the printer. You can also send the merged letters to e-mail or to a fax machine.

You can use mail merge to produce more than form letters. You can also use it to print envelopes or mailing labels, or even documents that don't have anything to do with mailing, such as a directory or a catalog. In short, mail merge is useful for any application in which a list of consistently formatted and repeating data must be converted into a document in which each record in the data source is formatted in a similar way.

Using the Mail Merge Wizard

To start the Mail Merge Wizard, first create a new blank document or open an existing letter. Then click the Mailings tab on the Ribbon, click Start Mail Merge in the Start Mail Merge group, and choose Step By Step Mail Merge Wizard from the menu that appears. The wizard appears in the task pane on the right side of the document window, as shown in Figure 3-1.

After you call up the wizard, you can follow the steps I outline in the following sections.

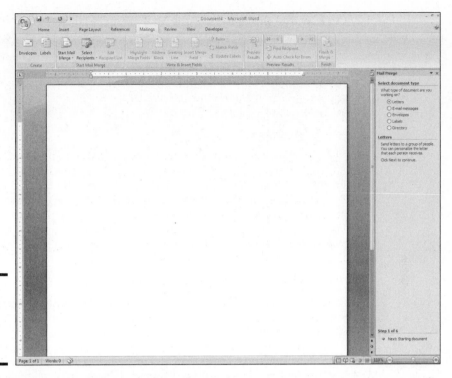

Figure 3-1:
The Mail
Merge
Wizard in
action.

Creating the main document

The first mail-merge task the wizard helps you accomplish is setting up your main document. Here are the steps:

1. **Select the type of documents that you want to create for your mailing.**

The choices are

- Letters
- E-Mail Messages
- Envelopes
- Labels
- Directory

For normal, run-of-the-mill mass mailings, select Letters.

2. **Click Next at the bottom of the Mail Merge Wizard.**

Step 2 of the Mail Merge Wizard appears, as shown in Figure 3-2.

3. **Click the Use the Current Document option if it isn't already selected.**

If you prefer to start a new document based on a template rather than using the current document, choose Start from a Template. Then click the Select Template link and select the template you want to use.

4. **Type the body of your letter.**

Leave out the address block and greeting line. You add those later.

5. **Choose Office⇨Save to save the file when you're done.**

Your letter looks something like the one shown in Figure 3-3.

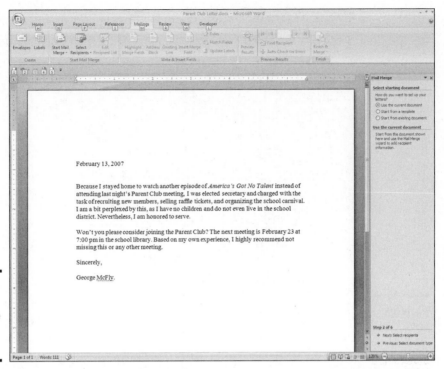

Figure 3-3:
A letter
ready to use
as a main
document.

Creating an address list

The next big step in the Mail Merge Wizard is to select the recipients who
will receive your letters. This step is usually the hardest part of the entire
procedure because it often involves creating an address list with the names
and addresses of your recipients. Here are the bothersome steps:

1. **If you haven't already done so, click Next at the bottom of the wizard
   to proceed to the Select Recipients step.**

   Step 3 of the wizard makes its appearance, as shown in Figure 3-4.

2. **Select the Type a New List radio button and then click the Create
   link.**

   The New Address List dialog box appears, shown in Figure 3-5.

Figure 3-4:
Select
the lucky
recipients.

Figure 3-5:
The New
Address List
dialog box.

If you already created the address list, you can call it up by selecting the Use an Existing List option instead of the Type a New List option. Then click Browse. When the Select Data Source dialog box appears, locate the file you previously saved the address list as and click Open. Then the Mail Merge Recipients dialog box appears, as shown in Figure 3-6, and you can skip ahead to Step 8.

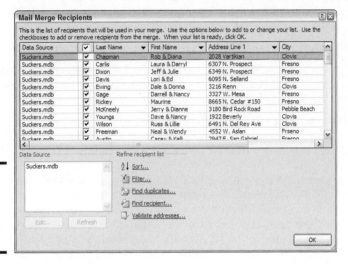

Figure 3-6:
The Mail
Merge
Recipients
dialog box.

3. **Type the information for a person that you want to add to the address list.**

   Press Tab to move from field to field or to skip over fields in which you don't want to enter any data. (You don't need to enter a value for every field.)

4. **After you type all the data for the person, click the New Entry button to add that person's data to the address list.**

5. **Repeat Steps 3 and 4 for each person that you want to add to the data source.**

   To delete a record, move to the record that you want to delete and then click the Delete Entry button.

6. **After you add all the names that you want to, click OK.**

   A Save Address List dialog box appears.

7. **Type a name for your address list and then click Save.**

   The file is saved to your computer's hard drive. Then the Mail Merge Recipients dialog box appears, as shown in Figure 3-6.

   From the Mail Merge Recipients list, you can get back to the New Address List dialog box by clicking the Edit button.

Book VII
Chapter 3

Using the Mail
Merge Wizard

8. **Click the column heading for the column that you want to sort the list by.**

   For example, if you want the letters to print in Zip Code sequence, click the heading for the Zip Code column. (You have to scroll the list to the right to see the Zip Code column.)

9. **Deselect any records that you don't want to include in the mailing.**

   The mailing will be sent to every record that's selected, and the records are all initially selected. So you can manually remove people from the list by deselecting them.

   If the mailing will be sent to only a few people on the list, click the Clear All button to remove all the check marks. Then go through the list and select the ones you want to send the mailing to.

The Address List feature is actually a built-in database program designed especially for Mail Merge. You can customize the fields that are used for each record in the address list by clicking the Customize Columns button in the New Address List dialog box. The Customize Address List dialog box appears, shown in Figure 3-7. This dialog box lets you add fields, remove existing fields, or change the order in which the Address List fields appear.

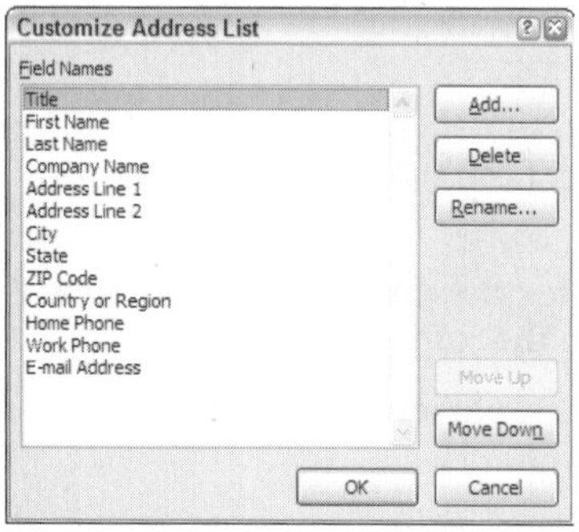

Figure 3-7:
The
Customize
Address List
dialog box.

Word offers ways other than the address list to store the names and addresses for your mailings. The two most popular choices are in an Access database or in your Outlook Address book. To use names and addresses from Outlook, choose the Select from Outlook Contacts option in Step 2. To use an Access database (or any other database), select Use an Existing List in Step 2 and then locate the database in the dialog box that appears.

Inserting the address block and greeting line

After you add names and addresses to the data source, finish your letter by adding placeholders for the address block, greeting line, and any other information you want to insert from the address list. In Wordspeak, these placeholders are called *merge fields*.

If the main document isn't already displayed, select it from the Window menu. Then, follow these steps:

1. **Click Next at the bottom of the wizard to bring up Step 4 of the wizard.**

As Figure 3-8 shows, this step allows you to add the address block and other merge fields to your letter.

Figure 3-8:
Completing
the letter.

2. **Position the insertion point where you want to insert the address block.**

3. **Click the Address Block link.**

The Insert Address Block dialog box appears, as shown in Figure 3-9.

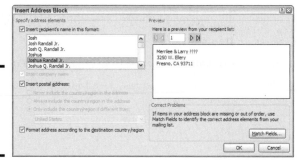

Figure 3-9:
The Insert
Address
Block
dialog box.

4. **Select the options that you want to use for the address block and then click OK.**

You can select the format to use for the recipient's name, whether to use the company name, and whether to use country and region information in the address.

When you click OK, the Insert Address Block dialog box is dismissed, and the address block is inserted.

5. **Position the insertion point where you want to insert the greeting line and click the Greeting Line link.**

The Insert Greeting Line dialog box appears, as shown in Figure 3-10.

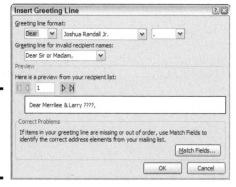

Figure 3-10:
The Insert
Greeting
Line
dialog box.

6. **Select the options that you want to use for the greeting line and then click OK.**

   The Insert Greeting Line dialog box lets you select several options for creating casual or formal greeting lines. When you click OK, the greeting line is inserted into the document.

7. **If you want to insert a field from the address list into the body of the letter, move the insertion point to where you want to insert the field and click the More Items link.**

   The Insert Merge Field dialog box comes up, as shown in Figure 3-11.

Figure 3-11:
The Insert
Merge Field
dialog box.

8. **Select the field you want to insert and click Insert.**

   The field is inserted into the document. The Insert Merge Field dialog box remains on-screen so that you can insert other fields, if you're so inclined.

9. **Repeat Step 8 for any other fields you want to insert and then click Close.**

   When you click Close, the Insert Merge Field dialog box is dismissed.

Figure 3-12 shows how a letter appears after you insert the Address Block, Greeting Line, and the First and Last Name fields in the body of the document. Notice that merge fields display within special chevron characters — for example, «AddressBlock» and «FirstName».

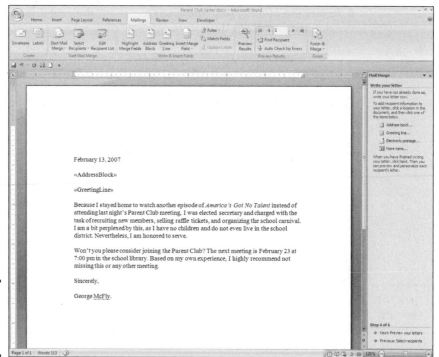

Merging the documents

After you set up the main document and the address list, you're ready for
the show. Follow these simple steps to merge the main document with the
data source to produce form letters:

1. **Click Next for the next step of the wizard — Preview Your Letters.**

The first letter in your mail merge appears on-screen, as shown in
Figure 3-13.

2. **Review each letter in the merge.**

You can click the >> or << button in the Mail Merge Wizard to move forward or backward through the letters. If you find a mistake in a name or
address, correct the mistake directly on the letter.

If you find a letter that you don't want to include, click the Exclude This Recipient button in the wizard.

If you review the first few letters and they look okay, you can skip ahead to the next step without reviewing them all.

3. When you review the entire mailing, click Next at the bottom of the wizard.

The final step of the wizard appears, as shown in Figure 3-14.

4. Click the Print link to print your letters.

The letters are printed.

If you want to edit the letters individually and print them later, click the Edit Individual Letters link instead of the Print link. The merged letters move to a new document, which you can then edit and save.

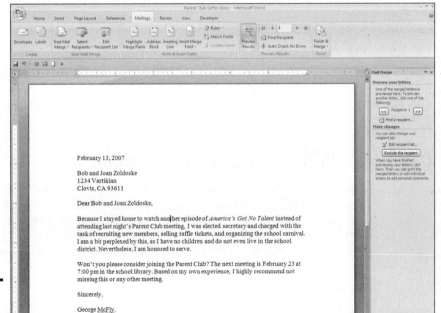

Figure 3-13:
Previewing the mail merge.

Mail Merge ▼ ×

Complete the merge

Mail Merge is ready to produce your letters.

To personalize your letters, click "Edit Individual Letters." This will open a new document with your merged letters. To make changes to all the letters, switch back to the original document.

Merge

   📄 Print...

   📄 Edit individual letters...

Step 6 of 6

⇤ Previous: Preview your letters

Figure 3-14:
Print the
mail merge.

Using the Mailings Tab on the Ribbon

If you're an experienced mail-merge user, you can save time by skipping the Mail Merge Wizard and just using the controls on the Mailings tab on the Ribbon to complete your mail-merge tasks. The following table lists the Mailings tab controls used to complete a mail merge. In general, you use these buttons in sequence from left to right to complete a mail merge.

Table 3-1	Controls on the Mailings Tab	
Button	*Name*	*What It Does*
Start Mail Merge	Start Mail Merge	Lets you choose Letters, E-Mail Messages, Envelopes, or Labels for the main document type. Also lets you start the Mail Merge Wizard.
Select Recipients	Select Recipients	Lets you select the data source by typing a new list, selecting an existing list, or using Outlook contacts.

Button	Name	What It Does
Edit Recipient List	Edit Recipient List	Lets you select which recipients in the list will be included in the merge.
Highlight Merge Fields	Highlight Merge Fields	Highlights the merge fields in the merge document so they are easy to spot.
Address Block	Address Block	Inserts an address block.
Greeting Line	Greeting Line	Inserts a greeting line.
Insert Merge Field	Insert Merge Field	Inserts a merge field, which lets you add more information from the data source.
Rules	Rules	Lets you add more fields that control which records to include in the merge field.
Match Fields	Match Fields	Lets you specify which fields in a database to use for certain mail-merge functions.
Update Labels	Update Labels	Copies the contents of the first label on the page to all subsequent labels.
Preview Results	Preview Results	Previews the merge operation.
First Record	First Record	Goes to the first record in the data source.
Previous Record	Previous Record	Goes to the previous record.
1	Go To Record	Goes to a specific record in the data source.
Next Record	Next Record	Goes to the next record in the data source.
Last Record	Last Record	Goes to the last record in the data source.

(continued)

**Book VII
Chapter 3**

Using the Mail
Merge Wizard

Table 3-1 *(continued)*

Button	Name	What It Does
Find Recipient	Find Recipient	Searches for records.
Auto Check for Errors	Auto Check for Errors	Checks for merge errors.
Finish & Merge	Finish & Merge	Merges the main document and data source.

Chapter 4: Advanced Mail Merge Tricks

In This Chapter

✔ Doing an e-mail merge

✔ Printing envelopes or labels from an address list

✔ Creating a directory

✔ Sorting and filtering data

✔ Pondering a computer science lesson that tastes like chicken

✔ Eliminating duplicate records

*T*his chapter covers some of the more interesting things you can do with Word's mail-merge feature, such as print mailing labels, choose only certain names to print letters for, use data from sources other than Word, and create an address directory.

This chapter assumes you already know the basics of performing a mail merge. If you're completely new to mail merge, stop where you are. Back up very slowly, make no sudden moves, and read the previous chapter. Only after that should you return to this chapter.

Other Types of Merges

Although creating form letters is the most popular use for mail merge, the Mail Merge Wizard can also send e-mail, create personalized envelopes, print address labels, and even create a directory. The following sections show you how to do all these things.

Merging to e-mail

If you want to send your letters via e-mail rather than snail mail, you can use the Mail Merge Wizard to merge your letters and then send them to e-mail addresses rather than print them. For this merge to work, your computer must have an e-mail program such as Microsoft Outlook installed.

Don't be a spammer! You should send e-mail merges only to people you know or to customers you've done business with and who have agreed to let you send them e-mail.

All you have to do is select E-Mail Messages rather than Letters as the document type in the first step of the Mail Merge Wizard. Then you follow the normal steps for using the Mail Merge Wizard as I describe in Chapter 3 of this minibook, until you get to the last step. Instead of the normal choices (Print and Edit Individual Letters), you have only one choice: Electronic Mail. Click this link to summon the Merge to E-Mail dialog box, as shown in Figure 4-1.

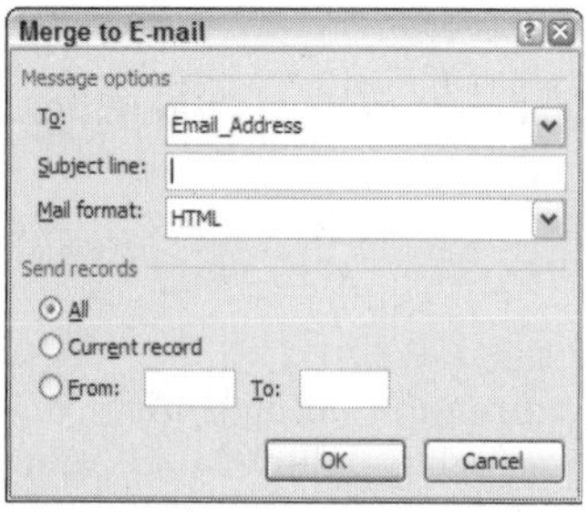

Figure 4-1:
The Merge
to E-Mail
dialog box.

Use this dialog box to specify the options you want to use for the e-mail merge. The options are

✦ **To:** Use this drop-down list to choose the field in the data source that contains the recipients' e-mail addresses.

✦ **Subject Line:** Type the subject line you want to appear in the e-mail messages.

  Unfortunately, Word doesn't let you personalize the subject line for each recipient. Each recipient in your mailing gets exactly the same subject line.

✦ **Mail Format:** This drop-down list lets you select one of three ways to send e-mail. You can format the messages as Plain Text, HTML, or Attachments. Choose HTML if you applied text formats or included images in the message. Otherwise, choose Plain Text.

✦ **Send Records:** Use these radio buttons to choose whether to send messages to all of the recipients in the merge, just the current recipient, or a range of recipients.

Merging envelopes

Ever spend 30 minutes printing 50 personalized letters by using mail merge and then another 30 minutes hand-addressing envelopes? Never again! Word can easily transform a mail-merge address list into a set of nicely printed envelopes.

For business mail, a good alternative to printing addresses on envelopes is to simply use window envelopes. That way, the address on the letters inside the envelope shows through the window. This feature has two advantages. First, you don't have to mess around with printing the envelopes. And second, you eliminate the risk of mixing up the letters and the envelopes and inadvertently sending Mr. Smith's overdue notice to Mr. Jones.

If you still insist on merging envelopes, follow the normal Mail Merge Wizard procedure, with these variations:

✦ In Step 1 of the Mail Merge Wizard, select the Envelopes option rather than Letters as the document type.

✦ In Step 2 of the Mail Merge Wizard, click Envelope Options to bring up the Envelope Options dialog box, shown in Figure 4-2. Use this dialog box to select the envelope size and to format the font used for the delivery and return addresses. You can also click the Printing Options tab to adjust Word's envelope layout to match the way envelopes feed into your particular printer. You might need to fiddle with these settings in case your envelopes print upside down or on the wrong side.

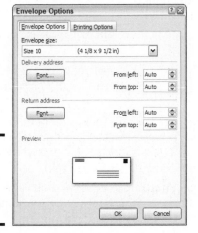

Figure 4-2: The Envelope Options dialog box.

✦ In Step 4 of the Mail Merge Wizard, click in the recipient address area in the center of the envelope and then click the Address Block link to insert a standard address block. Then click in the return address area in the upper-left corner of the envelope and type your return address (unless you're using preprinted envelopes). Figure 4-3 shows how the envelope appears when it's been set up properly.

You can also use this step of the Mail Merge Wizard to add a postal bar code to the envelope. And, if you subscribe to an electronic postage service such as Stamps.com, you can print e-postage right on the envelope so that you don't have to use stamps.

The postal bar code is not a secret password that gets you into pubs where mail carriers hang out — it's a bar code that speeds mail delivery. If you do bulk mailing and have the proper permits, using this bar code can earn postage discounts. (Unfortunately, the USPS has recently changed the bar code rules and the current version of Word doesn't print barcodes that qualify for bulk mail discounts. But hopefully Microsoft will issue an update to Word to correct this problem.)

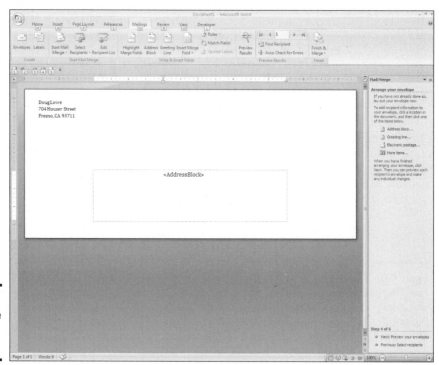

Figure 4-3:
An envelope all ready to be merged.

You can complete the rest of the Mail Merge Wizard steps as you do for a printed letter.

Merging to labels

If you want to create mailing labels instead of envelopes, choose Labels as the document type in the first step of the Mail Merge Wizard. Then follow the normal Mail Merge Wizard steps, with these exceptions:

✦ In Step 2 of the wizard, click Label Options to bring up the Label Options dialog box, as shown in Figure 4-4. Use this dialog box to specify the type of labels you're using.

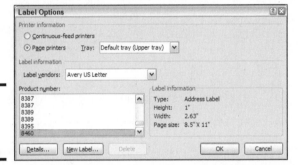

Figure 4-4: The Label Options dialog box.

✦ In Step 4 of the wizard, you format the labels. To do that, click in the first label and then click the Address Block link to insert an address block in the label. If you want, change the font or size of the address block. Then click the Update All Labels button at the bottom of the Mail Merge Wizard. The contents of the first label copy to all the other labels on the page. It also adds a Next Record field to each label except the first to tell Word to skip to the next recipient. When you're done, your main document resembles Figure 4-5.

You can complete the rest of the Mail Merge Wizard the usual way.

If the addresses don't fit properly in the labels, first check to make sure that you selected the right type of label in the Label Options dialog box. If the labels are correct and the addresses still don't fit, return to Step 4 and try reducing the font size for the address block. You can do this by changing the size for the first label. Then click the Update All Labels button to propagate the change to all the other labels.

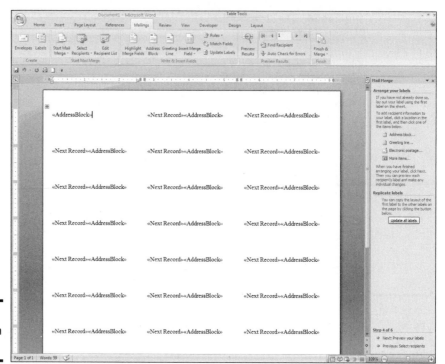

Figure 4-5:
A label main
document.

Creating a directory

You can use the Mail Merge Wizard to create a directory that lists all the addresses in a data source by choosing Directory as the document type in Step 1 of the wizard. Then follow the wizard's normal steps with these variations:

✦ In Step 4, add the merge fields you want to appear for each item in the directory. For a simple address listing, you can just click the Address Block link. Or, you can create a more customized directory by clicking the More Items link to bring up the Insert Merge Field dialog box, as shown in Figure 4-6.

For example, here's one way to format an address listing that lists people in alphabetical order, with last name first:

```
«LastName», «FirstName»
    «Address_Line_1»
    «Address_Line_2»
    «City», «State» «ZIP_Code»
    «HomePhone»
```

Figure 4-6:
The Insert
Merge Field
dialog box.

✦ When the preview of the document appears in Step 5, only the first record is shown. Don't panic. All the records appear when you complete the merge.

✦ In Step 6, click the To New Document link. A new document is created for your directory. Then choose Office➪Save to save the directory to a file.

Fun Things to Do with the Data Source

Mail merge is useful enough if all you do with the data source is store your names and addresses. But Word's data sources have more tricks up their sleeves than meet the eye. With a little chutzpah and a bit of wrestling with the dialog boxes, you can do several cute and moderately useful tricks with the data source. The following sections explain these amazing feats.

Sorting records

Suppose that you enter all the names in whatever sequence they were sitting in the pile, but you want to print the letters in alphabetical order. No problem! Just sort the data source.

Sorting is controlled from the Sort Records tab of the Filter and Sort dialog box. To get to this dialog box and sort your merge records, follow these steps:

1. **Start a mail merge as usual. When you get to Step 3 of the Mail Merge Wizard, click Edit Recipient List.**

The dialog box that opens lets you edit recipient addresses, as shown in Figure 4-7.

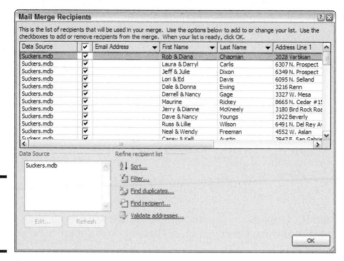

Figure 4-7:
Editing the
recipient
list.

2. Click the Sort link.

The Filter and Sort dialog box comes up, as shown in Figure 4-8.

Figure 4-8:
Sorting the
recipient
list.

**3. From the Sort By drop-down list, select the merge field that you want
to sort the data source by.**

Click the down arrow in the Sort By drop-down list to reveal a list of all
the merge fields in the data source and then select the one you want to
sort the data by. (In Figure 4-8, I already chose LastName for the first
sort field.)

If you want to sort records in reverse order, select the appropriate
Descending option. Records are then sorted on that field in reverse
order, beginning with the Zs and working back up to the As.

4. **If you want a second or third sort field, set them in the two Then By fields.**

The Then By field is used as a tiebreaker when two or more records have the same main Sort By field. For example, in Figure 4-8, I chose FirstName as the second sort field. Then, if the data source has more than one record with the same LastName, they sort into sequence by their first names, like this:

```
King    Larry
King    Martin Luther
King    Stephen
```

If you have a third field you can use as a tiebreaker, set it in the next Then By field.

5. **Click OK twice.**

You return to the Mail Merge Wizard.

6. **Finish the merge.**

Your letters (or envelopes, labels, or whatever) now print in the proper sequence.

Filtering records

Filtering lets you automatically select certain names from your database based on some arbitrary criteria. For example, you might want to send letters only to bald-headed starship captains of French descent. Sending letters to this group is possible if you have fields in your data source for Starfleet rank, degree of baldness, and country of origin.

Unlike the filters in your car, mail merge filters don't fill up with gunk, so you don't have to change them every 5,000 miles. You do have to be careful about how you set them up, though, to be sure that they choose just the records you want to include in your mail merge.

To mail letters to only those lucky few, follow these steps:

1. **Start a mail merge as usual. When you get to Step 3 of the Mail Merge Wizard, click Edit Recipient List.**

The Mail Merge Recipients dialog box appears. (If you already have chosen a recipient list, click Edit Recipient List to summon this dialog box.)

2. **Click the Filter link.**

The dialog box shown in Figure 4-9 appears.

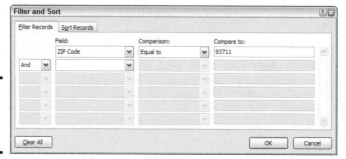

Figure 4-9:
Filtering the
recipient
list.

3. **Set the criteria for including records in the mail merge by specifying a Field, Comparison, and Compare To value for each criteria.**

   To create a letter only for people who live in the 93711 zip code, for example, set the first Field to ZIP Code, the first Comparison to Equal To, and the Compare To field to 93711. This filter means the mail merge includes only the records whose ZIP Code field is equal to 93711. (That's how the filter shown in Figure 4-9 is set up.)

   The following section contains an explanation of the options in the Comparison fields.

4. **Click OK twice.**

   You're returned to the mail Merge Wizard.

5. **Finish the mail merge.**

   Now only the records that match the filter criteria are included in the merge.

Understanding relationships

You can set up ten different kinds of tests in the Comparison fields. Computerniks call these tests *relational tests* because they test the relationship between two things (in this case, a merge field and a specific value). You can use the following relational tests to create different kinds of selection filters:

✦ **Equal To:** Selects records if the field matches the Compare To value exactly.

✦ **Not Equal To:** Selects records if the field doesn't match the Compare To value exactly.

✦ **Less Than:** Selects records if the field is less than the Compare To value.

- ✦ **Greater Than:** Selects records if the field is greater than the Compare To value.

- ✦ **Less Than or Equal:** Selects records if the field is less than or equal to the Compare To value.

- ✦ **Greater Than or Equal:** Selects records if the field is greater than or equal to the Compare To value.

- ✦ **Is Blank:** Selects records in which the field is blank.

- ✦ **Is Not Blank:** Selects records in which the field isn't blank.

- ✦ **Contains:** Selects records if the field contains the Compare To value.

- ✦ **Does Not Contain:** Selects records if the field doesn't contain the Compare To value.

You can set up complicated queries that check the contents of several fields. You might want to mail letters only to people who live in a particular city and state, for example. You set up the query like this:

```
City Equal to Bakersfield
And State Equal to CA
```

In this query, the merge includes only records whose City field is equal to *Bakersfield* and whose State field is equal to *CA*.

You can also set up queries that test the same field twice. To mail to addresses with zip codes 93711 or 93722, for example, set up the query like this:

```
Zip Code Equal to 93711
Or Zip Code Equal to 93722
```

Notice that I change the And/Or field from And to Or. That way, a record is selected if its Zip Code field is 93711 or 93722. If you test the same field for two or more specific values, don't leave the And/Or field set to And. If I left the And/Or field set to And in the preceding example, a record is selected only if its Zip Code field is equal to 93711 and if it is also equal to 93722. Obviously, this situation isn't possible: The zip code may be 93711 or 93722, but it can't be both at the same time. Leaving the And/Or field set to And is natural because you want to "mail letters to everyone in the 93711 *and* 93722 zip codes." But when in this situation, you have to specify Or, not And.

On the other hand, suppose that you want to mail to anyone whose zip code is 93711, 93722, or any value in between. In that case, you use two condition tests linked by And, as shown in this example:

```
Zip Code Greater Than or Equal to 93711
And Zip Code Less Than or Equal to 93722
```

Unprecedented stuff about precedence

Be careful when you set up a query that uses three or more field tests and mixes And and Or. You're confronted with the issue of precedence, which means, in layperson's terms, "The Chicken or the Egg?" You might suppose that Word tests the conditions you list in the Filter and Sort dialog box in the order in which you list them. Not necessarily. Word groups any condition tests linked by And, and then checks them out before combining the results with tests linked by Or.

Confused? So am I. The following example shows how it works. Suppose that you open the menu at a restaurant and see that the fried chicken dinner comes with a "leg or wing and thigh." Which of the following statements represents the two possible chicken dinner combinations you can order?

✔ You can order a meal with a leg and a thigh, or you can order a meal with a wing and a thigh.

✔ You can order a meal with a leg, or you can order a meal with a wing and thigh.

According to the way Word processes queries, the answer is the second one. Word lumps together as a group the two options linked by And.

If you want the first example to be the right answer, you have to state the menu choice as "leg and thigh or wing and thigh."

For a more realistic Word for Windows example, suppose that you want to mail to everyone who lives in Olympia, WA, just across the way in Aberdeen, WA. You might be tempted to set the query up like this:

> State Equal To WA
>
> And City Equal To Olympia
>
> Or City Equal To Aberdeen

Unfortunately, that doesn't work. You end up with everyone who lives in Olympia, WA, plus anyone who lives in any town named Aberdeen, regardless of the state. (You can find an Aberdeen in Maryland and South Dakota.)

You could just petition the federal government to make Aberdeen, MD, and Aberdeen, SD, change their names. But the better way is to set up the filter like this:

> State Equal To WA
>
> And City Equal To Olympia
>
> Or State Equal To WA
>
> And City Equal to Aberdeen

For an even more interesting twist concerning And/Or, see the sidebar "Unprecedented stuff about precedence."

Weeding out duplicates

The bigger your recipient list gets, the harder it is to keep track of who you've already entered into the list. Over time, you're bound to end up with duplicate entries.

To save postage, you can use the Find Duplicates feature to spot potential duplicate records. Here are the steps:

1. **Start a mail merge as usual. When you get to Step 3 of the Mail Merge Wizard, click Edit Recipient List.**

The Mail Merge Recipients dialog box appears. (If you already have chosen a recipient list, click Edit Recipient List to summon this dialog box.)

2. **Click the Find Duplicates link.**

The Find Duplicates dialog box shown in Figure 4-10 appears. This dialog box lists the records that might be duplicates.

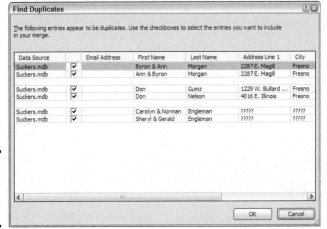

Figure 4-10:
The Find Duplicates dialog box.

3. **Deselect the records you don't want to include in the merge.**

You have to double-check each group of records in the Find Duplicates dialog box. If you have found a true duplicate, you should deselect the record or records you don't want to send mail to.

4. **Click OK and then click OK again.**

5. **Finish the mail merge.**

Now the merge doesn't include duplicate records.

Book VIII

Customizing Word

"Roger! Check the sewing machine's connection to the PC. I'm getting Martha's English papers stitched across my curtains again."

Contents at a Glance

Chapter 1: Customizing the User Interface

In This Chapter

✔ Playing with the Quick Access toolbar

✔ Dealing with old custom toolbars

✔ Adding custom keyboard shortcuts

*O*ne of the great strengths of previous versions of Word — up to and including Word 2003 — has been that the menus, toolbars, and keyboard shortcuts that make up the user interface have been almost completely customizable. If you didn't like the way the toolbars were arranged, you could rearrange them to your liking. Need a new menu command? You could write a macro to carry out the command and then assign the macro to a new menu item. You could even create entirely new toolbars or menus.

Unfortunately, this strength was also one of Word's most annoying weaknesses. In its studies prior to developing Word 2007, Microsoft found that far more people *accidentally* customized Word's user interface than did it on purpose. It was all too easy to accidentally drag a toolbar to a weird location or make it disappear altogether.

Thus, Microsoft decided to make the Ribbon interface of Word 2007 decidedly more difficult to customize. However, you can still create your own customized keyboard shortcuts. To simplify what you have to customize, Microsoft endowed Word with a single customizable toolbar — the Quick Access toolbar — where all custom buttons would live.

In this chapter, you find out how to create custom keyboard shortcuts and customize the Quick Access toolbar.

 It turns out that the Ribbon itself is almost completely customizable — in fact, it's actually more customizable than the old toolbars and menus. However, you can't customize it from within Word the way you could create custom toolbars and menus in previous versions. Instead, customizing the Ribbon is more of an advanced programming thing. As such, it isn't covered in this book.

Customizing the Quick Access Toolbar

The Quick Access toolbar, also known as the QAT, is the closest thing Word 2007 has to a customizable toolbar. You don't have the same options for customizing it as you did with ordinary toolbars in previous versions of Word. But you can choose one of two positions for it, and you can choose which buttons you want it to contain. I describe these simple customizations in the following sections.

Relocating the Quick Access toolbar

By default, the Quick Access toolbar appears above the Ribbon near the document title. Most users find this to be the most convenient location. However, Word lets you position it beneath the Ribbon, as shown in Figure 1-1.

There are two ways to change the Quick Access toolbar location. The easiest is to click the arrow that appears to the right of any buttons on the QAT. This action reveals a menu that includes two commands. The second of these commands moves the Quick Access toolbar. If the QAT is currently below the Ribbon, the command is called Place Quick Access Toolbar above Ribbon. If the QAT is already above the Ribbon, the command is called Place Quick Access Toolbar below Ribbon.

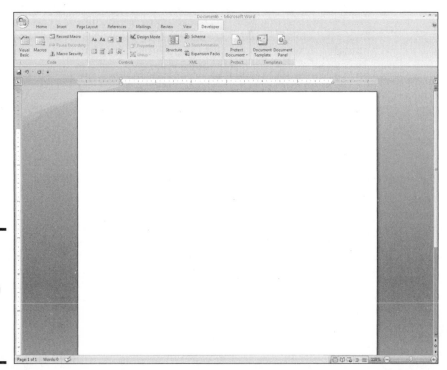

Figure 1-1:
The Quick Access toolbar can live above the Ribbon as well as below it.

The second way to move the QAT is to follow these steps:

1. **Choose Office➪Word Options.**

   This brings up the Word Options dialog box.

2. **Click the Customization tab.**

   The Customization tab appears, as shown in Figure 1-2.

3. **Deselect the Place Quick Access Toolbar below the Ribbon check box to place the QAT above the Ribbon.**

   Or, if you've already deselected the box, select it to move the QAT back below the Ribbon.

4. **Click OK.**

   The Quick Access toolbar moves to its new location.

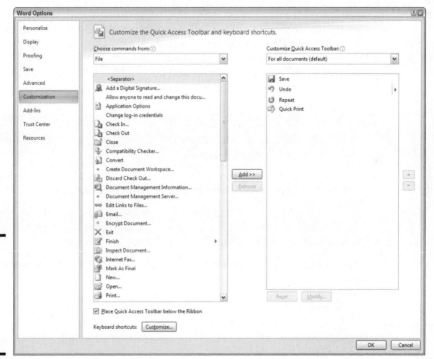

Figure 1-2:
The Customiza-
tion tab of
the Word
Options
dialog box.

Here are a few points to ponder concerning the position of the QAT:

+ You can move the QAT, but you can't remove it. In other words, there's no option to hide the QAT.

+ If you've used previous versions of Word, your first instinct for relocating the QAT is to simply grab it with the mouse and drag it to a new location. Microsoft has completely disabled this feature.

Adding and removing buttons

By default, the Quick Access toolbar includes the following three buttons:

+ Save

+ Undo

+ Redo

This is a pretty minimalist collection of buttons. You don't have to think hard to come up with some other buttons that would be useful here, such as Open, Save As, New Document, or Print.

Fortunately, Word 2007 lets you add any number of buttons to the Quick Access toolbar. To add a button, just follow these simple steps:

1. **Right-click the Quick Access toolbar and choose More Commands.**

This brings up the Customization tab of the Word Options dialog box (refer back to Figure 1-2).

2. Choose a category from the Choose Commands From drop-down list that appears above the list of available buttons.

This drop-down list lets you select buttons from any of the several categories. These categories include Popular Commands, Commands Not In the Ribbon, All Commands, and Macros.

3. Select the button you want to add to the Quick Access toolbar.

4. Click the Add button.

The button is added to the QAT.

Here are a few additional tips for customizing the Quick Access toolbar:

+ To remove an item from the QAT, call up the Customization tab of the Word Options dialog box, select the button you want to remove in the list of buttons currently on the QAT, and click the Remove button.

✦ You can change the order of buttons in the QAT from the Customization tab of the Word Options dialog box. First, select a button from the list of buttons currently in the QAT. Then use the Move Up or Move Down buttons (they're on the right side) to change the location of the selected button.

✦ The Popular Commands category includes the most commonly used buttons. You probably want to add several of the commands in this category to your QAT, including New, Open, and Quick Print.

✦ The Commands Not in the Ribbon category lists a variety of Word commands that don't appear on any of the Ribbon tabs. You can find more than a hundred interesting commands in this category.

✦ If you're not sure what category a command resides in, you can choose the All Commands category.

✦ You can also assign a macro to a QAT button by choosing the Macros category. For more information about creating macros, see Book IX.

As you scroll through the Choose Commands From drop-down list, you might notice that the buttons shown in the Commands section of the dialog box are context sensitive; they change to indicate which buttons are available for a category. As you examine the categories, you see familiar buttons, such as the New, Open, and Save buttons. But you also find many unfamiliar buttons. These represent Word commands you didn't know existed because they aren't on any of the menus or toolbars by default.

Dealing with Old-Style Custom Toolbars

Previous versions of Word let you create custom toolbars. Although Word 2007 doesn't use toolbars in the same way that previous versions did, Word 2007 does provide a way for you to access custom toolbars you created for documents and templates in previous versions of Word. Old-style custom toolbars are displayed in the Add Ins tab, as shown in Figure 1-3. Here I've opened a document I created with Word 2003, and it has two custom toolbars.

Note that all of the custom toolbars in an old-style Word document are displayed together in a single group, named Custom Toolbars. You have no way to turn the individual toolbars on or off and no way to drag them to a new location or dock them to the side. But at least the custom toolbars are accessible.

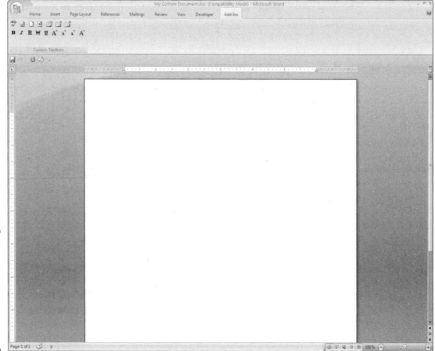

Creating Custom Keyboard Shortcuts

If you're a keyboard shortcut junkie (as I am), you probably want to create your own keyboard shortcuts. Then you can assign the styles, macros, and other goodies you use most often to handy keyboard shortcuts.

Follow these steps to assign a new keyboard shortcut:

1. **Call up the Customization tab of the Word Options dialog box.**

To open the dialog box, click the Office button and then click Word Options. Then click the Customization tab. Refer to Figure 1-2 for a refresher of what this dialog box looks like.

2. **Click the Customize button.**

The Customize Keyboard dialog box appears, as shown in Figure 1-4.

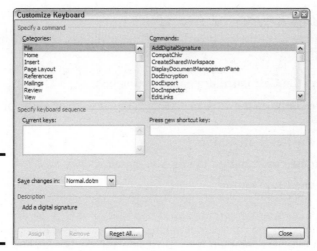

Figure 1-4:
The
Customize
Keyboard
dialog box.

3. Click a Category, and then select the command, style, macro, font, or other item for which you want to create a keyboard shortcut.

Spend some time exploring these lists. Lots of useful commands are buried amongst a bunch of strange-looking gobbledygook. You can create a shortcut for any command, style, macro, font, or just about any other item.

4. Click in the Press New Shortcut Key text box and then type the new keyboard shortcut.

When you type the shortcut, Word lets you know whether the key is already assigned to some other command.

5. Click Assign to assign the keyboard shortcut. Then click Close.

You're finished! Try the shortcut to see whether it works.

You can also assign a keyboard shortcut to a style. Open the Styles window by clicking the Styles button at the bottom right of the Styles group on the Home tab on the Ribbon. Select the style you want to assign a keyboard shortcut to and then click the down-arrow to reveal its shortcut menu. Choose Modify and then click the Format button to reveal the formatting shortcut menu for the style. Then choose the Keyboard Shortcut command to create your keyboard shortcut.

**Book VIII
Chapter 1**

**Customizing the
User Interface**

Resetting keyboard shortcuts

You can erase all of the keyboard shortcuts stored in a template by following these steps:

1. **Call up the Customize Keyboard dialog box.**

   For the steps on how to call up this dialog box, refer to the preceding section.

2. **Click the Reset All button.**

3. **When the confirmation dialog box appears, click Yes.**

4. **Click the Close button.**

If you have keyboard shortcuts saved in both Normal.dotm and the template attached to the current document, you need to use Reset All for both templates to revert completely to Word's default keyboard shortcuts. And, to make the return to default shortcuts permanent, you must save the template file as well.

Printing your keyboard shortcuts

If you lose track of your custom keyboard shortcuts, you can print a complete list of them for the current document by following these steps:

1. **Open a document that's attached to the template with the keyboard shortcuts you want to print, or open the template itself.**

2. **Choose Office➪Print➪Print to display the Print dialog box.**

3. **In the Print What drop-down list, select Key Assignments.**

4. **Click OK.**

Keyboard assignments print, starting first with the keyboard assignments derived from the template attached to the document and listing the global keyboard assignments taken from the Normal.dotm template. Word's built-in keyboard shortcuts do not print; if they did, the listing would go on for many pages.

Chapter 2: Opting for Options

In This Chapter

✔ Finding out what's up with all these options

✔ Personalizing Word

✔ Dealing with Display options

✔ Perusing the Proofing options

✔ Setting the Save options

✔ Adjusting the Advanced options

✔ Looking at other Word options

Sometimes I long for the old pre-Windows days, when my favorite word processor was WordPerfect 4.2 and the only real options I had to worry about were whether to change WordPerfect's screen colors or take the afternoon off and catch a quick round of golf. My golf game fell all to pieces after I began using Word. Now I spend all my free time playing with the options in the Word Options dialog box, so I don't have any time left over for such luxuries as golf.

You should read this chapter when you finally decide to give in to the Word Options dialog box and you want to know what all those options do. This chapter describes the most useful options, but more importantly, it also tells you which options you can safely ignore so that you (unlike some people I know — me, for example) can catch up on your golf.

I'm aware, of course, that for many people, golf is a more frustrating game than playing with Word. And for some, golf is more boring than reading Word's online help resources. If you're one of those poor, unenlightened souls, feel free to substitute your favorite non-golf pastime in the preceding paragraphs.

What's with All the Options?

The Word Options dialog box is one of the most heavily laden dialog boxes of all time. This dialog box has so many options that it earned Microsoft a Lifetime Achievement Award from the American Society of Windows Programmers.

Like many other dialog boxes in Word, the Options dialog box organizes its settings into tabs. Each tab has its own set of option controls. To switch from one tab to another, just click the tab label on the left side of the dialog box.

Most Word dialog boxes that use tabs have two or three tab labels, but the Word Options dialog box has nine — that's right, *nine* — tabs:

+ **Popular:** These are the most popular options for working with Word.

+ **Display:** Contains options that control the way your document displays on-screen and how your documents print.

+ **Proofing:** Controls the proofing tools such as the spell checker and the AutoCorrect feature.

+ **Save:** Has important options that control the way Word saves your documents.

+ **Advanced:** Contains a hodgepodge of options that control features Microsoft considers to fit in the category of "Advanced." Unfortunately, Microsoft has inexplicably placed options it considers advanced here even if the option would more logically be placed on one of the other tabs. For example, you can find options that affect the way documents are displayed or printed on this tab rather than on the Display tab. And your mailing address goes on this tab rather than the Personalize tab. Go figure.

+ **Customization:** This tab is where you customize the Quick Access tool-bar. For more information, turn to Chapter 1 of this minibook.

+ **Add-Ins:** This tab lets you activate a variety of cool add-in features.

+ **Trust Center:** This tab contains security information and lets you access the Trust Center dialog box, where you can change various security settings.

+ **Resources:** This tab provides easy access to a variety of Web-based services that support Microsoft Office.

The ten best options

Direct from the home office in sunny Fresno, California, here are my top ten favorite options:

1. **Save AutoRecovery Information (Save tab):** This option can be a real lifesaver. Set it to save your work every five minutes or so, and you won't have to worry about losing an entire day's work because of a power failure.

2. **Use Smart Cut and Paste (Advanced tab):** No more worrying about whether the space is before or after the text cut to the Clipboard. This option handles that for you. In fact, the good people at Microsoft turn this option on by default.

3. **Show Paragraphs and Show Tabs (Display tab):** Displays paragraph marks and tab characters.

4. **Automatic Word Selection (Advanced tab):** Without this option, you have to select an entire word and then press Ctrl+B or Ctrl+I to make the word bold or italicized. With this option set, you can just put the cursor anywhere in the word (or select portions of two or more words), and any formatting you apply is applied to the entire word (or all the words).

5. **Recently Used File List (Advanced tab):** Saves you from navigating through the Open dialog box. Set it to as high a number as you can tolerate.

6. **Print in Background (Advanced tab):** Why wait for the computer while it prints? With this option turned on (which it is by default), Word prints in the background while you can do other work.

7. **Embed Fonts in the File (Save options):** Saves fonts with the file so another user who doesn't have the font installed can use the document. Of course, this option works only if the license for the fonts permits sharing.

8. **File Locations (Advanced tab):** Brings up a dialog box that lets you set the locations of various Word files, including the location where documents are stored by default and a network location where users of the network can share templates.

9. **Update Fields Before Printing (Display):** Use this option to ensure that fields (such as dates) are always updated whenever the document is printed.

10. **Eighteen holes of golf:** Better than the other nine options put together.

To set options in Word, follow these steps:

1. **Click the Office button and then click the Word Options button.**

The Word Options dialog box appears.

2. **Click the tab that contains an option you want to change.**

If you're not sure which tab contains the option you're looking for, just cycle through the tabs until you find the option.

3. **Set the option however you want.**

Most of the options are simple check boxes that you click to select or deselect. Some require you to select a choice from a drop-down list, and some have the audacity to require that you type a filename or otherwise demonstrate your keyboard proficiency.

4. **Repeat Steps 2 and 3 until you exhaust your options or until you're just plain exhausted.**

5. **Click OK.**

You're done!

As you fritter away your day playing with these tabs, keep the following points in mind:

✦ Several of the Options tabs have more than one road that leads to them. You can reach the Display tab, for example, by choosing Office⇨Print⇨Print and then clicking the Options button.

✦ As big as the Word Options dialog box is, it still isn't big enough to hold all of Word's options. As a result, some of the Options tabs have buttons that bring up additional dialog boxes that have additional tabs. Sheesh!

✦ To move to a tab, just click the tab label. You can also move from tab to tab by pressing the arrow keys. To move from the General tab to the Edit tab, for example, press the right-arrow key.

Some settings that a normal person would consider *options* are located else-where on the Ribbon. For example, the option that controls whether the ruler is displayed is found on the View tab on the Ribbon, not in the Word Options dialog box.

The Popular Tab

The Popular tab, shown in Figure 2-1, features the most popular options for working with Word. These options are described in the following sections.

Top Options for Working with Word

Microsoft has gathered what its programmers believe are the most useful options in this section. The options are

✦ **Show Mini Toolbar on Selection:** When this option is enabled, a special toolbar called the *Mini Toolbar* is displayed whenever you select text. This toolbar lets you set the most common formatting options, such as the font, size, bold, italic, color, and so on.

✦ **Enable Live Preview:** Shows a preview of how various Word features will affect your document when you hover the cursor over different choices.

✦ **Show Developer Tab in the Ribbon:** Enables the Developer tab, which lets you access macros, customize forms, and so on.

✦ **Always Use ClearType:** *ClearType* is a display option that improves the way text appears, especially on LCD displays.

✦ **Open E-Mail Attachments in Full Screen Reading View:** When this option is enabled, Word documents sent as e-mail attachments are opened in Reading view. Personally, I'm not a fan of Reading view, so I usually disable this option.

✦ **Color Scheme:** Lets you choose one of two color schemes for Office.

✦ **ScreenTip Style:** Lets you control whether ScreenTips are displayed.

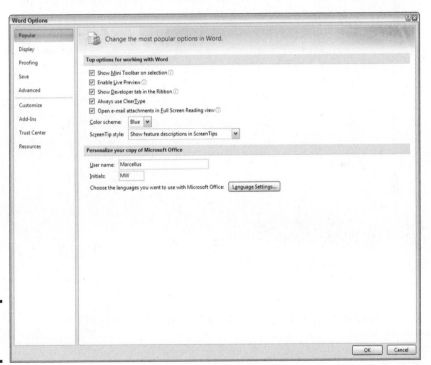

Figure 2-1:
The Popular tab.

Personalize Your Copy of Microsoft Office

This section lets you personalize your copy of Office by supplying your name, initials, and the language you want to work with. This information is used in several ways:

✦ In the document properties when you save a document

✦ In comments and in revision marks when you track changes

✦ On envelopes, labels, and letters

The Display Tab

The options on the Display tab, shown in Figure 2-2, let you customize the appearance of Word's humble display. The Display options are arranged in three groups: Page Display Options, Always Show These Formatting Marks on the Screen, and Printing Options.

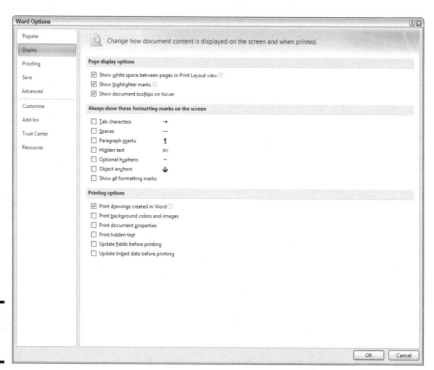

Figure 2-2:
The Display tab.

Page Display Options

The Display options grouped under the Page Display Options heading control the amount of detail displayed in the document window. The following list gives you the lowdown on each of the options you can set from this tab:

✦ **Show White Space between Pages in Print Layout View:** This option displays the space between pages in Page Layout view. Otherwise, you don't see that white space created by margins.

✦ **Show Highlighter Marks:** Deselect this option to turn off the highlighting made by Word's Highlight feature. Note that the highlighting isn't actually removed; it just isn't shown. This option can be helpful if you want to highlight something on-screen, but not in the printout.

✦ **Show Document Tooltips on Hover:** Select this option to enable tips that appear when you hover the cursor over certain Word items, such as comments or hyperlinks.

Always Show These Formatting Marks on the Screen

This group of options lets you control which special characters display in the document window:

✦ **Tab Characters:** Displays tab characters as an arrow. I usually leave this option selected so that I can keep track of tabs.

✦ **Spaces:** Displays spaces as little dots. I usually leave this option deselected, but some people like to see the little dots so they can tell where they type spaces.

✦ **Paragraph Marks:** Displays paragraph marks. I usually leave this option selected so that I can quickly find extraneous paragraphs.

✦ **Hidden Text:** Displays hidden text. Hidden text is text in your document that isn't printed. It's marked as hidden via the Font dialog box. (For more information, see Chapter 2 of Book II.)

✦ **Optional Hyphens:** Displays optional hyphens, which are helpful when you want precise control over hyphenation.

✦ **Object Anchors:** Shows the anchors that tie objects to a specific location in your document.

✦ **Show All Formatting Marks:** Displays all hidden characters. Selecting this option is the same as clicking the Show/Hide button on the Home tab on the Ribbon.

When the Show/Hide button on the Ribbon is depressed, all nonprinting characters display. When the button is not depressed, only those nonprinting characters specified on the View tab display. Set the options on the View tab so that only those nonprinting characters you *always* want to display — such as tab characters and paragraph marks — are selected. You can display the other nonprinting characters at any time simply by clicking the Show/Hide button.

Printing Options

This section contains several options that affect how documents are printed. Specifically:

✦ **Print Drawings Created in Word:** If you turn off this option, the document's text is printed, but any graphics are not printed.

✦ **Print Background Colors and Images:** Turn on this option if you want to print the page background color or image. Leave this option off if you're printing on colored or preprinted paper.

✦ **Print Document Properties:** If you want document properties to print as a separate page, select this option.

✦ **Print Hidden Text:** Select this option to print text that has been marked as hidden.

✦ **Update Fields before Printing:** Updates the contents of fields before printing. I recommend turning on this option. (For more information, see Chapter 3 of this minibook.)

✦ **Update Linked Data before Printing:** Likewise, this option should also be turned on. For instance, if you link a table in Word to an Excel spreadsheet, leaving this option turned on ensures that the most up-to-date info in the Excel spreadsheet is included in your Word table.

The Proofing Tab

Figure 2-3 shows the Proofing tab of the Word Options dialog box, which lets you control the way the various Office proofing tools work. Because the settings on this tab are covered elsewhere in this book, I don't belabor them here. For more information about setting AutoCorrect options, please see Chapter 5 of Book II. And for more information about the spelling and grammar options, please go to Chapter 6 of Book II.

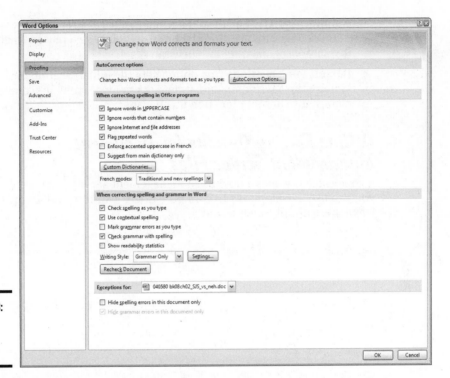

Figure 2-3:
The
Proofing
tab.

The Save Tab

Figure 2-4 shows the Save tab, which lets you specify how you want documents to be saved. The following sections describe the options on this tab.

Save Documents

This section contains basic options for how files are saved:

- ✦ **Save Files in This Format:** Specifies the default format for saving Word files. This option is initially set to Word Document (*.docx) to save files in the new Word 2007 format.

- ✦ **Save AutoRecovery Info Every *N* Minutes:** Automatically saves recovery information at regular intervals. The default setting is to save the recovery information every 10 minutes, but you can change the time interval if you want. I like to set it for 5 minutes.

✦ **AutoRecover File Location:** Specifies the hard drive folder where AutoRecover files are stored. Rarely do you have a reason to change this option.

✦ **Default File Location:** This option sets the initial location for files when you use the Save command. It defaults to My Documents, but you can change it to another location if you want.

Offline Editing Options for Document Management Server Files

If your company uses a document management server (such as SharePoint), you can use these options to configure how it works. Usually, you should leave these options unchanged.

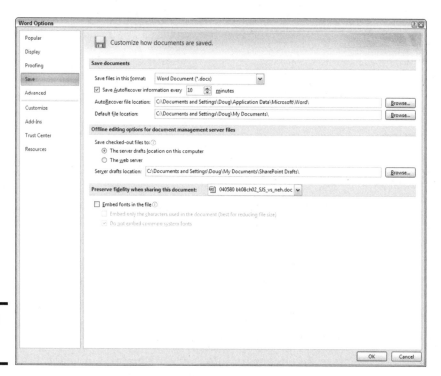

Figure 2-4:
The Save
tab.

Preserve Fidelity When Sharing This Document

The one option in this section, Embed Fonts in the File, lets you specify whether to include Truetype font files in your documents. Embedding the fonts in the document increases the size of the document file, so this option is usually left deselected. However, if you intend to share the file with other users and you use any uncommon fonts in the document, you should select this option. (As for the two check boxes beneath this option, it's best to leave them set as they are.)

The Advanced Tab

The Advanced tab, shown in Figure 2-5, is the catch-all tab of the Word Options dialog box. It contains a plethora of options, as described in the following sections.

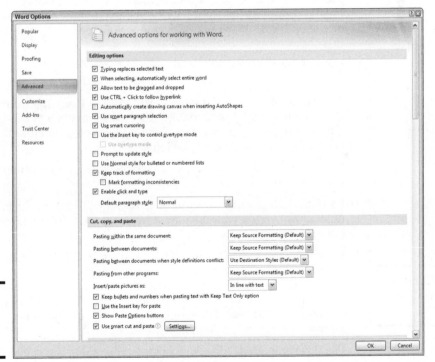

Figure 2-5: The Advanced tab.

Editing Options

The Editing Options section contains the following options that affect the way you can edit documents:

✦ **Typing Replaces Selected Text:** If you highlight text by dragging the cursor over it or by holding down the Shift key while moving the cursor and then type something, the whatever-it-was-you-typed obliterates the whatever-it-was-you-highlighted. If this behavior drives you bonkers, you can turn it off by deselecting the Typing Replaces Selected Text check box.

✦ **When Selecting, Automatically Select Entire Word:** This option is one of the niftiest features in Word. It causes Word to assume that you meant to select an entire word. This tool can be disconcerting at first, though, so be prepared. If it's against your religion, you can turn it off by deselecting the When Selecting, Automatically Select Entire Word check box.

✦ **Allow Text to Be Dragged and Dropped:** More commonly known as dragon dropping, this option lets you move text by selecting it and then dragging it with the mouse. If it annoys you, turn it off by deselecting this check box.

✦ **Use CTRL + Click to Follow Hyperlink:** If you select this option, the usual clicking action doesn't automatically activate a hyperlink.

✦ **Automatically Create Drawing Canvas When Inserting AutoShapes:** If this option is on, Word automatically creates an object called a Drawing Canvas whenever you insert a shape into your documents. This option is off by default, and should be left off.

✦ **Use Smart Paragraph Selection:** Keeps paragraph formatting intact when you cut and paste paragraphs.

✦ **Use Smart Cursoring:** This option automatically moves the insertion point as you scroll your document by using the scrolling keys (such as Page Up or Page Down).

✦ **Use the Insert Key to Control Overtype Mode:** If this option is selected, the Insert key switches from Overtype mode to Insert mode. In Overtype mode, anything you type replaces text that's already on the screen. If you want to insert content in the middle of a paragraph and you care whether the text that is already there *stays* in your document, you want Word in Insert mode as much as possible.

✦ **Use Overtype Mode:** Speaking of Overtype mode, sneak into someone's office late at night, click the Word Options button on the Office menu, then select this option. Then let out an evil laugh when he shouts obscenities every time he starts up Word and doesn't discover that it's in Overtype mode until it's too late.

I don't know what got into me. Don't, under any circumstances, do this. Please. Playing with other people's computers isn't nice.

✦ **Prompt to Update Style:** If this option is on, Word asks what you want to do if you modify the format of some text, and then reapply the previously applied style. The prompt asks whether you want to revert to the formatting specified by the style or whether you want to update the style to reflect the new formatting.

✦ **Use Normal Style for Bulleted or Numbered Lists:** If this option is selected, bulleted or numbered lists are formatted using the Normal paragraph style. Best leave this at its default.

✦ **Keep Track of Formatting:** This option tells Word to automatically create a style every time you apply formatting. This feature is pretty cool because you can then modify the style to make consistent changes to your document. On the other hand, Word can go a little overboard creating styles. You might find that your style list fills up with dozens of styles that Word created as it tracked every little formatting change you made.

✦ **Mark Formatting Inconsistencies:** If this option is selected, text that is formatted similar to but not exactly like other text in the document will be marked with a wavy blue underline.

✦ **Enable Click and Type:** This option enables the Click and Type feature, which lets you place text anywhere on a page by double-clicking where you want to place the text and typing. Word automatically adds paragraphs or tabs necessary to get the text at the right place.

✦ **Default Paragraph Style:** Sets the default paragraph style for new paragraphs created with the Click and Type feature. Best to leave it set to Normal.

Cut, Copy, and Paste

The Cut, Copy, and Paste options affect the way the clipboard works:

✦ **Pasting within the Same Document:** Lets you pick one of three behaviors for pasting text that's cut or copied from one location of a document and pasted to another location within the same document. The three choices are

  • *Keep Source Formatting:* Retains the formatting applied to the original text.

  • *Match Destination Formatting:* Changes the formatting of the pasted text to match the formatting of text where it is pasted.

  • *Keep Text Only:* Doesn't apply any formatting to the pasted text.

✦ **Pasting between Documents:** The same three choices exist for copying or cutting text from one document and pasting it into another.

✦ **Pasting between Documents When Style Definitions Conflict:** Determines how style formatting is handled when text is copied or cut from one document and pasted into another and the styles in the two documents specify different formatting.

✦ **Pasting from Other Programs:** Specifies how formatting is handled when text is copied or pasted from a program other than Word.

✦ **Insert/Paste Pictures As:** Specifies the default layout option to use for pasted pictures.

✦ **Keep Bullets and Numbers When Pasting Text with Keep Text Only Option:** Hmm. This one is obscure. If you specify Keep Text Only for one of the previous pasting options, this option determines whether bullets or numbers are considered part of the text or just formatting. If you select this option, the bullet or number is pasted. If this option is deselected, bullets or numbers are not pasted.

✦ **Use the Insert Key for Paste:** If you select this option, the Insert key serves as a handy shortcut for the Paste command.

✦ **Show Paste Options Buttons:** This option displays a Paste Options button at the bottom corner of text you paste into your document. You can click this button to reveal a menu of options for formatting the pasted text.

✦ **Use Smart Cut and Paste:** Adjusts spaces before and after text you cut and paste so that you don't end up with two spaces between some words and no spaces between others. Leave this option selected; it's too good to turn off.

Show Document Content

The following options, located in the Show Document Content section, let you refine the way Word documents are displayed:

✦ **Show Background Colors and Images in Print Layout View:** If you want to see page backgrounds in Print Layout view, leave this option selected.

✦ **Show Text Wrapped within the Document Window:** You should leave this option deselected if you want the text wrap to reflect the way the document will actually print (which you probably do). If page count is an issue in the work you do, selecting this option will give you a migraine.

✦ **Show Picture Placeholders:** If you insert a picture into a document, you notice that Word hesitates a little when you scroll the picture into the document window. If you add 200 pictures to a document, the hesitations might come so often that you want to scream. Selecting this option causes Word to display a simple rectangle where the picture goes. This step eliminates the hesitation, but of course hides the pictures so you can't see what they look like until you print the document.

✦ **Show Drawings and Text Boxes on Screen:** You can deselect this option to hide any drawings or text boxes in your document. I don't know why you would, though, unless you're using a slow computer that's barely able to display the drawings and text boxes in your document.

✦ **Show Animated Text:** This option enables text animation effects.

✦ **Show Bookmarks:** Takes text referred to in a bookmark and sandwiches it between gray brackets.

✦ **Show Smart Tags:** Controls whether smart tags are highlighted.

✦ **Show Text Boundaries:** Displays faint lines that indicate the boundaries within which text will be placed. This is often a very helpful option.

✦ **Show Crop Marks:** This has nothing to do with cropping pictures. Instead, crop marks are little lines that print in the corners of the page to indicate where the page should be physically cut to fit the margins.

✦ **Show Field Codes instead of Their Values:** Shows the codes inserted for each field rather than the results of the field. Use this option when you're struggling with a maniacal mail merge. For more information, see Chapter 3 of this minibook.

✦ **Field Shading:** You might apply shades to a field to draw attention to them. You can set this option to Never (which never shades field results), Always (which always shades field results), or When Selected (which shades field results only when some or all of the field is selected).

✦ **Use Draft Font in Draft and Outline Views:** Choose this option if you want to display text in a standard font (usually Courier New) when the document is viewed in Draft or Outline view. The main reason for this feature is to help you focus on your document's content rather than its appearance. You should consider using this option if you spend most of your time playing with fonts instead of improving your prose.

Display

The options in the Display section control various aspects of Word's display:

✦ **Number of Documents in the Recent Document List:** Tells Word how many files to list at the right of the Office menu. You can list as many as nine files.

✦ **Show Measurements in Units Of:** In case you don't like inches, you can change Word's measurements to centimeters, points, picas, fathoms, leagues, cubits, or parsecs.

✦ **Style Area Pane Width in Draft and Outline Views:** The style area pane appears at the left of the screen in Draft and Outline view and indicates the style assigned to each paragraph. You can adjust its width by dragging its border, or you can use this option to set the width. Set this option to 0 if you want to hide the style area pane.

✦ **Show Pixels for HTML Features:** Makes pixel the default choice for the measurement unit for Web documents.

✦ **Show All Windows in the Taskbar:** Indicates that each document should get its own icon in the taskbar.

✦ **Show Shortcut Keys in ScreenTips:** Indicates that ScreenTips should show shortcut keys whenever appropriate.

✦ **Show Horizontal Scroll Bar:** The scroll bar at the bottom of the screen. If you discover one day that you've been using Word for two years and didn't know that a horizontal scroll bar was available, deselect this option to free up more space to display your document.

✦ **Show Vertical Scroll Bar:** At the right edge of the window. If your text is just a wee bit wide for the screen, consider deselecting the Show Vertical Scroll Bar option to remove the scroll bar. This action frees up a little space, and you can still press the Page Up and Page Down keys to scroll through your document.

✦ **Show Vertical Ruler in Print Layout View:** Indicates whether a vertical ruler should be displayed when you're working in Print Layout view. This option is off by default.

Print

The Print section of the Advanced tab displays several options that let you control printing. To wit:

✦ **Use Draft Quality:** Prints the document in draft format, with very little formatting. This option can result in faster printing and can save ink because draft quality usually uses less ink than final quality.

✦ **Print in Background:** Speeds printing and allows you to continue working while a long document is printing. I suggest you leave this option on.

✦ **Print Pages in Reverse Order:** Prints the document backwards, starting with the last page in your document. This is useful if your printer stacks the printed pages in the wrong order.

✦ **Print XML Tags:** If this option is set, any XML codes in your document will be printed.

✦ **Print Field Codes Instead of Their Values:** Prints field codes rather than field results. Use this option only if your document is filled with fields and you're trying to figure out why they aren't working right.

✦ **Print on Front of the Sheet for Duplex Printing:** Sets the order of pages on the front of each sheet. Normally, the odd-numbered pages are printed in order on the top of each page. Select this option to reverse the print order of the odd-numbered pages.

✦ **Print on Back of the Sheet for Duplex Printing:** Normally, even numbered pages are printed in order on the back of each page.

✦ **Use Your Locale's Standard Paper Size:** Select this option if you want Word to use your computer's Locale setting to decide what paper size to use by default.

✦ **Default Tray:** Lets you specify the default tray to use.

✦ **Print PostScript Over Text:** This option is important only if you're converting documents from Macintosh Word format. In that case, turn this option on.

✦ **Print Only the Data from a Form:** If your document contains a form and you're printing on preprinted form paper, this option prints just the data rather than the form itself.

Save

This section contains a few options that aren't on the Save tab:

✦ **Prompt before Saving Normal Template:** If you select this option, Word asks your permission before it saves any changes to the Normal template.

✦ **Always Create Backup Copy:** This option isn't nearly as useful as you might think at first, especially if you frequently save your documents, which you should. Still, it's a good safety net, so I recommend it.

✦ **Copy Remotely Stored Files onto Your Computer, and Update the Remote File When Saving:** This option can improve performance when you're working over a network. In some cases, the performance improvement is significant. So I recommend leaving this option selected.

✦ **Allow Background Saves:** Use this option if you work on large documents that take a long time to save. Avoid it if your documents are small and save quickly.

Preserve Fidelity When Sharing This Document

These options provide additional control over data that's stored with the document. Specifically, you can choose to save the following information with the document:

✦ Smart tags in XML format

✦ Form data as a delimited text file

+ Linguistic data

+ Embedded smart tags

General

Finding a section of General options in the middle of a huge collection of Advanced options seems a little backwards to me, but here they are nevertheless:

+ **Provide Feedback with Sound:** Causes Word to beep, boop, and otherwise chortle whenever it needs to get your attention. Turn this option on if you want to constantly remind your neighbors that you haven't yet mastered Word.

+ **Provide Feedback with Animation:** Lets Word show off by displaying clever animations when you perform certain actions, such as saving files or printing.

+ **Confirm Conversion at Open:** This option isn't some kind of religious awakening. Instead, it merely instructs Word to ask for your consent before opening a document that was created by some other program.

+ **Update Automatic Links at Open:** Automatically updates any files that are linked to a document when you open the document. Leaving this option on is usually best.

+ **Allow Opening a Document in Draft View:** Select this option if you want documents to display in Draft view when you open them.

+ **Allow Background Open of Web Pages:** When you open HTML pages that take a long time to load, this option allows you to continue working on other documents while the Web page loads.

+ **Enable Background Repagination:** Ever notice that when you take a breather from your sustained typing rate of 90 words per minute, Word sometimes causes page breaks to dance about? This dance is Word's Background Repagination feature at work, constantly surveying the length of your document and inserting page breaks where they rightfully belong. If you deselect this check box, Word repaginates the document only when you print it; when you create a Table of Contents, index, or other table; or when you work in Page Layout or Print Preview view.

Turning off Background Repagination might make your computer run a little faster, but you'll always be wondering whether you're at the top or bottom of the page. I don't recommend it. (You can't turn off Background Repagination when you're in Page Layout view because Page Layout view requires that page breaks always be up-to-date.)

✦ **Show Add-In User Interface Errors:** Always leave this option selected. It alerts you to errors in an add-in template's attempt to customize the user interface.

✦ **Mailing Address:** Enter your mailing address here.

At the bottom of the General section, you find three buttons that bring up additional dialog boxes stuffed with options:

✦ **File Locations:** Brings up the dialog box shown in Figure 2-6. This dialog box lets you change the location of various Word files, including

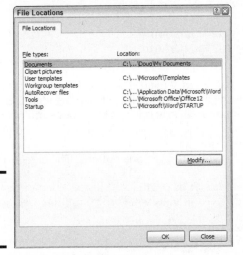

Figure 2-6:
The File
Locations
dialog box.

- *Documents:* Changes the default folder for the Open and Save As commands.

- *Clipart Pictures:* If you have your own collection of clip art, you might want to modify this file type to make your clip art easier to find.

- *User Templates:* You should probably leave this one alone. It tells Word where it can retrieve templates from.

- *Workgroup Templates:* This option lets you set up a secondary location for template files.

- *All the rest:* Leave the rest of the options alone.

**Book VIII
Chapter 2**

Opting for Options

✦ **Web Options:** Brings up the dialog box shown in Figure 2-7, which lets you set various options related to how Word accesses the Web.

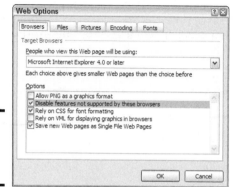

Figure 2-7:
The Web
Options
dialog box.

✦ **Service Options:** Brings up the dialog box shown in Figure 2-8. This dialog box lets you control several options that come into play when you connect to the Internet. For some reason, Microsoft decided not to provide tabs in this dialog box. Instead, you choose one of the categories in the Categories list to display the various options. The categories are

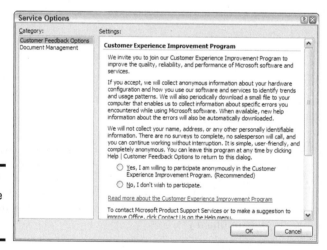

Figure 2-8:
The Service
Options
dialog box.

- *Customer Feedback Options:* Lets you grant Microsoft permission to snoop on you as you use Word. Microsoft promises that this snooping is anonymous and that it gathers only information about how you use Microsoft products.

- *Document Management:* Provides additional options for managing your documents, especially if you use the Shared Workspace feature.

Compatibility Options

The last section on the Advanced tab lets you set backwards compatibility for previous versions of Word or other word-processing programs. You can set the following compatibility options:

✦ Microsoft Office Word 2007

✦ Microsoft Office Word 2003

✦ Microsoft Word 2002

✦ Microsoft Word 2000

✦ Microsoft Word 97

✦ Microsoft Word 6.0/95

✦ Word for Windows 1.0

✦ Word for Windows 2.0

✦ Word for Macintosh 5.x

✦ Word for MS-DOS

✦ WordPerfect 5.x

✦ WordPerfect 6.x for Windows

✦ WordPerfect 6.0 for DOS

This section also includes an innocuous-looking button called Layout Options. If you click it, the already huge list of options shown in the Advanced tab expands to show an additional 60+ options that control how your document is laid out. These options let you revert specific features to the way they worked in previous versions of Word or in WordPerfect. I suggest you avoid these options if you can.

The Customize Tab

The Customize tab lets you customize the buttons that appear on the Quick Access toolbar. For more information about working with this tab, go to Chapter 1 of this minibook.

The Add-Ins Tab

The Add-Ins tab is where you manage global templates and other types of add-ins. For more information about working with this tab, please turn to Chapter 3 of Book I.

The Trust Center Tab

The Trust Center tab, shown in Figure 2-9, lets you access several security-related features for Windows, Office, and Word. This tab includes links to several useful Web sites. In addition, you can click the Trust Center Settings tab to reach the Trust Center dialog box, as shown in Figure 2-10.

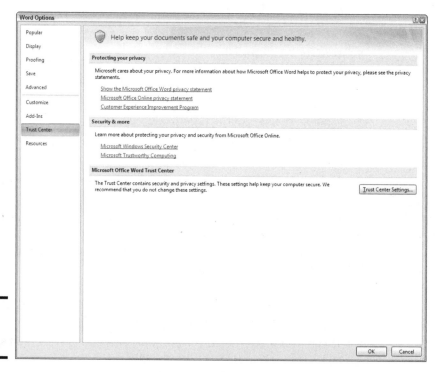

Figure 2-9:
The Trust
Center tab.

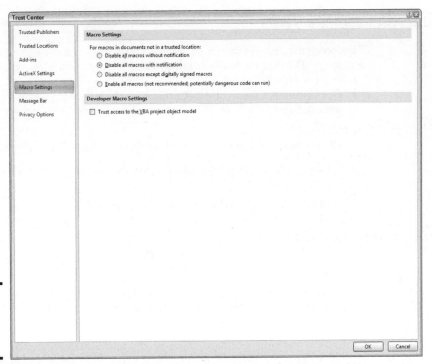

Figure 2-10:
The Trust
Center
dialog box.

The Trust Center dialog box resembles the Word Options dialog box in that it has tabs that let you access specific security-related options. The tabs are

✦ **Trusted Publishers:** Identifies sources of add-ins that have been digitally signed and can therefore be trusted.

✦ **Trusted Locations:** Identifies file locations that contain files such as add-ins and templates that you trust.

✦ **Add-Ins:** Various security options for add-ins. You should leave these options at their default settings.

✦ **ActiveX Settings:** Security options for ActiveX controls. You should leave these options at their default settings.

✦ **Macro Settings:** Security options for macros. You should leave these options at their default settings.

✦ **Message Bar:** Lets you activate or deactivate the message bar, which notifies you when suspicious content has been blocked. You should leave these options at their default settings.

✦ **Privacy Options:** Options that help protect your privacy. You should leave these options at their default settings.

The Resources Tab

The Resources tab, shown in Figure 2-11, contains links to useful information and helpful Web sites. In particular:

✦ **Get Updates:** Links you to Microsoft's Office Update Web site, which automatically updates your copy of Office with the latest security and other fixes.

✦ **Office Diagnostics:** Follow this link if you're having a problem with Word.

✦ **Contact Us:** This link takes you to a page that lists various ways to contact Microsoft.

✦ **Activate Microsoft Office:** When you first install Office, you must activate it within 30 days. Follow this link to do so, if you haven't already.

✦ **Register for Online Services:** This link takes you to a page where you can register with Microsoft Office Online, a Web site that has plenty of useful information and tools for working with Office 2007.

✦ **About Microsoft Office Word 2007:** This link displays a page of important information about your copy of Word 2007, such as the exact version number, the product key, and so on.

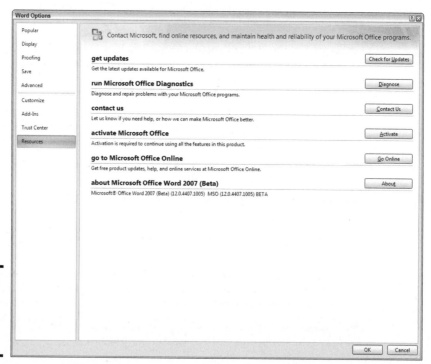

Figure 2-11:
The
Resources
tab in all its
glory.

Chapter 3: Working with Fields

A *field* is a special placeholder code that tells Word to insert something (usually text of some sort) into the document. A date field, for example, tells Word to insert the current date into the document. No matter when you edit or print the document, the date field causes the document to contain the current date.

Fields are everywhere in Word. Many of the commands you've come to know and love rely on fields to do their business. Fields let you put the page number in a header or footer, create a Table of Contents or an index, and print mail-merged letters. These fields are often inserted into your document without your knowledge, as a result of you using some other feature such as footnotes or indexes.

This chapter shows you what you need to know to insert fields directly, using the Quick Parts button on the Insert tab. Word provides many different types of fields (more than 60). At the end of this chapter is a table that lists them all.

Understanding Fields

A *field* is a code that Word translates into some result, usually text, which then inserts into the document. When you insert a date field, for example, you're really saying to Word, "Insert the current date right here, and make sure that you get the date right. When I print this document, I want to see today's date. If I print it tomorrow, I want to see tomorrow's date. Next week, I want to see next week's date. A year from now. . . ." Get the idea? A date field is like a placeholder for an actual date, which Word inserts automatically. Other fields work in a similar way.

The text Word inserts in place of the field code is called the *result.* For a date field, the result is the current date. For a page-number field, the result is the current page number. Other field types produce more complicated results, such as a Table of Contents or an index. For some fields, the result isn't text at all, but a picture or a chart.

When you print a document, you can't distinguish between text you typed directly into the document and text that is a field result. Consider, for example, the following text you may use in a letter:

> As of today, Saturday, December 2, 2006, you have been banished from Remulak and sentenced to live out the remainder of your existence among the Blunt Skulls of Earth.

You can't tell that *Saturday, December 2, 2006* is a field result.

When you edit a document in Word, you must have some way to distinguish between regular text and field results. Word normally displays field results so that the document appears on-screen just as it does when you print it. If the result isn't quite what you expect, however, or if you want to make sure that you used the correct field to produce a result, you can switch the display to show field codes.

The preceding letter fragment with field codes displayed looks like this:

> As of today, { TIME \@ "dddd, MMMM d, yyyy" }, you have been banished from Remulak and sentenced to live out the remainder of your existence among the Blunt Skulls of Earth.

The field is the stuff marked by the curly braces ({ }), which are called *field characters.* Their whole purpose in life is to tell Word that a field lives there. They look just like the curly braces you can type with the keyboard, but they're not the same.

Sandwiched between the field characters is the field itself. Each field begins with a *field type* that tells you what type of field you have there. In the preceding example, you're looking at a TIME field, which provides the current date or time in many different formats.

Following the field type are *instructions,* which tell the field what to do. The TIME field in the preceding example contains an instruction that tells Word how to format the time: *dddd, MMMM d, yyyy.*

Inserting a Field

Follow these steps to insert a field in your document:

1. **Move the insertion point to the spot where you want to insert the field.**

2. **On the Insert tab on the Ribbon, click the Quick Parts button, found in the Text group. Then choose Field from the menu that appears.**

   The Field dialog box appears, as shown in Figure 3-1.

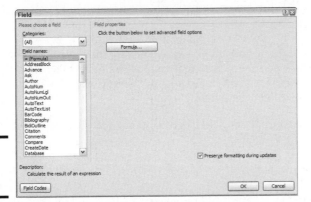

Figure 3-1:
The Field
dialog box.

3. **Select the field type you want to insert.**

   Because so many field types exist, Word breaks them down into categories so that you can find them easier. First, pick the category that contains the field you want to use. Then pick the field from the Field Names list box. If the field you want doesn't appear, try a different category. If you're not sure which category contains the field you want to insert, choose All as the category. This action lists all of Word's field types in the Field Names list box.

4. **Use the other controls in the Field dialog box to add more instructions required by the field.**

   I'd like to be more specific here, but I can't. The appearance of the Field dialog box changes when you select a field because each type of field accepts a different combination of options. For example, Figure 3-2 shows how the Field dialog box appears if you select an Info field. The Field dialog box for an Info field includes a New Value text box, an Info Categories drop-down list, and a Format drop-down list.

5. **Click OK to insert the field.**

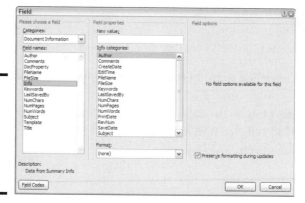

Figure 3-2:
The Field dialog box changes when you select a field type.

You can add more options to a field by clicking the Field Codes button in the Field dialog box and then clicking the Options button. The Field Options dialog box appears, shown in Figure 3-3. The options presented in the dialog box vary depending on the field.

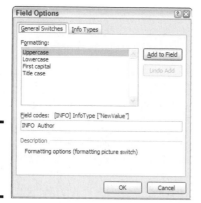

Figure 3-3:
The Field Options dialog box.

You can add options to the field codes by choosing an option you want to add in the list and then clicking the Add to Field button. Every time you click the Add to Field button, the selected option is added to the Field Codes text box. Also, a terse description of each field option appears at the bottom of the Field Options dialog box.

When you insert a field, either the field code or the result displays, depending on whether the Fields Codes view option is set. You can switch between field codes and field results by pressing Alt+F9, or you can right-click the field and choose the Toggle Field Codes command.

If you see something like Error! Unknown switch argument rather than the field result you expect, you made a mistake when you composed the field instructions. You have to edit the field directly by pressing Alt+F9 to reveal the field codes and then clicking in the field and typing your correction. (Or, once again, right-click the field and choose the Toggle Field Codes command.)

Keyboard Shortcuts for Working with Fields

A whole bevy of specialized keyboard shortcuts are available for working with fields. Table 3-1 summarizes them for your convenience.

Table 3-1	Keyboard Shortcuts for Fields
Keyboard Shortcut	*What It Does*
F9	Updates the selected field or fields.
Shift+F9	Switches the display between field codes and field results for the selected field or fields. You must place the insertion point in a field to use this command.
Alt+F9	Switches the display between field codes and field results for all fields in the document. You don't have to select a field before using this command.
Ctrl+F9	Inserts a blank field into a document.
Ctrl+Shift+F9	Converts a field to text (unlinks the field).
F11	Finds the next field in the document.
Shift+F11	Finds the previous field in the document.
Ctrl+F11	Locks a field so that it cannot be updated.
Ctrl+Shift+F11	Unlocks a field.

Another Way to Insert Fields

If you're good at typing commands, you can insert a field by typing it directly in your document. Just follow these steps:

1. **Position the insertion point where you want to insert the field.**

2. **Type the field name and instructions for the field you want to insert.**

   Don't worry about the curly braces for now. Just type the field and its instructions.

3. Select the text you typed in Step 2.

4. Press Ctrl+F9.

Ctrl+F9 converts the selected text to a field by enclosing it in field codes: those curly little braces that look just like the curly braces you can type with the keyboard but aren't the same thing at all.

If you prefer, you can reverse these steps: Position the insertion point where you want to place the field and press Ctrl+F9. An empty field appears, which you can select. Then you can type the field name and instructions within the braces. Or, you can right-click the empty set of braces and then choose Edit Field to bring up the Field dialog box. Then you can use the Field dialog box to choose the field name and the instructions.

Formatting Field Results with Switches

Word provides several switches you can use on almost any field to control the formatting applied to the field result. You don't have to use any of these switches if you don't want to. If you omit them, Word makes an educated guess about the format of the field result.

You can use three switches to format a field's result:

+ **The Mergeformat switch (*)** tells Word to preserve the formatting you include.

+ **The Format switch (*)** tells Word whether to capitalize the field results and, for fields that produce numeric results, which type of numbers to create (Arabic or Roman numerals, for example).

+ **The Numeric Picture switch (\\#)** controls the format of numbers.

+ **The Date-Time Picture switch (\\@)** sets the format of dates and times.

Each of these switches has numerous options that you can mix and match to format the field in just about any way you want. I explain the various uses of these three switches in the following sections.

Preserving formatting when you update fields: The * Mergeformat switch

When you update a field, Word usually removes any formatting, such as bold or italics, you applied to a field result. If you want Word to keep this type of formatting, include the * Mergeformat switch in the field. Preserving formatting is usually a good idea, so I recommend you use this switch most of the time.

You can tell Word to automatically add a * Mergeformat switch to a field by selecting the Preserve Formatting During Updates check box in the Field dialog box.

Capitalizing field results

Use the Format switch (*) options I list in Table 3-2 to control capitalization in a field result. The following field, for example, inserts the name of the current file in lowercase letters:

{ filename * lower * mergeformat }

Table 3-2	Capitalizing Field Results
Switch	*What It Means*
* caps	The First Letter Of Each Word Is Capitalized.
* firstcap	The first letter of the first word is capitalized.
* lower	all the letters are lowercase.
* upper	ALL THE LETTERS ARE UPPERCASE.

Setting the number format

Numbers usually display with Arabic numerals. You can change the format of numbers in field results, however, by using the switches listed in Table 3-3. Consider this text, for example:

This is the { page * OrdText * mergeformat } page.

This line produces a result like this:

This is the thirty-third page.

In this case, the * OrdText switch spells out the page number.

The capitalization used in the table doesn't matter except for the Alphabetic and Roman formats. In that case, the capitalization determines whether upper- or lowercase letters display for the field value.

Table 3-3	Setting the Number Format
Switch	*What It Means*
* alphabetic	Converts numbers to lowercase letters (*1* becomes *a*, *2* becomes *b*, and so on).
* ALPHABETIC	Converts numbers to uppercase letters (*1* becomes *A*, *2* becomes *B*, and so on).
* Arabic	The usual number format (nothing special here).
* CardText	Spells out the number (for example, *1994* becomes *one thousand nine hundred ninety-four*).
* DollarText	Spells out a dollar amount the way you write it on a check (*289.95* becomes *two hundred eighty-nine and 95/100*).
* Hex	A favorite of computer nerds, converts numbers from the normal Earth dweller base 10 numbering system to base 16 (for example, *492* becomes *1EC*).
* Ordinal	Adds *st, nd, rd,* or whatever is appropriate to the end of the number (for example, *307* becomes *307th*).
* OrdText	Spells out the number and adds *st, nd, rd,* or whatever is appropriate to the end (for example, *307* becomes *three hundred seventh*).
* roman	Converts the number to lowercase roman numerals. Film directors use this format to mark copyright dates (for example, *1953* becomes *mcmliii*).
* ROMAN	Converts the number to uppercase roman numerals (for example, *1953* becomes *MCMLIII*).

Creating custom number formats

If you don't like the way Word displays numbers, you can create your own custom number formats by using the Numeric Picture switch (\#). Numeric pictures are created by stringing together a bunch of pound signs, zeros, commas, decimal points, plus or minus signs, dollar signs, and other characters to show how you want numbers to appear. Table 3-4 lists the numeric picture switches you're most likely to use.

Table 3-4	Sample Numeric Picture Switches
Picture Switch	*Description*
\# #,##0	Prints whole numbers with commas to separate groups of thousands (for example, 1,024 and 1,244,212).
\# #,##0.00	Prints numbers with commas to separate groups of thousands and two decimal positions. Both decimal positions print even if one or both of them is zero (for example, 1,024.00 and 8.47).

Picture Switch	Description
\# $#,##0.00;($#,##0.00)	Prints numbers as money: commas to separate groups of thousands, two decimal positions, and a leading dollar sign; for example, $1,024.00. Negative numbers are enclosed in parentheses; for example, ($97.38).
\# 0	Prints whole numbers without commas (for example, 38 and 124873345).
\# 0%	Prints whole numbers without commas, followed by a percent sign (for example, 98%).
\# 0.00	Prints numbers without commas but with two decimal positions (for example, 1024.00 or 3.14).
\# 0.00%	Prints numbers without commas, with two decimal positions, and followed by a percent sign (for example, 97.99%).

Creating custom date and time formats

When you insert a date field, you can click the Options button and choose from one of 17 different formats. If you don't like any of the 17 formats, you can compose your own custom date format by using the Date-Time Picture switch (\@). You just string together the various components of the date or time by using combinations of characters, such as MMM to stand for the three-letter month abbreviation, and dddd to stand for the day of the week, spelled out.

You'd think with 17 date formats to choose from, you could always find the one you need. That's not always the case, though. For example, if you want just the year (as in 2006), you have to create a custom date format using the switch \@ **"yyyy"**. Word doesn't provide this seemingly basic date format among its 17 formats.

Updating a Field

When you first insert a field, Word calculates the field's result. Thereafter, the field result might become out of date. To recalculate a field result to make sure that it is up-to-date, follow one of these procedures:

+ Click the Office button and then click Word Options and select the Display tab. Then select the Update Fields Before Printing check box and then click OK. Word automatically updates all the fields every time you print the document.

✦ To update a specific field, select the field and press F9. If you select several fields, pressing F9 updates all of them. You can quickly update all the fields in a document by pressing Ctrl+A to select the entire document and then pressing F9 to update the fields.

✦ If you point to a field with the cursor and right-click, a shortcut menu appears. Choose the Update Field command from this menu to update the field.

Preventing a Field from Being Updated

If you do *not* want to update a field, you can either lock the field or unlink the field. If you lock the field, Word prevents it from updating until you *unlock* the field. If you *unlink* the field, Word deletes the field code and replaces it with the result text. Locking a field temporarily prevents it from being updated; unlinking the field is permanent.

To lock, unlock, or unlink a field, first select it. Then use the keyboard shortcuts I list in Table 3-5.

How I learned to love the Seq field

Seq is one of my favorite fields because it lets me create a type of numbered list that I use all the time and that can't be done easily using Word's numbering feature. When I plan the Table of Contents for a book, I have to create a list that looks something like this:

Part I: Basic PowerPoint 2007 Stuff

Chapter 1: Opening Ceremonies

Chapter 2: Editing Slides

Chapter 3: Outlining Your Presentation

Part II: Making Your Presentations Look Mahvelous

Chapter 4: Fabulous Text Formats

Chapter 5: Working with Pictures and Clip Art

Chapter 6: A Slide of a Different Color

Do you see in this example how the chapters are numbered sequentially (1 through 6) and the parts also are numbered sequentially (I, II, and so on)? You can't easily create this type of list by using Word's built-in numbering feature. But you can do it if you use a Seq field. For the part numbers, use the Seq field like this:

{ seq part * ROMAN *mergeformat }

For the chapter numbers, use the Seq field like this:

{ seq chapter * mergeformat }

The *part* and *chapter* in the fields let Word keep track of two separate lists at the same time.

Table 3-5	Keyboard Shortcuts for Locking, Unlocking, or Unlinking a Field
Keyboard Shortcut	*What It Does*
Ctrl+F11	Locks the field.
Ctrl+Shift+F11	Unlocks the field.
Ctrl+Shift+F9	Converts the field to results text (unlinks the field).

Field Code Reference

Table 3-6 lists all of the field codes available in Word 2007, along with a brief description of what each code does. For more detailed information about each field code, check the information available via the Insert Field Code dialog box.

Table 3-6	Word Field Codes
Field Code	*Description*
AddressBlock	Inserts a mail-merge address block.
Advance	Moves the text that follows the Advance field to the right or left, up or down, or to a specific position. In most cases, adjusting the positioning with the Font or Paragraph dialog box is better.
Ask	Prompts for information from the user and stores the result in a bookmark. A separate dialog box displays to ask the question.
Author	Obtains the Author name from the document properties or sets the Author property to a new value.
AutoNum	Automatically numbers the paragraph.
AutoNumLgl	Automatically numbers heading paragraphs using legal or technical format (for example, 1.1, 1.2, and so on). Place an AutoNumLgl field at the beginning of each paragraph that you want numbered. This field has been rendered obsolete by Word's built-in numbered lists.
AutoNumOut	Automatically numbers heading paragraphs using outline form. Place an AutoNumOut field at the beginning of each paragraph that you want numbered. This field has been rendered obsolete by Word's built-in lists.
AutoText	Inserts an AutoText entry.
AutoTextList	Creates a shortcut menu in the document that allows the user to select AutoText entries.
BarCode	Inserts a postal bar code based on an address.

(continued)

**Book VIII
Chapter 3**

**Working
with Fields**

Table 3-6 *(continued)*

Field Code	Description
BidiOutline	This field code wins reverses the direction of outline numbering in documents that mix languages that are left-to-right (such as English) and right-to-left (such as Hebrew or Arabic).
Comments	Shows the contents of the comments field from the document's properties and allows you to change the comments.
Compare	Compares two expressions and returns a value of 1 if the comparison is true and 0 if false. It is similar to the If field code.
CreateDate	Inserts the document's creation date.
Database	Inserts the result of a database query into the document as a table.
Date	Inserts the current date into the document. (Word gets the date from Windows. If the date appears wrong, double-click the date that appears at the right side of the Windows task bar to reset the date.)
DocProperty	Retrieves a specified document property. Many of these document properties are also available via their own field codes, such as Author, TotalEditingTime, and so on. Some are also available via the Info field.
DocVariable	Inserts the value of a document variable into your text.
EditTime	Inserts the total editing time in minutes since the document was created. Don't be fooled into thinking that this number somehow reflects a meaningful measure of how long you spent working on the document because the clock continues to run while a document is open whether or not you're working on it. (If you get paid based on this field, I recommend you leave your documents open overnight.)
Eq	The Eq field creates rudimentary mathematical equations and is left over from the days before Word had built-in equations.
FileName	Inserts the filename of the current document, with or without the complete path.
FileSize	Inserts the size of the document file in bytes, kilobytes, or megabytes.
Fillin	Prompts the user for text and then inserts the text into the document as the field result. It is similar to the Ask field, except that Ask places the user's input in a bookmark rather than in the document.

Field Code	Description
GoToButton	Creates a button that moves the insertion point to a specified location when clicked.
GreetingLine	Inserts the greeting line for a mail merge.
HyperLink	Inserts a hyperlink.
If	Compares the results of two expressions and supplies one of two result values depending on the outcome of the comparison.
IncludePicture	Inserts a picture into the document. Inserting a picture is much easier with the Insert tab (click Picture in the Illustrations group on the Insert tab) so this field is pretty much obsolete.
IncludeText	Inserts another document into the current document.
Index	Inserts an index. You must first mark entries to be included in the index with XE fields. Note that creating an index is much easier by using the References tab.
Info	Retrieves the specified document information. Many of these document properties are also available via their own field codes, such as Author, TotalEditingTime, and so on. Most are also available via the DocProperty field. The Info field also lets you set a new value for several of the properties.
Keywords	Displays the keywords from the document properties.
LastSavedBy	Displays the name of the user who last saved the document.
Link	Inserts a file or portion of a file created by another application into the document.
MacroButton	Inserts a button that, when clicked, runs a macro.
MergeField	Sets up a merge field that is replaced by data from the data source when the mail merge is processed.
MergeRec	Sets up a merge field that displays the number of the data record being processed during a mail merge.
MergeSeq	Displays a count of the number of records that are merged so far.
Next	Skips to the next record in the data source without starting a new merge document. Use this field if you want each merge document to include data from two or more records.
NextIf	Skips to the next merge record if the specified condition is true. The Mail Merge Wizard (found on the Mailings tab) handles conditional merging better.

(continued)

Table 3-6 *(continued)*

Field Code	Description
NoteRef	Allows you to refer to a footnote or endnote that is already marked so that if the footnote or endnote changes, the reference changes along with it.
NumChars	Inserts the number of characters in the document.
NumPages	Inserts the number of pages in the document.
NumWords	Inserts the number of words in the document.
Page	Inserts the current page number. This field is inserted into the header or footer when you click the Page Number button.
PageRef	Inserts the number of the page on which a specified bookmark appears.
Print	Sends printer codes directly to the printer when the document prints. To use this field properly, you need to be an expert in the printer codes used by your printer. It works best with HP LaserJet printers or PostScript printers.
PrintDate	Displays the date the document was last printed.
Private	Holds information stored when a document converts from one format to another. This field is intended for use only by the document converters.
Quote	Inserts text into a document.
RD	Allows you to create a Table of Contents or index for a multi-file project without dealing with Word's master document feature. Unfortunately, this method doesn't automatically number pages consecutively from one document to the next. Instead, you must manually set the page numbers and update any TOC, TOA, or Index fields in the separate documents.
Ref	Inserts the contents of the specified bookmark. This is the only field for which the field code itself is optional. As a result, you can just cite the name of the bookmark if you want.
RevNum	Inserts the number of times the document is saved. Thus, if you save a document ten times in the course of an hour (not an unreasonable rate), you produce ten revisions. Unfortunately, this result probably isn't what you or I think of as a true revision number, because most users frequently save their work.
SaveDate	Inserts the date the document was last saved.
Section	Inserts the current section number.

Field Code	Description
SectionPages	Inserts the total number of pages in the current section.
Seq	Creates sequence numbers, such as a numbered list, chapter or heading numbers, and so on. For simple lists, using the Numbering button found in the Paragraph group on the Home tab.
Set	Allows you to create a bookmark for text that isn't visible in the document.
SkipIf	Conditionally skips the next merge record during a mail merge, based on the results of a comparison. The Mailings Ribbon tab has better tools for handling conditional merging, so avoid using this field.
StyleRef	Inserts text that is formatted with a particular style. This field is most useful for creating dictionary-style headers or footers that cite the first or last heading on the page.
Subject	Inserts the document subject taken from the document's properties.
Symbol	Inserts a symbol into the document. This result is far easier to accomplish by using the Symbol button found in the Symbols group of the Insert tab.
TA	Marks a citation to be included in a table of authorities. This field is inserted when you press Alt+Shift+I to mark a citation.
TC	Marks an entry to be included in a Table of Contents. You can more easily compile Tables of Contents based on heading styles, but if you must do it the hard way, use TC fields instead.
Template	Inserts the filename of the template attached to the document.
Time	Inserts the current time.
Title	Inserts the document title taken from the document's properties.
TOA	Compiles a table of authorities based on TA fields inserted into the document. This field is inserted when you use the References ribbon tab to insert a table of authorities.
TOC	Compiles a Table of Contents. This field is inserted when you use References tab to insert a Table of Contents.
UserAddress	Inserts the user's address taken from the Popular tab of the Word Options dialog box (choose Office➪Word Options to access the Word Options dialog box).
UserInitials	Inserts the user's initials.

**Book VIII
Chapter 3**

**Working
with Fields**

(continued)

Table 3-6 *(continued)*

Field Code	Description
UserName	Inserts the user's name.
XE	Marks an entry for inclusion in an index. XE fields insert when you press Alt+Shift+X.
= (Formula)	Lets you insert formulas into your documents.

Chapter 4: Creating Custom Forms

In This Chapter

✔ **Getting to know forms**

✔ **Making a form template**

✔ **Inserting a text field**

✔ **Inserting a check box field**

✔ **Adding a drop-down field**

✔ **Entering data into a form**

✔ **Adding help to a field**

*M*y guess is that Microsoft had a big contract with the government — probably the military — to sell a million copies of Word to the government if the program provided a feature for creating and filling in forms, preferably in triplicate. So here I am, ready to write another chapter for this book. I'd really rather call it a day and maybe catch a quick round of golf, but who knows — maybe the government will buy a truckload of copies of this book at $913 each if I throw in a chapter about creating and filling in forms. So what the heck.

You might not realize it, but creating a form that you or someone else can fill out later qualifies as a type of programming. As such, you must adopt a bit of a programmer's mentality, distasteful as that might seem. In this chapter, I use the word *user* to refer to the person — you or someone else — who fills out a form that you create, just to keep you alert.

Also, be aware that Word 2007 introduces a new type of form that is designed to work with data stored in files in XML format. These types of forms are usually created by application developers who are intimately familiar with XML. The forms I show you how to create in this book are simply documents that restrict the user's input to specific parts of the document and don't have anything to do with XML.

Understanding Forms

A *form* is a special type of document in which parts of the document are protected from the user modifying it. The user is allowed to enter information only in predefined, fill-in-the-blank portions of the document, which are called *form fields*.

Figure 4-1 shows an example of a form that I created with Word. Most of the text you see in the document is protected. The only parts of the document that the user can modify are the shaded parts: the name and address fields, the answers to the two questions, and the check boxes.

I provide the exact steps for creating and filling out a blank form later in this chapter, but the general idea goes something like this: First, you create a new template. Then you add any text that you want to appear in the form to the template and you add the form fields using buttons available on the Controls section of the Developer tab. When you finish the blank form, use Protect Document command (found on the Developer tab) to prevent the user from modifying any part of the document other than the form fields, and finally, you save the template.

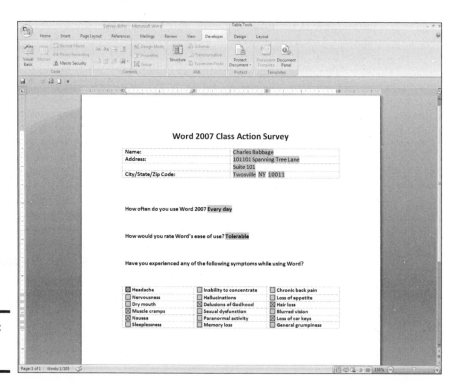

Figure 4-1:
A Word form.

To fill in a form, you have to create a new document based on the form template. Then fill in the blanks. Word doesn't allow you to move the insertion point anywhere outside the form fields, so you don't have to worry about accidentally messing up the form.

- ✦ Think of the template as a pile of blank forms. To fill out a form, first you have to grab a form off the pile by opening the template. After you fill out the form (the template), you can save it as a normal document. The saved document contains the form itself that's copied from the template, plus whatever information you typed into the form fields.

- ✦ Although it's not apparent from Figure 4-1, the form fields for the first two questions are actually drop-down list boxes. Instead of typing in a response to the question, the user selects one of several permissible responses. If, for example, the user clicks in the form field for the first question ("How often do you use Word 2007?"), the drop-down list shown in Figure 4-2 appears.

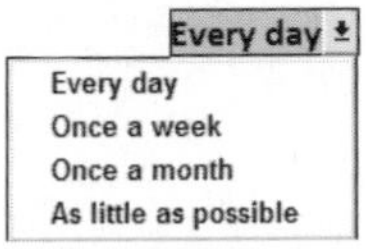

Figure 4-2:
A drop-down list.

- ✦ Microsoft offers several form templates for download at the Microsoft Office Online Web site. To see what you can do with forms, try downloading a few of these templates.

Creating a Form Template

Before you can fill out a form, you must create a template. The template contains any text and graphics that appear on the blank form as well as the form fields, into which the user enters information.

To create a form template, follow these steps:

1. **Choose Office⇨New to display the New Document dialog box, and then select Blank Document and click Create.**

This action creates a new blank document.

2. **Choose Office⇨Save As.**

The Save As dialog box appears.

3. Select Word Template from the Save as Type drop-down list.

4. Type a name for your new form template and click Save.

The initial copy of the template is saved.

5. Choose Office⇨Word Options.

This step brings up the Word Options dialog box.

6. On the Popular tab, click the Show Developer Tab in Ribbon option. Then click OK.

The Developer tab appears. It contains the commands you need to create a form, as shown in Figure 4-3.

Figure 4-3:
The
Developer
tab.

7. Create your form.

Type text where you want text to appear, insert graphics where you want graphics to appear, and insert form fields where you want form fields to appear. (Much of the rest of this chapter is devoted to this task.)

To insert form fields, click the Legacy Tools button in the Controls group of the Developer tab. This reveals the menu of controls shown in Figure 4-4. The form controls are in the top row of this menu, labeled Legacy Forms. For more specific information on creating these fields, see the following three sections.

Figure 4-4:
The Legacy
Forms
menu.

8. Click the Protect Document button, found in the Protect group of the Developer tab on the Ribbon, and then choose Restrict Formatting and Editing from the menu that appears.

The Restrict Formatting and Editing task pane appears, as shown in Figure 4-5.

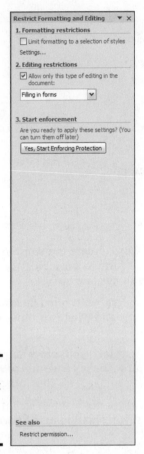

9. **Select the Allow Only This Type of Editing in the Document check box and then select Filling in Forms from the drop-down list.**

   This action protects the document so that the user can enter data into the form fields only.

10. **Click the Yes, Start Enforcing Protection button in the Protect Document task pane.**

   The dialog box shown in Figure 4-6 appears.

11. **Type the password you want to use to protect the document in both text boxes and then click OK.**

   Using a password helps ensure that only you can unprotect the form to make changes to the form's layout. If you don't care about password protecting the form, just click OK without typing a password.

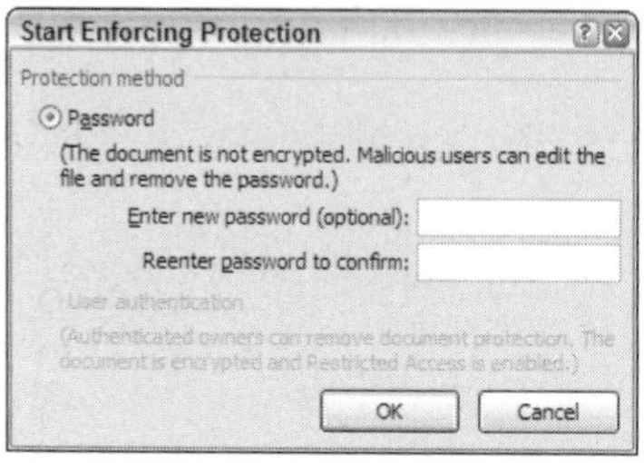

Start Enforcing Protection

Protection method

◉ Password

(The document is not encrypted. Malicious users can edit the file and remove the password.)

Enter new password (optional):

Reenter password to confirm:

○ User authentication

(Authenticated owners can remove document protection. The document is encrypted and Restricted Access is enabled.)

OK   Cancel

Figure 4-6:
The Start
Enforcing
Protection
dialog box.

12. **Choose Office⇨Save to save the template.**

That's all. You're done.

Here are some suggestions for creating forms:

✦ If you're converting a paper form to Word, create the Word form so that it looks as much like the current paper form as possible. Work in Print Layout view so that you can see how things line up.

✦ If you want the form to be laid out on a grid with ruled lines and boxes, use tables, text boxes, borders, shading, and whatever other Word features you can muster.

✦ If you're creating a template for the first time, you may want to refer to Book I, Chapter 3 to make sure you know the ins and outs of working with templates.

✦ Creating a form is tedious work. You might not want to wait until the very end to save the template. In fact, you should press Ctrl+S to save your work every few minutes.

✦ If you protect the template by using the Protect Document command, you must unprotect the template if you need to change the layout of the form later. Click Protect Document (in the Protect group of the Developer tab) and choose Restrict Formatting and Editing to bring up the Restrict Formatting and Editing task pane. Then click the Stop Protection button found at the bottom of the task pane. If you used a password when you protected the document, you're asked to enter the password to unprotect the document. Don't forget to protect the form again when you finish!

Creating a Text Field

A *text field* is a form field that the user can type information into. You use text fields to provide a space on the form where the user can enter information, such as a name or address. The form shown in Figure 4-1 uses four text fields: one for the name and three for the address lines.

To create a text field in a form, follow these steps:

1. **Position the insertion point on the template where you want the text field to appear.**

2. **In the Controls group of the Developer tab, click Legacy Tools and then click the Text Form Field button.**

ab|

A text form field is inserted.

Typing some sort of text in the template next to the field to tell the user what to type into the field is a good idea. For example, in Figure 4-1, I typed **Name:** next to the text field that is supposed to contain the name.

If you want to provide a *default value* for the text field — that is, a value that the field assumes if the user doesn't type anything into the field — double-click the text field to summon the Text Form Field Options dialog box, as shown in Figure 4-7. Type a default value for the field in the Default Text box and then click OK.

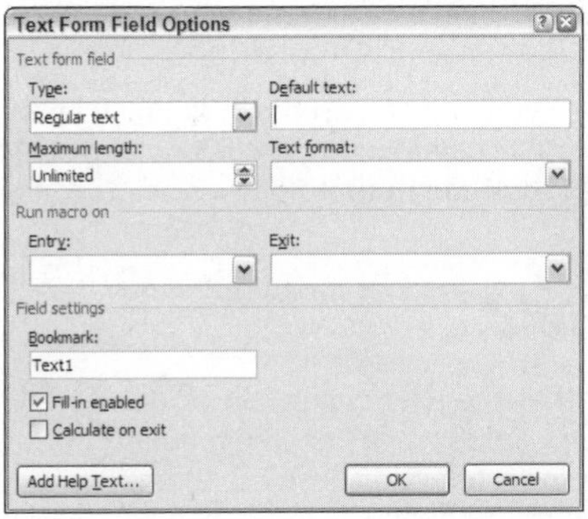

Figure 4-7:
The Text Form Field Options dialog box.

The Text Form Field Options dialog box also enables you to set the field type. Word lets you create six different types of text fields, as I summarize in Table 4-1.

Table 4-1	The Six Types of Text Fields
Text Field Type	*What It Does*
Regular Text	This field consists of ordinary text, like a name or address. The user can type anything into the field.
Number	The user must type a number into the field.

(continued)

Table 4-1 *(continued)*

Text Field Type	What It Does
Date	The user must type a date into the field. The date must be in the month/day/year date format (for example, 05/31/04 or 6-24-04) or may include the month spelled out (as in March 28, 2004).
Current Date	Word automatically inserts the current date into the field. The user can't type anything in the field.
Current Time	Word automatically inserts the current time into the field. The user can't type anything in the field.
Calculation	The field contains a formula field (=) to calculate a result value, usually based on the value of one or more number fields. The user also can't type anything into this field.

If you deselect the Fill-In Enabled check box in the Text Form Field Options dialog box (see Figure 4-7), Word displays the text field, but the user can't modify it. Use this field only if you plan on doing some fancy macro programming, in which a macro enables or disables the field at will. This kind of macro programming requires programming knowledge that is way beyond the realm of reasonableness.

After you create a text field, you can call up the Text Form Field Options dialog box by double-clicking the field or right-clicking the field and choosing Properties from the shortcut menu that appears.

Creating a Check Box Field

A *check box field* is a field that the user can select or deselect to provide a yes or no answer. Check box fields work just like regular check boxes in dialog boxes: You click them to select or deselect them.

Follow these steps to create or insert a check box field:

1. **Position the insertion point in the template where you want the check box field to appear.**

2. **In the Controls group of the Developer tab, click Legacy Tools and then click the Check Box Form Field button.**

   A check box form field is inserted.

3. **If you want the check box to not be selected when the form first displays, you're done. Otherwise, double-click the Check Box form field.**

   The Check Box Form Field Options dialog box appears, as shown in Figure 4-8.

Figure 4-8:
The Check
Box Form
Field
Options
dialog box.

4. Select the Checked option.

The check box will be selected when the form first displays.

5. Click OK.

The check box is now inserted in the document.

Here are some pointers for creating a check box field:

✦ Obviously, a check box by itself is of little worth. You want to place some text in the template right next to the check box so that the user knows what the check box field means.

✦ Unless you're into writing macros, the only thing you can do with a check box is select it or deselect it. If you want to roll up your sleeves and do some heavy-duty macro programming, you can come up with all sorts of exotic uses for check box fields.

✦ If you want to change the default size of the check box field, select Exactly (at the top of the Check Box Form Field Options dialog box) and type the size of the check box in points.

✦ If you deselect the Check Box Enabled check box, Word displays the check box field, but the user can't modify it. Use this field only if you plan to do some fancy macro programming, in which a macro enables the field if the user enters a certain value into another field. To re-enable the check box again, check the Check Box Enabled check box.

Sounds like a scene from *Airplane,* doesn't it?

Roger: Chuck, check the Check Box Enabled Check Box.

Chuck: Roger, Roger. Now checking the Check Box Enabled check box. Chuck out.

Roger: Check, Chuck.

✦ You can call up the Check Box Form Field Options dialog box after you insert a check box field by double-clicking the field or right-clicking the field (that is, pointing to it and clicking the right mouse button) and selecting the Properties command from the shortcut menu that appears.

Creating a Drop-Down Field

A *drop-down field* is like a text field, except that the user isn't allowed to type text directly into the field. Instead, the user must select from a list of preset choices that are given in a list box. List boxes are great for fields such as marital status, shipping instructions, or gender (in other words, fields that have only a limited set of correct answers).

Follow these steps to create, or insert, a drop-down field:

1. **Position the insertion point in the template where you want the drop-down list field to appear.**

2. **In the Controls group of the Developer tab, click Legacy Tools and then click the Drop-Down Form Field button.**

A drop-down form field is inserted.

3. **Double-click the drop-down form field.**

The Drop-Down Form Field Options dialog box appears, as shown in Figure 4-9.

Figure 4-9: The Drop-Down Form Field Options dialog box.

4. **To add an item to the drop-down list, type some text in the Drop-Down Item box and then click the Add button.**

The text is added to the Items in Drop-Down List field.

5. **Repeat Step 4 for each item you want to include as a choice in the drop-down list.**

6. **When you add all the items you want in the list, click OK.**

   That's it!

If you're going to the trouble of creating drop-down list fields, keep the following hot tips in mind:

✦ The first item in the drop-down list is the default selection — that is, the item that is initially selected for the field.

✦ To rearrange items in the drop-down list, call up the Drop-Down Form Field Options dialog box, select the item that you want to move to another position in the list, and click the up or down Move buttons.

✦ To delete an item from the list, select the item and click the Remove button.

✦ To correct a mistake in a list item, delete the incorrect item. Word copies the deleted item to the Drop-Down Item box, where you can correct the mistake and click the Add button to reinsert the item.

✦ If you deselect the Drop-Down Enabled check box, Word displays the drop-down list field, but the user can't modify it. Use this field only if you plan to do some fancy macro programming, in which a macro enables or disables the field on the fly. Better con a computer nerd friend into doing this macro for you.

✦ You can call up the Drop-Down Form Field Options dialog box after you insert a drop-down field by double-clicking the field or right-clicking the field and selecting the Properties from the shortcut menu that appears.

Filling Out a Form

After you create a form template and protect it, it's time to put the form to good use collecting the vital information that you so carefully designed it to record. In other words, it's time to fill out the form.

To fill out a form by using a form template that you or someone else created, follow these steps:

1. **Choose Office⇨New.**

   The New Document dialog box appears.

2. **Click My Templates and then select the correct form template from the list of templates.**

3. Click OK.

4. Fill in the form fields.

When you fill in the form fields, you can use any of the keyboard actions I list in Table 4-2. For the most part, you use the Tab key to move from field to field.

Note that the spell checker doesn't work in form fields. So you have to be careful about your spelling when you work with a form.

5. Print the document.

Click the Office button, then click Print.

6. Save the file, if you want.

Choose Office⇨Save.

Table 4-2	Keys You Can Use When Filling Out a Form
Key	*What It Does*
Enter, Tab, or ↓	Moves the insertion point to the next field
Shift+Tab, or ↑	Moves the insertion point to the previous field
Alt+↓ or F4	Displays a drop-down list
↑ or ↓	Moves up or down in a drop-down list
Spacebar or X	Selects or deselects a check box field
F1	Displays the help text for a field
Ctrl+Tab	Inserts a tab character into a text field

Adding Help to a Form Field

Word lets you add your own help text to form fields. Then if you forget what a field is for when you're filling out a form, the help text reminds you.

You can create two types of help text for each field. The status bar help is a single line of text that appears on the status bar whenever the insertion point moves into the field. Word limits this help text to 138 characters so that it fits in the space provided on the status bar. If the status bar help isn't enough, you can supply help text, which the user can summon by pressing F1. You can provide up to 256 characters for help text. Figure 4-10 shows an example of help text.

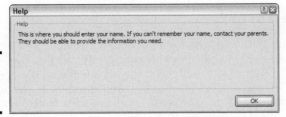

Figure 4-10:
Help text for
a form field.

To create help text for a field, follow these steps:

***1.* Select the field you want to add help text to.**

Make sure the form is unprotected. You can't add help text to a field while the form is protected.

***2.* Double-click the field to call up the Form Field Options dialog box.**

***3.* Click the Add Help Text button.**

The Form Field Help Text dialog box appears, as shown in Figure 4-11.

Figure 4-11:
Adding help
to a form
field.

***4.* Type the status bar help text on the Status Bar tab and the help text on the Help Key (F1) tab.**

***5.* Click OK.**

The help text is now attached to the field. The user can display it by pressing F1.

Using Preprinted Forms

If you're creating an online form for a document for which you have preprinted forms that you can use with your printer, format the form template so that its fields align exactly with the form fields on the preprinted form. Then, when you want to print to the preprinted form, choose Office➪Word Options. In the Word Options dialog box, click the Advanced tab, scroll down to the When Printing This Document options, and then select the Print Only Data For a Form option. Word prints just the data you enter into the form fields, not the form template itself. If your preprinted forms and your form template are lined up properly, the data fits snugly in the fields on the preprinted form.

Book IX

Features for Developers

The 5th Wave

By Rich Tennant

"It's a ten step word-processing program. It comes with a spell-checker, grammar-checker, cliche-checker, whine-checker, passive/aggressive-checker, politically correct-checker, hissy-fit-checker, pretentious pontificating-checker, boring anecdote-checker and a Freudian reference-checker."

Contents at a Glance

Chapter 1: Recording and Using Macros

In This Chapter

✔ **Recording a macro**

✔ **Running a macro**

✔ **Editing a macro**

✔ **Using auto macros**

A macro is a sequence of commands or keystrokes that Word records and lets you play back at any time. Macros allow you to create your own customized shortcuts for tasks you do over and over again. For example, Word comes with built-in keyboard shortcuts to make text bold (Ctrl+B) and to make text italic (Ctrl+I), but no built-in shortcut exists to make text bold and italic all at the same time. To perform that formatting task, you have to press Ctrl+B and then press Ctrl+I. If you do that a million times a day, pretty soon that extra keystroke becomes bothersome. Wouldn't having a shortcut for bold-italic be nice? With Word's macro recorder, you can create one.

This chapter shows you how to record and play back simple macros. It doesn't show you how to create complex macros by using Word's macro programming language, Visual Basic for Applications. That's the topic of the remaining chapters in this minibook.

Where Do All the Macros Go?

You can store macros in documents or in templates. When you create a macro, you have three choices for where to store the macro:

✦ **The current document:** This is the best place to create macros that you will use only in a single document.

✦ **The template that's attached to the current document if it is macro-enabled:** This is the best place to create macros that you want to use in a large number of similar documents. Then, the macros will be available to any document you create from the template.

✦ **The `Normal.dotm` template:** This is the place to create macros that you want to be available all the time, no matter what document you are working on.

Note: If the current document is based on `Normal.dotm`, you really have only two choices — the current document or the `Normal.dotm` template.

When you create a macro, you need to think about when you're going to want to run the macro. If you need to run the macro only from within a specific document, create the macro in that document. If you want the macro to be available only to documents based on a particular template, create the macro in that template. But if you want the macro to always be available no matter what document you're working on, store the macro in `Normal.dotm`.

Actually, you can store macros in a fourth place: in a *global template.* A global template is a great place to create a library of macros that are available to all of your documents. For more information about using global templates, turn to Book I, Chapter 3. *Note:* To create or edit macros in a global template, you must open the template. After you create macros in a template, you can close the template, attach it as a global template, and then run any macros it contains.

Doing the Macro Recorder Dance

The easiest way to create a macro is to use the *macro recorder,* which is kind of like a videocassette recorder. After you turn on the macro recorder, it follows you around and makes a precise record of everything you do until you turn off the recorder. Well, not really *everything.* The Word macro recorder records only the stuff you do in Word. It doesn't notice when you dribble coffee down your chin or sneeze on the monitor. But when you turn on the recorder, anything you do in Word — whether you're typing text, applying formatting, calling up a command, or filling out a dialog box — is carefully recorded.

Then when you turn off the recorder, you can replay the recorded macro to repeat the exact sequence of steps that Word recorded in the macro.

About the only things that are *not* recorded by the macro recorder are mouse movements within the document. The macro recorder records buttons or Ribbon choices you click, but Word won't let you navigate about your document or select text with the mouse while the macro is recording. As a result, use the keyboard for navigating or selecting text while recording a macro.

To record a macro, follow these steps:

1. **Try to talk yourself out of it.**

Fiddling around with macros can be a bit of a time-waster. Ask yourself whether you really will use the macro after you go to the trouble of recording it. If not, go directly to Step 12.

2. **Think about what you're going to do.**

Think through all the steps you have to follow to accomplish whatever task you want to automate with a macro. To create a macro that makes text bold and italic, for example, all you have to do is press Ctrl+B and then press Ctrl+I. That's a pretty simple macro, but other macros can be much more complex, involving dozens of steps. If necessary, rehearse the steps before you record them as a macro.

3. **Click the Developer tab on the Ribbon and then click the Record Macro button in the Code group.**

The Record Macro dialog box appears, as shown in Figure 1-1.

Book IX
Chapter 1

**Recording and
Using Macros**

Figure 1-1:
The Record
Macro
dialog box.

If the Developer tab isn't visible, choose Office⇨Word Options to summon the Word Options dialog box. Then, click the Personalize tab and select the Show Developer Tab in the Ribbon check box.

4. Type the name of the macro you want to create in the Macro Name text box.

The name can be anything you want, but it cannot include spaces, commas, or periods. When the Record Macro dialog box first appears, the macro name is set to something like Macro1 or Macro2 (or Macro783 if you've been busy). Surely you can come up with a better name than that. (I know . . . "Yes, I can . . . and stop calling me Shirley.")

5. To make your macro accessible from a toolbar or the keyboard, click the Button or Keyboard button.

This step calls up the Customize dialog box, which is ready to add your macro to a toolbar, the Ribbon, or a keyboard shortcut. Figure 1-2 shows the Customize Keyboard dialog box that Word displays if you click the Keyboard button. Type the shortcut key combination you want to assign to the macro (in this case, I pressed Alt+Ctrl+B), click the Assign button and then click Close.

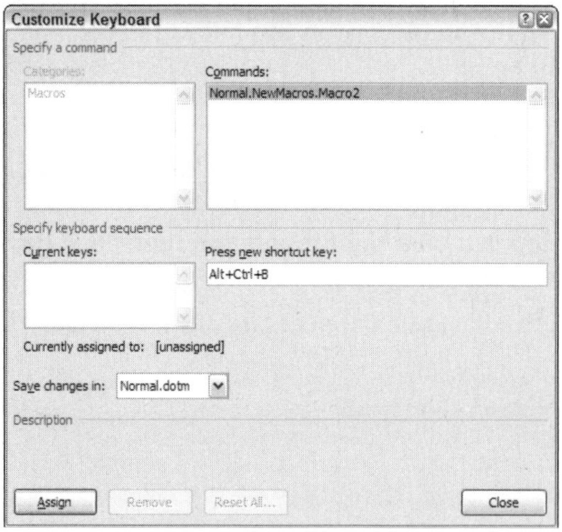

Figure 1-2:
Assigning a
macro to a
keyboard
shortcut.

If you click the Button button instead, the Word Options dialog box appears with the Customize tab selected. Then, you can create a button on the Quick Access toolbar to run the macro. For more information, refer to Book VIII, Chapter 1.

6. Set the Store Macro In drop-down list to the location where you want to store the macro.

The default setting stores the recorded macro in the `Normal.dotm` template so that it's always available. The other choices available in this drop-down list are storing the macro in the document that you were working on when you called up the macro recorder or storing the macro to the template that document is based on.

7. Click OK to begin recording the macro.

8. Type the keystrokes and Ribbon commands you want to record in the macro.

To record the ***BoldItalic*** macro, for example, press Ctrl+B and then press Ctrl+I.

9. If you have to stop recording temporarily, click the Pause button. Click it again to resume recording.

❚❚◉ Pause Recording

You might forget how to do something, for example, especially if you skipped Step 2. If you click the Pause button, you can call up Word's Help command, look up the procedure for whatever it is you forgot, dismiss Help, and click the Pause button again to resume recording.

▢ Stop Recording

10. After you finish recording the macro, click the Stop button.

Word adds the macro to the template or document. You're almost done.

11. Test the macro.

If you assigned the macro to a keyboard shortcut, use the shortcut now to see whether the macro works. Otherwise, follow the steps in the later section, "Running a Macro."

12. You're finished.

Congratulate yourself.

If the function of the macro isn't obvious from the macro name, type a more elaborate description of the macro in the Record Macro dialog box's Description field. You'll thank yourself later when you forget what the macro does.

Macro Recording Tips

Here are some tips to keep in mind as you record macros:

✦ You can call up the Record Macro dialog box directly by clicking the Record Macro button on the status bar. It appears as a little red dot.

✦ If the macro doesn't work, you might have made a mistake while recording it. If the macro is short enough, the best thing to do is to record the macro again. If the macro is long and you don't have anything important to do, try editing the macro to expunge the problem. See the section "Editing a Macro" later in this chapter.

✦ Macros are normally stored in the global `Normal.dotm` template. To store a macro in the template attached to the current document, change the setting of the Record Macro dialog box's Store Macro In drop-down list.

✦ Don't make any assumptions about where the insertion point will be when you run the macro. If necessary, begin the macro with a positioning command by moving the insertion point to the beginning of the document, the beginning of the line, or the beginning of a word. (Not all macros require a positioning command. But if your macro depends in any way on the position of the insertion point, this step is a must.)

✦ Don't use the mouse to select text or navigate through the document. Word doesn't record these mouse actions. You can use the mouse to select Ribbon commands, but not to move the insertion point.

✦ Use Ctrl+Home or Ctrl+End to move to the beginning or end of a document. Don't use repeated Page Up or Page Down keys for this purpose. Pressing Page Up three times might get you to the top of your document when you record the macro, but when you run the macro, it might not. Similarly, use Home and End to move to the start or end of a line rather than the left or right arrow keys.

✦ If you use the Find or Replace commands, be sure to move to the beginning of the document first.

✦ Avoid any commands that depend on the contents of a document that's active when you record the macro. If your macro is based on information that will never be replicated, it's a pretty useless macro.

Running a Macro

If you assigned a macro to the Quick Access toolbar, the Ribbon, or a keyboard shortcut, you can run the macro by clicking the QAT button, choosing

Avoiding unexpected side effects

Sometimes a macro has unexpected side effects. Suppose that rather than record the keystrokes Ctrl+B and Ctrl+I for the *BoldItalic* macro, you decide to record these steps instead:

1. Call up Format⇨Font.

2. Choose Bold Italic as the font style.

3. Click OK.

The macro seems to work, but sooner or later, you discover that in addition to recording the Bold Italic font style, the macro recorded other character attributes — such as font, size, and effects. If the text to which you applied the

Format⇨Font command when you recorded the macro was 10-point Times New Roman font, every time you apply the macro, the font is switched to 10-point Times New Roman.

You can avoid these side effects in two ways:

✔ Avoid recording dialog boxes in macros whenever a keyboard shortcut or a Ribbon button can do the trick. Whenever you record a dialog box in a macro, you record all the dialog box's settings.

✔ Fix the macro later by editing it and removing the extraneous information. See the section "Editing a Macro."

the Ribbon command, or pressing the keyboard shortcut. If you didn't, you can run it by following these steps:

1. **Select the Developer tab on the Ribbon and then click the Macros button in the Code group.**

The Macros dialog box, shown in Figure 1-3, appears.

As a shortcut, you can press Alt+F8.

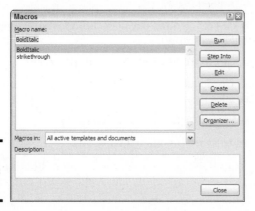

Figure 1-3:
The Macros
dialog box.

2. **If the macro you want to run isn't already selected, select it now. If the macro you want doesn't appear, try changing the Macros In setting.**

The macro might be in a different template.

3. **Click Run.**

Editing a Macro

If you make a mistake while recording a macro, you can abandon the recording and start over. Or you can finish the recording and edit the macro to correct the mistake. When you edit the macro, the macro's commands appear in a separate window. You can delete or modify erroneous commands, you can insert new commands if you know how, or you can merely study the macro to try to figure out how it works.

When you edit a macro, you're exposed to Visual Basic for Applications (VBA). VBA is not as deadly as the Ebola virus, but it can cause severe headaches and nausea if you're not inoculated with the Programmer Vaccine. For more information about VBA and its editor, turn to Chapter 2 of this minibook.

Here are the steps for editing a macro:

1. **Click the Macros button on the Developer tab on the Ribbon or on the status bar.**

The Macros dialog box appears. (Refer to Figure 1-3.)

2. **Select the macro you want to edit and click the Edit button.**

Word launches the Visual Basic editor, with the macro you selected visible in its own window. See Figure 1-4.

Notice that the Visual Basic editor uses good old-fashioned menus instead of the new-fangled Ribbon.

3. **Make whatever changes are necessary to the macro.**

Correct misspelled words, delete extraneous commands, and if you're brave, add more commands.

4. **Choose File⇨Save Template to save your changes.**

5. **Choose File⇨Close to close the macro window.**

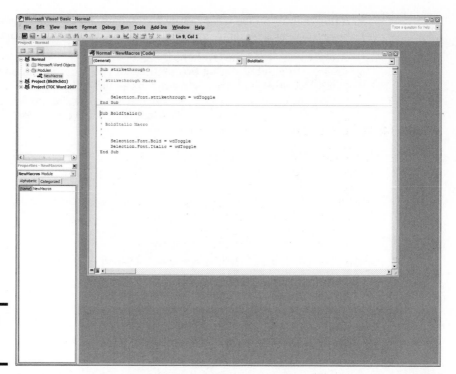

Figure 1-4:
Editing a
macro.

Simple Macro Edits That Don't Require a Ph.D. in VBA

Before you make massive changes to a macro, you need a pretty good knowledge of VBA. However, you can make certain types of changes without knowing much about VBA at all. Here's a sampling:

+ **Correct spelling errors.** If you inserted text into a document and misspelled it, don't hesitate to edit the macro to correct the misspellings. Text you insert into a document while recording a macro is included in a `Selection.TypeText` command, like this:

```
Selection.TypeText Text:="This is some simple text."
```

You can correct any spelling mistakes or change the inserted text altogether, provided you take care not to remove either of the quotation marks that appear before and after the text. For example, you can correct the preceding line to:

```
Selection.TypeText Text:="This is some sample text."
```

✦ **Remove extraneous commands.** If you inadvertently used a command while recording a macro, you can clean up your macro by removing the unnecessary command.

✦ **Remove unwanted dialog box settings.** If you record a dialog box in a macro, Word includes every setting in the dialog box. You can remove the settings that you do NOT WANT the macro to change. For example, if you use Font dialog box to format text with small caps, Word inserts the following commands into the macro:

```
With Selection.Font
       .Name = "Times New Roman"
       .Size = 9.5
       .Bold = False
       .Italic = False
       .Underline = wdUnderlineNone
       .UnderlineColor = wdColorAutomatic
       .strikethrough = False
       .DoubleStrikeThrough = False
       .Outline = False
       .Emboss = False
       .Shadow = False
       .Hidden = False
       .SmallCaps = True
       .AllCaps = False
       .Color = wdColorAutomatic
       .Engrave = False
       .Superscript = False
       .Subscript = False
       .Spacing = 0.3
       .Scaling = 100
       .Position = 0
       .Kerning = 0
       .Animation = wdAnimationNone
   End With
```

This command looks complicated at first, but if you study it, you see that it is little more than a list of all the dialog box controls that appear in the Font dialog box. The periods look strange appearing in front of each command argument as they do, but they're required. You can safely delete the lines that specify those dialog box controls you don't want to use so that the resulting command looks like this:

```
With Selection.Font
           .SmallCaps = True
   End With
```

Actually, with a little more VBA knowledge, you can also remove the `With` and `End With` commands and substitute just the following:

```
Selection.Font.SmallCaps = True
```

Using Auto Macros

An *auto macro* is a macro that runs automatically whenever some key event happens, such as when Word starts or when a document closes. Word recognizes auto macros by their names. For example, a macro named AutoNew automatically runs when you create a new document from a template, and a macro named AutoClose automatically runs when you close a document.

To create an auto macro, you simply create a macro by using one of the following special macro names:

✦ **AutoExec:** Runs when Word starts. Store it in the `Normal.dotm` template.

✦ **AutoExit:** Runs when Word exits. Store it in the `Normal.dotm` template.

✦ **AutoNew:** Runs whenever a new document is created by using the template that contains the AutoNew macro.

✦ **AutoOpen:** Runs whenever an existing document opens. You can create an AutoOpen macro in the `Normal.dotm` template or in the template that's attached to the document. Or both.

✦ **AutoClose:** Runs whenever an open document closes. This macro can reside in `Normal.dotm` or in the template attached to the document.

You can prevent any auto macro from executing by holding down the Shift key while performing the action that otherwise triggers the macro. For example, holding down the Shift key while creating a new document prevents the AutoNew macro from running.

Macro security

Computer viruses can exploit Word's auto macro feature to infect your computer. As a result, you need to take some steps to protect yourself from the possibility of being hit by a macro virus. Here are some things you can do:

✔ Set your macro security to at least the Medium setting to protect yourself from malicious macros. To set the macro security, click the Macro Security button on the Developer tab on the Ribbon. Then choose the security level you're most comfortable with.

✔ Don't open documents from people you don't know or trust, especially documents that arrive as attachments in unsolicited e-mail messages.

✔ Install an antivirus program. These programs sniff out and smash all known macro viruses, as well as other more common types of viruses and worms.

Chapter 2: Programming with VBA

In This Chapter

- ✔ Using variables, strings, and other VBA elements
- ✔ Working with objects, properties, and methods
- ✔ Executing macros with If, While, and Select Case
- ✔ Displaying information and obtaining input from the user
- ✔ Working with user-defined subroutines and macros

I cover the basics of recording and playing macros in Chapter 1 of this minibook. Chapter 1 touches on the subject of VBA programming just enough to whet your appetite and give you the skills needed to create and use the various macros that appear throughout this book. But I reserve the real meat of VBA programming for this chapter. Here I show you VBA in-depth so that, with a little practice and a lot of trial and error, you can create VBA macros of your own.

This chapter is admittedly a bit of a whirlwind introduction to VBA program-ming. If you have absolutely no programming experience, this chapter might be a bit overwhelming. Don't let the details of VBA bog you down. Study the sample macros that appear in this chapter and in the remaining chapters in this book, experiment a lot, and keep your chin up. You'll catch on soon enough. If you're not sure about how to create and edit macros, check out Chapter 1 of this minibook before proceeding.

The Basic Structure of VBA Macros

If you want to create a blank macro that you can then edit yourself, you can do so by summoning the Macros dialog box, typing a name for the macro you want to create, and clicking the Create button. Then Word switches you to the VBA editor and creates a skeleton of a macro for you, like this:

```
Sub BoldItalic()
'
' BoldItalic Macro
' Macro created 2/18/2004 by Doug Lowe
'
End Sub
```

The lines that begin with apostrophes are comments. VBA ignores them completely, but you can use them to remind yourself what the macro does or how it works. Comments can appear on lines all by themselves, or they can appear at the end of a line, like this:

```
Sub BoldItalic()   'The BoldItalic macro
```

The `Sub` and the `End Sub` statements mark the beginning and end of the macro's main procedure. As you see later, a macro can call upon other procedures or functions that you define elsewhere in your code. However, the simplest macros consist of these lines with some additional VBA statements in between.

For example, the following macro contains two VBA statements, one to make the selected text bold, and the other to make it italic:

```
Sub BoldItalic()
    Selection.Font.Bold = wdToggle
    Selection.Font.Italic = wdToggle
End Sub
```

The net effect of this command is to make the selected text both bold and italic.

Well, not quite. Actually, the effect of this macro is to change both the bold and italic attributes of the selected text. If the text isn't already bold or italic, the macro makes it bold and italic. But if the text is already formatted as bold but not italic, the macro turns off the bold attribute but turns on italic. And if no text is selected at all, the macro sets the bold and italic attributes for text you subsequently type.

So here, just a page into this chapter, you already have an example of the Undeniable Truth of VBA programming: Even simple macros sometimes don't work the way you expect them to. The outcome of a macro usually depends a great deal on whether text is selected; how the selected text (if any) is formatted; the view (Normal, Page Layout, or Outline); and many other factors. The moral of the story: *Test everything.*

Basic Elements of VBA

The following sections present a whirlwind tour of some of the basic elements of writing VBA macros.

Rules for writing VBA statements

The normal way to write VBA statements is one per line. You can gang up several statements on a single line by separating the statements with colons, as in this example:

```
Dim i As Integer : i = 100
```

However, your macros are easier to read if you stick to one statement per line.

You can indent lines to show the relationships among statements by using tabs or spaces. For example:

```
If Weekday(Now()) = 1 Then
    MsgBox "Time for football!"
End If
```

Spacing *within* a VBA statement generally isn't important. You can omit spaces when different elements of a statement are separated by a comma, colon, or other punctuation. However, don't be surprised if VBA automatically inserts spaces around such elements as you type them.

If you need to continue a statement onto two or more lines, end each line except the last one with an underscore character, like this:

```
MsgBox ("This is a really " _
  & "long message.")
```

The underscore character indicates to Word that the statement continues on the next line, so the successive lines are treated as a single statement.

Comments

Comments are marked with apostrophes. When you use an apostrophe anywhere on a line, VBA completely ignores everything on the line after the apostrophe. This treatment allows you to place comments directly on the lines where they relate:

```
Sub BoldItalic()  ' This macro applies both bold and italic.
    Selection.Font.Bold = wdToggle     'Toggles Bold
    Selection.Font.Italic = wdToggle   'Toggles Italic
End Sub
```

Projects, modules, procedures, and macros

At the simplest level, a macro is a single VBA procedure that you can run from an application such as Word. However, VBA lets you gather procedures together to form modules and projects to help you organize your macros. The following paragraphs describe each of these organizational units:

✦ **Procedure:** A procedure is a named collection of VBA statements that's contained between a `Sub` and `End Sub` statement.

✦ **Macro:** A macro is a specific type of procedure that you can invoke directly from a Word document. You can run a macro from the Macros dialog box or by associating it with a customized Quick Access toolbar button or a keyboard shortcut.

✦ **Module:** A module is a named collection of procedures. All Word documents include a module named New Macros. When you create a macro from the Macros dialog box, the new macro is created in this module. If you're working with a lot of macros, you can create additional modules to help keep them organized.

✦ **Project:** A project is a collection of modules and other Word objects. Every document and template is a project.

Working with Variables and Data

A *variable* is a name assigned to a bit of computer memory that is used to hold a value. Variables are key features of any programming language, and VBA is no exception. Variables play an important role in all but the most trivial VBA macros.

Using assignment statements

You use an assignment statement to assign values to variables. For example:

```
Pi = 3.14159
X = 0
MessageText = "Hello from Planet Earth"
```

In a concession to the 40-year-old legacy of BASIC programming, VBA allows you to preface assignment statements with the keyword `Let`:

```
Let Pi = 3.14159
Let x = 0
Let MessageText = "Hello from Planet Earth"
```

The `Let` keyword is not required, however, and is considered quaint.

Declaring variables

You declare a variable by using a `Dim` statement, like this:

```
Dim i As Integer
```

This statement declares a variable named `i`. The type of the variable is `Integer`.

Variable names can be up to 40 characters, must start with a letter, and can contain only letters, numerals, and the underscore (`_`). Also, you cannot use any of VBA's reserved words (such as function names), the names of VBA statements, and so on.

You use the `As` keyword to specify the data type for variables. VBA provides a number of data types you can use for variables. The valid data types are

✦ **Boolean:** True or False values.

✦ **Byte:** Integers from 0 to 255.

✦ **Integer:** Integers from –32,768 to +32,768.

✦ **Long:** Large integers. Values can be from approximately –2 billion to +2 billion.

✦ **Currency:** Decimal numbers with up to 19 digits.

✦ **Single:** Single-precision, floating point numbers, not used often in Word macros.

✦ **Double:** Double-precision, floating point numbers, used even less often in Word macros.

✦ **Date:** A date or time value.

✦ **String:** A bit of text, such as "Humpty-Dumpty."

✦ **Object:** Any object, such as a Word document or a window.

✦ **Variant:** A generic number or string.

If you omit the data type, `Variant` is assumed.

Placing your declarations

The normal place to declare variables is within a procedure before you need to use the variable. Some programmers like to place all variable declarations at the start of the procedure, but that isn't necessary. You can declare a variable any time up to the first time you use the variable.

You can also declare variables at the module level. *Module-level variables* are available to all procedures in the module. Place any module-level variables before the first procedure in the module.

Using static variables

A *static variable* is a variable whose value is preserved between executions of the procedure in which it's declared. You can find many excellent uses for static variables in Word macros. For example, you may use a static variable to temporarily keep track of text entered by the user, to remember the location in the document where an operation was performed, or to keep track of actions taken since the last time the macro was run.

To create a static variable, use the `Static` keyword rather than the `Dim` keyword, like this:

```
Static iCaseCount As Integer
```

You can use static variables only in procedures. You can't create a static variable at the module level.

Using Option Explicit

Unlike in many other programming languages, such as C and Pascal, you don't have to define variables before you can use them in VBA. The first time you use a variable in a VBA macro, the variable is automatically defined.

Most experienced programmers consider the fact that you don't have to define variables to be *the* major weakness in BASIC and all of its dialects, including VBA and Visual Basic. The trouble is that you never know when you've misspelled a variable name because if you misspell a variable name, VBA assumes that you want to create a new variable. For example, suppose at the start of a macro you ask the user to enter a string value, and you store the value entered by the user in a variable named `InputString`. Then later in the macro, you use the variable in a statement, but misspell it `InputStrign`. Does VBA point out your error? No. It just assumes that you want to create a new variable named `InputStrign`. This `InputStrign` variable is given a default value of `" "` rather than the value entered by the user.

Such problems are very common in VBA programming. Any time you're faced with a macro that looks like it should work, but doesn't, carefully double-check all your variable names to see whether you misspelled any.

You can avoid the problem of misspelled variable names by adding the following line to the very beginning of your VBA module:

```
Option Explicit
```

This line forces you to declare variables before you use them. Then, if you use a variable that you haven't declared, an error message displays.

Using Strings

Strings are the most common data types for macros when working with Word documents. You need to know how to manipulate string data if you hope to accomplish anything meaningful in Word VBA.

For starters, you can create string *literals* — that is, strings that are simply quoted in your macro. To use a string literal, enclose a string value in quotation marks; full-fledged double quotes, not apostrophes. For example:

```
MessageText = "Hi there!"
```

In this example, `"Hi there!"` is a string literal whose value is assigned to the string variable named `MessageText`.

You can use an apostrophe within a string literal with no ill effects, as in the following example:

```
MessageText = "Hi y'all"
```

But you cannot include quotes within quotes. For example, the following produces an error:

```
MessageText = "Say, "Cheeseburger!""
```

To include a quotation mark within a literal quoted with quotation marks, you must double the quotation marks, like this:

```
MessageText = "Say, ""Cheeseburger!"""
```

Concatenation

A technique called *concatenation* allows you to join two or more strings together end to end to make a single, larger string. For example:

```
Entre = "Cheese" & "burger"
```

This line results in the string `"Cheeseburger"` being assigned to the `Entre` variable. The ampersand (`&`) is used for this purpose. The spaces around the ampersand are optional; if you leave them out, Word adds them when you run the macro.

Concatenation becomes very useful when combined with string variables and, as you see in the following section, string functions. For example, consider this statement:

```
Message = "Could not deliver message to " & Recipient
```

Here, a literal string value is concatenated with a variable string value. If the value of the `Recipient` variable is `"Jimmy Hoffa"`, the `Message` variable is set to `"Could not deliver message to Jimmy Hoffa"`.

The number of concatenations you can string together in a single statement has no limit.

String functions

VBA provides several built-in functions that work on strings. Table 2-1 summarizes these functions. Most of these functions come in handy from time to time.

One of the most commonly used string function is `Len`: It returns the number of characters in a string. For example:

```
Message="Hello world!"
LengthOfMessage = Len(Message)
```

In this example, the `LengthOfMessage` variable is assigned the value `12`, the number of characters in the string `Message`. ***Note:*** The `Len` function returns a number, not a string. And the quotation marks that indicate the start and end of string literals aren't counted.

A final group of string functions you need are those used to clean up string values that may contain unnecessary leading or trailing spaces or unprintable characters. These functions include `LTrim()`, `RTrim()`, and `CleanString()`. For example, to remove spaces from the beginning and end of a string variable, use this statement:

```
TrimmedString = Trim(InputText)
```

Table 2-1	VBA Functions for Manipulating Strings
Function	*What It Does*
Chr(*value*)	Generates the character that corresponds to the numeric (ANSI) code value. Common uses are: Chr(9): Tab Chr(11): New line Chr(13): Carriage return Chr(30): Nonbreaking hyphen Chr(32): Space Chr(160): Nonbreaking space
InStr([*n*,]*string1*, *string2*)	Returns the character position within *string1* at which *string2* begins, or 0 if *string2* is not found in *string1*. If *n* is used, the first *n-1* characters of *string1* are ignored.
LCase(*string*)	Converts *string* to lowercase.
Left(*string*,*n*)	Returns the leftmost *n* characters of *string*.
Len(*string*)	Returns the length of *string*.
LTrim(*string*)	Removes leading spaces from *string*.
Mid(*string*,*x*,*y*)	Returns *y* characters from *string* starting at character *x*.
Right(*string*,*n*)	Returns the rightmost *n* characters of *string*.
RTrim(*string*)	Removes trailing spaces from *string*.
Str(*n*)	Converts the number *n* to a string variable. For example, Str(3.15) becomes the string "3.15".
UCase(*string*)	Converts *string* to uppercase.
Val(*string*)	Returns the numeric value of *string*. For example, Val("3.15") becomes the numeric value 3.15.

Of Objects, Properties, and Methods

VBA is inherently *object oriented,* which means that it deals extensively with programming elements known as *objects.* Simply put (as if that's possible), an object is a named entity that represents some component of a Word document. For example, a Document object represents an entire Word document, whereas a Selection object represents the text that's currently selected in a document.

Objects have three components:

+ **Properties:** Define the data that's associated with an object. For example, the `Selection` object has a `Text` property that contains the text that's in the selection.

+ **Methods:** Define actions that the object can perform. For example, the `Selection` object has a `Copy` method that copies the selection to the Clipboard.

+ **Events:** Defines actions that an object can respond to. For example, when the user closes a document, the `Document` object raises a `Close` event. Then you can write a macro routine that is executed to add special processing for the `Close` event.

Although events can be important in certain types of macros, most macros work with just the properties and methods of various Word objects.

Using objects

The basic trick for working with objects in VBA is that you use the period to separate the name of the object you want to work with from the name of the property or method you want to use. For example, `Selection.Text` refers to the `Text` property of the `Selection` object, and `Range.Copy` refers to the `Copy` method of the `Range` object.

One of the most important points about object-oriented programming is that the properties of an object can themselves be other objects that have properties and methods. For example, the `Selection` object has a `Font` property, which is itself a `Font` object. The `Font` object, in turn, has its own properties, such as `Name` and `Size`. So, you can refer to the `Name` property of the selection's font like this: `Selection.Font.Name`.

Another key to understanding objects is knowing that you can create variables to refer to them. You specify the type of a variable with the `As` keyword. For example, the following line declares a variable named `f` that represents a `Font` object:

```
Dim f As Font
```

Then you can assign an object to the variable.

You can't use the normal assignment statement to assign objects, however. Instead, you must use a `Set` statement, like this:

```
Set f As Selection.Font
```

Here, the Font variable f is set to the object referred to by the Font property of the Selection object.

You can then refer to properties of the object variable in the usual way. For example, f.Name refers to the Name property of the f object.

Getting to know the object model

Much of the trick to writing VBA macros for Word is knowing Word's *object model* — that is, the objects available in a Word macro and the properties and methods available for each type of object. You find out more about Word's object model in Chapter 3 of this minibook.

One way to get to know the object model is to let the VBA editor tell you about it. When you type a period after an object name, the VBA editor pops up a helpful list of the properties and methods available for that object. Then you can scroll down to the property or method you want to use and press Tab to insert it into your macro. This way is one of the best to discover what properties and methods are available for any given object.

Another way to find out about what objects, properties, and methods are available — perhaps the best way — is to record a macro that comes close to accomplishing what you want to do, and then switch to the VBA editor to see what code was generated for the macro. For example, suppose you want to write a macro that marks index entries. If you record a macro and then press Alt+Shift+X to mark an index entry, Word generates VBA code similar to this:

```
ActiveDocument.Indexes.MarkEntry Range:=Selection.Range, Entry:= _
    "Object model", EntryAutoText:="Object model", CrossReference:="",
    CrossReferenceAutoText:="", BookmarkName:="", Bold:=False, Italic:=False
```

Here, you can tell that you use the MarkEntry method of ActiveDocument.Indexes to mark an index entry, and that this method takes several arguments: Range, Entry, EntryAutoText, CrossReference, CrossReferenceAutotext, BookmarkName, Bold, and Italic.

Using methods

A method is an action that an object can perform. When you call a method, the object performs the action associated with the method. For example, the following statement copies the contents of the current selection to the Clipboard:

```
Selection.Copy
```

Some methods require *arguments,* which supply data for the method to work with. For example, the `Selection` object's `InsertAfter` method accepts a text string as an argument. The text string contains the text that's inserted after the selection.

To use arguments, simply list the argument values you want to pass to the method, like this:

```
Selection.InsertAfter "Some text"
```

Here, `Selection` is an object, `InsertAfter` is a method, and `"Some text"` is an argument.

If a method requires two or more arguments, separate them with commas, like this:

```
Selection.StartOf wdParagraph, wdExtend
```

In this example, the arguments are called *positional* because Word interprets the meaning of each argument based on the order in which you list them. Word also allows you to pass arguments by using argument names, as in this example:

```
Selection.StartOf Unit:=wdParagraph, Extend:=wdExtend
```

When you use methods that require arguments, the VBA editor displays tips that let you know what arguments the method expects.

VBA also allows you to enclose the arguments in parentheses, like this:

```
Selection.InsertAfter("Some text")
```

However, the parentheses aren't required. Note that it's okay to use both styles — with and without parentheses — within a macro.

Using the With statement

The `With` statement is a special VBA shortcut that lets you refer to an object in several statements without having to refer to the object each time. You simply list the object in the `With` statement. Then any statement that appears between the `With` and its corresponding `End With` statement and that begins with a period uses the object listed in the `With` statement.

For example, suppose you want to set the Bold and Italic properties of
the Font property of the Selection object for a document named Temp.
You can use these lines:

```
Documents("Temp").ActiveWindow.Selection.Font.Bold = True
Documents("Temp").ActiveWindow.Selection.Font.Italic = True
```

Or you can place these lines within a With/End With block, like this:

```
With Documents("Temp").ActiveWindow.Selection.Font
    .Bold = True
    .Italic = True
End With
```

Granted, the With statement adds two lines of code. But if the object reference is complicated, it can save you typing even if you need to set only two
property values.

Working with collections

A *collection* is a special type of object that holds one or more occurrences of
some other object. The Word object model, which I discuss further in the
next chapter, has many collections that help organize the various objects
used in Word. For example, you can store all the currently open documents
in a collection called Documents. And you can access all the paragraphs in a
document via a collection called Paragraphs.

All collections have a Count property you can use to determine how many
items are in the collection. For example, the following code displays the
number of currently open documents:

```
MsgBox "There are currently " & Documents.Count _
    & " documents open."
```

Many collections have an Add method that adds a new item to the collection. In many cases, the Add method creates a new object of the type appropriate for the collection, adds it to the collection, and returns the new object
as its return value. For example, the following code creates a new document
and then displays the document's name:

```
Dim d As Document
Set d = Documents.Add
MsgBox "The new document's name is " & d.Name
```

You can access the individual items in a collection by using an index number. For example, the following code displays the name of the first document in the `Documents` collection:

```
MsgBox Documents(1).Name
```

In many cases, you can use the name of an item instead of an index. For example, this statement closes the document named `TempDoc`:

```
Documents("TempDoc").Close
```

Note: If no document is named `TempDoc`, the statement generates an error.

Controlling Your Programs

The simplest macros execute their statements one at a time, in the sequence in which the statements are listed in the macro, until they reach the `End Sub` statement.

More sophisticated macros need more control over the sequence in which statements are executed. For example, you might need to skip over some statements based on the result of a condition test. Or you might need to create a loop of statements that repeats itself a given number of times or until a certain condition — such as reaching the end of the document — is met.

The following sections describe the VBA statements that let you control the flow of execution in your macro.

The If statement

Do you remember that Robert Frost poem that begins, "Two roads diverged in a yellow wood . . ."? That poem is an apt description of how the `If` statement works. The macro is rolling along, executing one statement after another, until it comes to an `If` statement. The `If` statement represents a fork in the road, and a choice must be made about which path to take.

Many macros need to make such decisions as they execute. For example, a macro that creates an index entry for text selected by the user has to first determine whether the user has indeed selected any text. If so, the macro proceeds to create the index entry. If not, the macro does nothing, or perhaps it displays an error message saying something along the lines of, "You didn't select any text!" To handle this decision processing, the macro uses an `If` statement.

VBA's If statement is remarkably flexible, with several formats to choose from. All these forms involve three basic parts:

✦ A *condition test* that is evaluated to yield a value of True or False

✦ A *then* part, which supplies one or more statements that execute only if the result of the condition test is True

✦ An *else* part, which supplies one or more statements that execute only if the result of the condition test is False

For example, consider these lines that may be used in an index-marking macro:

```
If Selection.Type = wdSelectionNormal Then
    ActiveDocument.Indexes.MarkEntryRange:=Selection.Range,
    Entry:="index"
Else
    MsgBox ("Please select something to mark.")
End If
```

Here, the If statement begins with a condition test that checks to see whether the selection is a normal text selection. If so, the ActiveDocument.Indexes.MarkEntry statement executes to insert an index field code. If not, a message box displays.

Each component of the If statement must fall on a separate line, as shown in the preceding example. In other words, you cannot place the statements on the same line as the Then or Else keywords.

The Else part of the If statement is optional. However, End If is not optional: Every If statement must have a corresponding End If. (The only exception to this rule is the single-line If format that I explain later, in the section "The single-line If.")

Although indenting the statements isn't strictly required, using such indentation makes the structure of the If statement much more apparent. Consider the preceding example without any indentation:

```
If Selection.Type = wdSelectionNormal Then
ActiveDocument.Indexes.MarkEntry Range:=Selection.Range,
Entry:="index"
Else
MsgBox ("Please select something to mark.")
End If
```

Now imagine that instead of a single statement between the Then and Else lines, the macro has a dozen, with a dozen more lines between the Else and End If lines. Indentation is the only way to keep track of the overall structure of the If statement.

Nested If statements

You can *nest* If statements — that is, you can include one If statement within the Then or Else part of another. For example:

```
If expression Then
    If expression Then
        statements
    Else
        statements
    End If
Else
    If expression Then
        statements
    Else
        statements
    End If
End If
```

Nesting can be as complex as you want. Just remember that you need an End If for every If. And be certain to use indentation so that each set of matching If, Else, and End If lines are properly aligned.

The ElseIf structure

VBA supports a special type of If structure, using the ElseIf keyword. The ElseIf form is a shorthand notation that allows you to simplify If structures that follow this form:

```
If expression Then
    statements
Else
    If expression Then
        statements
    Else
        If expression Then
            statements
        End If
    End IF
End If
```

Using the `ElseIf` keyword, you can express the same structure like this:

```
If expression Then
    statements
ElseIf expression Then
    statements
ElseIf expression Then
    statements
End If
```

If that's a little too abstract, consider a macro that displays one of three messages, depending on the day of the week. For Sunday, the macro displays "Time for Football!" For Saturday, it displays "Time to mow the lawn!!" And for any other day, it displays "Time to go to work!!!"

Here's how to code this macro by using ordinary `If` statements:

```
DayOfWeek=Weekday(Now())
If DayOfWeek = 1 Then
    MsgBox("Time for football!")
Else
    If DayOfWeek = 7 Then
        MsgBox("Time to mow the lawn!!")
    Else
        MsgBox("Time to go to work!!!")
    End IF
End If
```

Notice that the first `Else` clause contains a nested `If` statement. By using the `ElseIf` keyword, the second `If` statement is subsumed into the first, so a single `If` statement handles the whole thing:

```
DayOfWeek=Weekday(Now())
If DayOfWeek = 1 Then
    MsgBox("Time for football!")
ElseIf DayOfWeek = 7 Then
    MsgBox("Time to mow the lawn!!")
Else
    MsgBox("Time to go to work!!!")
End If
```

In this example, only one `End If` line is required because it has only one `If` statement. In other words, the `ElseIf` keyword doesn't require its own matching `End If`.

In most cases, a `Select Case` statement implements `If` structures that require `ElseIf` clauses more easily, which I describe later in this chapter, in the section "The Select Case statement."

The single-line If

VBA also allows you to use a single-line form of the `If` statement, which looks like this:

```
If condition Then statement [Else statement]
```

To use this form of the `If` statement, you must code the condition, `Then` clause, and `Else` clause (if any) all on the same line. For example:

```
If x > 0 Then MsgBox("X is " & x)
```

The preceding example displays the message `X is` *n*, where *n* is the value of x. But the message displays only if x is greater than zero.

You can include more than one statement in the `Then` part by separating the statements with colons. But if more than one statement is required, or if an `Else` part is required, I suggest you use the basic multi-line `If` form instead of the single-line form.

For/Next Loops

`For/Next` loops allow you to set up a basic looping structure in which a series of statements execute over and over again, with the value of a counter variable increased by one (or more) each time until the counter variable reaches a certain value.

As a simple — if not very practical — example, the following snippet inserts the numbers 1 through 100 in the current document, one number on each line:

```
For x = 1 to 100
    Selection.InsertAfter Str(x) & Chr(13)
Next x
```

This `For/Next` loop causes the `Insert` statement it contains to execute 100 times. The first time through, the variable x is set to the value 1. The second time, x is 2; the third time, 3; and so on, all the way up to 100.

The general form of a `For/Next` loop is

```
For counter-variable = start To end [Step increment]
    statements...
Next [counter-variable]
```

You can specify any starting and ending value you want for the counter variable. In addition, you can specify an increment value by using the `Step` clause. You can use `Step` to create `For/Next` loops that count by twos, threes, or any other value you want. If you omit `Step`, the default is 1.

The term *iteration* is often used to refer to each execution of a `For/Next` loop. For example, a `For/Next` loop that starts with the line `For x = 1 To 10` iterates ten times.

While/Wend loops

`While/Wend` loops provide a more sophisticated form of looping, in which the loop continues as long as a specified condition remains `True`. The general form is

```
While condition
    statements
Wend
```

The `While` loop starts by evaluating the condition. If it is `True`, the statements in the loop execute. When the `Wend` statement is encountered, the condition is evaluated again. If it is still `True`, the statements in the loop execute again. This cycle continues until the condition evaluates as `False`.

At this point, you really need to know just what it means to say a condition is `True`. In VBA, `False` is defined as the numeric value 0, and any nonzero value is considered to be `True`. For example, consider this `While` loop:

```
x = 5
While x
    Selection.InsertAfter Str(x) & Chr(13)
    x = x - 1
Wend
```

This loop continues to execute as long as x is not zero. The moment x becomes zero, VBA considers the condition expression to be `False` and the loop terminates. As a result, this `While` loop displays five message boxes, showing the values 5, 4, 3, 2, 1, and then it terminates.

To continue a loop as long as an expression evaluates to `False`, use `Not` as part of the condition test. For example:

```
x = 0
While Not x = 5
    Selection.InsertAfter Str(x) & Chr(13)
    x = x + 1
Wend
```

Here, the loop repeats as long as `x` is not equal to 5.

The Select Case statement

Life would be easy if it consisted entirely of either/or choices. But in the real world, you're often faced with many alternatives to choose from. And so it is in VBA. More than a few VBA functions return more complicated results than a simple yes/no, true/false, 0/1. For example, `Selection.Style.Name` returns the name of the style applied to the current selection. You can use this information to cause your macro to take a different action depending on which style is applied to the selected paragraph.

The `Select Case` statement is designed just for such situations. It lets you test an expression for various values, executing different statements depending on the result. Its general form is

```
Select Case expression
    Case case-condition
        statements
  [ Case case-condition
        statements ]
  [ Case Else
        statements ]
End Select
```

The `Select Case` statement starts by evaluating the expression. Then, it compares the result with the case conditions listed in the `Case` clauses, one at a time. When it finds a match, it executes the statements listed for the `Case` clause that matches, and it skips the rest of the `Select Case` statement. If none of the case conditions match, the statements in the `Case Else` clause execute. The key point is that only one of the `Case` clauses is selected for execution.

For each `Case` clause, *values* can be any of the following:

+ **A single value, such as `Case 4`:** The `Case` clause is selected if the expression is equal to the value.

+ **A list of expressions, such as `Case 4, 8, 12, 16`:** The `Case` clause is selected if the expression equals any of the listed values.

✦ **A range of values, separated with the keyword `To`, such as `Case 4 to 8`:** The `Case` clause is selected if the expression falls between the two values, inclusively.

✦ **The word `Is` followed by a relational comparison, such as `Is > 4`:** The relation is tested against the expression, and the `Case` clause is selected if the result of the comparison is `True`.

Here's an example of a `While` loop that includes a `Select Case` statement to count the number of Heading 1, Heading 2, and Heading 3 styles from the current selection to the end of the document:

```
Dim Heading1Count As Integer
Dim Heading2Count As Integer
Dim Heading3Count As Integer
Dim s As Style
While Selection.Move(wdParagraph, 1)
    Select Case Selection.Style.NameLocal
        Case "Heading 1"
            Heading1Count = Heading1Count + 1
        Case "Heading 2"
            Heading2Count = Heading2Count + 1
        Case "Heading 3"
            Heading3Count = Heading3Count + 1
    End Select
Wend
```

In this example, the variables `Heading1Count`, `Heading2Count`, and `Heading3Count` count the number of headings for each level. The `Select Case` statement evaluates the `NameLocal` property of the selection's `Style` object. Then the `Case` clauses check for the values `"Heading 1"`, `"Heading 2"`, and `"Heading 3"`. If the `NameLocal` property returns one of these three values, 1 is added to the appropriate counter variable.

You can use `Case Else` to handle any values that aren't specifically mentioned in `Case` clauses.

User Input and Output

The following sections describe various methods of displaying information and obtaining input from the user.

MsgBox

The MsgBox command allows you to display a dialog box containing an informative message. MsgBox temporarily halts the macro until the user closes the message dialog box.

The MsgBox command has the following form:

```
MsgBox message [,buttons [,title] ]
```

message is the text to display in the message, *buttons* is a constant that indicates the type of buttons to display, and *title* is the title displayed in the dialog box title bar.

To display a simple message, use a command such as this:

```
MsgBox "It's Saturday night!"
```

This command displays the dialog box shown in Figure 2-1.

Figure 2-1:
A MsgBox
dialog box.

Here's a MsgBox call that specifies the type of buttons and a title:

```
MsgBox "It's Saturday night!", vbOKCancel, "Live from New
    York!"
```

Its output is shown in Figure 2-2.

Figure 2-2:
A MsgBox
dialog box
with a title
and a button
style.

The *buttons* argument actually controls three things at once: what buttons appear in the dialog box, what icon appears in the dialog box, and which button is the default. Table 2-2 lists the values for these settings.

You can add these constants together to create composite styles. For example, this `MsgBox` command displays OK and Cancel buttons, a Stop symbol, and makes the Cancel button the default:

```
MsgBox "It's Saturday night!", vbOKCancel + vbExclamation +
    vbDefaultButton2, "Live from New York!"
```

Figure 2-3 shows the resulting dialog box.

Figure 2-3:
A MsgBox
dialog box
with an icon
and default
button.

Table 2-2	MsgBox Type Values	
Group	*Constant*	*Meaning*
Buttons	vbOKOnly	OK only
	vbOKCancel	OK and Cancel
	vbAbortRetryIgnore	Abort, Retry, and Ignore
	vbYesNoCancel	Yes, No, and Cancel
	vbYesNo	Yes and No
	vbRetryCancel	Retry and Cancel
Icon	vbCritical	Critical icon
	vbQuestion	A question mark
	vbExclamation	An exclamation mark
	vbInformation	Information only
Default button	vbDefaultButton1	First button (OK, Yes, or Abort)
	vbDefaultButton2	Second button (Cancel, No, or Retry)
	vbDefaultButton3	Third button (Cancel or Ignore)

MsgBox returns a value that indicates which button was clicked, as described in Table 2-3.

Table 2-3		MsgBox Return Values
Constant	*Numeric Value*	*Which Button Was Pressed*
vbOK	1	OK button
vbCancel	2	Cancel
vbAbort	3	Abort
vbRetry	4	Retry
vbIgnore	5	Ignore
vbYes	6	Yes
vbNo	7	No

InputBox

InputBox is a VBA function that displays a dialog box that includes a single text field into which the user can type a response. The user's input is then returned to the macro as the function's return value.

The InputBox function accepts three arguments:

```
InputBox(prompt [,title] [,default])
```

For example, the following InputBox function asks the user to enter a name:

```
Name=InputBox("Type a name:")
```

This example shows how to provide your own title for the input dialog box and display a default choice:

```
Name=InputBox("Type a name:", "The Name Game", UserName)
```

The user's response returns in the Name variable. Figure 2-4 shows the dialog box that displays.

Figure 2-4:
An Input
dialog box
with an icon
and default
button.

User-Defined Procedures and Functions

Most VBA macros consist of a single procedure. However, VBA lets you
create additional procedures and functions that you can call from within the
macro's main procedure. Procedures and functions are useful when you have
a series of VBA commands or a complex calculation that you need to call
upon several times in a macro. By placing these commands in a procedure
or function, you can code them once and call upon them as many times as
needed.

Using procedures

To create a procedure, use a Sub/End Sub command pair outside the
Sub/End Sub command pair for the macro's main procedure. The statements that make up the procedure go between the Sub and End Sub commands, and the Sub command supplies the name of the procedure and any
arguments that are passed to the subroutine. For example:

```
Sub SayHello
    BeepMsg "Hello World!"
End Sub
Sub BeepMsg(Message As String)
    Beep
    MsgBox Message
End Sub
```

In this example, the BeepMsg procedure displays a message and sounds a
tone to get the user's attention. In the macro's main procedure (called
SayHello), you can use BeepMsg as if it were a built-in VBA command.

If you want, you can type the keyword Call before the subroutine name
when calling the subroutine. For example:

```
Call BeepMsg "Hello World!"
```

The Call keyword is optional, but some VBA programmers like to use it to help distinguish user-written subroutines from built-in VBA commands.

Using functions

A function is similar to a subroutine, with one crucial difference: A function returns a value. Here's an example:

```
Sub GetAnAnswer
    If GetYesNo("Yes, or no?") Then
        BeepMsg "You said yes."
    Else
        BeepMsg "You said no."
    End If
End Sub
Sub BeepMsg(Message As String)
    Beep
    MsgBox Message
End Sub
Function GetYesNo(Message As String) As Boolean
    If MsgBox(Message, vbYesNo) = vbYes Then
        GetYesNo = True
    Else
        GetYesNo = False
    End If
End Function
```

Here, the GetYesNo function uses a MsgBox function to display a message box with Yes and No buttons. The return value from the MsgBox function determines which button the user pressed, and the return value of the GetYesNo function is set to True if the user clicked Yes, False if the user clicked No. Back in the Main routine, the GetYesNo function is used in an If statement to display You said yes if the user clicks Yes or You said no if the user clicks No.

Here, StringVar is passed by value rather than by reference to BeepMsg. As a result, the MsgBox command in Main displays Original Value rather than New Value.

Call-by-value looks peculiar when used with a function call because the parentheses must be doubled. For example:

```
Sub Main
    Prompt = "Yes, or no?"
    Reply = GetYesNo((Prompt))
    MsgBox Prompt
End Sub
Function GetYesNo(Message)
    GetYesNo = MsgBox(Message, 36)
    Message = "New Value"
End Function
```

Here, Prompt is passed by value to the GetYesNo function, so its value is unchanged.

Chapter 3: More Programming: Using Word's Object Model

In This Chapter

✔ Understanding the basic objects of Word's object model

✔ Wrestling with documents

✔ Discovering selections and ranges

✔ Creating macros that manipulate text

✔ Creating macros that adjust text formatting

*W*ord's *object model* is the programming interface that lets you manipulate Word documents from VBA. The object model consists of a collection of different object types, such as documents, paragraphs, styles, tables, and so on. Each of these objects has its own properties and methods you can use from VBA. The most difficult aspect of writing Word macros is dealing with this object model, in part because Word's object model is huge. The people at Microsoft who designed Word's object model weren't minimalists.

However, after you get your mind around a few basic concepts, such as the difference between selections and ranges, the object model begins to make sense. So, without further ado, this chapter presents an overview of the most commonly used parts of Word's object model.

An Overview of Important Word Objects

Word's object model is far too complex to completely cover in a single chapter. All told, the object model has more than 130 types of objects, more than 100 types of collections, and hundreds of methods and properties.

Fortunately, you don't have to know about all the objects, collections, methods, and properties that make up the complete object model to start writing useful VBA macros. To give you an idea for the overall structure of the Word object model, Table 3-1 summarizes the function of the 30 or so most commonly used Word objects and the collections that contain them. You get more details about many of these objects throughout the rest of this chapter.

Please don't let this table overwhelm you. I include it here simply to familiarize you with the name and general purpose of Word's most commonly used objects. Don't feel like you have to memorize it or give it more than a casual glance for now. Just know it's here when you need it.

Also, notice that some of the objects listed in this table have a corresponding *collection*. For example, all of the bookmarks for a document are stored in a `Bookmarks` collection, with each individual bookmark represented by a single `Bookmark` object. Not all of the objects in this table have a corresponding collection, however. For example, just one `Application` object exists, so there's no need for a collection to store this object type.

By the way, AutoComplete can come in handy when you're working with objects in your VBA macros. When you type an object name and then type a period, the AutoComplete feature displays a list of the methods and properties that are available for the object.

Table 3-1	Major Objects in the Word Object Model	
Object	*Collection*	*Description*
Application		The Microsoft Word application itself. This object is considered to be the start of the Word object model. Use the `Application` object to access other top-level objects. For example, use the `ActiveDocument` property to access the `Document` object for the current document.
Bookmark	Bookmarks	Used to access bookmarks. You can access the `Bookmarks` collection via a `Document` object.

Object	Collection	Description
Cell	Cells	Used to access cells in a table. You can access the Cells collection via a Row or Column object. You can also access an individual cell by using the Cell method of a Table object.
Column	Columns	Represents a column in a table. You can access the Columns collection via a Table object.
Diagram	Shapes	Represents a diagram. Diagrams are stored along with other shapes in a Shapes collection. You can access the Shapes collection via a Document object.
Document	Documents	Represents a single document. The Documents collection (available via the Application object) contains all of the currently open documents.
Email		Represents the e-mail information for a document. Accessed via the Email property of a Document object.
Envelope		Represents a document's envelope. Accessed via the Envelope property of a Document object.
Field	Fields	Represents a field. The Fields collection is accessed via a Document, Range, or Selection object.
Find		Provides the function of the Find command on the Home tab.
Font		Represents a font. Accessed via the Font property of a Selection, Range, or Style object.
HeaderFooter	HeaderFooters	Represents a header or footer for a section of a document. The HeaderFooters collection is accessed via the Headers or Footers property of a Section object.
List	Lists	Represents a list in a document. The Lists collection is accessed via a Document object.
Options		Represents the settings in the Word Options dialog box.

(continued)

Table 3-1 *(continued)*

Object	Collection	Description
Page	Pages	Represents the pages in a document. The Pages collection is accessed via a Pane object, not a Document object as you may expect. Go figure.
PageSetup		Represents the page setup, including margins and columns. Accessed via a Document or Section object.
Pane	Panes	Represents an open window pane used to view a document. The Panes collection is accessed via a Window object.
Paragraph	Paragraphs	Represents a paragraph. The Paragraphs collection is accessed via a Document, Selection, or Range object.
ParagraphFormat		Represents the format for a Paragraph or Style object.
Range		Represents a range of a document. Many Word objects have a Range property, including Document, Section, Paragraph, and Bookmark.
Replacement		Provides the function of the Replace command on the Home tab.
Row	Rows	Represents a row in a table. The Rows collection is accessed via a Table object.
Section	Sections	Represents a document section. The Sections collection is accessed via a Document object.
Selection		Represents the current selection. Accessed via a Selection or Range object.
Shape	Shapes	Represents a shape. The Shapes collection is accessed via a Document object.
Style	Styles	Represents a style. The Styles collection is accessed via a Document object.
Table	Tables	Represents a table. The Tables collection is accessed via a Document, Range, or Selection object.

Object	Collection	Description
Template	Templates	Represents a template. All the available templates (normal template, attached templates, and global templates) are available in the `Templates` collection, which you can access via the `Global` object. Use the `AttachedTemplate` property of a `Document` object to access the template attached to a document.
TextColumn	TextColumns	Represents a column. The `TextColumns` collection is accessed via a `PageSetup` object.
Variable	Variables	Represents a document variable. The `Variables` collection is accessed via a `Document` object.
View		Represents the view settings, such as whether paragraph marks or field codes are visible. Accessed via a `Window` or `Pane` object.
Window	Windows	Represents an open window. The `Application.Windows` collection has all open windows. The Windows collection for a Document object has just those windows that are open for the document.

Using the Application Object

The `Application` object is the starting point for Word's object model. It represents the Word application itself. Here are a few of its more interesting properties:

✦ `ActiveDocument`: A `Document` object that represents the active document — that is, the document from which the user ran the macro.

✦ `ActiveWindow`: A `Window` object that represents the active window.

✦ `Documents`: A collection that contains all the currently open documents.

✦ `Options`: An `Options` object that represents the current settings for Word. You can usually set the options via the Word Options dialog box, which you access by choosing Office➪Word Options on the Office menu.

- ✦ ScreenUpdating: Controls whether the screen updates to reflect changes made to the document as a macro runs. Some macros run faster if you set ScreenUpdating to False.

- ✦ Selection: The text that is currently selected in the active document.

- ✦ Templates: A Templates collection that contains all the currently available templates.

- ✦ UserAddress: The user's mailing address.

- ✦ UserInitials: The user's initials.

- ✦ UserName: The user's name.

- ✦ Version: The version of Word being used.

- ✦ Windows: A collection of Window objects that represents all the currently open windows.

The Application object also has several methods that can be useful. In particular:

- ✦ CleanString: This method removes non-printable characters from a text string.

- ✦ GoBack: Moves the insertion point back to previous locations where editing occurred.

- ✦ GoForward: After using the GoBack method, the GoForward method moves forward to previous editing locations.

- ✦ ListCommands: Creates a new document that lists all of Word's commands along with their keyboard shortcuts.

- ✦ OnTime: Starts a timer that runs a macro at a specified time.

- ✦ Quit: Quits Microsoft Word.

- ✦ Repeat: Repeats the most recent editing action.

- ✦ Run: Runs another macro.

- ✦ ScreenRefresh: Updates the screen. This method is useful if you've suppressed screen updating by setting the ScreenUpdating property to False.

- ✦ ShowClipboard: Shows the Clipboard task pane.

You can use many of the properties and methods of the `Application` object without explicitly specifying `Application`. For example, the following two lines of code are equivalent:

```
Application.Options.AllowFastSave = True

Options.AllowFastSave = True
```

The `Application` object properties and methods you can use without specifying the `Application` object are called *global members.*

Working with Documents

You use the `Document` object to access a document in Word. The `Document` object has many useful properties and methods. Here are a few of the more interesting properties:

+ `Name`: The document's name.
+ `Path`: The hard drive path for the document.
+ `ReadOnly`: Indicates whether the document is read-only.
+ `Saved`: False if the document has changed since it was last saved.
+ `Windows`: Returns a `Windows` collection that contains all the windows in which the document is open.
+ `AttachedTemplate`: Returns a `Template` object for the template that's attached to the document.

Here are some of the methods of the `Document` object:

+ `Activate`: Makes the document the active document.
+ `Close`: Closes the document.
+ `PrintOut`: Prints all or part of the document.
+ `Save`: Saves the document. Prompts the user for a name if the document hasn't been saved before.
+ `SaveAs`: Saves the file with a specified name and path.

Accessing documents

If the document you want to access is the active document — that is, the document from which the user ran the macro — you can just specify `ActiveDocument` to access its properties and methods. For example, the following statement saves the active document:

```
ActiveDocument.Save
```

You can access all the documents that are currently open via the `Documents` collection. For example, the following code displays a message box that lists the name of each open document:

```
Dim msg As String
Dim d As Document
For Each d In Documents
    msg = msg & d.Name & VbCr
Next
MsgBox msg
```

You can use the `Documents` collection to access a document by name, like this:

```
Documents("Document1").Save
```

Creating a document

You can create a new document by using the `Add` method of the `Documents` collection. The `Add` method returns the document that was created. The following code creates a new document and then displays the document's name in a message box:

```
Dim d As Document
Set d = Documents.Add
MsgBox d.Name
```

Creating a document makes the new document the active document. If your macro needs to return to the original active document, it needs to save the active document's name in a string variable and then use the variable later to return to that document. For example:

```
Dim s As String
s = ActiveDocument.Name
Dim d As Document
Set d = Documents.Add
Documents(s).Activate
```

Working with Documents **605**

Book IX
Chapter 3

More Programming:
Using Word's
Object Model

Here, the active document's name is saved in the string named s. Then, a new document is created, and the original active document is reactivated.

Opening a document

You might have noticed that the Document object doesn't have an Open method. However, the Documents collection does. The following example opens the document named QuarterlyReport.doc and assigns it to the Document variable named report:

```
Dim report As Document
Set report = Documents.Open("QuarterlyReport.doc")
```

When the Open method opens a document, it creates a Document object, adds it to the Documents collection, and makes the new document the active document. If the document specified by the string argument doesn't exist, an error message displays.

Understanding stories

A Word document actually consists of one or more *stories,* which represent distinct areas of a document. All documents have a *main story* that contains the text displayed within the page margins. In addition, documents can have other stories, such as headers and footers, footnotes and endnotes, text that appears in frames, and comments.

If your macro works only with the contents of the main story, you don't need to worry about stories at all because the main story is the default story of the Document object. But if you want to create a macro that manipulates text in another story, such as the footnote story, you have to know how to get to the right story.

To do that, you use the StoryRanges collection of the Documents object. One of the constants listed in Table 3-2 indexes this collection. For example, the following macro displays the number of paragraphs in the footnotes story:

```
Dim fr As Range
Set fr = ActiveDocument.StoryRanges(wdFootnotesStory)
MsgBox fr.Paragraphs.Count
```

In this example, wdFootnotesStory is used as the index for ActiveDocument.StoryRanges to get the footnotes story. Then the Paragraphs.Count property displays the number of paragraphs in the story.

The Word object model doesn't have a separate `Story` object. Instead, each item in the `StoryRanges` collection is a `Range` object. I further discuss `Range` objects in the next section.

Table 3-2	Constants for Story Types
Constant	**Description**
wdCommentsStory	Comments made by reviewers
wdEndnoteContinuationNoticeStory	Endnote continuation notices
wdEndnoteContinuationSeparatorStory	Endnote continuation separators
wdEndnoteSeparatorStory	Endnote separators
wdEndnotesStory	Endnotes
wdEvenPagesFooterStory	Footers for even pages
wdEvenPagesHeaderStory	Headers for even pages
wdFirstPageFooterStory	Footers for the first page
wdFirstPageHeaderStory	Headers for the first page
wdFootnoteContinuationNoticeStory	Footnote continuation notices
wdFootnoteContinuationSeparatorStory	Footnote continuation separators
wdFootnoteSeparatorStory	Footnote separators
wdFootnotesStory	Footnotes
wdMainTextStory	The main text of the document
wdPrimaryFooterStory	Footers
wdPrimaryHeaderStory	Headers
wdTextFrameStory	Text that appears in frames

Understanding Selection and Range Objects

One of the most confusing aspects of Word's object model is that two distinct objects refer to portions of a document: `Selection` and `Range`. The `Selection` and `Range` objects are similar, with many overlapping features. However, selections can do some things that ranges can't, and vice versa.

In a nutshell, a `Selection` object refers to a portion of a document that is selected. The selection can be made by the user prior to running the macro, or the macro itself can select text.

Like a selection, a *range* is a portion of a document. However, a range isn't actually selected, so it isn't highlighted in the document window. Ranges allow you to work on document text without drawing attention to the text.

A document can have only one selection at a time, unless the same document is open in two or more windows or window panes. In that case, each window or pane can have its own selection in the document. However, you can create as many ranges for a document as you want. And the ranges can overlap. For example, you can create a `Range` object that refers to the entire document, another `Range` object that refers to a particular paragraph within the document, and a third `Range` object that refers to a single word within that paragraph.

Working with the Selection object

The `Selection` object refers to the portion of the document that is currently selected. If you're writing a macro that manipulates the text selected by the user, you most likely need to use the `Selection` object. For example, this statement copies the selection to the Clipboard:

```
Selection.Copy
```

And the following code formats the selected text as both bold and italic:

```
Selection.Font.Bold = True
Selection.Font.Italic = True
```

You can access the text that's contained in a selection by using the `Text` property. For example, the following statement displays the selected text in a message box:

```
MsgBox Selection.Text
```

Getting the right selection

When you refer to a `Selection` object by using just the word `Selection`, you're accessing the selection in the currently active document window. This method is the most common way to use a `Selection` object.

However, you can also refer to other `Selection` objects. You can display each open document in more than one window, and you can split each of those windows into two panes. Because you can select text in any window pane, Word's object model lets you access a `Selection` object for each window pane. To access a selection in another document, use the `Document` object's `ActiveWindow` property, like this:

```
Documents("QuarterlyReport.doc").ActiveWindow.Selection
```

This statement accesses the selection in the active pane of the active window for the QuarterlyReport document.

If the window is split into panes, you can use the `Panes` property to access the selection in either pane. For example, the following code displays a message box that lists the text selected in both panes of the active window:

```
Dim msg As String
msg = ActiveWindow.Panes(1).Selection.Text + VbCr _
    + ActiveWindow.Panes(2).Selection.Text
MsgBox msg
```

Dealing with selection types

A user may make many different types of selections before running your macro. Any macro that works with the `Selection` object needs to first make sure that the right type of selection is made. You can do that by checking the `Type` property. For example, this code checks to make sure that the user makes a normal selection before copying the selection to the Clipboard:

```
If Selection.Type = wdSelectionNormal Then
    Selection.Copy
End If
```

The `Type` property can have any of the constant values listed in Table 3-3.

Table 3-3	Constants for the Selection.Type Property
Constant	*Description*
`wdNoSelection`	No selection is made.
`wdSelectionBlock`	A vertical block of text is selected, as when the Alt key is used with the mouse.
`wdSelectionColumn`	A table column is selected.
`wdSelectionFrame`	A frame is selected.
`wdSelectionInlineShape`	An inline shape is selected.

Constant	Description
wdSelectionIP	The selection is just an insertion point.
wdSelectionNormal	A normal block of text is selected.
wdSelectionRow	A table row is selected.
wdSelectionShape	A drawing shape is selected.

Working with Range objects

A Range object identifies a portion of a document. The range can be as short as a single character or as long as the entire document. Range objects let you access text from within a macro without actually selecting the text on-screen or affecting the text that's currently selected.

Getting ranges

Many objects with the Word object model have a Range property that you can use to create a range that represents a portion of the document. For example, suppose you want to access the first paragraph of the active document as a range. To do so, you can use this code:

```
Dim r As Range
Set r = ActiveDocument.Paragraphs(1).Range
MsgBox r.Text
```

Here, the Paragraphs collection accesses the first paragraph in the active document.

The following table lists the objects that have a Range property:

Bookmark	HeaderFooter	Selection
Cell	Hyperlink	SmartTag
Comment	InlineShape	Subdocument
Endnote	List	Table
Footnote	Paragraph	TableOfAuthorities
Formfield	Revision	TableOfContents
Frame	Row	TableOfFigures
HeaderFooter	Section	

Notice that among these objects is the `Selection` object. As a result, you can get a `Range` object that corresponds to the current selection, like this:

```
Dim r As Range
Set r = Selection.Range
```

 Several properties of other objects also return `Range` objects. For example, the `Document` object has a `Content` property that returns a `Range` object representing the entire content of a document. For more ways to get ranges that represent portions of a document, see the section "Accessing text," later in this chapter.

Getting a range from a bookmark

Book III, Chapter 1 explains how you can use bookmarks to assign names to portions of a document. In effect, a bookmark is simply a named range that's saved along with the document. Bookmarks are commonly used in macros because they allow you to refer to a predefined area of text by name. If your macro needs to insert text into a document at predefined locations, bookmarks are the easiest way to do it.

To create a `Range` object for a bookmark, use code similar to this:

```
Dim r As Range
Set r = ActiveDocument.Bookmarks("FromAddress").Range
```

This code is fine if you're certain that the bookmark is always there. If you can't make that guarantee (and you can't, really), check first to make sure the bookmark exists, like this:

```
If ActiveDocument.Bookmarks.Exists("Customer") Then
    Dim r As Range
    Set r =ActiveDocument.Bookmarks("FromAddress").Range
Else
    MsgBox "Missing bookmark!"
End If
```

Here, the `Exists` method of the `Bookmarks` collection determines whether the `Customer` bookmark exists before it's accessed.

Creating a range from scratch

You can also create a `Range` object by using the `Range` method of the `Document` object. Note that I said the `Range` *method,* not the `Range` *property.* The `Range` method of the `Document` object creates a new range for the portion of the document you specify. In the Range method, you must provide the starting and ending character position for the range. Here's an example:

```
Dim r As Range
Set r = ActiveDocument.Range(0, 100)
```

Here, a Range object that includes the first 100 characters of a document is created.

Selecting a range

The Range object has a Select method that you can use to make a range the current selection. For example:

```
Dim r As Range
Set r = ActiveDocument.Range(0, 100)
r.Select
```

Here, a Range object is created for the first 100 characters of a document. Then the Range object is selected.

Moving Selections and Ranges

The Selection and Range objects both have Start and End properties that indicate the character position of the start of the section or range and the position of the end of the section or range. You can set these properties directly to change a selection or range. For example, to collapse the active selection, you can use this code:

```
Selection.End = Selection.Start
```

The preceding statement leaves the insertion point at the start of the selection. If you want to collapse the selection and leave the insertion point at the end of the selection, use this code instead:

```
Selection.Start = Selection.End
```

You can also add or subtract values to the selection Start or End properties. For example, the following code extends the selection by one character:

```
Selection.End = Selection.End + 1
```

Methods for moving the selection

The `Selection` and `Range` objects sport several methods that let you move the start or end of the selection or range:

+ `Collapse`: Makes the `Start` and `End` values the same. You can specify a direction as an argument to indicate which direction the selection or range collapses. Specify `wdCollapseStart` to collapse to the start of the selection or range. Specify `wdCollapseEnd` to collapse to the end.

+ `EndOf`, `StartOf`: Moves the start or end of the selection or range to the start or end of a specified unit. Table 3-4 lists the possible unit values, which are used in several other methods as well.

+ `Expand`: Expands the selection to include the next unit.

+ `Move`: Collapses the selection or range and then moves the selection or range the specified number of units.

+ `MoveStart`, `MoveEnd`: Moves the start or end of the selection or range the specified number of units.

+ `MoveStartUntil`, `MoveEndUntil`: Moves the start or end of the selection or range until one of the specified characters is found.

+ `MoveStartWhile`, `MoveEndWhile`: Moves the start or end of the selection or range until a character that is not one of the specified characters is found.

+ `MoveUntil`, `MoveWhile`: Similar to `MoveStartUntil`/`MoveEndUntil` and `MoveStartWhile`/`MoveEndWhile`, but collapses the selection or range first.

+ `Next`, `Previous`: Moves the selection to the next or previous specified unit.

Table 3-4	Constants for Word Units
Constant	*Description*
wdCharacter	Character
wdWord	Word
wdSentence	Sentence
wdParagraph	Paragraph
wdSection	Section
wdStory	Story
wdCell	Table cell
wdColumn	Column
wdRow	Table row
wdTable	Table

A macro that moves the selection

To illustrate how you can move the selection in a macro, the following example shows a macro that displays a message indicating how many times the font has changed in a selection:

```
Sub CountFontChanges()
    Dim iCount As Integer
    Dim iEnd As Integer
    Dim sFont As String
    Dim r As Range
    Set r = Selection.Range
    iEnd = r.End
    r.Collapse
    sFont = r.Font.Name
    While r.Start < iEnd - 1
        Set r = r.Next(wdCharacter, 1)
        If r.Font.Name <> sFont Then
            iCount = iCount + 1
            sFont = r.Font.Name
        End If
    Wend
    MsgBox "The selected text has " & iCount _
        & " font changes."
End Sub
```

This macro starts by assigning the selection to a Range object named r. It then saves the ending character position of the range in a variable named iEnd and collapses the range. Next, it saves the name of the font used for the first character in the selection in a variable named sFont. Then it launches into a While loop that continues until the start of the range reaches the character that was just before the last character of the original selection.

Within the loop, the Next method moves the range to the next character in the document. Then the font of this character is compared with the previously saved font name. If it's different, the iCount variable is incremented to indicate that the font has changed, and the name of the new font is saved in the sFont variable. When the loop finishes, the message box displays how many times the macro determined that the font changed.

You can accomplish this type of character-by-character movement through a selection or range in many different ways. For example, I could have coded the `While` loop like this:

```
While r.Start < iEnd - 1
    r.Start = r.Start + 1
    r.End = r.Start + 1
    If r.Font.Name <> sFont Then
        sFont = r.Font.Name
        iCount = iCount + 1
    End If
Wend
```

Also, as I discuss in the next section, you can code this macro by using the `Characters` collection of the `Selection` object.

Working with Text

The following sections describe various ways to work with text in a macro.

Accessing text

The `Document`, `Selection`, and `Range` objects have several properties you can use to access the contents of a selection or range. These properties work the same whether you're using a `Document`, `Selection`, or `Range` object. The following paragraphs describe how they work:

✦ `Text`: Returns a string that contains the text marked by the selection or range.

✦ `Characters`: Returns a collection of `Range` objects, each representing one character of the selection or range. *Note:* There is no `Character` object. Instead, each character is represented by a separate `Range` object.

✦ `Words`: Returns a collection of `Range` objects, each representing one word of the selection or range. As with characters, there is no separate object for words. Instead, each word is represented by a `Range` object.

✦ `Sentences`: A collection of `Range` objects, each representing one sentence of the selection or range. Again, there is no separate object for sentences. Each sentence is represented by a `Range` object.

✦ `Paragraphs`: A collection of `Paragraphs`, each representing one paragraph of the selection or range. Once again, there is no — made you

look! Word's object model *does* have a separate `Paragraph` object.
That's because many formatting options, such as line spacing, indentation, and tabs, are applied to paragraphs via the `Paragraph` object.

✦ `Sections`: Returns a collection of `Section` objects, representing the
sections in the selection or range.

You can easily implement the `CountFontChanges` macro that I present earlier in this chapter (in the section "A macro that moves the selection") by
using the `Characters` collection of the `Selection` object:

```
Sub CountFontChanges()
    Dim iCount As Integer
    Dim sFont As String
    Dim r As Range
    sFont = Selection.Characters(1).Font.Name
    For Each r In Selection.Characters
        If r.Font.Name <> sFont Then
            sFont = r.Font.Name
            iCount = iCount + 1
        End If
    Next
    MsgBox "The selected text has " & iCount _
        & " font changes."
End Sub
```

Here, the `For Each` loop accesses the characters in the selection one at a
time, so the macro doesn't have to keep track of the start and end of the
range as it loops.

Inserting text

The `Selection` and `Range` objects offer the following methods for inserting
text into your document:

✦ `InsertAfter`: Inserts the specified text after the selection or range.
The selection or range expands to include the new text. For example, the
following statement inserts text after the selection:

```
Dim s As String
s = "So let it be written, so let it be done."
Selection.InsertAfter(s)
```

✦ `InsertBefore`: Inserts the specified text before the selection or range.
The selection or range expands to include the new text. Here's an example that writes text before the selection:

```
Selection.InsertBefore("Listen up!")
```

✦ `InsertParagraph`: Replaces the selection with an empty paragraph.

✦ `InsertParagraphAfter`: Inserts an empty paragraph after the selection or range. The selection or range expands to include the new paragraph.

✦ `InsertParagraphBefore`: Inserts an empty paragraph after the selection or range. The selection or range expands to include the new paragraph.

Rather than using the `InsertParagraph` methods, you can also use the special VBA constant `vbCr` to insert a paragraph mark. For example, the following code moves to the end of the current paragraph, and then inserts the text "Listen Up!" as a separate paragraph:

```
Selection.Move (wdParagraph)
Selection.InsertAfter ("Listen up!" & vbCr)
```

You can use a similar constant, `vbTab`, to insert tab characters. For example:

```
Dim s1, s2 As String
s1 = "Hello"
s2 = "There"
Selection.InsertAfter (s1 & vbTab & s2 & vbCr)
```

Here, the words `Hello` and `There` are inserted into the document, separated by a tab.

Deleting text

I had an English teacher in the 10th grade who said that any book report that contained the words *stupid, dumb,* or *boring* would get an automatic F. Too bad, because I read a lot of books that were stupid, dumb, *and* boring. I probably would have passed the class if only I had a macro that automatically deleted those words from my book reports.

Here's a macro that uses the `Delete` method of a `Range` object to delete those three words from an entire document, and then it displays a message to tell you how many words were deleted:

```
Dim iCount As Integer
Dim r As Range
For Each r in ActiveDocument.Words
    Select Case Trim(r.Text)
        Case "stupid", "dumb", "boring"
            r.Delete
```

```
            iCount = iCount + 1
    End Select
Next
MsgBox "Deleted " & iCount & " words."
```

Here, any occurrence of the forbidden words is deleted from the document.

Copying, cutting, and pasting

Both the `Selection` object and the `Range` object support the standard copy, cut, and paste operations via the Clipboard. Not surprisingly, the methods are

✦ `Copy`: Copies the selection or range to the Clipboard.

✦ `Cut`: Cuts the selection or range to the Clipboard.

✦ `Paste`: Pastes the contents of the Clipboard into the selection or range. Use the `Collapse` method to collapse the selection or range if you don't want the Clipboard contents to replace the contents of the selection or range.

For example, the following code copies the contents of the first paragraph in the document to the selection:

```
ActiveDocument.Paragraphs(1).Range.Copy
Selection.Collapse
Selection.Paste
```

Note two things about this example: First, I had to use the `Range` property of the paragraph to get to the `Copy` method — because the `Paragraph` object doesn't have a `Copy` method. And second, I collapsed the selection before pasting it so that the macro doesn't overwrite any text.

You don't always have to use the Clipboard to copy text to another location in the document. For example, the following code does the job without involving the Clipboard:

```
Dim r As Range
Set r = ActiveDocument.Paragraphs(1).Range
Selection.Collapse
Selection.InsertAfter (r.Text)
```

Formatting Text

All the options for formatting text are available through objects you can access as properties of the `Selection` or `Range` objects. For example, to make the current selection bold, set `Selection.Font.Bold` to `True`.

The following paragraphs describe the formatting objects you can access via the properties of the `Selection` or `Range` objects:

✦ `Borders`: A collection of `Border` objects that define the borders for the selection or range.

✦ `Font`: A `Font` object that lets you set character formatting. For more information, see the section "Using the Font object" that's coming right up.

✦ `ParagraphFormat`: A `ParagraphFormat` object that controls paragraph formatting, such as line spacing, alignment, and indentation. For more information, see the section "Using the ParagraphFormat object."

Two other formatting properties you might want to use are

✦ `Style`: Sets the name of the style for the selection or paragraph. For example, to set the selected paragraphs back to the Normal style, use this code:

```
Selection.Style = "Normal"
```

✦ `TabStops`: A collection of `TabStop` objects. This collection is available only from a `Paragraph` object. For example, this code accesses the first Tab stop for the first paragraph in a selection:

```
Dim t As TabStop
Set t = Selection.Paragraphs(1).TabStops(1)
```

Using the Font object

The `Font` object gives you access to all of the character formatting options available via the Font dialog box (which can be accessed via the dialog box launcher in the Font section of the Home tab). As a result, most of its properties look familiar. Table 3-5 lists the properties you're most likely to use.

Although you must access most of these properties via the `Font` property of a `Selection` or `Range` object, the `Range` object has shortcuts to the `Bold`, `Italic`, and `Underline` properties. Thus, you can set a range to bold, italic, or underline without going through the `Font` object. For example, this statement sets the first sentence of the active document to bold:

```
ActiveDocument.Sentences(1).Bold
```

The Sentences collection is a collection of Range objects, so Sentences(1) returns a Range object for the first sentence in the collection.

Many font properties can be set to True, False, or the special Word constant wdToggle. The wdToggle constant changes the value of the property from whatever its current value is. So if the property is True, wdToggle changes it to False. If it's False, wdToggle changes it to True. This constant mimics the behavior of many formatting shortcut keys, such as Ctrl+B or Ctrl+I.

Table 3-5	Properties of the Font Object
Property	*Description*
Bold	Applies bold formatting
Color	Sets the font color
DoubleStrikeThrough	Applies double-strikethrough formatting
Emboss	Embosses the text
Engrave	Engraves the text
Hidden	Hides the text
Italic	Applies italic formatting
Kerning	Sets the smallest point size at which Word applies kerning
Name	Sets the font name
Outline	Applies outline formatting
Position	Raises or lowers the text by the number of points specified
Shading	Sets shading for the text
Shadow	Applies a shadow effect
SmallCaps	Applies small cap formatting
Strikethrough	Applies strikethrough formatting
Subscript	Applies subscript formatting
Superscript	Applies superscript formatting
Underline	Underlines the text
UnderlineColor	Sets the color for the underline

Using the ParagraphFormat object

The `ParagraphFormat` object gives you access to all of the paragraph formatting options available via the Paragraph dialog box. (You can access this dialog box by clicking the dialog box launcher in the Paragraph group on the Home tab.) As a result, most of its properties look familiar. Table 3-6 lists the most commonly used properties of the `ParagraphFormat` object.

The properties that require a measurement value (such as `FirstLineIndent`) require the measurement in points. There are 72 points in an inch. But if you don't want to do that calculation manually, you can use the `InchesToPoints` function to do the calculation for you. For example, this code sets the `FirstLineIndent` to 0.75 inches:

```
With Selection.ParagraphFormat
    .FirstLineIndent = InchesToPoints(0.75)
End With
```

Table 3-6	Properties of the ParagraphFormat Object
Property	*Description*
Alignment	Sets the alignment. The most common values are wdAlignParagraphLeft, wdAlignParagraphCenter, wdAlignParagraphRight, and wdAlignParagraphJustify.
Borders	Sets the borders for the text.
FirstLineIndent	The indentation for the first line, in points.
KeepTogether	Specifies whether the paragraph is kept on one page.
KeepWithNext	Specifies whether the paragraph is on the same page as the next paragraph.
LeftIndent	Specifies the left indent in points.
LineSpacing	Sets the line spacing in points.
LineSpacingRule	Sets the type of line spacing. The options are wdLineSpace1pt5, wdLineSpaceAtLeast, wdLineSpaceDouble, wdLineSpaceExactly, wdLineSpaceMultiple, and wdLineSpaceSingle.
PageBreakBefore	Specifies whether the paragraph begins a new page.
RightIndent	Specifies the right indent in points.
Shading	Sets the shading for the paragraph.
SpaceAfter	Sets the spacing after the paragraph, in points.

Property	Description
SpaceAfterAuto	Specifies whether Word automatically sets the space that appears after the paragraph.
SpaceBefore	Sets the spacing before the paragraph, in points.
SpaceBeforeAuto	Specifies whether Word automatically sets the space that appears before the paragraph.
Style	The name of the style for the paragraph.
TabStops	The TabStops collection for the paragraph.

Chapter 4: Creating UserForms

In This Chapter

✔ Adding a UserForm to a macro project

✔ Discovering labels and text boxes

✔ Fiddling with frames

✔ Carrying on with check boxes and option buttons

✔ Working with combo boxes

✔ Creating list boxes that allow multiple selections

*T*his chapter shows you how to create macros that display customized dialog boxes called *UserForms*. A UserForm is an interactive, customizable form in a Word document. Its reason for being is to collect information from users and then perform actions based on the information the user entered. UserForms are crucial to creating sophisticated Word macros that automate routine tasks. But UserForms aren't just for complicated macros. Sometimes even a simple macro can benefit from a modest UserForm to get a few critical items of data from the user before proceeding. You can find out more about macros in Chapter 1 of this minibook.

Understanding UserForms

UserForms help you obtain any kind of information you need from the user in a single interaction. For example, suppose that you need to know a person's name, company, and e-mail address. You could use a series of InputBox statements, such as this:

```
Dim Name, Company, EmailAddress As String
Name=InputBox("Name:", "Info", Name)
Name=InputBox("Address:", "Info", Address)
Name=InputBox("Email Address:", "Info", EmailAddress)
```

But wouldn't simply displaying a single dialog box to get all three items be more convenient for the user? With UserForms, you can, as shown in Figure 4-1.

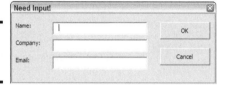

Figure 4-1:
A custom
UserForm.

UserForms aren't as powerful as the forms you can create with a full-fledged programming language, such as Visual Basic or C#. However, you can create forms with any of the dialog box controls listed in Table 4-1.

Table 4-1	UserForm Controls	
What It Looks Like	*What It's Called*	*Description*
Name:	Label	Displays text on the form
Type text here.	TextBox	Lets the user enter text
Arial / Courier New / Symbol	ComboBox	Displays a drop-down list
Times New Roman / Arial / Courier New	ListBox	Displays a scrollable list
Option 1	OptionButton	Used to select one of several alternative settings
Check Here	CheckBox	Supplies a yes/no or on/off setting
Toggle On Toggle Off	ToggleButton	Yet another way to select yes/no values
Options	Frame	Creates a group of controls
OK	CommandButton	Invokes a Sub procedure when clicked
Tab1 Tab2	TabStrip	Divides a form into multiple tabs

What It Looks Like	What It's Called	Description
Page1 Page2	`MultiPage`	Divides a form into multiple pages
	`ScrollBar`	Displays a scroll bar
	`SpinButton`	Allows the user to select from a range of values by incrementing or decrementing the value
	`Image`	Displays a picture

Creating a UserForm

The VBA editor includes a form designer that lets you create UserForms by dragging and dropping controls from a toolbar onto the form. You can then adjust the property settings for each control by using the Properties pane. Adjusting the properties is the fun part of creating a UserForm. Figure 4-2 shows a UserForm being created in the form designer.

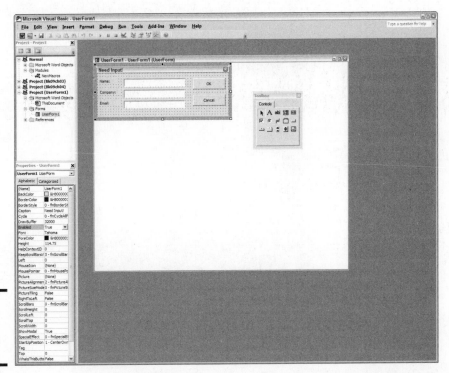

Figure 4-2:
Creating a custom UserForm.

To create a UserForm, follow these steps:

1. **Select the project you want to add the UserForm to in Project Explorer.**

   The Project Explorer window appears in the upper-left corner of the VBA editor. Each open document and template is listed as a project. If you want to create a UserForm in the `Normal.dot` template so that it's available to any document, you can just select Normal in Project Explorer. But if you want to create the UserForm in another template, you must first open that template by choosing File⇨Open. If you simply open a document that's attached to the template, the template is listed in Project Explorer, but you can't access it.

2. **Choose Insert⇨UserForm.**

   A blank UserForm is created, as shown in Figure 4-3.

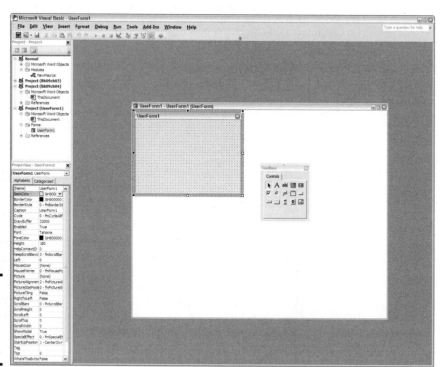

Figure 4-3:
A blank UserForm awaiting your design.

3. **To add a control to the form, click the control you want to add in the Toolbox and then click the form where you want to add the control.**

   You can add any of the controls that are listed earlier in Table 4-1. I explain each of the controls later in this chapter.

   After you add a control, you can drag it around the form to its final position. And you can resize the control by clicking the control to select it and then dragging one of its size handles.

4. **To change a property, select the control you want to change, and then use the Properties pane (in the lower-left part of the window) to set the property you want to change.**

   To set a property for the form itself, click the form anywhere outside one of its controls. You find more information about setting properties for form control in the next section.

   You can also use the drop-down list that appears at the top of the Properties pane to choose a form or control.

5. **To see how your form will appear when run, click the Run button.**

   Running the form from the VBA editor in this way is useful for making sure the form looks the way you want.

6. **When you're satisfied, click the form's Close button to close the form.**

7. **Write whatever code is necessary to implement the form's processing requirements.**

   You can write code that executes whenever the user clicks a button by double-clicking the button in the form designer. This action takes you to the VBA editor and creates a Sub procedure that's all set up to run when the user clicks the control.

   You might also want to write code that executes when the form first displays. To do that, switch to the code window by choosing View⇨Code. Then choose the form from the drop-down list at the top left of the code window and choose Initialize from the drop-down list at the top right of the code window. A Sub procedure automatically runs when the form is initialized. (One common use for the form Initialize procedure is to add items to a drop-down list or list box control.) For more information, see the sections "Using Combo Boxes" and "Using List Boxes," later in this chapter.

Here are a few other points to ponder as you create UserForms:

✦ Be sure to save your work often by clicking the Save button in the VBA editor.

✦ To remove a control from the form, click the control to select it and press Delete.

✦ If your form requires several similar controls, create one of them first and adjust its properties the way you want. Then use good old Copy and Paste commands to duplicate it. (Select the control, press Ctrl+C, and then click the form to select it and press Ctrl+V.)

✦ If you inadvertently double-click a control and the code window pops up, you can select and delete the Sub and End Sub statements that are generated. To get back to the form designer, choose View➪Object.

✦ If the Toolbox disappears on you, you can get it back by choosing View➪ Toolbox.

✦ If you accidentally create the form in the wrong template, you can use the Project Explorer window to drag the form to the correct template.

✦ If you want the form to appear automatically whenever you create a new document based on the template that contains the form, create an AutoNew macro in the template. This macro can then call the form's Show method to show the form. For example:

```
Sub AutoNew()
    UserForm1.Show
End Sub
```

✦ Even if you include an AutoNew macro to automatically call up the form when a new document is created, you might also want to provide another way for the user to access the form after the document opens. For example, you might want to create a macro similar to the preceding AutoNew macro to show the form. Then you can add a button to the Quick Access Toolbar to call up the form. If you really want to be ambitious, you can use the techniques described in the next chapter to add a button that displays the form to the Ribbon.

Working with Controls

Most of the work of creating macros that use UserForms is setting up the controls that appear on the form. After you add a control to a form, you need to adjust the control's properties. You can do that via the Properties pane. First, select the control whose properties you want to adjust. Then locate the property you want to adjust in the Properties pane and specify whatever settings you want to apply.

All controls have several properties in common. In particular:

+ Name: The name of the control, which is used to access the control from code. Provide a meaningful name for every control that you need to refer to in code. For controls, such as labels, that aren't referred to in code, you can leave the default names (such as Label1) as they are.

  When you create a name for a control, beginning the control with a short prefix to indicate the type of control is a good idea. For example, give text boxes names such as txtName and txtEmail, and give buttons names such as btnOK and btnCancel.

+ Caption: Not all controls have a Caption property, but most do. The Caption property sets the text that the control displays. The default value for the Caption property is the control's name, so you almost certainly want to change it to something more suitable.

+ Accelerator: This property specifies the letter that the user can use along with the Alt key to activate the control without using the mouse. The first occurrence of this letter is underlined in the control's caption. For example, if you specify Proceed for the Caption property and "o" for the Accelerator property, the caption appears as Proceed on the control.

+ TabStop: Indicates whether the user can move to the control by pressing the Tab key. Controls that accept input usually have this property set to True.

+ TabIndex: Specifies the order in which the Tab key cycles through the controls. After you have all the controls set up on a form, you can set the TabIndex property of each control to get the tab order right. For example, set the TabIndex to 1 for the control you want to be first in the tab order; 2 for the control you want to be second; and so on.

+ Enabled: Indicates whether the control is enabled. If you set this property to False, the control is dimmed.

+ ControlTip: This property supplies text that's displayed as a tip if the user hovers the cursor over the control for a few moments. You can use this property to provide additional information about what the control does or what happens if the user clicks the control.

When you have a control's properties set the way you want, you can add code for the control by double-clicking the control. Double-clicking takes you to the code window and creates a Sub procedure that executes if the user clicks the control. In most cases, you create a Sub procedure only for command button controls. However, you can create a procedure to handle clicks for any control on a UserForm, not just command buttons.

Using Command Buttons

Command buttons are the workhorses of most UserForms. You usually need to set one property for a command button: the `Caption` property. Use the `Caption` property to specify the text you want to appear on the button. You might also want to set the `Accelerator` property for command buttons.

The hard part of working with command buttons is writing the code that is supposed to execute when the user clicks the button. To create this code, simply double-click the button in the form designer.

Creating a Cancel button

All forms need a Cancel button that lets the user bail out of the form without doing anything. The click procedure for the Cancel button typically looks like this:

```
Private Sub btnCancel_Click()
    Hide
End Sub
```

The `Hide` statement is actually a call to the `Hide` method of the current form, which closes the form and returns the user to the document. You could specify the form name on this statement, but the current form is assumed by default if you don't, so just coding `Hide` is enough.

The `Hide` method doesn't stop the macro from running. If your macro needs to do additional work after it closes the form, it can include additional statements after the `Hide` method call.

Creating an OK button

Most UserForms also contain a button that processes the data that the user enters on the form. This button goes by various names, such as OK or Save, depending on what the form does. In many cases, the code for this button extracts the data the user entered in the form and inserts it into the document, either at the location of the insertion point or at predefined locations marked by bookmarks.

For example, the following code shows the click procedure for the OK button in the form shown earlier in Figure 4-1. Here, the information from the three text boxes is inserted into the document after the selection:

```
Private Sub CommandButton1_Click()
    Selection.InsertAfter txtName.Text & vbCr
```

```
        Selection.InsertAfter txtCompany.Text & vbCr
        Selection.InsertAfter txtEmail.Text & vbCr
        Selection.Collapse wdCollapseEnd
        Hide
End Sub
```

After the text is inserted, the selection collapses, and the form closes.

Suppose you want to insert the text in an area of the document marked by a `Customer` bookmark rather than in the selection. In that case, use code similar to this:

```
Private Sub CommandButton1_Click()
    If ActiveDocument.Bookmarks.Exists("Customer") Then
        Dim r As Range
        Set r =ActiveDocument.Bookmarks("Customer").Range
        r.InsertAfter txtName.Text & vbCr
        r.InsertAfter txtCompany.Text & vbCr
        r.InsertAfter txtEmail.Text & vbCr
        Hide
    Else
        MsgBox "Missing bookmark!"
    End If
End Sub
```

Using Labels

Label controls display text on the form. For plain, unexciting labels, just drag a label control from the Toolbox onto the form, set the label's `Caption` property to the text you want to display, and be done with it. For fancier labels, you can set the following properties via the Properties pane:

✦ `Font`: The font used for the `Caption` text. When you set the `Font` property in the Properties pane, a Font dialog box appears, allowing you to choose the font, style (such as bold or italic), and size.

✦ `TextAlign`: Lets you choose the text alignment: left, centered, or right.

✦ `SpecialEffect`: Lets you apply one of the four special effects shown in Figure 4-4.

✦ `WordWrap`: Indicates whether the text wraps onto multiple lines if the label isn't wide enough to display it all.

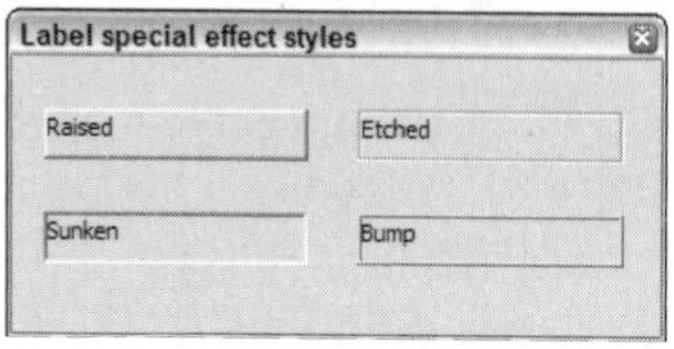

Figure 4-4:
Special
effects you
can use
with label
controls.

Using Text Boxes

Text boxes are the main tool you use to get text input from the user for your macro. The user's input is available via the Text property. The following code assigns the text entered into a text box named txtCompany to a variable named Company:

```
Company = txtCompany.Text
```

You can also use the Text property to assign an initial value to a text box. Then, if the user doesn't change the value, the initial value is retained. You can set the initial text value with an assignment statement such as this example in the form's Initialize procedure:

```
txtCompany.Text = "John Wiley & Sons, Inc."
```

Or you can set the initial value in the Properties pane when you design the form.

Text boxes have a few other noteworthy properties:

✦ MaxLength: Limits the number of characters the user can enter. When the entry exceeds the MaxLength limit, anything else the user types is ignored.

✦ MultiLine: If set to True, this property allows the user to enter more than one line of text into the text box. The user must press Shift+Enter to create a new line. You usually want to increase the height of the text box so that the additional lines can display.

✦ PasswordChar: Allows you to create a password entry field. Instead of displaying the text entered by the user, the password entry field displays the password character. That way, nosey bystanders can't see what the user typed.

Using Frames

A frame control is a container that lets you group controls on a form. A frame not only adds visual structure to the form, but it also helps out when you use option buttons, as I discuss in the next section.

To use a frame control, just drag a frame from the Toolbox onto the form and then resize it and position it however you want. Then you can drop other controls onto the frame.

The only property you're likely to set for a frame control is the Caption property, which sets the text displayed in the margin of the frame. You might also want to play with the SpecialEffect property if you want to give the frame a nonstandard look.

Using Check Boxes and Option Buttons

Check boxes and option buttons allow the user to select options. For example, Figure 4-5 shows a UserForm that gathers information needed to order a pizza. The user selects the size of the pizza from a group of option buttons and selects the toppings by using check boxes. (This UserForm also uses frames to provide nice borders around the Size and Toppings sections of the dialog box.)

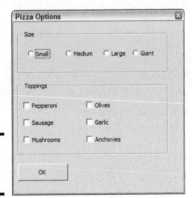

Figure 4-5:
A pizza
order form.

When you create a check box or option button, you use the `Caption` property to set the text that describes the option. Then, in your code, you can use the `Value` property to determine whether the check box or option button is selected.

Grouping option buttons

The main difference between check boxes and option buttons is that check boxes are independent of one another. In contrast, option buttons travel in groups, and a user can select only one option button in a group at a time. To indicate which group an option button belongs to, you need to set the `GroupName` property. If a form has only one group of option buttons, you can leave this property blank. You can also ignore the `GroupName` property if you place each group of option buttons in a separate frame. But if you have two or more groups of option buttons and they're not isolated in frames, you must set this property to indicate which group each option button belongs to.

Testing option button and check box values

You can test the setting of a check box or option button in code by testing the `Value` property for `True` or `False`. For example, here's the code that runs when the user clicks the OK button for the UserForm shown earlier in Figure 4-5:

```
Private Sub btnOK_Click()
    Dim s As String
    s = "Pizza size: "
    If obtnSmall.Value = True Then
        s = s & "Small" & vbCr
    ElseIf obtnMedium.Value = True Then
        s = s & "Medium" & vbCr
    ElseIf obtnLarge.Value = True Then
        s = s & "Large" & vbCr
    ElseIf obtnGiant.Value = True Then
        s = s & "Giant" & vbCr
    End If
    s = s & "Toppings: " & vbCr
    If chkPepperoni.Value = True Then
        s = s & vbTab & "Pepperoni" & vbCr
    End If
    If chkSausage.Value = True Then
        s = s & vbTab & "Sausage" & vbCr
    End If
    If chkMushrooms.Value = True Then
        s = s & vbTab & "Mushrooms" & vbCr
```

```
        End If
        If chkOlives.Value = True Then
            s = s & vbTab & "Olives" & vbCr
        End If
        If chkGarlic.Value = True Then
            s = s & vbTab & "Garlic" & vbCr
        End If
        If chkAnchovies.Value = True Then
            s = s & vbTab & "Anchovies" & vbCr
        End If
        Selection.InsertAfter s
        Hide
End Sub
```

In this example, a string variable named s constructs the text that's inserted into the document. First, the option buttons are checked in a series of `If/ElseIf` statements to determine which size was selected. Then a series of separate `If` statements determine which toppings to include in the order. (For more information about string variables, refer to Chapter 2 of this minibook.)

Suppose you run this form, select a large pizza, and select the Pepperoni, Garlic, and Anchovies check boxes. In that case, the following text is inserted into the document when you click OK:

```
Pizza size: Large
Toppings:
     Pepperoni
     Garlic
     Anchovies
```

You'd better be hungry because you'll probably end up eating this one by yourself. And you'd better have some breath mints handy, too.

Using Combo Boxes

A combo box displays a drop-down list that lists options from which the user can choose. Depending on how you configure the combo box, the user might also be able to type in a selection if one of the items in the list isn't suitable.

List boxes are similar to combo boxes. I discuss them in the next section, titled (surprisingly enough) "Using List Boxes."

When you create a combo box, you can set the `Style` property to indicate what type of combo box you want to create. The choices are `DropDownCombo` and `DropDownList`. `DropDownCombo` allows the user to enter a value in the text box part of the control. `DropDownList` forces the user to choose one of the items from the list.

To use a combo box in a macro, you have to know how to write code to do two things: load the items for the list into the combo box and determine which of the list items the user selected. I describe these coding techniques in the following sections.

Loading items into a combo box

To load items into a combo box, you use the `AddItem` method. The best time to use the `AddItem` method is when the form is initializing. For example, here's an `Initialize` procedure for a form that loads a combo box with items that can be included as toppings on a pizza:

```
Sub UserForm1_Initialize()
    cboSize.AddItem "Small"
    cboSize.AddItem "Medium"
    cboSize.AddItem "Large"
    cboSize.AddItem "Giant"
End Sub
```

And here's a `For Each` loop that loads the names of all the available fonts into a combo box:

```
Dim FontName As Variant
For Each FontName in FontNames
    cboFonts.AddItem FontName
Next
```

Determining which item was selected

To determine which item the user has selected from a combo box, use the `Value` property. For example:

```
Dim Size As String
Size = cboSize.Value
```

If, for some reason, you're interested in knowing the index number of the item chosen by the user, use the `ListItem` property instead. However, be aware that unlike most VBA indexes, the `ListItem` value for the first item in the combo box is 0, not 1.

Setting the selected item

In some cases, you want to set the item that's selected in a combo box from VBA. For example, you might want to force the first entry in the combo box to be selected when the form is initialized. You can use the `ListIndex` property to do that. For example:

```
cboSize.ListIndex = 0
```

Here, the first item is selected.

Combo boxes number their list items beginning with 0, not 1.

Using List Boxes

A list box is similar to a combo box, but it doesn't have the drop-down ability that combo boxes do. Instead, a list box displays one or more items from the list, depending on the vertical size of the list box. If all the items don't fit, a scroll bar appears so that the user can scroll through the list.

In most cases, list boxes are much less useful than combo boxes. However, list boxes have one feature that combo boxes don't have: the ability to let the user select more than one item from the list. For example, Figure 4-5 shows a form with a list box that lets the user select several choices from a long list of pizza toppings.

To get the effect shown in the list box in Figure 4-6, I set two properties for the list box:

✦ `MultiSelect`: I set this property to `Multi` to allow more than one selection.

✦ `ListStyle`: I set this property to `Option` to display check boxes next to each item in the list.

Loading items into a list box

You load items into a list box just like you load items into a combo box. For example, here is some of the code from the form `Initialize` procedure for the form shown in Figure 4-6:

```
lbToppings.AddItem ("Pepperoni")
lbToppings.AddItem ("Sausage")
lbToppings.AddItem ("Salami")
lbToppings.AddItem ("Linguica")
```

```
lbToppings.AddItem ("Pastrami")
lbToppings.AddItem ("Ground Beef")
lbToppings.AddItem ("Chicken")
lbToppings.AddItem ("Canadian Bacon")
```

Figure 4-6:
A pizza
order form
with a list
box and a
combo box.

Dealing with multiple selections

Determining which items are selected in a multiselect list box is tricky. You need to use three properties of the list box to do this:

✦ ListCount: The number of items in the list

✦ List *(index)*: Retrieves the specified item from the list

✦ Selected*(index)*: Indicates whether or not the specified item was selected

Putting these three properties together, the following For/Next loop creates a string variable named msg that lists all the toppings selected from the lbToppings list box:

```
Dim s As String
Dim i As Integer
For i = 0 To lbToppings.ListCount - 1
    If lbToppings.Selected(i) = True Then
        s = s & lbToppings.List(i) & vbCr
    End If
Next i
```

The If statement determines whether the item for the current index value is selected. If so, the item is appended to the string.

Index

Numerics

3-D effects
  adding to charts, 308
  adding to shapes, 269–271
  color, 270
  depth, 270
  direction, 270
  lighting, 270
  surfaces, 270
3-D On/Off button, 270

A

About Microsoft Office
  Word 2007 option
  (Resources tab), 524
accept/reject change, track
  changes, 399–400
account registration, blogs,
  376–378
Activate Microsoft Office
  option (Resources tab),
  524
ActiveX Settings option
  (Trust Center tab), 523
Add New Document dialog
  box, 389
Add Templates dialog
  box, 50
Add-Ins option
  Trust Center tab, 523
  Word Options dialog box,
  44, 50
Add-Ins tab, 502, 522
Address Block button, 475
addresses
  adding to Mail Merge, 467
  address blocks, 470
  creating in Mail Merge,
  465

customizing, 468
e-mail, 460
envelope creation, 450
existing Mail Merge
  address, 466
label creation, 452
naming, 467
records, deleting Mail
  Merge, 467
sorting in Merge, 468
Adjust List Indents dialog
  box, 234
advanced search option
  (Find and Replace
  dialog box), 145
Advanced tab
  Compatibility option, 521
  Copy option, 513–514
  Cut option, 513–514
  description, 502, 511
  Display option, 515–516
  Editing Options section,
  512
  General option, 518–521
  Paste option, 513–514
  Preserve Fidelity When
  Sharing This Document
  option, 517–518
  Print option, 516–517
  Save option, 517
  Show Document Content
  option, 514–515
  Word Options dialog
  box, 28
Align Bottom Center
  button, 327
Align Bottom Left button,
  327
Align Bottom Right button,
  327
Align Center button, 327

Align Center Left button,
  327
Align Center Right button,
  327
Align Top Center button,
  327
Align Top Left button, 327
Align Top Right button, 327
alignment
  numbered lists, 238
  object, 274
  page formatting, 201
  paragraph, 89, 99
  tab, 101–102
Alignment button, 355
All Programs command
  (Start menu), 10–11
All search option (Find and
  Replace dialog box),
  143
alternative word forms,
  finding text by, 145–146
Always Show These
  Formatting Marks on
  Screen option (Display
  tab), 507–508
Always Use ClearType
  option (Popular
  tab), 505
anchored frames, 349
anchors
  displaying, 507
  picture location, 292
animated text, 515
Application object,
  601–603
Apply As You Type section
  (AutoFormat feature),
  157–158
Apply Styles dialog box, 123

BUSINESS, CAREERS & PERSONAL FINANCE

0-7645-9847-3

0-7645-2431-3

Also available:
- Business Plans Kit For Dummies
  0-7645-9794-9
- Economics For Dummies
  0-7645-5726-2
- Grant Writing For Dummies
  0-7645-8416-2
- Home Buying For Dummies
  0-7645-5331-3
- Managing For Dummies
  0-7645-1771-6
- Marketing For Dummies
  0-7645-5600-2

- Personal Finance For Dummies
  0-7645-2590-5*
- Resumes For Dummies
  0-7645-5471-9
- Selling For Dummies
  0-7645-5363-1
- Six Sigma For Dummies
  0-7645-6798-5
- Small Business Kit For Dummies
  0-7645-5984-2
- Starting an eBay Business For Dummies
  0-7645-6924-4
- Your Dream Career For Dummies
  0-7645-9795-7

HOME & BUSINESS COMPUTER BASICS

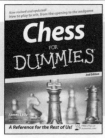

0-470-05432-8

0-471-75421-8

Also available:
- Cleaning Windows Vista For Dummies
  0-471-78293-9
- Excel 2007 For Dummies
  0-470-03737-7
- Mac OS X Tiger For Dummies
  0-7645-7675-5
- MacBook For Dummies
  0-470-04859-X
- Macs For Dummies
  0-470-04849-2
- Office 2007 For Dummies
  0-470-00923-3

- Outlook 2007 For Dummies
  0-470-03830-6
- PCs For Dummies
  0-7645-8958-X
- Salesforce.com For Dummies
  0-470-04893-X
- Upgrading & Fixing Laptops For Dummies
  0-7645-8959-8
- Word 2007 For Dummies
  0-470-03658-3
- Quicken 2007 For Dummies
  0-470-04600-7

FOOD, HOME, GARDEN, HOBBIES, MUSIC & PETS

0-7645-8404-9

0-7645-9904-6

Also available:
- Candy Making For Dummies
  0-7645-9734-5
- Card Games For Dummies
  0-7645-9910-0
- Crocheting For Dummies
  0-7645-4151-X
- Dog Training For Dummies
  0-7645-8418-9
- Healthy Carb Cookbook For Dummies
  0-7645-8476-6
- Home Maintenance For Dummies
  0-7645-5215-5

- Horses For Dummies
  0-7645-9797-3
- Jewelry Making & Beading For Dummies
  0-7645-2571-9
- Orchids For Dummies
  0-7645-6759-4
- Puppies For Dummies
  0-7645-5255-4
- Rock Guitar For Dummies
  0-7645-5356-9
- Sewing For Dummies
  0-7645-6847-7
- Singing For Dummies
  0-7645-2475-5

INTERNET & DIGITAL MEDIA

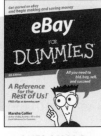

0-470-04529-9

0-470-04894-8

Also available:
- Blogging For Dummies
  0-471-77084-1
- Digital Photography For Dummies
  0-7645-9802-3
- Digital Photography All-in-One Desk Reference For Dummies
  0-470-03743-1
- Digital SLR Cameras and Photography For Dummies
  0-7645-9803-1
- eBay Business All-in-One Desk Reference For Dummies
  0-7645-8438-3
- HDTV For Dummies
  0-470-09673-X

- Home Entertainment PCs For Dummies
  0-470-05523-5
- MySpace For Dummies
  0-470-09529-6
- Search Engine Optimization For Dummies
  0-471-97998-8
- Skype For Dummies
  0-470-04891-3
- The Internet For Dummies
  0-7645-8996-2
- Wiring Your Digital Home For Dummies
  0-471-91830-X

* Separate Canadian edition also available
† Separate U.K. edition also available

Available wherever books are sold. For more information or to order direct: U.S. customers visit www.dummies.com or call 1-877-762-2974.
U.K. customers visit www.wileyeurope.com or call 0800 243407. Canadian customers visit www.wiley.ca or call 1-800-567-4797.

SPORTS, FITNESS, PARENTING, RELIGION & SPIRITUALITY

0-471-76871-5

0-7645-7841-3

Also available:
- Catholicism For Dummies
  0-7645-5391-7
- Exercise Balls For Dummies
  0-7645-5623-1
- Fitness For Dummies
  0-7645-7851-0
- Football For Dummies
  0-7645-3936-1
- Judaism For Dummies
  0-7645-5299-6
- Potty Training For Dummies
  0-7645-5417-4
- Buddhism For Dummies
  0-7645-5359-3

- Pregnancy For Dummies
  0-7645-4483-7 †
- Ten Minute Tone-Ups For Dummies
  0-7645-7207-5
- NASCAR For Dummies
  0-7645-7681-X
- Religion For Dummies
  0-7645-5264-3
- Soccer For Dummies
  0-7645-5229-5
- Women in the Bible For Dummies
  0-7645-8475-8

TRAVEL

0-7645-7749-2

0-7645-6945-7

Also available:
- Alaska For Dummies
  0-7645-7746-8
- Cruise Vacations For Dummies
  0-7645-6941-4
- England For Dummies
  0-7645-4276-1
- Europe For Dummies
  0-7645-7529-5
- Germany For Dummies
  0-7645-7823-5
- Hawaii For Dummies
  0-7645-7402-7

- Italy For Dummies
  0-7645-7386-1
- Las Vegas For Dummies
  0-7645-7382-9
- London For Dummies
  0-7645-4277-X
- Paris For Dummies
  0-7645-7630-5
- RV Vacations For Dummies
  0-7645-4442-X
- Walt Disney World & Orlando
  For Dummies
  0-7645-9660-8

GRAPHICS, DESIGN & WEB DEVELOPMENT

0-7645-8815-X

0-7645-9571-7

Also available:
- 3D Game Animation For Dummies
  0-7645-8789-7
- AutoCAD 2006 For Dummies
  0-7645-8925-3
- Building a Web Site For Dummies
  0-7645-7144-3
- Creating Web Pages For Dummies
  0-470-08030-2
- Creating Web Pages All-in-One Desk
  Reference For Dummies
  0-7645-4345-8
- Dreamweaver 8 For Dummies
  0-7645-9649-7

- InDesign CS2 For Dummies
  0-7645-9572-5
- Macromedia Flash 8 For Dummies
  0-7645-9691-8
- Photoshop CS2 and Digital
  Photography For Dummies
  0-7645-9580-6
- Photoshop Elements 4 For Dummies
  0-471-77483-9
- Syndicating Web Sites with RSS Feeds
  For Dummies
  0-7645-8848-6
- Yahoo! SiteBuilder For Dummies
  0-7645-9800-7

NETWORKING, SECURITY, PROGRAMMING & DATABASES

0-7645-7728-X

0-471-74940-0

Also available:
- Access 2007 For Dummies
  0-470-04612-0
- ASP.NET 2 For Dummies
  0-7645-7907-X
- C# 2005 For Dummies
  0-7645-9704-3
- Hacking For Dummies
  0-470-05235-X
- Hacking Wireless Networks
  For Dummies
  0-7645-9730-2
- Java For Dummies
  0-470-08716-1

- Microsoft SQL Server 2005 For Dummies
  0-7645-7755-7
- Networking All-in-One Desk Reference
  For Dummies
  0-7645-9939-9
- Preventing Identity Theft For Dummies
  0-7645-7336-5
- Telecom For Dummies
  0-471-77085-X
- Visual Studio 2005 All-in-One Desk
  Reference For Dummies
  0-7645-9775-2
- XML For Dummies
  0-7645-8845-1

HEALTH & SELF-HELP

0-7645-8450-2   0-7645-4149-8

Also available:
- Bipolar Disorder For Dummies
  0-7645-8451-0
- Chemotherapy and Radiation
  For Dummies
  0-7645-7832-4
- Controlling Cholesterol For Dummies
  0-7645-5440-9
- Diabetes For Dummies
  0-7645-6820-5* †
- Divorce For Dummies
  0-7645-8417-0 †

- Fibromyalgia For Dummies
  0-7645-5441-7
- Low-Calorie Dieting For Dummies
  0-7645-9905-4
- Meditation For Dummies
  0-471-77774-9
- Osteoporosis For Dummies
  0-7645-7621-6
- Overcoming Anxiety For Dummies
  0-7645-5447-6
- Reiki For Dummies
  0-7645-9907-0
- Stress Management For Dummies
  0-7645-5144-2

EDUCATION, HISTORY, REFERENCE & TEST PREPARATION

0-7645-8381-6   0-7645-9554-7

Also available:
- The ACT For Dummies
  0-7645-9652-7
- Algebra For Dummies
  0-7645-5325-9
- Algebra Workbook For Dummies
  0-7645-8467-7
- Astronomy For Dummies
  0-7645-8465-0
- Calculus For Dummies
  0-7645-2498-4
- Chemistry For Dummies
  0-7645-5430-1
- Forensics For Dummies
  0-7645-5580-4

- Freemasons For Dummies
  0-7645-9796-5
- French For Dummies
  0-7645-5193-0
- Geometry For Dummies
  0-7645-5324-0
- Organic Chemistry I For Dummies
  0-7645-6902-3
- The SAT I For Dummies
  0-7645-7193-1
- Spanish For Dummies
  0-7645-5194-9
- Statistics For Dummies
  0-7645-5423-9

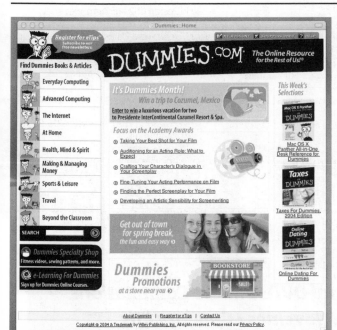

Get smart @ dummies.com®

- **Find a full list of Dummies titles**
- **Look into loads of FREE on-site articles**
- **Sign up for FREE eTips e-mailed to you weekly**
- **See what other products carry the Dummies name**
- **Shop directly from the Dummies bookstore**
- **Enter to win new prizes every month!**

* Separate Canadian edition also available
† Separate U.K. edition also available

Available wherever books are sold. For more information or to order direct: U.S. customers visit www.dummies.com or call 1-877-762-2974.
U.K. customers visit www.wileyeurope.com or call 0800 243407. Canadian customers visit www.wiley.ca or call 1-800-567-4797.